UNIVERSITY LIBRARIES

PICK YOURSELF UP

Geoffrey Block, Series Editor

Series Board

Stephen Banfield   Jeffrey Magee

Tim Carter   Carol Oja

Kim Kowalke   Larry Starr

"South Pacific": Paradise Rewritten
Jim Lovensheimer

Pick Yourself Up: Dorothy Fields and the American Musical
Charlotte Greenspan

PICK YOURSELF UP

DOROTHY FIELDS AND THE AMERICAN MUSICAL

CHARLOTTE GREENSPAN

OXFORD
UNIVERSITY PRESS

2010

OXFORD
UNIVERSITY PRESS

Oxford University Press, Inc., publishes works that further
Oxford University's objective of excellence
in research, scholarship, and education.

Oxford   New York
Auckland   Cape Town   Dar es Salaam   Hong Kong   Karachi
Kuala Lumpur   Madrid   Melbourne   Mexico City   Nairobi
New Delhi   Shanghai   Taipei   Toronto

With offices in
Argentina   Austria   Brazil   Chile   Czech Republic   France   Greece
Guatemala   Hungary   Italy   Japan   Poland   Portugal   Singapore
South Korea   Switzerland   Thailand   Turkey   Ukraine   Vietnam

Published by Oxford University Press, Inc.
198 Madison Avenue, New York, New York 10016

www.oup.com

Oxford is a registered trademark of Oxford University Press

Library of Congress Cataloging-in-Publication Data
Greenspan, Charlotte Joyce, 1941–
Pick yourself up : Dorothy Fields
and the American musical / Charlotte Greenspan.
p. cm. — (Broadway legacies)
Includes bibliographical references.
ISBN 978-0-19-511110-1
1. Fields, Dorothy, 1905–1974. 2. Lyricists—United States—Biography.
3. Librettists—United States—Biography. I. Title.
ML423.F4G74 2010
782.1'4092—dc22
[B]
2009036378

1   3   5   7   9   8   6   4   2

Printed in the United States of America
on acid-free paper

For my husband,

JERROLD MEINWALD,

and our daughter,

JULIA EVE MEINWALD

ACKNOWLEDGMENTS

• • •

This book has taken a long time to come to fruition, and I am delighted to have the opportunity here to thank many of the people who helped me along the way.

When I first decided to write a biography of Dorothy Fields, I contacted her daughter, Eliza Lahm Brewster, and her son, David Lahm. Eliza was from the start gracious, supportive, and generous, sharing memories and thoughts about her mother as well as photos. David came into the project when it was nearing completion, meticulously going over every word of the manuscript more than once. Many improvements in the text are his. Needless to say, the remaining flaws are all my own.

This project has taken more than a decade to complete, and in that time I have had the privilege of working with several excellent editors at Oxford University Press. The first of these was Sheldon Meyer, who, when I told him I wanted to write a book about Dorothy Fields, kindly replied, "You've made my day!" He was succeeded by Maribeth Payne, Kim Robinson, and Suzanne Ryan, all of whom found the right balance between encouraging me and "holding my feet to the fire" (Maribeth's term). In the difficult home stretch, Norman Hirschy did a remarkable job of reassuring me that it would all work out in the end—and finding ways to make that come true.

Some of the work for this book was done in the congenial setting of the American Academy of Arts and Sciences. I am grateful to the helpful staff and particularly the chief executive officer, Leslie Berlowitz, for the hospitality shown to me.

I am also grateful to Rita Pirsic, working in Ithaca, for her assistance in the final preparation of the manuscript.

I would also like to thank a number of librarians, archivists, and other resource persons who helped me to work with materials that were a fundamental necessity for the writing of this book. They include Marty Jacobs, theater curator of the Museum of the City of New York, where many of Dorothy Fields's papers, scrapbooks, and other documents are kept; Robert Scott, visitor services library coordinator at the Museum of Television and Radio (now the Paley Center for Media); the staff of the Columbia University Oral History Research Center Office; and the staff of the Music Division and Theater Division of the New York Public Library at Lincoln Center. Forrest and Leslie Perrin and Michael and Joy Brown were kind enough to invite me into their homes and share with me their recollections of Dorothy Fields and the time in which she worked.

A number of colleagues shared information, opinions, and strategies. They include Geoffrey Block, Mimi Daitz, Jon Finson, Sarah Fuller, Claudia Gorbman, Paul Machlin, Jeffrey Magee, Severine Neff, Vicki Ohl, Annette Richards, David Rosen, Wayne Schneider, Ann Sears, Rose Subotnik, Judith Tick, Katharine Weber, and David Yearsley. This may look like a lengthy list, but I trust they know that I am grateful to each of them individually. I also wish to express my indebtedness, too late for them to see it in print, to Edward Murray, Lenore Coral, Scott McMillin, and Adrienne Block.

Last, and most important, I want to thank my family and friends for the many ways they contributed to the book—not least by just staying interested: my husband, Jerrold Meinwald; our daughter, Julia Eve Meinwald; my husband's daughters, Constance Meinwald and Pamela Meinwald; and friends Diane Ackerman, Mary Lash, Judy Levitt, Lisa Liss, Jeanne Mackin, Anna Matusiewicz, Margaret Dieter Miller, Anna Salamone, and Paul West.

CONTENTS

• • •

FOREWORD

• • •

The book you are reading is the second volume in a new series called Broadway Legacies, published by Oxford University Press. The series will offer engrossing books on Broadway composers, composer-lyricist teams, choreographers, directors, and other creative artists who have made Broadway one of America's most celebrated, recognizable, and popular cultural institutions. Other books in the series will be devoted to singular sensational musicals that have made a major cultural and artistic impact on the genre. All the volumes will provide original research and new ideas by leading scholars in engaging and accessible prose. Among the coming attractions are books on *Oklahoma!* and *Carousel* choreographer Agnes de Mille; Jerry Bock and Sheldon Harnick (the composer and lyricist team that created *Fiddler on the Roof*); the Broadway career of American icon Irving Berlin; and the pioneering Broadway classic *Show Boat*.

If you didn't know this already, you will soon discover that Dorothy Fields (1904–74) was one of the foremost lyricists and librettists in a career that spanned from the late 1920s to the early 1970s. Her legacy of lyrics from composer Jimmy McHugh's "I Can't Give You Anything but Love" (*Blackbirds of 1928*) to composer Cy Coleman's "Big Spender" and "If My Friends Could See Me Now" (*Sweet Charity*, 1966) have long since entered the American consciousness, although, for most of us, subliminally and anonymously. Paradoxically, unless they are part of a famous team such as Rodgers and Hammerstein or Lerner and Loewe, lyricists tend to inhabit a relatively unsung position on the Broadway stage. Librettists receive even shorter shrift. But if we don't pay attention to their nominal identity, we often remember what they said and especially how they said it. Who, for example, could top the simple elegance of this delicious Dorothy Fields lyric from the musical film *Swing Time* (1936): "A fine ro-mance! / with *no* kiss-es! / A fine ro-mance, / my friend / this is!"

Fields was a lyricist *and* a librettist, sometimes one or the other and sometimes both at the same time depending on her partner and the situation. For example, Cole Porter and Irving Berlin were composer-lyricists and needed a book writer, whereas Cy Coleman had Neil Simon to write the book for *Sweet Charity* and needed only a lyricist. For the three musicals she wrote with Porter and the one show she wrote with Berlin, Dorothy shared the book-writing labors with her brother Herbert, who had previously gained distinction as the librettist for some of Rodgers and Hart's and Porter's biggest hits in the 1920s and 1930s. Fields's versatility demonstrates persuasively that there were many ways to create a hit show.

To convey how a memorable lyric can also be an anonymous lyric, I can think of no better example than President Obama's call to action at his inaugural address on January 20, 2009: "Starting today, we must pick ourselves up, dust ourselves off, and begin again the work of remaking America." As far as I know, none of the commentators that day noted that Obama's reference was taken from Dorothy Fields's lyric from Ginger Rogers and Fred Astaire's opening song and dance in *Swing Time*, "Pick Yourself Up."

A few days later, however, op-ed columnist and former theater critic Frank Rich, writing in the *New York Times*, described the inaugural passage as "one subtle whiff of the Great Depression" and "a paraphrase of the great songwriter Dorothy Fields" (for the record, following the words "Pick Yourself Up," the song hook actually continues slightly differently and more concisely with "dust yourself off, start all over again"). One grumpy pundit, although he did not seem to recognize its poet, singled out Field's inspirational phase not only as the most memorable in Obama's speech but the *only* memorable line. *Swing Time*, which complements Fields's words with music by Jerome Kern, remains for many the high point of the popular Astaire and Rogers collaborations and one of the acknowledged masterworks of musical film. It also marked the first time a female lyricist won the Oscar for Best Song, for "The Way You Look Tonight" in 1936.

Dorothy Fields came from one of Broadway's first families. In addition to Herbert (*A Connecticut Yankee*, *Du Barry Was a Lady*), her brother Joseph was also a successful playwright and screenwriter with three hit musical books to his credit (*Gentlemen Prefer Blondes*, *Wonderful Town*, and *Flower Drum Song*). Her father, Lew Fields, the tall half of the long-lived nineteenth-century vaudeville team of Weber and Fields, was a leading Broadway producer during his daughter's early years. Her family is a major part of her story, and, despite all the films, for almost all her creative life it is mainly a Broadway story.

Dorothy Field's career was launched when, with Jimmy McHugh, she created hit songs for Duke Ellington's famous venue in the late 1920s, the Cotton Club, and for the hit Broadway show *Blackbirds of 1928*. Later highlights of her career include the songs she and Kern added for the film version of *Roberta* (mainly for Astaire and Rogers in expanded roles) and *Swing Time* in the 1930s, librettos to three Porter hits from the early 1940s and the book that supported Berlin's lyrics and music for the beloved classic *Annie Get Your Gun* (1946), almost certainly her most well-known legacy to Broadway. She also wrote the books or lyrics to interesting shows by composers as diverse as

Sigmund Romberg's *Up in Central Park* in 1945 (as the sole lyricist and a book with Herbert) and Arthur Schwartz's *A Tree Grows in Brooklyn* in 1951 (lyrics), and even a few songs with Harold Arlen and Burton Lane in the 1940s and 50s before concluding her career on a high note with Coleman.

It was truly an amazing life's output, one that included more than four hundred songs, lyrics for nineteen Broadway shows, librettos for nine others, and work on more than thirty films. She also led a rich life with many personal and professional friendships. Charlotte Greenspan writes about all this and much more. In refreshing contrast to many show business stories of ascent and decline, the story of Dorothy Fields is a heartwarming story of an optimistic and productive life from beginning to the end.

To use Cap'n Andy's recurring phrase in *Show Boat*, I'll conclude with "jest a sample" from Greenspan's *Pick Yourself Up*: "Without the benefit of a banner or movement, she made the field of songwriting more woman-friendly, teaching by example. Some commentators continue the debate over whether the lyrics are distinctly female, but to me her body of work makes the question pleasantly irrelevant. For millions who know her lyrics but do not know who wrote them, she made an anonymous gift."

GEOFFREY BLOCK
Series Editor, Broadway Legacies

PREFACE

● ● ●

In the past decade I have had the following conversation, or some variant of it, numerous times.

"I am writing a biography of Dorothy Fields."

"Who?"

"She was a lyricist. You many not know her name, but you know her songs."

"Like what?"

"'I Can't Give You Anything but Love,' 'On the Sunny Side of the Street,' 'I'm in the Mood For Love,' 'I Feel a Song Coming On,' 'Close as Pages in a Book,' 'Lovely to Look At,' 'The Way You Look Tonight,' 'A Fine Romance,' 'Don't Blame Me,' 'If My Friends Could See Me Now.'"

"Oh! Of course."

Sometimes, after I have gotten through only a part of the list of Dorothy Fields's greatest hits, the person I am speaking with will burst into song. I have never met anyone who could not sing at least one chorus of "I Can't Give You Anything but Love"—not that I have been searching for such an unfortunate individual.

Dorothy Fields (1904–74) was one of the most significant and intriguing figures in twentieth-century American musical theater and film. Her career was a long one, spanning almost fifty years. None of the songs she wrote in the 1920s or in the 1970s, nor at any time between those points, sound dated, which must be some sort of definition of classic. The number, scope, and popularity of Dorothy Fields's lyrics place her in a rank with Ira Gershwin, Lorenz Hart, Yip Harburg, and Oscar Hammerstein II.

Dorothy Fields made her way very successfully in what had been before her an almost exclusively male endeavor. She was not the first woman ever to pen the lyric for a popular song. But she was one of the first to write lyrics that were not particularly ladylike. Her most important predecessors, such as Rida Johnson Young (*Marietta* and *Maytime*) and Dorothy Donelly (*The Student Prince* and *Blossom Time*), wrote sentimental texts for European-influenced operettas. Dorothy Fields's lyrics, in contrast, are colloquial and urbane, sometimes slangy and sometimes sensuous, capturing the rhythm and impulse of the language of the here-and-now, from "I Can't Give You Anything but Love" in 1927 to "Nobody Does It Like Me" in 1973. She is closer in spirit to Dorothy Parker than to Dorothy Donelly.

Like many of her colleagues in the business of songwriting, Dorothy Fields was a first-generation American, the descendant of eastern European Jewish immigrants. Unlike most of her colleagues, she was a second-generation show-business personality.[1] Her father was Lew Fields, the taller member of the famous Weber and Fields comedy duo. When Weber and Fields ended their performing partnership in 1904, Fields remained in show business as an actor and producer. He was responsible for bringing hits such as *Peggy-Ann* and *A Connecticut Yankee* to the stage. Dorothy's brothers, Joseph and Herbert, had successful careers as librettists both on Broadway and in Hollywood. Richard Rodgers and Lorenz Hart wrote songs for her high school musical. Cole Porter gave her her first rhyming dictionary. Lehman Engel accurately observed that, "it is impossible that anyone could have been born and reared in the midst of a larger and more impressive musical theatre environment than Dorothy Fields."[2] Perhaps more important than the contacts she had (in fact, her father tried to block her entrance into show business), she grew up in an atmosphere in which words—their meanings and their sounds, the way they are used and misused—were highly valued.

Dorothy Fields was a central figure in the world of popular song during its most vibrant period, and her career mirrors important trends during that time. The unlikely launch pad for her career was New York's Cotton Club, a speakeasy with lavish Negro stage revues and a posh clientele. The revues at the Cotton Club were a curious and delicately balanced example of integration and separation: the production team, including songwriters, choreographers, and costume designers, was all white, and the performers were all black. In the decade from the mid-'20s to the mid-'30s, songwriters at the Cotton Club included Jimmy McHugh and Dorothy Fields as well as Harold Arlen and Ted Koehler; performers included Duke Ellington, Ethel Waters, and Cab Calloway. While working for the Cotton Club, Fields and McHugh wrote the Broadway review, *Blackbirds of 1928*. Featuring Bill Robinson, Aida Ward, and Adelaide Hall, *Blackbirds of 1928* was one of the ten longest-running musicals of the decade.

By 1930, Dorothy Fields and Jimmy McHugh were in Hollywood, under contract to MGM studios. It is likely that their experience writing for revues (as opposed to book musicals) was an excellent preparation for Hollywood's fragmentary approach to putting together a musical. In the course of the 1930s, Dorothy's whole family, with the exception of her sister Frances, moved to Los Angeles, where they all continued to work—mostly independently but sometimes with one another. Dorothy's exclusive partnership with Jimmy McHugh ended in Hollywood, and she began to join her words to the melodies of composers as different as Oscar Levant, Fritz Kreisler, and—probably her favorite partner—Jerome Kern. With him she wrote the songs for *Swing Time*; the song "The Way You Look Tonight" from that movie won them an Oscar in 1936.

Dorothy returned to New York before the beginning of the 1940s, as did her brothers and mother. Although she continued to write songs for movies, she also wrote songs for book musicals, beginning with *Stars in Your Eyes* (1939) with music by Arthur Schwartz and *Up in Central Park* (1945) with music by Sigmund Romberg. She also began writing the books for musicals—*Let's Face It* (1941), *Something for the Boys* (1943), and *Mexican Hayride* (1944), all with music and lyrics by Cole Porter; and *Annie Get Your Gun* (1946), with music and lyrics by Irving Berlin. These books were all written in collaboration with her brother Herbert.

The years from 1951 to 1974 represent the longest and in a sense the steadiest period in Dorothy Fields's life. The groundwork for her career had been established, and there were no major shifts in direction in her professional life in her final two and a half decades. However, she did work with some composers she had not worked with before, including Burton Lane, Morton Gould, Harold Arlen, Albert Hague, and she worked in a medium she had not written for before, the television musical. The last two shows she wrote lyrics for were *Sweet Charity* (1966) and *Seesaw* (1973), both with music by Cy Coleman. In these late works, Fields adds to her customary well-crafted, apt turns of phrase a certain mature feminine insight that allows her to examine the shifting interplay between what a woman feels, what she says, and what she means.

A NOTE ABOUT THE LYRICS

• • •

As the reader will see, there are no full lyrics in this book. My original intention when writing this book was to publish about seventy-five of Dorothy Fields's lyrics. It seemed natural to me to present together the life and the works for which I have so much admiration.

There are two reasons, both having to do with copyright, contributing to my change of plan. One of the publishers that issues the print licenses for many of the lyrics I had hoped to reprint requested $150 per song. The total amount for the number of lyrics I wanted to publish would have been formidable. Furthermore, it was necessary to get permission to reprint lyrics from the executor of Dorothy Fields's estate, her son, David Lahm. Although Mr. Lahm has been very generous with his time, going over the manuscript and offering many suggestions and opinions, his generosity did not extend to granting permission to reprint the lyrics.

Fortunately, there are several means, outside of this book, for accessing the lyrics of Dorothy Fields. Three books are particularly useful: *Reading Lyrics*, by Robert Gottlieb and Robert Kimball; *On the Sunny Side of the Street*, by Deborah Grace Winer; and *Their Words Are Music*, by Lehman Engel. Many of her lyrics can be heard in context, in original-cast recordings of Broadway shows and DVDs of movies. Information for all of these sources is in the two appendices and the endnotes. And, of course, there is the Internet. There is an excellent Dorothy Fields Web site, maintained by Jon Aldous, that provides a wealth of information including CDs, DVDs, and Web performances of Fields's songs. There are also many Web sites—I found more than a dozen in a brief search—on which lyrics by Dorothy Fields can be found. I think that the readers of this book will come to agree that the search is well worth their time.

PICK YOURSELF UP

1

THE WORLD OF HER FATHER

• • •

Dorothy Fields made her entrance into the world in a theatrical fashion. This was only fitting, as she was born into a theatrical family. In her own words, "When I was born my family was spending the summer down at the Jersey shore. I must have arrived ahead of time, because I've always heard how Lee Shubert and Willie Collier, the actor, who were both good friends of my father, Lew Fields, ran through the streets looking for a doctor or a midwife."[1]

It is unlikely that Dorothy, who weighed nine pounds upon her birth on July 15, 1904, was premature, even if the family legend has her arriving ahead of time. Perhaps her mother miscalculated the date. Perhaps, as a twenty-nine-year-old mother of three healthy children, Rose Fields was relaxed to the point of casualness about arrangements for Dorothy's arrival. In any case, it is characteristic that the family member Dorothy mentions first in the tale of her birth is her father, not her mother. As a youngster, indeed for much of her life, Dorothy's world was very much the world of her father.

Lew Fields's entrance into the world, and his entry into the United States five and a half years later, was less dramatic than Dorothy's. In the autumn of 1872, Solomon and Sarah Schoenfeld arrived at the State Immigration Depot at Castle Gardens, New York, from the *shtetl* west of Warsaw where they had lived and owned a tailoring business. With them were their sons Marx, age eleven; Abel, age eight; Moses, age five; and Henry, age one. As was the case for many immigrants to the United States, one aspect of their lives that underwent change was their names. For immigrants whose first language was Yiddish, which is written using the Hebrew alphabet, at the very least their names would be transliterated. When they wrote their names in Roman characters, they might need to choose between preserving spelling or pronunciation. Moreover, whatever name they entered the country with might well undergo further transformation over the years. Hence, the elder sons of Solomon (or Samuel) Schoenfeld (or Schanfield) would by 1900 be called Max, Sol, and Lew (sometimes Maurice Lewis) Fields.

Their family history does not preserve a specific reason for their emigration. They may have been seeking greater economic opportunity. Sarah's older brother, David Frank, had already established himself in New York City. With four healthy sons, the Schoenfelds may well have been fleeing the threat of future conscription into the army. Jews were not allowed full rights of citizenship in that time and place, but the privilege of serving five years in the army of Czar Alexander II was freely and forcefully extended to them.

The Schoenfelds were not pioneers, but they came ahead of the largest wave of immigrant Jews from Eastern Europe, which began in the 1880s. The outbreak of pogroms following the assassination of Czar Alexander II in 1881 meant that the Jews living in the Pale of Settlement, who had been suffering the gradual misery of increasing pauperization, now felt immediate fears for their physical safety as well. The trickle of Jewish immigration became a flood.

According to the eminent interpreter of the immigrant Jewish-American experience, Irving Howe, what "uniquely characterized the east European Jews [in the last third of the nineteenth century] was the explosive mixture of mounting wretchedness and increasing hope, physical suffering and spiritual exaltation. And what was new in their experience was that for the first time they could suppose there was someplace else to go, a new world perceived as radically different from the one in which they lived."[2] The Schoenfeld family, arriving in the 1870s, were not only ahead of the great wave of eastern European immigration, they were ahead of the concomitant backlash: the outpouring of nativist fears about threats to the American way of life. Over the years, reflecting shifts in popular prejudices, Lew Fields would variously describe himself as American-born, German-born, or Polish-born. For some immigrants or children of immigrants, the step from inventing a new family name to inventing a new family history was a small one. Moreover, the shifting political boundaries in eastern Europe at this time made it difficult to be precise about one's place of origin even if one had a desire to do so. Did one come from Danzig or Gdansk, a city in Poland or in Germany? Lemberg or L'vov? The answer might depend on when the question was asked.

The Schoenfelds moved into a three-room apartment on Division Street on the Lower East Side, which served as their living place and workplace. A few months after they arrived, Charles was born—the first American-born member of the family. The family was completed by the births of Anna (1874), Nathan (1877), and Renee, nicknamed Ray (1879).

Apart from coming to the United States, probably the most significant event in the first decade of Lew Fields's life was a simple and undramatic one. At age eight, he became friends with Joe Weber. Lew and Joe had many things in common. They both came from large, poor, immigrant Jewish families (Joe was the youngest of thirteen children). They lived in the same neighborhood and went to the same school. More important, they both loved clowning around—first for their classmates and later for anyone who would pay to see them. Of course, this was not what they were supposed to be doing. They were supposed to be going to school or working at jobs their fathers understood as jobs—assisting in the tailoring business, working in a factory, or peddling.

School ended for Joe and Lew in the fourth grade. Some biographers report that they were expelled from the Allen Street school for cutting up in class. However, the early end to their formal education should be put in the perspective of their time. Four years of primary school was all that New York law demanded at the time. The generally overcrowded classrooms were far from seductive. And the pressure to earn money to help support the family was unrelenting. Education may have provided a means to a better future for a later generation, but the first crop of immigrants needed more immediate means of sustaining themselves.[3] Joe Weber once reminisced, "We had to make some money to help our families along and we tried our hands at a whole lot of different things to earn a little. We sold cakes and I did pretty well imitating a stuttering boy. All the ladies felt sorry for me and made the men who were with them buy something out of pity. But one day there was a heavy shower and our whole stock was dissolved. At one time Fields sold soda water and I made cigarettes, but no matter what else we were doing we kept practicing and going to whatever shows we could."[4] For Weber and Fields, all the world was a stage and a training ground, a place to observe human nature and to practice what they saw.

The 1880 U.S. Census has Lew Fields listed as a tailor, as it does his older brothers, Max and Sol. That designation, one must assume, illustrated the parents' view of their sons' present and future occupation. But in fact, Weber and Fields began to be paid as entertainers from the time they were twelve, in 1879. Employed in dime museums and variety houses in the Bowery, they earned between $6 and $25 a week for their act. One summer on Coney Island, their earnings climbed as high as $30 a week. Of course, the work was not steady, but the income from tailoring was likewise far from secure. If Lew ever felt tempted to return to the family tailoring trade (and there is no evidence that he was ever so tempted), the mass immigration of eastern European Jews in the early 1880s, followed by the overall lowering of wages for garment workers, could have reminded him that there was no financial security in the needle trades. As the number of immigrants grew in the 1880s, there was an oversupply of semiskilled workers, and their pay plummeted.

Men who typically earned $15 per week in 1883 earned half that in 1885; women generally were paid half the hourly rate men received. When Weber and Fields were in their early teens, they learned the irresistible lesson that by doing what they most enjoyed doing—playacting and clowning around—they could also earn more money than they could at drudge work.

The act that Weber and Fields first developed was a patchwork of entertaining bits—songs, dances, and humor, both verbal and physical. Their fundamental stance was as outsiders, addressing themselves to an audience of outsiders. At the beginning of their careers, just what kind of outsider they represented was not very important. They could be a blackface duo, an Irish duo, or a Dutch (i.e., German) duo by making only slight adjustments to their material and more substantial adjustments to their makeup and costumes. Their basic entrance song was:

> Here we are, a jolly pair
> With no troubles or care.
> We are here once more
> To make the people roar,
> Before we go to the ball.

It worked equally well whether they sang, "Here we are an Irish pair" or "Here we are a colored pair" or "Here we are a German pair." The choice of ethnicity came not so much from who they themselves were but from what acts they could observe and imitate. What they never presented themselves as, not out of pride or respect but for lack of models, was a Yiddish pair. Among the best of the blackface teams performing when Weber and Fields were young were George McIntyre and Thomas Heath; surely the most famous of the Irish pairs were Harrigan and Hart. Later there were German and Italian duos, the comic acts generally reflecting the shifting waves of immigration.

The journeyman years of Weber and Fields were years literally spent journeying, mainly by railroad, and the lessons they learned were many and varied. When their act went over poorly in Philadelphia, John L. Carncross, the manager of the Carncross Minstrels, advised them to reassure the audience, after many minutes of slapstick violence, by making up onstage before the end of the act. The advice proved apt, and the team eventually developed a line that became one of their trademarks: "When you are away from me, I can't keep my mind off you. When you are with me, I can't keep my hands off you" (followed by mock choking). Weber and Fields did not need the guidance of Freud to mine the rich vein of material coming from exaggerated emotional ambivalence. The same Philadelphia manager advised that they increase the comic incongruity of their act by performing in formal evening dress instead of the loud, checkered jackets they had been wearing.

A different lesson was learned in Providence, Rhode Island, when their trunk did not arrive in time for their first performance. Working with hastily assembled costumes and props, Fields whacked a too-heavy cane over a too-thinly padded wig on Weber's head, and blood flowed. The audience laughed uproariously. Years later, Weber complained in an interview, "All the public wanted to see was Fields knock the hell out of me." Fields concurred, "Providence liked our murder act. It was rough work. . . . When we bled the audience seemed to like us all the better."[5] The experience may not have given Weber and Fields a warm view of human nature, but they incorporated a safer version of increased mayhem into their act.

The many hours they spent on trains were another source of comedy for Weber and Fields—or at least the events seemed comic in retrospect, when they turned their trials into anecdotes for interviewers. Well into their teens, they tried to dupe ticket sellers and train conductors into letting them travel on children's fares. They spent a few months in 1887 working with a two-ring railroad circus but found this did not suit them well. The subculture of the circus troupe was alien to them; moreover, although the team could present themselves as Negro, Irish, or German, their material was intended for urban rather than rural audiences.

From their earliest working days, both Weber and Fields had made it a practice to send the greater part of what they earned back to their families. The death of Weber's father in 1883 probably increased his sense of responsibility for the care of his mother and older siblings. Lew's father was not only alive and well; he continued to disapprove of his son's chosen career. Hence, subterfuge was needed for Lew to contribute to his family's finances—the weekly checks were sent to Lew's older brother Max. Before they were out of their teens, Weber and Fields were not only independent, self-made men, but were on their way to becoming the chief financial support of their families. At this stage in their careers, touring was most profitable, both for financial returns and for the artistic benefit of continually honing and sharpening material before changing audiences.

By the end of their journeyman period, Weber and Fields had developed the comic personae—Mike and Myer—that would serve them for the rest of their lives. Physiology played a role. By the end of their teen years, they had attained their full height; Joe Weber was five foot four, and Lew Fields was five foot eleven. Weber wore clothing that was heavily padded around the middle, and when standing together Weber and Fields looked like a globe and an obelisk, respectively. It was clear who would be the bully and who the bullied.

They also took into their personae a central feature of ethnic humor—the contrast of the stupid and the canny. Both Mike and Myer are outside mainstream American life, but Myer is just one step ahead of Mike and relates to him as both teacher and exploiter. What distinguished Weber and Fields from other knockabout comic teams was the acuity of their verbal wit, which focused on the absurdities of life and of the English language.

MIKE: In two days, I vill be a murdered man.

MYER: A vot?

MIKE: I mean a married man.

MYER: I hope you vill always look back upon der presendt moment as der habbiest moment uff your life.

MIKE: But I aind't married yet.

MYER: I know it, und furdermore, upon dis suspicious occasion, I also vish to express to you—charges collect—my uppermost depreciation of der dishonor you haf informed upon me in making me your bridesmaid.

MIKE: Der insuldt is all mein.

MYER: As you standt before me now, soo young, soo innocent, soo obnoxious, there is only one void dat can expres mine pleasure, mein dissatisfaction—

MIKE: Yes, yes?

MYER: Und I can't tink of der void.[6]

For five years, until 1889, Weber and Fields moved around the country as members of assorted traveling variety shows: three seasons with Gus Hill's Company and one season each with Austin's Australian Novelty Company and Harry Kernell's Company. This time was valuable not only for developing their own act but also for observing how touring companies operated. Even as teenagers, Lew and Joe exhibited different but complementary skills. Lew had an eye for burgeoning talent and a knack for developing warm professional relationships. Joe had an excellent grasp of financial details and a clear-eyed notion of practical realities.

In 1890, when they were twenty-three, Weber and Fields felt ready to produce and manage their own traveling show. Felix Isman, Weber and Fields's earliest biographer, suggests that they were motivated to start their own company, in part, by the anger and hurt they felt over their treatment at the hands of Harry Kernell, the manager of the company they worked for in 1889. Annoyed by Weber and Fields's request for higher wages, Kernell hired the Rogers Brothers, Max and Gus, to duplicate Weber and Fields's act, and placed them earlier on the program, forcing Weber and Fields to create a new act or look like pale imitators of the Rogers Brothers. Isman stated, "In the mutual rage generated by this grotesque vendetta, Weber and Fields' sense of humor failed them. . . . Their bluff to Kernell of taking out their own show became a point of honor."[7]

It should be remembered, though, that the American dream did not stop at the ability to enter a profession based on one's own talents rather than training received from one's father in the father's trade. The American dream extended to becoming a boss as well as a worker, to owning as much as possible of the resources and the profits resulting from the products of one's talents. Thus, Irving Berlin was not only a self-made songwriter but also a publisher of songs. He became a partner in the publishing firm Waterson, Berlin, and Snyder in 1911 and formed his own publishing company, Irving Berlin Inc., in 1914. Douglas Fairbanks and Mary Pickford were not only actors but, together with Charlie Chaplin and D. W. Griffith, were the owners of United Artists, formed in 1919. In 1890, several decades before these entertainment entrepreneurs, Weber and Fields moved up from being a knockabout comic act to being the producers of Weber and Fields' Own Company, financed in part by the $2,000 profits they gained performing in San Francisco and Oregon.

As was true for filmmaking in the 1910s and 1920s, theater in the 1890s—particularly comic or variety shows—was an area in which self-taught men of talent could rise quickly to the top. The first company of their own that Weber and Fields took on the road was made up of more than a dozen people, including various ethnic comedians (Irish, blackface, or "Dutch"), trained animals, acrobats, and alluring women. In thirty-seven weeks they traveled to Paterson, Newark, Philadelphia, Providence, Montreal, Toronto, Buffalo, Chicago, and Milwaukee; they also played in several New York venues—the Olympia Theater in Harlem, the Grand Theater in Brooklyn, and the London Theater in the Bowery. They never operated with much of an economic cushion, and the diamond studs they purchased when they first took on the personae of managers were in and out of hock several times, but all in all the operation was enough of a success to take Weber and Fields' Own Company on the road again the next season.

His success as an employer may have encouraged Lew Fields to take another step into the world of responsible adulthood and become a husband. Rose Harris was fifteen when she first met Lew Fields. They were introduced by Annie Schanfield, Rose's friend and Lew's sister. Rose came from a slightly smaller family than Lew—four siblings instead of seven—and worked in a department store in Brooklyn. After a three-year acquaintance, which must have grown in large part through letters, since Weber and Fields toured for well over half the year, Lew and Rose married on January 1, 1893. She was eighteen, and he twenty-six.

A detail of the wedding, a matter of names, suggests that the growing security and stability of Lew's professional and personal life was not accompanied by a clarification of his own personal identity. The man who came into the world as Moses Schoenfeld, who was known to the theatergoing public as Lew Fields, was called Louis M. Schoenfields on his marriage certificate and L. Maurice Fields in the report of the wedding that appeared in the *New York Herald*. These were not slips of the pen, I believe, but signs of a division within the self. In an event as deeply personal and family-centered as a wedding (Rose's bridesmaids were her sister, her sister-in-law, and a girl who was to marry one of Lew's brothers), Lew Fields seems to have struggled with what face (that is, what name) to present to the world.

The day after the wedding, Lew went back to work. January 2, 1893, marked the first appearance of Weber and Fields uptown on Broadway; they played at the New Park Theatre at Broadway and Thirty-fifth Street. Vaudeville was not the typical fare for the uptown audience, but Weber and Fields gambled that this was an audience they could entertain. Their faith was not misplaced. Weber and Fields were booked to play the New Park Theatre once again in April, this time for an unprecedentedly long (for the theater) run: two weeks.

Playing in theaters in New York and Brooklyn continued to alternate with touring, but here too expansion took place. In the 1893–94 season, Weber and Fields's talent for management allowed them to expand to two road companies: Weber and Fields' Own Company toured twenty-nine cities in twenty-eight weeks, and the Russell Brothers Company toured thirty-three cities in thirty-two weeks. Two seasons later, they added a third touring company, the Vaudeville Club.

In May 1896, Weber and Fields played an even grander uptown venue, the Olympia Theater on Broadway between Forty-fourth and Forty-fifth Streets. Designed by the impresario Oscar Hammerstein, the Olympia comprised three different performance spaces plus a roof garden, a café, and a billiard room. The team was paid the princely salary of $750 per week.[8] Their success was a reaffirmation of the belief that the team could entertain audiences not only on the Lower East Side where they had spent their childhood or touring across the nation where they had spent much of their adolescence, but also on Broadway, which in some ways may have seemed a greater distance from the Bowery than did San Francisco.

After the triumph at the Olympia, Weber and Fields took one more step toward professional independence and growth. In 1896, they leased their own theater and hired an all-star company to perform in it. The theater, at various times called the Imperial Music Hall and the Broadway Music Hall, was on Twenty-ninth Street, but leasing an adjoining shop made it possible to construct an entrance to the theater on Broadway. In an area populated with several hotels, theaters, and fashionable stores, the location should have been ideal. However, the previous leaseholder had not been successful, and in some people's minds the house was an unlucky one. For Weber and Fields, though, it was opportunity calling.

They could not get a bank loan, lacking collateral, but once again there was family to draw on. Leo Teller, identified by Felix Isman as the brother-in-law of Lew Fields (which would make him Renee's husband), put up $1,500 and left his job as a department manager in the A. I. Namm store in Brooklyn to become a house manager for the Weber and Fields music hall.

The lease of the music hall was the start of a new era for Weber and Fields, marked by a change in audience and a change in material. The audience Weber and Fields were now aiming at was socially upscale. Opening nights at the music hall soon became major social events attended by entertainment figures such as Tony Pastor, Fred Hamlin, Florenz Ziegfeld, publisher Julius Witmark, political figures such as Tammany Boss Richard Croker and Mayor Van Wyck, and social lions such as Jesse Lewisohn, William Randolph Hearst, and Stanford White. Tickets for opening night were sold at auction with prices for box seats as high as $500 and orchestra seats as high as $100. The take from opening night helped finance the entire season.

In addition, Weber and Fields, both members of which were now family men themselves, was courting a family audience—or at least a mixed-sex audience. To make the enterprise more suitable to an upper-class audience of both sexes, the team paid attention to the quality of the show and of the theater's decor. One year, the color scheme was red and gold; another year, pink and gold; another, green silk brocade with gold trim.

For this new, uptown, theatergoing audience, Weber and Fields ventured into a new-for-them form of entertainment; they began to burlesque successful Broadway shows. When Belasco presented *The First Born*, Weber and Fields gave its audiences *The Worst Born*. Similarly, *Quo Vadis* was transformed into *Quo Vas Iss?*, *The Stubbornness of Geraldine* metamorphosed into *The Stickiness of Gelatine*, and *Madame du Barry* became *Du Hurry*. Weber and Fields's cleverness did not end at the invention of titles. There was verbal humor, costumes and stage props verging on the surreal, and occasionally pointed social satire. The dramatic premises of the source plays were either exaggerated or inverted. Overweening virtue, rather than vice, could bring a character down, but a smiling mask softened implied criticism.

In a sense, the focus and butt of Weber and Fields's humor never changed. It was always themselves and their audiences. When they viewed themselves and their audiences as laboring-class immigrants, the comic personae they took on were just such people. They saw these people as most humorous in the times (rare enough, perhaps) when they were free to pursue leisure activities. Their most famous routine, which they created in 1892 and revived and repeated for four decades, shows Mike and Myer playing pool. In 1894, audiences saw Mike and Myer at a shooting gallery; in 1895, there was a bowling skit. When Weber and Fields leased the music hall, they were no longer of the newly arrived laboring classes; nor, for the most part, was their audience. They were still newly arrived, perhaps, but newly arrived to the middle class. As such, they had a clear-seeing eye for moral ambiguities and fraudulent pieties and skewered these, to the glee of their audiences.

The company that played at the music hall was built more from the standpoint of a performer than that of a bookkeeper. The first question was who would make the company strongest. The question of how to run such a company at a profit came second. Weber and Fields were not careless about money, but the bottom line was not their first thought. Nor were they interested in the biggest stars, the biggest drawing powers that money could buy—which might be a fair description of Oscar Hammerstein's approach before them or Florenz Ziegfeld's after them. They needed the best possible talents who could work together in a stock company—who would work in shows in the Weber and Fields style. In the eight years that Weber and Fields occupied the music hall, their company included, at a minimum, two or three women who could sing and play comic roles, two or three men in addition to Weber and Fields who played comic roles, and a male romantic lead. All of the performers needed to be skilled at improvising comedy.

The women in the company were Mabel Fenton, Fay Templeton, and, from 1900 on, Lillian Russell. These women were all seasoned performers before coming to Weber and Fields. Templeton and Russell had both started out in vaudeville and had crossed over to the legitimate stage. The male comics included Sam Bernard, John T. Kelley, David Warfield, and Peter Dailey. These men were all fluent in but not dependent on ethnic humor—Irish, German, or Jewish. De Wolf Hopper, the resident leading man for many years, was replaced in 1902 by Willie Collier, mentioned in Dorothy's anecdote about her birth.

In 1904, Weber and Fields ended their partnership after eight epoch-making seasons in the music hall. They were only thirty-seven years old but they had been a team for twenty-five years, and to many it seemed the end of an era. As with political revolutions, there were both immediate and underlying causes for the breakup. The short-term cause was the fire in the Iroquois Theater in Chicago on December 30, 1903, in which 575 people died. In New York

City and elsewhere, officials began to look more seriously at rewriting—or at least enforcing—the fire codes in theaters. Weber was willing to spend the money to have their theater rebuilt, but Fields wanted to move on. In the end, each man got his way. The two comedians agreed to separate—after one last moneymaking tour across the United States—and on May 1, 1904, Fields sold his interest in the music hall to Weber for $40,000.

Even before the fire at the Iroquois Theater, artistic, personal, and financial disagreements—sometimes exacerbated by assorted members of Fields's and Weber's families—placed ever greater stress and strain on the partnership. Performers whose reputations had been made or greatly enhanced at the music hall moved on—David Warfield to work for David Belasco, Sam Bernard to run his own company, Mabel Fenton and Fay Templeton to prosperous retirements. Lew watched them go, benevolently, but sometimes, perhaps, with a touch of envy. For example, David Warfield had been doing only comic roles under Weber and Fields's auspices, but he went on to serious dramatic roles. Lew might well have felt he had similar or greater abilities himself but had no arena in which to show this. Weber had little sympathy for Fields's aspirations outside of their acts together. "I don't think I am cut out to play Romeo, and I have my doubts what kind of a Hamlet you would make, Lew," he once commented.[9] Each time a star departed, Weber and Fields attempted to replace him or her with a star of even greater magnitude—at a higher salary. But the music hall sat fewer than seven hundred patrons. Should they move to a larger hall? Should they raise ticket prices? In the past, Weber and Fields had managed to sustain their very expensive New York season through far more profitable summer touring seasons during which they played in larger houses, which could ask higher ticket prices for a limited-engagement run. But the best touring houses were coming under ever-tightening, monopolistic control of theater syndicates such as Klaw and Erlanger, whose practices Weber and Fields found unacceptable. So a variety of factors brought an end to Weber and Fields's partnership, and in 1904, the year Dorothy Fields was born, one era ended and another began in the world of her father.

2

THE WORLD OF HER FAMILY

• • •

Dorothy Fields was born on July 15, 1904, in Allenhurst, New Jersey, in a residence the Fields family was renting for the summer. The *American Society of Composers, Authors, and Publishers Biographical Dictionary* gives her year of birth as 1905, as do several other works. In an oral-history interview for Columbia University, given in 1958, she states that she was born in 1905. Nevertheless, 1904 is the year on her birth certificate. Her birth certificate is revealing on several additional points. The birthplace of her father is listed as New York City, which was a convenient fiction. The birth certificate also reveals that as of July 18, three days after her birth, she had not yet received a given name.

Baby girl Fields was given the name Dorothy after the heroine in *The Wizard of Oz*, which at that time was popular as both a novel and a musical play. What type of heroine is this Dorothy? For one thing, she is ultra-American—a midwesterner from deep in the heartland, Kansas. Any ties her family may have had with Europe are long forgotten, consigned to oblivion (as were Lew Fields's ties to his real birthplace, Poland, on Dorothy's birth certificate). There is no Old World in the fictional Dorothy's past, and the New World she discovers is magical and theatrical. In this magical and theatrical world, she keeps her wise-child common sense. Also, she is throughout her adventures a child, not a woman.

Perhaps one should not make too much of the choice of the name Dorothy. After all, in the period from 1900 to 1910, "Dorothy" was one of the ten most popular names for girls in the United States. When she was an adult, two of Dorothy Fields's best friends were Dorothy Hammerstein and Dorothy Rodgers. Nevertheless, for assimilating Jewish immigrants at this time, the taking, changing, and giving of names was bound up with their sense of self, their identities, and their aspirations. Dorothy's brother Joseph was named after Joe Weber—someone adult, someone real. Frances and Herbert, the names given to her sister and another brother, were names borne by other members of their mother's family. So the general popularity of the distinctly American name Dorothy may have been less important than the implication that it designated a special, almost magical, child—at least in Lew's mind.

When Dorothy was born, Lew and Rose Fields already had three children, a girl and two boys. The three older Fields children were born in close succession, starting when Rose was nineteen. When Frances was born, in 1894, Lew was on tour, and Rose was living with his parents, Solomon and Sarah Schoenfeld. This arrangement made sense financially and socially. Moreover, keeping two or more generations of Fieldses together in a single living unit was clearly a family preference. At different times, daughters-in-law lived with parents (Rose with the Schoenfelds) or parents with children (Solomon and Sarah with their daughter Annie and her husband, Morris Warschauer). Herb, after he was an employed adult, lived with Rose and Lew. Dorothy and Joseph joined Herb at the parental home when their first marriages ended. In the 1930s, Lew and Rose lived in the house in Hollywood that Herb and Dorothy rented. The Fieldses' nuclear family had a rather large nucleus, with strong bonds.

By the time their second child, Joseph, was born, on February 21, 1895, Rose and Lew had moved to an apartment of their own at Fifty-ninth Street and Lexington Avenue. This was part of a large-scale family migration. Lew's parents, brothers, and sisters left the Bowery and spread out along the East Side of Manhattan from Fifty-ninth Street to 107th Street. Herbert was born in 1897. There was a seven-year hiatus before the birth of Dorothy, putting her in a special position in the family.

The start of the new century had been shadowed with deaths or close brushes with death in the Fields family. In December 1900, all three of the Fields children were critically ill with diphtheria and scarlet fever—diseases often fatal in the time before antibiotics—but they all recovered. Max, Lew's older brother and closest ally in the Fields family, had succumbed to tuberculosis in 1901. Dorothy's birth in 1904 may have made the cliché "blessed event" seem a simple statement of fact.

Dorothy's family environment differed from that of her siblings, even beyond the fact that she was the baby and that her father was no longer an itinerant entertainer. Some things remained much the same. The family pattern of Rose making the household decisions continued. Although he was no longer touring, Lew was seldom at home because he spent long hours at the theater. No longer partnered with Joe Weber, Lew Fields was very active as a producer and actor. Moreover, one could say that Rose represented Lew's aspirations of what the family would become—something more solidly middle class and secure. A generation earlier, a stay-at-home mother in a poorer Jewish family would have worked in the at-home family business. In

Lew Fields's family, Rose's sole occupation was the family. The next generation brought another reversal; Dorothy, even while a wife and mother, was devoted to her profession. In any case, Rose had more say in how the family was reared. Temperamentally, Rose was the stabler figure, whereas Lew was the more expressive: he showed both more affection and more anger. But although Rose probably was a stronger influence on the lives of the older children, Lew, despite his absences, exerted a stronger influence on Dorothy. By the time Dorothy was born, success and a certain measure of wealth were what the Fields family had come to expect for itself. And the success of a father in show business meant that Dorothy, more than her older siblings, was born to life as a public figure. The day after her birth, a newspaper article appeared under the headline "Oh Joy! Lew Fields Once More a Proud Father. It's a Baby Girl This Time." The article, with a picture of Rose Fields, went on to state:

> The golden hue in the southwesterly heavens last evening, which many attributed to a tardy sunset, was in reality the glow of bonfires and red fire ignited by the joyful residents of Allenhurst. At exactly two o'clock in the afternoon Lew Fields became the proud father of another daughter, and all villagers, together with the summer colonists, set out to make the day and night memorable.
>
> By 2:30 Broadway had learned over the telephone of the latest Fields edition deluxe and the theatrical district rushed to the nearest telegraph offices in order to send hearty congratulations. Less than an hour before the birth of Miss Fields (first name still in doubt) Mrs. Fields was chatting with her husband and Grace George in front of her cottage. When a physician arrived at the household little Miss Fields was crying lustily, and Mr. Fields was jumping up and down on the veranda in the ecstasy of his emotions. Further details, as Broadway learned then, was that Miss Fields weighs nine pounds and that both she and her mother are doing nicely.
>
> With the latest recruit to Mr. Fields' stock company, the aggregate of juvenile players is four. The others are named Francis [sic], Joseph, and Herbert.[1]

It is not clear to what extent Lew Fields cultivated celebrity. Certainly, he seemed to like to theorize about his art in the newspapers. Over the years, newspaper interviews appeared with titles such as "Coherency What the Public Wants Now" and "Exaggerated Truth Lew Fields' Laugh Formula." But by the time of Dorothy's birth, all sorts of events in Lew's private life, and that of his extended family, were grist for the publicity mill. In 1906, just a few days before Dorothy's second birthday, the *New York Telegraph* informed its readers, "Lew Fields' Brother Sol Is Married." The same newspaper ran an article on the fiftieth wedding anniversary of Lew's parents in 1907. Rose Fields's efforts on behalf of various charities were covered in the papers, as were Herb's and Joe's activities at school or camp. The embarkation of the Lew Fields family for Europe in May 1911 was covered with a story under the headline, "Lew Fields to Have First Vacation in Four Years." The death of Lew's father at age seventy-one, in November 1911, was also covered by the press. Thus, Rose Fields's somewhat Dickensian remark to her children, "You must be polite to strangers because your father is an actor," may be understood as a practical assessment that the family was in the public eye.

Dorothy's childhood years were also better documented in photographs than were those of her older siblings. A photo of Dorothy Fields at about the age of six shows her well dressed and unsmiling. Granddaughter of a tailor and daughter of a refugee from the tailoring business, Dorothy, her sister, and her brothers were always meticulously well dressed. Her apparel in the photo suggests a child well taken care of: she has a large bow in carefully combed hair, a lacy dress, shining shoes. Dorothy must have been fond of this photo, for she kept it framed and on dislay in her home later on in her life. This suggests she felt a certain comfort with her past and with herself. Her father, on several occasions, reinvented his past, telling the press he was American-born, or German-born, when in fact he was born near Warsaw. But Dorothy was the child of a celebrity and her childhood was, at least in part, documented in the public record.

Other photos, published in newspapers and periodicals, show Dorothy with her family. There is always a bow in her hair—probably her mother's touch. The photos reveal a close, comfortable physical connection between father and daughter. In one, Lew is on his hands and knees, and Dorothy, with a gleeful smile, is riding on his back. In another, a family picnic scene, Dorothy is sitting on the grass, and Lew is reclining with his head on her lap. A more formally posed photo, from 1910, shows Dorothy with her family, standing outside their new residence on Riverside Drive. It must be summer; Lew and Joseph are wearing straw boaters. Dorothy is wearing a short-sleeved dress, and her calves are bare. Lew's arms encircle Dorothy protectively, his right arm around her back, his left hand over her right hand. She is seated on a banister, and the older members of the family are all standing. All the adults are looking directly into the camera and their roles are set—the men all look earnest, ready to take on what life has to offer; the women are all smiling, prepared to look decorative and be taken care of.

Photos of the entire family together no doubt marked special occasions, partly because Lew was seldom home during the children's waking hours. He spent long hours, every day, at work. When Lew was a child, home and workplace were the same place. For subsistence tailors, renting a place to work as well as a place to live would have been an absurd expense. As an adult, when Lew was home he was not only in a different place; he was, in his own mind, a different person. He told an interviewer, "If you ask me if I am a comedian in my private life, do clowning in my house, at my dinner table, no! I am very serious. . . . I come to the theater and do my job with the tools of my profession which I keep [there], just as the mechanic goes to work and uses his tools."[2]

John Lahr has eloquently described the great contrast between the onstage and offstage personalities of his father, the comedian Bert Lahr, who created the role of the cowardly lion in the 1939 movie of *The Wizard of Oz.* "Onscreen the Lion was panic-stricken but fun; his despair was delightful. . . . The Lion had words for what was going on inside him; he asked for help and got it. At home, there were no words or even tears, just the thick fog of some ontological anxiety, which seemed to have settled permanently around Dad and was palpable, impenetrable—it lifted only occasionally, for a few brilliant moments. . . . He was perpetually distracted from others, and, despite his ability to tease the last scintilla of laughter from a role, he had no idea how to brighten his own day."[3]

One should not take a comparison between Lew Fields and Bert Lahr very far, however. There is very little to suggest that Lew Fields was moody or morose at home. Indeed, he may have been protesting too much by insisting on the difference between his onstage and offstage personae. The Fields household was often a lively and laugh-filled place. Moreover, Dorothy recalled observing her father work at home. "I remember so well hearing his lines—he always did this, with any new play, whether it was a musical play or a straight play. I always heard his lines. He was a good study and a very thorough study. The house was always filled with scripts and things that were sent to him. He always had bits and pieces of paper, gags that he'd figured out or that he'd heard, that he thought he might use."[4] Dorothy's perception of her father's love for the theater must have come in part from her sense of the joy that radiated from him when he was at work. It is hard to know how much wistfulness, or longing, or even resentment one should read into her statement, "My father had always been in the theater as an actor and a producer, and that was the only thing he cared about, actually."[5]

It is likely that in the children's minds, Rose stood for reality and stability, Lew for mystery and exciting potential. Rose was Lew's lifelong mate and partner. But she saw her motherly role in part as shielding the children from some aspects of Lew's life—to some extent from his life as a performer and certainly from his life as a gambler. A love for gambling was the shadow side of the hardworking, clean-living, uxorious, family-loving Lew Fields. In 1958, Dorothy commented, "My father was a great gambler. He would play the races in the afternoon, and roulette at night. Mother left him twice on account of that. She just wouldn't have it. One time she packed up at Saratoga, took all of us and came home. He promised he wouldn't gamble, and he gave her all his cash except a $20 gold piece, and excused himself and said New York was calling. He went into the gaming tables at the hotel. Mother caught him and she said, 'That's the end, Lew. I'm leaving! And I'm taking the children with me!' . . . He didn't stop. He was just incorrigible. But he was such an angel, and a fascinating guy."[6]

Nobody knows how much money Lew won or lost at gambling. Sometimes he won big. Fields's biographers note that around the time of Dorothy's birth, Lew had a winning streak both at the roulette tables and at the racetrack, winning more than $16,000 in a few days.[7] In a life that was never financially predictable, roulette and horse races may have seemed just a more ritualized form of fiscal insecurity.

In the United States at the turn of the century, gambling houses and race-tracks were, like the theater, venues where social classes mixed—where money spoke louder than family background. Gambling was one of Lew's connections to a higher social class. It was at the racetrack that Lew first met, and hired, Lillian Russell. According to Armond Fields and L. Marc Fields,

> One version of the racetrack meeting, perhaps apocryphal, has Lillian Russell, seated in [Jesse] Lewisohn's box, picking a winner by jabbing a hatpin into the program with her eyes closed. Fields suggested that if she used a fork, she could pick win, place, and show. The quip broke the ice, and Fields asked her if she would consider joining his company. This too, brought a smile to her face. How could they afford to pay her price, with their small theater? Swallowing hard, Fields asked her to name her price: twelve hundred and fifty a week, a thirty-five week guarantee, and all costumes to be paid for by the producers. Drawing on all of the reserves of self-control he had learned at the roulette table, Fields calmly replied, "That's fine. We'll be expecting you at rehearsals in August." He shook hands with a surprised Lillian Russell, and the deal was sealed. For the next five seasons that was the only contract they needed.[8]

The deaths of Dorothy's maternal grandmother in 1909 and paternal grandfather in 1911 had important ramifications for her family life. When Rose Harris Fields's mother died in 1909, she left a fourteen-year-old son, Herbert Harris, whom Lew and Rose took into their home. Herb Harris and Joseph Fields, though uncle and nephew, were just about the same age. They were to become lifelong friends and occasional business partners. Indeed, although the family groupings would shift several times in the next decade, certain patterns of alliance remained strong. Frances was, in a sense, an outsider among her siblings. Nicknamed "the princess," she was closest to her mother in her attitudes and in the pattern her life would take. While Joe Fields and Herb Harris forged a strong bond, an even stronger one was formed between the two youngest children, Herbert and Dorothy.

Lew's father, Solomon, died on November 7, 1911, with his wife, his two daughters, and his one non-theatrical son, Henry, at his bedside. Over the years, Solomon had become reconciled to Lew's profession to the point of not merely accepting money from him but even taking his son's surname. Lew's parents may have been disappointed with their son's assimilated ways: neither of his own sons had a formal bar mitzvah ceremony, the Fields family did not keep kosher, and they even celebrated Christmas with a tree and gifts. But the Fields family script was not *The Jazz Singer*; the patriarch was not inflexible, and differences in the ways the generations lived did not cause irreconcilable divisions.

The reconciliation that took place at Solomon's funeral was not between family members but between Fields and Weber. As Felix Isman tells the story:

> Fields' father died and Weber attended the funeral. He and Lew rode together returning from the cemetery. Their route led through the Bowery. There was Miner's, here Donaldson's London, farther down the street the old Bowery Theater, there what once had been the Chatham Square and the Globe Museums; a moving panorama of their youth. Newer immigrants had displaced their generation from these crowded tenements. They saw themselves in the urchins that played in the noisome streets and fell silent.
>
> "So you're giving up the old music hall, Web," Fields asked at length.
>
> "Yes," Joe said. "It has been losing money in recent years. It has seen its day."
>
> "We ought to go together again, Web."
>
> Lew read Joe's answer in his eyes.[9]

The reunion of the Weber and Fields comedy team after a hiatus of almost eight years was greeted with intense enthusiasm. Several of the former members of the Weber-Fields theatrical company—including Faye Templeton, who had gone into happily married retirement several years earlier, and Lillian Russell—joined Joe and Lew for a show that brought the audience to transports of nostalgia. Tickets for opening night, February 8, 1912, were auctioned off, as they had been for Joe and Lew's music hall shows a decade earlier. Prices for tickets were astronomical by 1912 standards—$35 for an orchestra seat and $900 for a box. Lew could have sold the box he reserved for his family for more than $1,000, but in this instance family came first.

Although the Fields children had been shielded from a close involvement with Lew's work by their mother, this opening-night performance, attended by noted industrialists, politicians, and a Supreme Court justice, was not one for them to miss. They sat in their center box and saw not only Lew's astounding talent but also the immense outpouring of affection for him. The show continued for 110 performances and, even at more normalized ticket prices, took in more than $300,000. The company then went on the road, playing in thirty-six cities and taking in an additional $105,000.

The tour brought along not only the Weber-Fields theatrical family but the biological families as well. Weber traveled with his wife, Lillian (they had no children). The Fields entourage consisted of Lew, Rose, Frances, Joe, both Herbs, Dorothy, and a governess. This was not the first time the Fields family traveled together. Sometimes it seemed as though the only way the entire Fields family could spend an extended period of time together was when they were away from home. In 1911, the whole family took a six-week European vacation. They left New York on June 24 on the *Lusitania* and returned home on August 4. While in Europe, they traveled by automobile to Paris, Berlin, Vienna, Dresden, Leipzig, Munich, and Amsterdam. The family trip was not entirely separate from Lew's work, however. In his role as producer, Lew was looking for performers and musical plays that might be well received in New York. After the spectacular success of *The Merry Widow* in New York in 1907, Broadway producers sought out other European operettas that might do as well. *The Chocolate Soldier*, with music by Oscar Straus, was a great hit in 1909, and *Madame Sherry*, with music by Karl Hoschna, did well in 1910. Lew, however, was not impressed with what he saw in Europe. Upon his return he told reporters, "I did not bring back any musical plays from Europe. To be perfectly frank, I saw nothing which I considered worthwhile. During my stay abroad I was convinced more than ever that America is capable of producing its own librettists, composers and lyricists."[10] He could not have known, when he made that statement, that in a few decades some of the best of America's own librettists and lyricists would be his own children, Joseph, Herbert, and Dorothy.

The European tour drew Lew Fields more closely into the world of his family; the Jubilee tour of 1912 brought the family into Lew's world of the theater. Dorothy had fond recollections of that time. She recalled "the coast-to-coast tour of the Weber and Fields Company—Lillian Russell, Willie

Collier, Louis Mann, Faye Templeton—in a long private [railway] car that said 'Weber and Fields Jubilee,' with a big light in front. We had our own private car and slept in it. They played [one-]night stands. It was really a wonderful experience. I went on the tour, and Mother went too. I was such a baby—I had no idea about the theater then—but it was loads of fun for Buster [Willie Collier's son] and me, because we'd get off and run around. We were left behind twice. They just pulled out without us."

She went on, "The other thing that I remember so vividly about that trip was this. You know, Lillian Russell wore wigs. Of course, nobody knew. I think Pop knew, and everybody who worked with her knew. She had the most beautiful wigs in the world. I never can decide to this day whether I actually remember this. Buster Collier and I used to run through the trains—you know, being kids and restless, we couldn't sit all the time. She had two staterooms, I think one for the wigs and one for Lillian Russell. . . . The door was open a bit, and Buster and I looked in, and there she was, sitting in a peignoir, with no wig. We both said, 'Not a spear of hair on her head.' We screamed. It was pretty frightening for kids to see. Of course, we were sworn to silence—not that we would have talked to anybody but maybe the conductor or the porter. Nobody was interested in what we had to say."[11]

The Weber and Fields Jubilee Tour ended in Pittsburgh, and there Lillian Russell married Alexander Moore, a Pittsburgh newspaper publisher and later ambassador to Spain. Dorothy recalled, "Though I was only about five [she was seven], I remember her wedding to the ambassador in Pittsburgh. I remember so well this beautiful wedding cake, and I can remember the wonderful candy flowers on it. I remember that I was a flower girl, and William Collier's son, Buster Collier, was a page."[12]

The Jubilee tour disrupted the pattern of winters in the city and summers in the country, a pattern that had been established before Dorothy was born. Sometimes the summer house was on the Jersey shore, sometimes in Far Rockaway, or Edgemere, Long Island. Joe and Herbert, as they entered their teen years, spent summers away at summer camp. Rose Fields no doubt thought that the camp environment would be a buffer between Lew's theatrical life and the boys' theatrical ambitions. How could she have known that summer camp was a breeding ground for young men's musical and theatrical talents? One of the earliest summer camps, the Weingart Institute in the Catskill Mountains in upstate New York, had as campers Lorenz and Teddy Hart, two of the Selznick brothers, and Oscar Hammerstein II. When Herb Fields went to Camp Paradox in 1910, among his fellow campers were Lorenz Hart; Eugene Zukor, the son of film producer Adolph Zukor; and Mel Schauer, who later became a producer at Paramount Studios. When songwriter Arthur

Schwartz was at Brant Lake Camp, he got to meet Billy Rose and Lorenz Hart. Dorothy Fields remembered a song that her brother Herb and Richard Rodgers wrote when they were both counselors at Camp Paradox, a song memorializing a swimming feat of a camper named Ovid Rose:

"O" stands for Ovid, who swam to the raft.
"V" stands for "Vhy did he svim to the raft?"
"I" stands for I who seen him swim to the raft.
"D" stands for "Did you see him swim to the raft?"
"R" stands for the raft out to which Ovid swam.
"O" stands for Ovid who swam to the raft.
"S" stands for swimming to the raft.
"E" stands for excellency in swimming to the raft.

"If I had tried to write lyrics then," Dorothy noted, "I wouldn't have learned much from that little gem."[13] But instead of going to camp, Dorothy spent her summers with her mother, developing some of the athletic talent she inherited from her father. She was a good swimmer, tennis player, and golfer.

In 1914, there was another shift in the family constellation: Frances, at the age of twenty, got married. Her husband was Charles Lionel Marcus, described in the *New York Times* wedding announcement as "First Vice President of the Bank of the United States of which his father is President. He is a graduate of Columbia University, class of 1906, and of the Columbia Law School."[14] Though the Bank of the United States sounds very official, it was actually a family affair founded by Charles's father, Joseph, who had been in the used-clothing business before he went into banking. The chief executive officers were Charles and his younger brother, Bernard. Joseph Marcus was active not only in financial affairs but also in Jewish charitable work and in politics.

The match must have seemed a very satisfactory one to Rose and Lew Fields. The Marcus family was not so far from them socially as to seem alien, but they did appear more respectable and financially secure—just the sort of upwardly mobile step they would want for their daughter. Dorothy and Herbert Fields took a more skeptical view, referring to the marriage as "the merger." This suggests a precocious awareness of the social and financial aspects of the marriage but also, perhaps, a certain emotional opacity, an inability or unwillingness to perceive the emotional bonds that Charles and Frances had established.

The wedding itself reflected both assimilationist and upwardly mobile trends in the Fieldses' lives. Rose and Lew Fields had been married in a synagogue, the Congregation Khul Adath Jeshrun, on the Lower East Side. Frances's wedding and reception were staged at the gold room at Delmonico's, a well-known restaurant with an elite clientele. Aaron Eiseman, the rabbi at Temple Beth El in New York, officiated at the ceremony, and a choir sang in the musicians' gallery behind a screen of smilax. The ceremony was performed under a bower of white hydrangeas and pink roses; after the ceremony, there was dancing between the dinner courses. Members of both families played significant supporting roles: Joseph Fields and Herbert Harris were ushers, and Dorothy was a flower girl, while the groom's brother was best man, and his sister maid of honor. There were about 150 guests at the dinner after the ceremony.

The engagement of Frances and Charles had been announced in April. Their wedding was on a Monday, August 24. Between those two dates, the Archduke Francis Ferdinand was assassinated in Sarajevo, and war had broken out in Europe. The couple had originally planned to honeymoon in Europe, but instead decided to spend two months visiting Yellowstone Park and resorts in California. In a few years, Charles would travel to Berlin as a representative of the Hebrew Sheltering and Immigrant Aid Society, and Frances would work in Switzerland for the Red Cross.

A curious coincidence: one column over from the *New York Times* announcement of the Fields-Marcus wedding is a review of a new show: *The Girl from Utah*. It was in this show that Jerome Kern interpolated a song that would be his first huge hit, "They Didn't Believe Me" (Kern and his song are not mentioned in this review). Two decades later, Kern and Dorothy Fields would be composing songs together in Hollywood. But before that, Dorothy would complete her schooling and test the theatrical waters as an actor and singer in high school and amateur college productions.

THE TEEN YEARS

• • •

The dispersal of Dorothy's nuclear family, which had begun with Frances's marriage in 1914, continued in 1917, after the United States entered World War I. Both Joseph Fields and Herbert Harris enlisted. A newspaper photo captioned "Lew Fields and His Fighting Sons" shows Lew standing with Joe and Herb Harris, both in military uniform. The article accompanying the photo explained that "this gives an idea of what the theatrical profession is doing for Uncle Sam. It shows Lew Fields, the comedian, enjoyed as one of the stars of *Miss 1917* with his two sons. . . . Joe Fields, oldest son of the actor . . . enlisted in the U. S. Navy Reserve Corps and is now doing active duty 'somewhere in America.' . . . Herbert Harris, younger brother of Mrs. Lew Fields, whom the actor adopted when he was a boy . . . is now with the Rainbow Division at Camp Mills. Both young men gave up a profitable poster advertising business to enlist in the service."[1] Joe had finished DeWitt Clinton High School and had enrolled in Columbia University. It was not clear what course he would pursue. Engineering was mentioned, as was law, but Joe seems to have left these potential careers behind him without regrets.

Joe's entrance into the armed forces was also his entry into show business. The "somewhere in America" at which he was stationed was the Pelham Naval Training Station. From there, he helped put together a revue called *Biff! Boom!*, which premiered in New York on May 30, 1918. The music was by William Schroeder, and lyrics were provided by William Israel, Robert D. Cohen, Frank Mills, and Joseph Fields. A reviewer for *Theatre Magazine* commented, "William Schroeder, whose songs heretofore have been too complicated to be widely popular, wrote a consistently tuneful and stick-to-you score, with a waltz called 'Love' that will be this year's successor to the 'Sweetheart' number in *Maytime*."[2] A highlight of the show was its female impersonators. The same reviewer stated, "The real hit of the show was scored by a ravishing row of 'show girls,' so magnificently gowned as to bring tears of envy to Ziegfeld's eyes."[3] Joe himself played a female stevedore. He might well have seen his namesake, Joe Weber, playing comic transvestite roles in productions with his father. Echoes of burly sailors comically playing buxom females turn up in the second act of Rodgers and Hammerstein's *South Pacific* several decades later.

It was reported in a contemporary magazine that *"Biff! Bang! [sic]* proved to be a real money-maker, and . . . several of the Broadway managers literally begged Admiral Usher to book the boys for a long run. But their purpose was to raise enough money to build a theatre at Pelham, and as this was practically accomplished by the opening night, it was a great concession of the authorities to allow the engagement to be extended as it was."[4]

Herb Harris also used his service in the armed forces as an entrée into show business. While at Camp Upton, he too put together a benefit show. For whatever reason, he seemed more willing than Joe to seek Lew Fields's help in the endeavor. Rather than using the soldiers at Camp Upton, he mounted a single-performance show with the volunteered talents of Elsie Janis, Bessie McCoy, the Dolly Sisters, Jim Corbett, and, of course, Lew Fields himself. Certainly, the more famous armed forces show coming out of Camp Upton was *Yip! Yip! Yaphank*, the music for which was written by Irving Berlin. Berlin used the Navy show as leverage to persuade his superior officers to allow him to put on an army show. Berlin biographer Philip Furia noted, "With the example of Ziegfeld before him, and the resources of the United States Army behind him, Berlin commandeered the huge Century Theatre, summoned 300 soldiers to be his cast and crew, and started rehearsals for a review he called *Yip! Yip! Yaphank.* . . . Knowing that the navy show at the Century Theatre had featured sailors in drag, Berlin also used his production to spoof Ziegfeld's lavish glorification of the American girl."[5] *Yip! Yip! Yaphank* launched a number of song hits, among them "Oh, How I Hate to Get Up in the Morning" and "Mandy." The contents of *Biff! Boom!* faded into oblivion.

Frances and her husband were in Europe in 1918, working with the Red Cross in Switzerland. The impetus to do charitable works was strong in all the Fields women. Rose Fields received some attention in newspapers in 1907 and 1908 for managing entertainment for charity for the Young Women's Hebrew Association (YWHA) and for arranging a raffle to benefit the Poor Children's Sanitarium.[6] Later, Dorothy would be active in the Girl Scouts (drawn in, in part, by a request from Irving Berlin's wife, Ellin) and assorted Jewish charitable organizations. The Marcus family, the family Frances married into, was also active in charitable endeavors.

By 1918, then, Herb Fields and Dorothy were the only children left at home. Dorothy's teen years were spent as an upper-middle-class young lady. She received piano lessons. She probably received tennis lessons—or at least she learned to play tennis, a sport she enjoyed on both coasts. A naturally athletic young woman, she swam and occasionally played golf. In high school, she won a basketball prize.

The high school that Dorothy attended was the Benjamin School for Girls. An advertisement for this school in the *New York Times* read: "The Benjamin School For Girls, Resident and Day School. The Benjamin School is located at 107th Street, overlooking Riverside Drive. DEPARTMENTS: Primary, Junior, High School (General, Academic, College Preparatory), Post Graduate (Academic and Secretarial). Music, Gymnasium, and Swimming . . ."[7] Going to a school at this location certainly made logistic sense, as it was walking distance from the Fieldses' family residence. Private school for Dorothy was a less obviously wise choice because at this time Lew Fields's finances were precarious. In 1921, he was forced to declare bankruptcy, with liabilities of more than $82,000, and was unable to continue to pay Herb's tuition at Columbia University. Typically in Jewish families at this time, if there was money to be spent on the education of children, it would have been spent on a son rather than a daughter. Perhaps Dorothy's going to private school was a sign of her special place in the family. At school, Dorothy's strongest subjects, not surprisingly, were English and dramatics. Although the Benjamin School offered secretarial courses, it is not clear if Dorothy ever learned to type. She wrote all her lyrics longhand, using a pad and pencil. In a *Life Magazine* photo from the 1940s, showing her and her brother Herbert working on a project, Herbert is at the typewriter.

Lew's career underwent a gradual evolution during Dorothy's childhood and adolescence. Over the years, Lew spent less of his time and energy being a performer (and when he did perform, he preferred roles that were not purely comic) and more time and energy being a producer. After the death in 1902 of John Stromberg, who had been the regular house composer for the Weber and Fields productions, Lew worked with a number of young composers whom Dorothy and Herbert would collaborate with as lyricist or librettist in later decades.

In 1904, Lew Fields interpolated into the score of *An English Daisy* three songs by an unknown eighteen-year-old songwriter named Jerome Kern. *An English Daisy* ran for only forty-one performances, and so Kern's songs (one was called "Wine, Wine!") did not get much exposure. Indeed, Kerns's apprenticeship was a long one. He added songs to some three dozen more shows over a period of a decade before he had his first great hit with "They Didn't Believe Me," interpolated into the score of *The Girl from Utah* in 1914. Half a lifetime later, Kern joined creative forces with Dorothy for six movies.

In 1915, Fields bought, for the musical *Hands Up*, some songs by another young unknown, Cole Porter. Fields's biographers wrote of Cole, "The fact that a Broadway producer of Fields' stature had paid money for his songs was worth writing home about. Porter immediately wired his sister: 'Tell Grandad that Lew Fields gave me $50 for each song I sold him.'"[8] As did Jerome Kern, Cole Porter united his talents with the next generation of Fieldses many years later.

Hands Up, which Lew Fields produced but withdrew from performing in, had a score by E. Ray Goetz and Sigmund Romberg. In 1920, Fields called on Sigmund Romberg to supplement the score written by the still wet-behind-the-ears team of Richard Rodgers and Lorenz Hart for *Poor Little Ritz Girl*. Decades later, Dorothy and Herbert teamed with Romberg to write his last musical, *Up in Central Park*. It was with Rodgers and Hart that Herbert and Dorothy took their first tentative steps into show business.

According to Dorothy, "Herbert, of course, was the first one of us to start writing for the theatre. As a matter of fact, I introduced him to Richard Rodgers when I was sixteen and Dick eighteen. When Dick came to see me at the house one night, we introduced him to my father, who was attracted by this fresh, delightful music."[9] Rodgers's own version of this story is different in some details:

> One sweltering Sunday afternoon I journeyed to the Fields' summer home to unveil the first Rodgers and Hart songs before their first audience. . . . Expecting to play my songs before an audience of one, I was surprised to find the entire Fields clan assembled to appraise my maiden efforts. In addition to Mr. and Mrs. Fields, the family consisted of their four children: Joseph, the eldest [*sic*], who bore a close physical resemblance to his father; Herbert, wavy-haired and clean-cut looking; fourteen-year-old Dorothy with the most dazzling eyes I had ever seen; and Frances, the only Fields sibling who would not pursue a career in the theatre. All six of them did what they could to make me feel comfortable, though I must admit that most of the time I found myself trying harder to impress young Dorothy than her father. When I had finished, I felt a genuine sense of accomplishment in hearing so many favorable comments from so knowledgeable a group, and I would have considered my trip worthwhile even if I had nothing more concrete than admiration and encouragement to take home with me.[10]

Most of the discrepancies between Dorothy's and Richard's recollections are slight. He accurately dates the meeting as taking place in 1919. He remembers Dorothy being fourteen at the time, and he sixteen, while in fact she had just turned fifteen. She remembers introducing Rodgers and Herb Fields prior to the visit, whereas he remembers meeting the entire family for the first time en masse.

It is likely that the person who introduced Richard Rodgers to Herbert Fields and thence to the rest of the family was in fact Lorenz Hart. Joe and Herb Fields and Larry Hart were all campers together at Camp Paradox, in the Adirondacks, in 1910. Hart and Joseph Fields attended DeWitt Clinton High School at the same time, but there is no evidence of friendship or even any contact between them then. Hart transferred to Columbia Grammar, from which he graduated in 1914. All three boys continued on a more or less parallel path and entered Columbia University. Herb attended Columbia for only one year; after 1916, neither Herb's father nor his brother-in-law, the banker Charles Marcus, was able to pay Herb's tuition. But even one year at Columbia was enough for Herb to establish contact with members of the Dramatic Society and the Columbia University Players, whose ranks included, one time or another, Lorenz Hart, Richard Rodgers, and Oscar Hammerstein II. Hart often quipped that his major at Columbia was "neither literature nor journalism but Varsity Shows."[11] Had Herb remained at Columbia, he might well have followed Hart's lead. Another Columbia acquaintance of Larry Hart's was Phil Leavitt who, by most accounts, gets credit both for bringing Larry Hart and Richard Rodgers together and for bringing the songwriting team of Rodgers and Hart to the attention of the Fields family.

The Weber and Fields Jubilee tour of 1912 was the start of the breakdown of Rose's carefully erected barrier between the children and some inside knowledge of theatrical life. After 1912, the tide had turned and there was no going back, although it took many years for that fact to emerge clearly. Lew and Rose tried to maintain the illusion that the theater was no place for their children. Joe lamented in later years that when he tried to watch rehearsals of shows his father was involved in, his father would insist that he leave the theater. Lew would complain to the press that Herbert showed "symptoms of being funny but I am in hopes that he will outgrow it."[12] Dorothy was allowed to be interested in the theater from the safe distance of a spectator. She kept a scrapbook filled with clippings and reviews of her father's theatrical activities. And she was allowed to see shows, in a ladylike way, in a box with her friends. She recalled, "We all went to the theater very frequently. I remember distinctly that every Saturday I had a box for one show or another, mostly musical shows or comedies. . . . I remember Willie Collier was playing in a show that Pop produced called *Never Say Die* [which opened November 12, 1912]. As usual, Saturday matinee, I had a front lower box with some girl friends, and there was a breakfast scene. They served some scrambled eggs, and we all went, 'Ooooh!' so he went right over to the box and said, 'Dorothy, would you like some?' Stepping out of character on a Saturday matinee! You know, we were all very giggly."[13]

As a teenager, Dorothy was even allowed to perform on occasion, in venues with impeccably nonprofessional credentials. She appeared in two productions put on for charitable purposes by the Akron Club, which Richard Rodgers characterized as "a local social-athletic group," many of whose members—her brother Herbert, Phillip Leavitt, Oscar Hammerstein II, and Mortimer Rodgers, older brother of Richard Rodgers—were connected with Columbia University. *You'd Be Surprised*, in which Dorothy had a starring role as a flower seller named Carmen, was presented at the Plaza Hotel once on March 6, 1920, and once on April 11. In the chorus were women whose surnames suggest a Jewish social register—Emily Guggenheim, Elise Bonwit, and Dorith Bamberger. Dorith was described by Richard Rodgers as "a very pretty little girl whom I used to see fairly regularly and fairly innocently."[14] Many people on the creative staff for this show would go on to greater theatrical fame. The songs were by Richard Rodgers and Lorenz Hart, one of their earliest collaborations. Oscar Hammerstein II also contributed a lyric. The Fields family was represented not only by Dorothy but by Herbert, who contributed a lyric for a much-applauded song about Mary, Queen of Scots, and by Lew, who is credited with giving "professional assistance."

The next year, the Akron Club presented *Say Mama* "for the benefit of the Oppenheim Collins Mutual Aid Association of Brooklyn, at the Brooklyn Academy of Music, February 10, 1921, and for the benefit of the Save-A-Home Fund of the *New York Evening Mail*, at the Hotel Plaza, February 1, 1921."[15] Many of the players and creative staff from *You'd Be Surprised* reappeared in *Say Mama*. Added to the group was Herbert Fields, who had joined Richard Rodgers and Lorenz Hart in two earlier Columbia University Varsity shows. No doubt Herb's parents expected him to keep a watchful eye over his younger sister during rehearsals—and perhaps he did.

Dorothy also participated in theatrical activities at her high school. She even induced Richard Rodgers to provide music for three of the Benjamin School for Girls' shows. The first was *The Chinese Lantern*, presented in 1922. Dorothy was seventeen years old, perhaps a senior in the high school; she stayed on at the Benjamin School after graduation as a part-time drama instructor. In March 1923 the Benjamin School presented *If I Were King*. The source for the musical was the play *If I Were King* by Justin Huntly McCarthy. Set in fifteenth-century France, the play shows the poet François Villon helping to save France by changing places with King Louis XI for a day. Directed by Herbert Fields, with a cast drawn from the students of the Benjamin School and Dorothy Fields in the starring role, the musical had its single performance in the Maxine Elliott Theatre on March 25.

In retrospect, Rodgers considered his work in amateur shows to have been a valuable experience. In his autobiography, he lists the titles of eleven amateur shows for which he composed the scores between 1920 and 1924. All of these shows involved the participation of Herbert or Dorothy Fields, or both. Rodgers does not discuss any of these shows in detail, but he makes clear that the process of mounting an amateur theatrical show blurs the distinction between professional and nonprofessional:

> There is a great deal more to writing for the musical theatre than learning notation, the meaning of a diminished seventh, or banging away at a typewriter in some lonely room. . . . Reject at the start the idea that "amateur" is a dirty word, and remember that while the qualitative differences between amateur and professional productions may be vast, the resemblances are equally great. Both require singers, actors, lighting, scenery, costumes, musical accompaniment and eventually an audience. On the way to that audience, writers, whether amateur or professional, are constantly polishing and making changes; through trial and error they learn what makes dialogue funny or touching and what makes a song not only suitable but remembered. As a showcase, the amateur production can even have immediately practical results. In the audience may be someone's uncle who knows an agent or a producer—or who may even be an agent or a producer—and the amateur may have taken the first giant step toward becoming a professional. This isn't just wishful thinking; it happened to me.[16]

Rodgers was proud enough of his score for *If I Were King* that he had hopes of bringing it to Broadway. He discussed the project with Broadway producer Russell Janney, but at that time they could not find enough financial backing for a team of relative unknowns. Janney did not lose interest in the project. Two and a half years later he hired Rudolph Friml, composer of *The Firefly* (1912) among other operettas, to compose a score for this story. Rodgers noted, ruefully, "Since the show, now retitled *The Vagabond King*, became one of the triumphs of the decade, I don't suppose Janney ever had any cause for regret."[17]

The third show for the Benjamin School in which Herbert Fields, Dorothy Fields, and Richard Rodgers all participated was another swashbuckler. *The Prisoner of Zenda*, based on a novel by Anthony Hope, was performed in March 1924. As with *If I Were King*, Dorothy played a man's role in this production. At the same time, there was a single performance of Rodgers's *Temple Belles*, a Purim entertainment produced by Irving Strouse at the Park Avenue Synagogue, New York, on March 20, 1924. The production was staged by Herbert Fields who, atypically, supplied the lyrics.

It would have been unnatural, even grotesque, for Lew and Rose to prevent their children from engaging in school, synagogue, or charity shows. But as soon as matters with Dorothy threatened to turn even semiprofessional, Lew stepped in. Dorothy said, "Pop wouldn't hear of the stage, although I had got a chance to do character parts. I was young, but I always looked pretty old. I had a chance at a playhouse in Tarrytown, but Pop squashed that, so I thought I would have to get in some other way."[18] The means Lew used to "squash" Dorothy's theatrical ambition was simply to intercept the letter of acceptance sent from the Tarrytown Playhouse to Dorothy. Although this action seems high-handed or authoritarian, one's judgment of it can be tempered by the knowledge that Lew did not think highly of summer stock as the starting point for an acting career. He made this explicit in a letter he wrote to Herbert in January 1916. Herbert had been considering the same route into the theater. It is interesting that in a family that did not hoard souvenirs, this is one letter that Herbert Fields held on to. Lew advised, "I haven't much confidence in stock work. You must learn to create. People in stock are given parts that have been created by other actors and only suffer by comparison.... Stock is a place where a great many bad actors go before they die."[19] Of course, Lew Fields was speaking from his own perspective. He honed his craft by working for several years in traveling variety shows. A number of actors a generation younger than he, among them Bette Davis, Gregory Peck, and Henry Fonda, started their careers in community theaters or in summer stock.

Dorothy knew—either first- or secondhand—women who had performed in shows produced by her father and who had had successful acting careers. But it is hard to say if a close knowledge of these actresses would have inspired or discouraged her. Although vivacious and attractive, with alluring dark brown eyes, Dorothy was not showgirl pretty. The strength of her features, the pronounced nose and lips, were not the rosebud ideal of feminine beauty of the time. If Dorothy compared herself to the actresses she knew in terms of talent and physical attributes, it is hard to guess what conclusions she might have drawn. Even as a teenager, she seemed to see herself more in character roles, frequently male, than in ingénue parts. Lew and Rose may have looked at the same actresses' offstage lives more than their onstage abilities, and they may have concluded that this was not the life they wanted for their daughter.

Nevertheless, it was easier for the two younger Fields children, Herbert and Dorothy, to sidle their way into show business. Perhaps with the two older children realizing their parents' upwardly mobile dreams, the two younger children had a little more slack—a little more room to negotiate in.

Or maybe the two older children lived out their mother's ambitions more because they were more subject to her influence; Lew simply was not around as much when the older children were growing up. Herbert and, especially, Dorothy saw a bit more of Lew, and they were united by their subversive love for the theater.

In Dorothy's teen years, there seemed to be a parting of the ways between Frances and Joseph on one hand and Herbert and Dorothy on the other. In 1919, five years after her wedding, Frances took the natural next step in domestic life and became a mother. The notice in the *New York Times*, typically, did not feature the new parents' names first, but rather Lew's. "Lew Fields Has Twin Grandchildren," the headline proclaimed. The text, too, leads by congratulating Lew on the accomplishment: "Lew Fields, the comedian, may be congratulated upon two grandchildren, both boys, and his first. They were born about 3 o'clock yesterday morning to Mr. and Mrs. C. L. Marcus at their home in Far Rockaway, at 232 Grand View Avenue. . . . The twins, named Raymond and Lawrence, are their first children."[20]

Almost a year and a half later, Joseph Fields married. Again, the *New York Times* notice began with Lew's name:

Lew Fields, the actor, received a cablegram last evening from Paris informing him that the marriage of his son Joseph Fields, to Henrietta Levey had taken place yesterday in Paris. The cable, which was from Mrs. [Rose] Fields, who attended the ceremony, also stated that Mr. and Mrs. Joseph Fields would spend their honeymoon in Monte Carlo, and would return to this country in about four weeks and make their residence in this city. The bride is the daughter of Otto Levey, one of the largest cotton and jute manufacturers on the Continent. The marriage is the culmination of a romance which began when Mr. Fields met his bride in Paris at an armistice celebration dance, when he was serving with the American forces overseas as an ensign in the navy. He is now in the employ of the American Corporation of International Commerce.[21]

Clearly Joseph, like his sister Frances, married up the financial ladder. While Rose was free to travel to Paris for the wedding, undaunted by the thought of a November sea crossing, Lew was fully occupied with his production of *Poor Little Ritz Girl*, which opened on July 28, 1921, ran for ten weeks, and then went on tour for twelve weeks.

Herbert Fields, meanwhile, was acquiring experience in many aspects of the theater. He appeared on Broadway with his father in *A Lonely Romeo*, which premiered on June 19, 1919. After that, his theatrical work was all behind the scenes. He staged the musical numbers and dances for *Fly with Me*

(1920), *You'll Never Know* (1921), and *Jazz a la Carte* (1922), all of which had music by Richard Rodgers, and he directed *If I Were King* (1923). His first libretto, written in 1922 with Oscar Hammerstein II, was *Winkle Town*; the work was never produced.

As we will see, Dorothy tried for a while to stay on both forks in the road—domestic and professional—before choosing the theater.

MARRIAGE AND THE START OF A CAREER

• • •

Dorothy's post–high school years show a certain lack of direction. Probably, she never seriously intended to pursue a higher education. When she spoke of not going to college, in later years, Dorothy placed the blame on her lack of math skills—she failed to master algebra. Trouble with numbers may have played a role in keeping Dorothy from college, but more likely it was bank account numbers. Lew Fields declared bankruptcy in August 1921. The *New York Herald* reported that his liabilities amounted to $82,126.

It should be pointed out, though, that academic life did not hold a strong attraction for any of the Fields children. When she was seventeen, Frances considered going to Wellesley or Vassar, but this idea seems not to have gone past the daydreaming stage (and whether it was Frances's daydream or her parents' is not clear). After completing DeWitt Clinton High School, Joseph attended New York University, where he studied law at his father's urging. But in 1917, when he enlisted in the Navy, he did not leave a law practice but rather a profitable poster advertising business, which he worked at with Herbert Harris. Herbert Fields started Columbia in 1915 and probably would have been happy to continue, in large part because of his involvement with theatrical activities there. But Lew Fields's financial fortunes took a downward turn in 1915, as did those of his son-in-law, Charles Marcus, who had financially sustained Herbert through the spring semester of 1916, and Herbert dropped out of Columbia. Although various members of the Fields family pursued different highbrow cultural interests (Lew loved Shakespeare, and Herbert Fields was deeply attracted to Wagnerian opera), the academic approach to knowledge or life was deeply irrelevant to the Fieldses; after all, the family business revolved around not taking things too seriously and also on taking close observations from life itself.

More important than a lack of drive to get a college degree was a positive drive to do something else: for Frances, to get married; for Joe, to enter the business world and to serve his country; for Herb, to enter show business. But for Dorothy, who might have started a career as a performer had parental opposition not nipped that in the bud, the way was less clear. After completing her studies at the Benjamin School for Girls and staying on awhile as an instructor in drama, she had various workaday jobs that seem an ill fit for her talents. For a while, she worked as a lab technician, an occupation that seems so uncharacteristic of her it would be hard to believe if the information had not come from Dorothy herself.[1] With a friend, Mathilde Ferro, she had a go at running a dance studio. Just what her qualifications were for this work is not clear.

Finally, at age twenty, Dorothy did what her older sister had done at age twenty and what her mother had done at age eighteen: she got married. A Jewish joke goes: Two women meet in the street. The first woman says to the second, "What darling children you have! How old are they?" The second woman replies, "My daughter, the teacher, is three, and my son, the doctor, is four." The joke encapsulates a kernel of truth regarding one Jewish generation's hopes for its offspring, and in some sense Dorothy approached the start of her adulthood trying to live out these aspirations. She was "my daughter, the teacher," although she was not a licensed, full-time teacher but rather a dramatic arts teacher in the private school from which she had graduated. And she brought into the family "my son-in-law, the doctor."

The man Dorothy married, Dr. Jack Wiener, had a practice on Fifty-Eighth Street and Central Park South and was a surgeon on the staff of Montefiore Hospital. Like the Fields children, the five Wiener children were on an upwardly mobile track. Their father was a baker, but one son became a lawyer, one a dentist, and Jack a surgeon. Superficially, Jack and Dorothy appeared well matched. Both were attractive. Jack was tall, dark-haired, blue-eyed, in his early thirties. Dorothy, barely twenty, had dazzling dark eyes and a ready smile and wit. They both played tennis. They must have had some friends in common to have met in the first place. They came from similar-size families— Dorothy the youngest of four, and Jack one of the younger of five. They both had older sisters who had already married, which may have contributed to their mutual desire for a simple wedding. And both were Jewish. Although the Fieldses were secular Jews, marrying outside the faith, at that time, would have required much more motivation for marriage than Dorothy had. Jack offered Dorothy stability and upward mobility; Dorothy offered Jack a closer view (but still at a safe distance) of an alter-ego group he admired—theatrical types.

Dorothy and Jack's engagement had been announced in the autumn of 1924. Perhaps Lew and Rose were looking forward to a wedding for Dorothy as lavish as Frances's had been. But, as a Jewish proverb goes, *A mentsh tracht un got lacht* (Man thinks, and God laughs). In May 1925, Jack and Dorothy had a small, quiet wedding in the Upper West Side home of a rabbi, then jour-neyed to Denver, where Lew was performing in a Weber and Fields Vaudeville production, and announced the fait accompli to her mother and father. Con-sideration for Lew Fields's ever-insecure finances no doubt contributed to Dorothy and Jack's decision to forgo an expensive wedding. Having seen the weddings of their own sisters may have given them as much of a taste for this kind of display as either of them cared to have. And perhaps, on some level, Dorothy had profound doubts about her marriage.

According to her cousins, "When the two had finally gone on their honey-moon, they had rented a cottage in the Adirondacks, and Dorothy spent most of the first night pacing back and forth on the porch. Why they bothered marrying in the first place remains a mystery. Though they stayed legally married for ten years, they led separate lives almost from the start."[2] Dorothy returned to her parental home soon after her marriage. One might guess that Dorothy wanted to go ahead with the wedding before she lost heart for the enterprise entirely. If the "honeymoon" began only after the long round-trip from New York to Denver and back to the Adirondacks, it is hard to imagine that it was precipitous passion that led them to marry before Lew and Rose returned from the Weber and Fields tour.

It may well be that Dorothy had an inkling her marriage was a mistake from the very start. It may be that for her, marriage was like the reverse side of the coin of sowing wild oats. It was something she needed to do—a necessary nod toward convention—before she could get on with a life that was truer to herself. She did not feel that career and marriage could not or should not coexist. She did not end her marriage to have a career. Probably, she simply married the wrong man—or went into a marriage that had form but not content. It could be that none of the Fields children were really emo-tionally savvy when it came to choosing their first mates. In any event, none of their first marriages lasted. But the second marriages of Frances, Joseph, and Dorothy were all until-death-do-us-part unions.

Dorothy and Jack lived apart from one another, but they remained on amicable terms. She stayed in touch with his family. A relative of Jack Wiener's told Deborah Grace Winer that "she visited [the Wiener family] with her hus-band on occasions like Passover, and continued to keep track of [them] after their eventual divorce."[3] Jack was consulted at times of family medical emer-gencies. He was an attending physician for Lew Fields when he needed sur-gical treatment for an abdominal problem. He was also with the family on the first night Dorothy's songs were heard at the Cotton Club, in 1928.

When Dorothy had returned home to 562 West End Avenue, she rejoined not only her parents but also her two brothers. Herbert Fields remained a bachelor. He never was blatantly open about being gay, but he did not cover up his homosexuality to the point of entering into a marriage. Joseph had returned home from Paris in 1923. After the Armistice, he had remained in Paris, in part with the intention of studying art. But somehow business success pursued him. With Herb Harris, he opened a perfume exporting business, Parfums Charbert, that grossed $800,000 in the first year. Joe's first marriage, like Dorothy's, came apart quickly.

In 1925, Dorothy opened a dancing school at Carnegie Hall, just a short walk from her husband's medical offices. Her partner in this business was Mathilde Ferro, who, one or two decades later, would acquire fame as the author of the radio serial "Lorenzo Jones." In what way Dorothy was qualified to operate a dancing studio isn't clear, but the same might be said of Herb's forays into choreography. Perhaps she played piano for the classes. She had certainly seen a lot of dance in the theater. One wonders if any echoes of Dorothy's dance-school experience resounded ten years later in the opening scenes of *Swing Time*.

For three or four years Dorothy had no "public life"; she stayed on theater's sidelines. Herbert Fields appeared to be the only one of Lew's children who would be active in the theater. Throughout the 1920s, Herbert's star rose, although it took him some time to find his niche. The first occupation he tried and then rejected was that of performer. Lew had given his reluctant blessing to this endeavor in a letter of January 1916, just after he turned forty-four years old. "Some people say there is something in heredity, and I think that there is more in you than has yet appeared. . . . I am aware of the restlessness in a young boy's heart when he is ambitious. I approve your going on the stage, for you wouldn't be happy until you tried."[4] Herbert appeared on Broadway in *Miss 1917* and in *A Lonely Romeo* (1919), both times alongside his father.

He next tried his hand at staging and choreographing musical numbers, mostly in the college and charity productions to which Lorenz Hart and Richard Rodgers had contributed songs—*Fly with Me* (1920), *You'll Never Know* (1921), *Jazz a la Carte* (1922), and *The Garrick Gaieties* (1925 and 1926). He had had the opportunity to watch several choreographers associated with works his father either produced or performed in; the most important among them was Ned Wayburn. It must be acknowledged, however, that the qualifications for choreographer at the time Herb ventured into this field were not very stringent.

Dance numbers tended to be cheerful and decorative, placing no great demands on the dancers or the audience. It is hard to know, at this distance, how much ability or talent Herbert had for acting or staging. Perhaps he was discouraged by critics or friends, or perhaps he decided on his own that these activities were not his proper métier. He also placed on the reject pile, after a brief trial, work as a lyricist. Herb provided lyrics for one song in *Poor Little Ritz Girl* and all the songs for *The Prisoner of Zenda*.

By the middle of the decade, Herbert saw that his calling in the theater would be as a librettist, a supplier of books (dialogue) for musical works. His first attempt as a librettist was made in 1922, when he collaborated with Oscar Hammerstein II on a work called *Winkle Town*, with songs by Rodgers and Hart. Hammerstein had achieved success on Broadway sooner than the team of Hart, Rodgers, and Fields. After his graduation from Columbia in 1918, Oscar worked for his uncle, Arthur Hammerstein, as a production manager. By 1920, he had turned to writing. The early plays of his that were presented on Broadway included *Always You*, with music by Herbert Stothart, and *Tickle Me*, a comedy written in collaboration with Otto Harbach and Herbert Mandel. In asking for help on *Winkle Town*, Dick, Larry, and Herb may have been thinking of Oscar's contacts as much as his talent. If that was the case, the ploy did not work: *Winkle Town* was never produced.

As with his work as a choreographer, in becoming a librettist Herbert was entering a field whose practitioners ranged from hacks to people of substantial talent. There were many who wondered if the libretto of a musical comedy, whether good or bad, had much influence on the success of a show. Hugh Fordin, describing 1920s musicals, said that librettists were neglected when things went well but blamed if a show failed: "As for the librettist, he was a kind of stable boy; if the race was won he was seldom mentioned; if the race was lost he was blamed for giving the horse the wrong feed."[5] In a similar vein, the theater historian Ethan Mordden commented, "When a musical makes a hit, who gets the credit? The songwriters, the performers, the director, the choreographer, the designer, the producer, the orchestrator, the stage manager, even the audience—for its good taste. When a musical bombs, who gets the blame? The author of the book."[6] Of course there were people who had higher hopes for the words in a musical—among them, Hammerstein and Harbach, Bolton and Wodehouse. Nevertheless, the writing of a libretto was often a thankless task. But for that very reason, it was a relatively safe entryway into the theater for Herbert.

Herbert's next libretto after *Winkle Town* was *Dearest Enemy*, which opened at the Knickerbocker Theatre on September 18, 1925, immediately after the surprise runaway success of *The Garrick Gaieties*. The initial idea for the show came from Larry Hart, who paused at the corner of Thirty-seventh Street and Lexington Avenue long enough to read a plaque on a building announcing, "Howe, with Clinton, Tryon and a few others, went to the house of Robert

Murray, on Murray Hill, for refreshment and rest. With pleasant conversations and a profusion of cake and wine, the good Whig lady detained the gallant Britons almost two hours: quite long enough for the bulk of Putnam's division of four thousand men to leave the city and escape to the heights of Harlem by the Bloomingdale road, with the loss of only a few soldiers."[7]

Larry discussed the idea of a musical comedy set at the time of the American Revolution with Herb, who developed a script that he showed to the young actress Helen Ford. She was particularly charmed by the heroine's first entrance, wearing nothing but a barrel. The search for financial backers for the show, first titled *Sweet Rebel*, then *Dear Enemy* before *Dearest Enemy* was decided on, was long and arduous. Ford remembers having about fifty auditions for potential backers in the course of a year or so. Finally, in the elevator of the Roosevelt Hotel, she found a friend of a friend—or actually, the brother of a Dartmouth roommate of her husband's—Robert Jackson, who was willing to back the show.

With financial backing assured, Herb, Larry, and Dick began to gather the rest of the staff. Helen Ford was the romantic female lead. Her husband, George Ford, was the producer. Director and supervisor of the entire production was John Murray Anderson. There were tryouts in Akron, Ohio, and at Ford's Opera House in Baltimore, Maryland. Rodgers and Hart were acutely aware that, although the success of *The Garrick Gaieties* had helped smooth the way, success in a revue did not guarantee success in a book musical. The work also had a number of out-on-a-limb novel aspects. It located itself between genres: the setting indicated operetta, but the urbane, cynical attitude of the characters was clearly 1920s. Had they understood the competition that was opening on Broadway, they might have been even more worried. *No, No Nanette* opened two days before *Dearest Enemy* and ran for 321 performances; *The Vagabond King* (the Rudolph Friml version, not the Richard Rodgers one) opened a few days later and ran for 511 performances; *Sunny* opened the day after that and ran for 517 performances. But Broadway found room in its heart for *Dearest Enemy* as well. It ran for 286 performances.

The team of Fields, Rodgers, and Hart was launched. Max Dreyfus of T. J. Harms offered to publish their songs. They were invited to join the American Society of Composers, Authors and Publishers (ASCAP). Even Lew Fields was won over and agreed to produce their next show, *The Girl Friend*, which opened at the Vanderbilt Theatre on March 17, 1926. Following on the heels of *Dearest Enemy*, *The Girl Friend* shows something of the versatility of Fields, Rodgers, and Hart. *Dearest Enemy* is set about 150 years in the past, whereas *The Girl Friend* is aggressively contemporary—even trendy. The slim plot revolves around preparations for a six-day bicycle race. The stars were Sammy White as the budding bicyclist and Eva Puck, White's real-life wife, as his coach, manager, and promoter. Rodgers recalled, "We'd first met Sammy and Eva when they appeared in *The Melody Man*, and they'd impressed us so much that we promised that someday we'd write a show just for them. Unlike most such promises, this one was kept."[8] *The Girl Friend* started slowly at the box office, despite good reviews, but it went on to be an even bigger hit than *Dearest Enemy*, largely on the strength of its score, which included the hit "The Blue Room."

The Girl Friend showed an awareness of a sports trend of the 1920s. The next hit of Fields, Rodgers, and Hart, *Peggy-Ann*, was steeped in contemporary intellectual and artistic currents including surrealism and psychoanalysis. *Peggy-Ann* took as its starting point a comedy that Lew Fields had produced in 1910, *Tillie's Nightmare*, which had starred Marie Dressler. Tillie, an ill-used drudge, falls asleep when her boss goes out on the town, dreams of a better life, and wakes up at the end of the play. His cousins noted, "Herb's transformation of Tillie into Peggy-Ann was in fact a radical reworking of the Cinderella musical by way of Freud's couch and the Algonquin Round Table."[9] The years 1910 and 1926 were on opposite sides of a divide in terms of social attitudes and attitudes toward entertainment. The device of falling asleep, dreaming, and waking up was kept when *Tillie's Nightmare* became *Peggy-Ann*, but the content of the dream in the later work—a talking fish, a policeman dressed in pink, a horse race in which the winning horse has the same name as the heroine of the play, people taking charge of situations by putting on larger and larger hats—can be termed absurdist, or surreal, or irrational. (In 1919, when the German expressionist film *Das Kabinett des Dr. Caligari* was deemed too weird to be acceptable to an audience, it was then framed in terms of a person dreaming the action and went on to become a classic.) There were structural innovations in *Peggy-Ann* as well as novelty of content. There is no music (no overture, no opening chorus) for the first ten or fifteen minutes of the play; there is a quiet conclusion rather than a bring-on-everyone-for-the finale ending. As Ethan Mordden quips, "The show is famous for its lack of conventions, but it doesn't really lack them—it just stirs them around a little."[10]

Helen Ford, who finished touring with *Dearest Enemy* on November 27, had just enough time to rush from Columbus, Ohio, back to New York for rehearsals. Instead of making an entrance in a barrel, as she did in *Dearest Enemy*, in *Peggy-Ann* she got to do a wedding scene in her underwear. The dance numbers, which were remarkably well integrated with the plot and helped set the tone for the entire show (and this was two decades before *Oklahoma!*), were staged by Seymour Felix. The entire production was under the supervision of Lew Fields, but Lew had been ill in the early stages of production, so much of the hiring of staff fell to Herbert. Indeed, *Peggy-Ann*, which in some ways demonstrated how much had changed theatrically from Lew's time to Herb's time, strengthened a bond between them. It is to Lew Fields's credit that he was able to change with the times, even if that meant following his son's lead. *Peggy-Ann* ran for 333 performances, their biggest success to date.

With three hits in little more than a year, the team of Fields, Rodgers, and Hart became very well known to critics. Press reviews were glowing. After the premiere of *The Girl Friend*, Abel Green, writing in *Variety*, declared, "Considerably more is anticipated from Rodgers and Hart, who, as a team are touted as an American Gilbert and Sullivan."[11] After the premiere of *Dearest Enemy* a different comparison was offered by Frank Vreeland of the *Telegram*: "We have a glimmering notion that some day they [Fields, Rodgers, and Hart] will form the American counterpart of the once great triumvirate of Bolton, Wodehouse, and Kern."[12] And after *Peggy-Ann* opened, Robert Coleman announced in the *Mirror*: "I hereby go on record as placing this talented triumvirate in the foremost ranks of our youthful and talented show builders."[13] The comparisons with Gilbert and Sullivan and with Bolton, Wodehouse, and Kern were both apt in terms of association. Gilbert and Sullivan were a highly linked pair, whereas Wodehouse, Bolton, and Kern were more loosely knit. Richard Rodgers described the relationship of Rodgers, Hart, and Fields this way: "Larry and I never had any kind of agreement, either written or verbal. Even a handshake would probably have seemed too formal. We simply knew that as long as we both could do the work we did, we would always remain partners. Our relationship with Herb Fields was much looser. Although, curiously, Herb never seemed to have any great love for the theatre, he was easy to get along with and was always full of ideas, and we enjoyed working with him more than with any other librettist. But none of us ever thought of ourselves as part of an indissoluble trio, even though, up to 1927, Herb had never written with any other songwriters."[14]

Rodgers and Hart provided the songs for several musicals in the 1920s for which Herb Fields did not provide the book. For the 1926 edition of the revue *The Garrick Gaieties*, Herb went back to staging the musical numbers; he also wrote some of the sketch material. Two musicals that opened in London— *Lido Lady* (1926) and *One Dam Thing after Another* (1927)—had no contribution from Herb. In New York, Rodgers and Hart were lured by Florenz Ziegfeld into working on *Betsy* (1927) which had a book by Irving Caesar and David Freedman, revised by William Anthony McGuire.

Meanwhile, Herbert and Lew Fields joined forces with Vincent Youmans. After his hit *No, No Nanette* (1925), Youmans wanted to produce his next show as well as write the music for it and wisely allied himself with Lew Fields. The work they brought out was *Hit the Deck!*, which debuted on April 25, 1927, and ran for 352 performances. Herbert provided the book for *Hit the Deck!*, basing it on a 1922 play by Hubert Osborne called *Shore Leave*. Youmans had spent time in the Navy in World War I, as had Herb's brother Joe. Moreover, shaping a romance between a sailor and a coffee shop proprietor-cum-heiress gave the work its peculiar and characteristic color. The book was praised by critics of the time. One observed that it had "a real, live, traceable plot that tends strictly to business," and another that "the plot makes for sturdier amusement than the conventions of such productions generally supply."[15] Most enthusiastic was the critic at *Variety*, who noted, "Some theatergoers may say 'too much plot'; others will be pleased at the logical, legitimate and believable yarn which is worked out to its plausible conclusion, and which is never thrown overboard to make way for specialties. . . . This may be and should be a big asset for the show, but it will be something of an innovation, and there's no telling how it will strike the public."[16]

Dorothy Fields was no doubt elated at the theatrical success of her closest sibling. On the other hand, could she have been completely happy about being left behind as the team of Fields, Rodgers, and Hart moved into the professional sphere? Herbert had had a few false starts—as actor and choreographer—before arriving at his calling as a librettist. Performing appeared to be a dead end for Dorothy as well, but what direction should she take next? She recalled, decades later, "I didn't know what I wanted to do, except that I knew it was something in the theatre."[17]

As Dorothy told the story, she did not go in search of a composer or a career, she just happened upon it. She said, "One summer I met J. Fred Coots at the Woodmere Country Club. He played some of his hits. Next I sat at the piano and played some of the early Rodgers and Hart songs. Fred Coots asked me if I'd ever tried to write. 'No,' I said. 'Well, try,' he said, so I tried. We wrote a couple of things—music good, lyrics terrible."[18] In retrospect, Dorothy thought her first lyrics may have been unsatisfactory because she was too much in thrall of the unique talent of Lorenz Hart. "I was so impressed with the inter-rhyming and the feminine hybrid rhymes of Larry Hart that I was not writing like anybody but trying to be like Larry and consequently they weren't very good. I didn't realize then that that was a very special thing, but that the best lyric writing is the simple lyric writing, and if you don't have a good initial thought, no amount of rhyming dictionaries and thesauruses can ever pull you over the hump."[19]

J. Fred Coots was born in Brooklyn in 1897. His mother was an able pianist and taught him to play. In 1913, at age sixteen, Coots took a highly paid job at the Farmer's Loan and Trust Company, but he stayed for only one year. He left to work as a stock boy and pianist at the McKinley Music Company, earning a fraction of what he had been making. Coots's first published song, "Mister Ford You've Got the Right Idea," appeared in 1917. It was published by A. J. Stasny, who, according to song chronicler Jack Burton, "bought songs whose titles would make ornate covers and not on musical merit."[20] Mr. Ford's good idea, for the purposes of this song, was not the manufacture of cars but the attempt to send a peace ship to Europe during World War I. The song, being topical, belongs to a category that provided an early stepping-stone for several composers. One of Irving Berlin's earliest published songs, "Dorando" (1909), is a lament of a fan who has lost money betting on an unsuccessful Olympic runner. As we will see, one of the first songs Dorothy would be paid for was about an American woman who was planning to fly across the ocean. Topical songs were not expected to have a long shelf life, and perhaps for this very reason publishers entrusted them to neophyte songwriters.

Coots became a successful professional songwriter, though not a member of the pantheon. He wrote the scores for two successful Broadway musicals—*Sally, Irene and Mary*, which opened in 1922 and ran for 312 performances, and *Sons o' Guns*, which ran for 231 performances in 1929. He also wrote songs for a number of revues—*Artists and Models of 1924*, *Artists and Models of 1925*, and *The Merry World*. The works for which he is best known are Tin Pan Alley hits written neither for Broadway nor for Hollywood. In the 1930s, he wrote three ballads that attained the status of standards: "For All We Know," "Love Letters in the Sand," and "You Go to My Head." He also wrote a novelty number that made his fortune, "Santa Claus Is Coming to Town." Coots did not abandon the topical song. In 1942, he had a hit with "Goodbye Mama, I'm Off to Yokohama." Dorothy Fields was not the only talent Coots fostered. He gave Jimmy Durante's career a boost by introducing him to Eddie Jackson and Lew Clayton.

It would appear that Coots did not try to tell or show Dorothy how to write lyrics. "He was very charitable and took me around to a few publishers and their answers were pretty much alike. When Mr. Coots insisted I had talent the publishers answered, 'If she's so damned talented why doesn't her father do something for her.'"[21] Perhaps publishers said something of this sort, or perhaps Dorothy puts in their mouths what she was thinking herself, especially as she saw the help her father had given to other young talents, including Rodgers and Hart, Cole Porter, Jerome Kern, and—not least of all—her brother Herbert. She went on, "We finally wound up at Mills Music. We played what we had and Jimmy McHugh, their professional manager and composer of many pop songs, listened. He listened, period."[22] In another few years, Dorothy Fields and Jimmy McHugh would become a songwriting team. But initially, as Dorothy tells the story, only Coots was her supporter.

Coots's main contribution to Dorothy Fields's career was not the songs they wrote together, none of which seem to have been published or preserved. It is interesting, then, that Dorothy speaks of Coots as the person with whom her career as a lyricist began. He was a professional who took Dorothy seriously, and this was no small thing for her. He may have contributed to steering her in the direction of writing rather than performing. Dorothy had had a close-up look at the songwriting world of Rodgers and Hart. But from her vantage point at that time, songwriting may have seemed like a boys' club. Coots may have directed Dorothy's attention to other female lyricists or songwriters, such as Dorothy Donnelly, Anne Caldwell, or Mabel Wayne. Or, even better, perhaps he conveyed the message that gender was not an issue, an attitude Dorothy herself quickly assumed.

Once Dorothy got her foot in the door of Mills Music Co., she was persistent. She said, "Mills Music was the kind of firm that when Valentino died, the next day they had a song out, 'There's a New Star in Heaven since Valentino Passed Away.' When Caruso died, the next day there was "A Songbird In Heaven Named Caruso.' Now, at this time a lady named Ruth Elder was going to fly the Atlantic. So Mills says, 'She's going to fly today and we have to have a song. I'll help you out. I'll give you fifty dollars to do this if you can do it by tomorrow. I'll even give you a title—'Our American Girl.' The two lines of verse you have to use are, 'You took a notion to fly across the ocean.' I said, 'Mr. Mills you don't take a *notion* to fly across the ocean!' "[23]

Irving Mills probably did not know a lot about the motivations of an aviatrix. He may have had in his head the lyric of a song by Porter Grainger, Clarence Williams, Graham Prince, and Everett Robbins, published in 1922, "Tain't Nobody's Business If I Do." The song, first recorded in 1923 by Bessie Smith, begins, "If I should take a notion to jump into the ocean, 'tain't nobody's business if I do."

Swallowing her doubts, Dorothy wrote the lyric overnight. She commented, "Ruth Elder never made it and neither did my first song. Well, the Mills Music Co. couldn't get rid of me. I became their fifty dollars a night girl. For fifty dollars they got a hundred words."[24] For a time, then, Dorothy Fields and Jimmy McHugh both worked for Mills Music Co., but apparently they did not work with each other. Dorothy does not mention the names of any composers who wrote the melodies to which she set her "hundred words."

James McHugh was born on July 10, 1894, into a working-class family in an Irish-German neighborhood in Boston. His father was a plumber and hoped Jimmy would follow in his footsteps. His mother was an able pianist, and all five children in the McHugh family played musical instruments. As a teenager, Jimmy worked as a kind of general office helper for the managing director of the Boston Opera House. A benefit of that job, over and above the opportunity to hear operatic masterworks, was the availability of pianos, ready whenever Jimmy wanted to try out an idea. "We had fifty pianos throughout the opera house, including in the ladies' room and the men's room," he recalled. He also remembered, "A chap heard me playing piano there, and he said, 'Gee, you should be working for Irving Berlin. What do you want to hang around an opera house for?' "[25] McHugh agreed with this assessment and became a song plugger, singing songs for the Boston branch of Waterson, Berlin, and Snyder.

In 1921, McHugh moved to New York City, looking for greater opportunities for his talent than Boston could offer. He left behind a wife and young son. He started working as a song plugger for a company recently started by Jack Mills. Initially Jack Mills, Inc., specialized in novelty rags. The company published "Kitten on the Keys," by Zez Confrey, in July 1921, and the song became one of its greatest hits, selling more than a million copies of sheet music. The company also published many blues and jazz numbers. Through his energy and enthusiasm, McHugh went from song plugger to business manager and a 20-percent partner. He also published several of his own songs. His biggest song hits from the period before he started working with Dorothy Fields were "When My Sugar Walks Down the Street" (1924, lyric by Irving Mills and Gene Austin) and "I Can't Believe That You're in Love with Me" (1926, lyrics by Clarence Gaskill).

McHugh had hoped that his songs would be sung in a Broadway show. But, to his disappointment, he "found out that the Irving Berlins, Jerome Kerns, Vince Youmans, Frimls—some of these other wonderful writers—had all of the shows tied up, and you just couldn't get anywhere."[26] Although his initial assault on Broadway was unsuccessful, McHugh did receive an offer to compose songs for the Cotton Club in Harlem, which he did on and off for almost ten years. Like many Tin Pan Alley tunesmiths, McHugh wrote with several lyricists, catch-as-catch-can. In addition to Gene Austin and Clarence Gaskill, he worked with the talented but erratic Al Dubin. Many things changed for McHugh when he and Dorothy Fields became a songwriting team.

McHugh describes his initial meeting with Dorothy as promising. "There was this wonderful young lady I met, very gorgeous, with the most beautiful eyes. She was a school teacher. I looked over her lyrics. It was sort of prose. I said, 'There's a typical little something that you have to add to your words so that they come out more in song form. Maybe the tempos or the melodies will do it.' I asked her how would she like to do a Cotton Club show."[27]

Some parts of this anecdote seem more credible than others. McHugh, like Richard Rodgers, was much taken with Dorothy's beautiful eyes. But it is hard to believe that he found her lyrics were as amateurish as he seems to suggest, since he quickly offered her the chance to be his lyricist for a Cotton Club revue. If the lyrics she showed McHugh were "sort of prose," we must assume she was trying for a particular effect. She already had managed to get some of her verse published in Franklin Pierce Adams's column "The Conning Tower" in the *New York World*. Indeed, her assessment of her earliest lyrics was that they were too complex.

Dorothy acknowledged that initially McHugh "took a slightly dim view of my talent."[28] In another narrative of their first meeting, McHugh gave a different account of the advice he gave Dorothy Fields. "What I did say was that you were trying to write *up* to the people, and I told you to write *down*, give them that which they understood, something that should not tax their intelligence."[29] This version accords better with Dorothy Fields's self assessment. An often-quoted remark about Fred Astaire and Ginger Rogers is that he gave her class and she gave him sex appeal. McHugh's biographer gives a slightly more extended description of the contrasting attributes McHugh and Fields brought to their partnership. "His brash Irish personality helped Fields come out of her shell and develop the confidence to write lyrics that captured the flavor of the time, and she gave him an entrée into the theatrical establishment way beyond his experience as a plugger."[30] The collaboration that was begun in 1927 would last almost a decade and would produce some of Fields's and McHugh's most famous songs.

WHAT'S BLACK AND WHITE AND HEARD ALL OVER?

• • •

Dorothy Fields started her career at a felicitous time. The 1920s saw women in the United States going where they had not gone before—into voting booths, for example. The world of Dorothy's early adulthood was very different from the coming-of-age time of her mother or even that of her older sister; American women had new freedoms and were exercising them. To establish herself in songwriting, Dorothy needed not only talent, but also nerve and daring, and the Roaring Twenties fostered those qualities in women far more than previous decades had. Dorothy could look around for encouragement and see flappers of her day trying all sorts of things their mothers had not dared to do. The timing was of great importance, given what lay ahead. Getting a secure foothold in songwriting before the Great Depression hit would be crucial to Dorothy's career.

The 1920s were not only liberating years for women politically and socially. They were also a remarkably good decade for theater in New York, both quantitatively and qualitatively. In the 1927–28 season, for example, there were 264 productions on Broadway, 53 of them musicals, a number that has never been matched. Jack Burton, an important chronicler of popular music before 1950, has noted, "No decade before or since sponsored as many musicals as did the 1920s—a total in excess of four hundred, not counting the revivals, and twelve hitting the 500-or-better continuous performance mark. Moreover, this record was set in the face of competition from two fronts— the movies and newborn commercial radio, which offered entertainment at bargain prices or for free, respectively."[1]

In the 1920s, Broadway was receptive to the operetta and the book musical and also to the revue, which could be a spawning ground for fresh talent but which, by its very nature, could be a rag-tag assemblage of lowest-common-denominator entertainment. Sometimes quality was assured by the producer whose name was prominently displayed on the marquee—Florenz Ziegfeld, George White, or Earl Carroll. Other times the title of a revue—*Broadway*

Brevities, The Broadway Whirl, Nic Nax of 1926, or *Bare Facts of 1926*—
blatantly declared that the audience should expect nothing but froth. New
Yorkers of the 1920s had a seemingly insatiable appetite for entertainment
and, until the end of 1929, the money to pay for it.

A coherent plot line or concept was not a necessity or even a desideratum
of the revue at that time; neither was a coherent score. Hence, the revue was
an arena where neophyte songwriters could hope to place a few songs and,
with luck, build a reputation which would encourage a producer to trust them
with the full score of a musical. The first Broadway show to use a song by
Jimmy McHugh and Dorothy Fields was indeed a revue, *Harry Delmar's
Revels,* which opened at the Shubert Theatre on November 28, 1927. Harry
Delmar had been a dancer on the vaudeville circuit for several years before he
turned his hand to producing. He assembled a cast that included comedians
Frank Fay and, making his Broadway debut, Bert Lahr; female singers
included Winnie Lightner and Patsy Kelly. The *Revels* was lavishly staged.
Billboard heralded the show as "extravagant as anything Ziegfeld could offer."
The *New York Times* reviewer commented on an undersea ballet with "one of
the best collective impersonations of jelly fish that have been seen on the
New York stage this season."[2]

As was often the case in Broadway revues of the time, several people contributed songs. Credits for the music for *Delmar's Revels* went to Jimmy Monaco,
James Greer, and Lester Lee and, for the lyrics, to Billy Rose and Ballard
MacDonald. Jimmy McHugh's and Dorothy Fields's contribution to the show
was "I Can't Give You Anything but Love." Since it was their first hit, and one of
their greatest hits, it is not surprising that legend and lore has accumulated
around this song, especially regarding its genesis and early reception.

Jimmy McHugh reminisced, "One day as Dorothy Fields and I were walking along Fifth Avenue, we stopped to glance in Tiffany's window. A boy and
girl walked up to us as we stood there, and we heard the young man remark
to his girl, 'Gee, I wish I could give you everything, Baby, but I'm afraid all I
can give you is plenty of love.' Needless to say, this was real inspiration, so
Dorothy and I hurried home to put it down in music and words."[3]

Dorothy Fields liked to talk about the song's initial failure. She said, "[Harry
Delmar] asked us to do a song about a poor little Brooklyn boy, who was Bert
Lahr, and a poor little girl named Patsy Kelly. They're sitting practically in
rags on a cellar step. The song we wrote was 'I Can't Give You Anything But
Love.' Well, they did one verse and one quick chorus, and the curtains parted
and there were the girls of the chorus, practically nude, dressed as rubies,
diamonds, opals, amethysts, sapphires, everything! Next day Delmar said,
'This is a lousy song. Take it and get out of my theatre.'"[4]

There are some problems with this story. Fields says the song was placed in *Delmar's Revels* at the start of an extravagant production number. If the song was tossed out after one night, was some other song used to replace it and, if so, what? We can assume on economic grounds that the entire production was not scrapped. Moreover, not even the most finicky producer would expect every song in a revue to be a smash hit. Some songs are simply functional.

A newspaper column called "Song and Dance" by Chas Weller, dated January 21, 1928, which is preserved in one of Dorothy Fields's scrapbooks, states, "Dorothy Fields, daughter of that famous comedian, Lew Fields, has become quite a composer since teaming up with that master of the art of writing melodies, Jimmie McHugh, general professional manager for Jack Mills, Inc. . . . These two great artists [wrote] the lyrics and music for the sensational *Cotton Club Revue* and *Petroff's Revue*. They also have two great songs in '*Delmar's Revels*,' now playing at the Shubert Theatre." The column does not mention the titles of the songs in *Delmar's Revels*, but it contradicts Dorothy's statement that the McHugh-Fields contributions to the show disappeared after the first night. The show itself ran for sixteen weeks.

Accretions of lore have also accumulated with regard to the authorship of the song. Bert Lahr, who debuted the song, brought songwriter Lew Brown into the authorship pool. He thought that Lew Brown, of the successful songwriting team of DeSylva, Brown, and Henderson, suggested the title "I Can't Give You Anything but Love" to Delmar, who passed the idea on to McHugh and Fields. Lahr remembered, "The number didn't do much in the show at all. It wasn't done by important people; and the public didn't consider *Harry Delmar's Revels* a hit show."[5] A newspaper article from 1929 stated that "Brown felt he was entitled to compensation. He consulted his attorney and determined to sue. When it came time to make an affidavit, however, Lew did not show up at the lawyer's office. He probably forgot to get up on time, and that was the end of the lawsuit."[6]

After Dorothy Fields and Jimmy McHugh died, claims surfaced in print that the authors of "I Can't Give You Anything but Love" were Fats Waller and Andy Razaf. Waller's son, Maurice, claimed in his 1977 biography of his father that Fats would fly into a rage when he heard his son sing the song, presumably because he felt cheated out of the credit for it. Waller said that his father "explained how he had sold that tune or other tunes just for drinking money and it bothered him terribly that they had become hits."[7] Mills Music was one among many houses at the time that would purchase songs for a lump sum, depriving the author of any claim to copyright, and Jimmy McHugh had been professional manager at Mills since 1921. But as Alyn Shipton noted in his recent book on McHugh, "It is true that as professional manager at Mills,

McHugh bought songs for cash from a range of would-be songwriters, black or white; but by 1927–28 Waller was already known as a marketable name, and there would be no reason for McHugh not to publish the song as Waller's own, had he bought it."[8]

Barry Singer's 1992 biography of Andy Razaf recounts that when Don Redman's widow, Gladys, was visiting Andy Razaf in the hospital in the early 1970s, she asked him to sing his favorite song, and he gave her a "bedside rendition" of "I Can't Give You Anything but Love."[9] Since, at least as the anecdote appears in print, Gladys Redman's request was for Razaf's favorite song, not his favorite of the songs he had written, his response of "I Can't Give You Anything but Love" constitutes no claim for authorship. Some have made a tenuous claim on the basis of style: the song just sounds like a Fats Waller tune to them. That the unsubstantiated claim for Waller's authorship of this song has lasted as long as it has makes it an interesting study in the power of rumor.

The song's later popularity is unquestionable. Some have suggested that the song grew popular during the Depression as an expression of unquench-able affection in the face of economic hard times. This may be so, but it is worth pointing out that the song became a great hit in 1928, a year before the stock market crashed. One might ask if the very popularity of "I Can't Give You Anything but Love" encouraged McHugh and Fields to surround the song with anecdotes. Did the authors feel a special need to legitimize this song and make it their own? Or was it a necessary part of Dorothy's notion of her life that she believed she had to overcome significant obstacles and failures before success shone on her? If so, it is interesting that she never speaks of being a woman in a man's field as an obstacle she needed to overcome.

Phillip Furia notes that "I Can't Give You Anything but Love" is a text in which one can see traces of Dorothy Fields's predecessors. He points out that the first four lines of Fields's first verse are practically a paraphrase of the last four lines of the second verse of "Where's That Rainbow?" by Lorenz Hart.[10] Hart writes, "My luck has changed—it's gotten/ From rotten to worse!" and Fields writes, "My luck is changing, it's gotten/ From simply rotten to some-thing worse." "Where's That Rainbow?" was first performed as a duet (as was "I Can't Give You Anything but Love") in the musical *Peggy-Ann*, which pre-miered in 1926. The first two lines of Hart's verse scan similarly to the first two lines of the refrain of "I Can't Give You Anything but Love." It would be easy to sing "Fortune never smiles, but in my case, [baby], It just laughs [it laughs] right in my face [baby]" to the first four measures of McHugh's song.[11] There can be little doubt that Dorothy Fields was familiar with this lyric since it came from a show produced by her father with a book by her brother. Recall that when Dorothy first met J. Fred Coots, she played for him the Rodgers and Hart songs she knew by heart, very possibly including "Where's That Rainbow?" But as similar as these lyrics in the two songs are, the tone of the two songs is a study in contrasts. Dorothy rejects the pessimism of the first few lines of her verse. That the speaker can give nothing but love at the moment does not seem to be such a bad thing.[12] Hart's entire lyric exhibits that smiling misery typical of many of his works.

The structure of Fields's lyrics also shows the imprint of her predecessors. The first line of the refrain of "I Can't Give You Anything but Love" returns as the last line, a useful trick to help hearers remember the name of the song. George M. Cohan, often economical in his use of words, favored this device. Sometimes he would bring the first line back unchanged, as in "Life's a Funny Proposition After All" or "When a Fellow's on the Level with a Girl That's on the Square." In other songs, Cohan puts the first line of the refrain as the penultimate line or varies the line slightly at the end. Phillip Furia points out that the "love/of" rhyme in the first two lines of Dorothy's refrain was earlier used by George M. Cohan in "You're a Grand Old Flag" in the line—"You're the emblem of the land I love." Furia notes, "Cohan's flippant 'of/love' rhyme [is] a desperate maneuver in a language that gives a lyricist fewer rhymes for 'love' than for almost any other four-letter word."[13]

Many other songwriters whose songs Dorothy likely knew used the device of bringing the first line of the refrain back as the last line. Irving Berlin's first published song (1907) places "My Sweet Marie from Sunny Italy" at the beginning and end of the refrain. The practice also served him well in "Alexander's Ragtime Band." Berlin sometimes would place just two or three key words or even a single word in the first and last lines of the refrain and sprinkle them in other lines as well. Examples of this appear in several of his most popular ballads of the 1920s such as "All Alone" (1924), "What'll I Do" (1924), "Remember" (1925), "All by Myself" (1926), and "Blue Skies" (1927). In "Always" (1925), Berlin places the title word at the end of almost every line of the refrain, a scheme Dorothy follows mutatis mutandis with the word "baby" in "I Can't Give You Anything but Love."

With the word "baby," Dorothy Fields shows, in one of her earliest lyrics, one of her most salient characteristics—a fine ear for the vernacular, for slang. Terms of endearment abound in popular song; they are a necessary part of saying "I love you" in thirty-two bars. Only some of these terms are slang, and only some are gender-specific. Some words only become terms of endearment when prefaced by a possessive; "gal" is neutral, but "my gal"—as in "Has Anybody Seen My Gal" (1925) or "The Bells Are Ringing for Me and My Gal" (1917)—is affectionate.

The terms of endearment lyricists use may be seen as a characteristic of their style. Lorenz Hart, a model for Dorothy Fields in other aspects of lyric writing, generally manages without terms of endearment. Berlin likes "honey" or the slightly more formal "dear," but at least once employs the more poetic "angel eyes." The word "baby" had served lyricists for several decades before Dorothy Fields employed it. One finds it in the titles of songs by Harrigan and Hart, Victor Herbert, George M. Cohan, and Gus Edwards. In 1900 Joe Howard covered all the bases in his million-copy song with the first line "Hello my baby, hello my honey, hello my ragtime gal." Other slang terms in "I Can't Give You Anything but Love" include the use of "swell" rhyming with "darn well" and also the youthful exclamation "Gee." In the verse, we hear about being "broke," not poor. Using a familiar proper name such as Woolworth is a trick Cole Porter liked to use in his list songs.

The most striking line is the second one of the second strophe, striking because of its telegraphic quality. Of course, song texts require concision, but this line goes beyond economy of expression. Because of its telegraphic quality it could contain several meanings if you stopped to think about it. But of course you don't stop to think about it; this is not lyric poetry, which you read at your own reflective pace, but a song lyric in which the melody pulls you on to the next thought. If this pair of lines were fleshed out they might read, "Gee, I'd like to see you looking swell, Baby, [I'd like to see you wearing] diamond bracelets [that] Woolworth doesn't sell." There are other possible readings, though. A frequent practice of Yiddish-American speech is to put the object of the phrase before the subject and verb. In this usage the statement "Diamond bracelets Woolworth doesn't sell" means the simple declarative statement "Woolworth doesn't sell diamond bracelets," and what is needed to complete the thought is "and the only place I can afford to shop these days is Woolworth." Sometimes poetry is valued because its ambiguity or incompletion demands that the reader, or listener, add something of his own to complete the meaning. That's what happens in this lyric.

Even if Dorothy's contribution to *Delmar's Revels* had been more immediately notable, it would have been overshadowed in the family by the clamorous success of *A Connecticut Yankee*, produced by Lew Fields, with a book by Herbert Fields and a score by Rodgers and Hart, which opened at the Vanderbilt Theatre on November 3, 1927. The seed of the idea for this musical was planted as early as 1921, when Herb, Dick, and Larry saw a silent film version of Mark Twain's *A Connecticut Yankee in King Arthur's Court*. They were sufficiently excited by the possibilities of this story to request from the Mark Twain estate permission to use it. The unknown team of youngsters received permission to use the story at no cost, but six years passed before their version came to fruition. An intermediate form of the idea was *A Danish Yankee in King Tut's Court*, a nonprofessional show for which Herb Fields wrote the book and most of the lyrics in 1923. *A Danish Yankee*, according to Lew Fields's biographers, "displayed in crude form the principal devices that they would employ in *A Connecticut Yankee*—anachronistic language, topical references, and an inter-epoch romance."[14]

It was only after Herb, Dick, and Larry had a number of successes under their belts, together and separately, that they returned to the idea of *A Connecticut Yankee*. No doubt Herb was helped by the experience he gained from other shows. In *Dearest Enemy*, he explored some of the possibilities for humor in the anachronistic clash of historical and contemporary attitudes. In *Peggy-Ann*, Herb had worked with the structure of the central body of the play being some kind of dream framed by a prologue and epilogue. In both *Peggy-Ann* and *A Connecticut Yankee*, the dream changes the protagonists' view of their present situation and allows them to make a better romantic choice. Peggy-Ann defies her mother and goes off with her boyfriend; Martin decides to marry Alice instead of Fay.

Financial backing for the show was supplied, in part, by Lyle Andrews, owner of the Vanderbilt Theatre, and by Herb Harris, Lew Fields's foster son, who had grown wealthy in the perfume importing business he started with Joe Fields. There was no stinting on this production, which included a cast of forty-two actors and a nineteen-piece orchestra. Indeed, the lavish production strained the capacity of the small stage of the Vanderbilt Theatre, and ingenuity was required to keep the actors from being impaled on the bulky props. The production staff included Alexander Leftwich as director and Busby Berkeley in one of his earliest choreographic assignments. For the leading role of Martin, Lew Fields brought in William Gaxton, who was established in vaudeville but untried on Broadway; Gaxton was also a partner of Herb Harris's in Parfums Charbert. Constance Carpenter, who played Dame Alisande, had previously been seen in *Oh, Kay! A Connecticut Yankee*, which received excellent reviews and was a big hit with the public. It ran at the Vanderbilt Theatre for 418 performances; the road company toured for over a year, taking the show to forty-nine cities across the United States.

The 1920s saw the flowering of another venue for live musical performance: the nightclub. Prohibition, brought about by the passage of the Eighteenth Amendment in 1920, caused the closing of many restaurants, in which drinking and eating were the main activities, and the rise of nightclubs, which offered drinking and entertainment. Nightclubs sprang up all over Manhattan—in midtown, downtown in Greenwich Village, and, most important for this story, uptown in Harlem.

The nightclubs of Harlem offered two transgressive activities for the price of one—drinking illegal booze and observing (if not exactly mingling with) people one did not usually mix with. The booze meant that the nightclubs were, at some level or other, connected to or run by bootleggers and gangsters. Social historian Lewis Ehrenberg noted, "New York criminals made crime a business by providing a consumption service in the 1920s. While the presence of criminals produced some violence in and about the nightclubs, especially in the late 1920s and early 1930s, for the most part they helped keep the peace in Harlem, making it safe for people in 'ermine and pearls' to go uptown."[15] Though some clubs in Harlem seemed to spring up and disappear almost overnight, others, famous for the entertainment they provided, were more stable. Three of the best known were Small's Paradise, where opening night in 1925 attracted more than fifteen hundred patrons; Connie's Inn, run by Connie Immerman and featuring the music of Don Redman; and the Cotton Club, run by Owney Madden.

Located at 142nd Street and Lenox Avenue, in a building that operated first as the Douglas Casino (1918) and then as the Club Deluxe (1920), the Cotton Club achieved relative stability when it was taken over by Madden, a bootlegger. Between 1923 and 1925, the Cotton Club shows were produced by Lew Leslie, who had previously operated the Plantation Club in midtown Manhattan, a cabaret presenting black entertainment patterned on all-black shows such as *Shuffle Along*. The Plantation Club featured, according to Ehrenberg, "log cabins, Negro mammies, picket fences around the dance floor, a twinkling summer sky, and a watermelon moon."[16]

In 1925, Madden's Cotton Club was padlocked by order of federal court judge Francis A. Winslow. When it reopened a few months later, Dan Healy had replaced Lew Leslie as the producer of stage shows, and Herman Stark was hired as stage manager. Cotton Club historian Jim Haskins observed, "Under Healy's direction the Cotton Club became probably the first night club to feature actual miniature stage sets and elaborate lighting as well as spectacular costumes."[17] Healy had a formula for a successful nightclub show. "The chief ingredient was pace, pace, pace! The show was generally built around types: the band, an eccentric dancer, a comedian—whoever we had who was also a star. The show ran an hour and a half, sometimes two hours; we'd break it up with a good voice. . . . And we'd have a special singer who gave the customers the expected adult song in Harlem."[18]

There is a wide range of opinion regarding just how segregated the Cotton Club was. At the shrillest, most polemical end of the spectrum are the remarks of Ellington biographer Dempsey J. Travis. "The mob-controlled Cotton Club was operated by twentieth-century slave masters. Talented jazz musicians were chained to specific night clubs and saloons in the North in the same manner as slaves were shackled to the large cotton and tobacco plantations in the antebellum South. Duke Ellington, Louis Armstrong, Cab Calloway, Earl Hines, Jimmie Lunceford and many others were inmates behind the Cotton Curtain at various periods in their careers from 1924 to 1941 and beyond."[19]

The published remarks of at least one of the musicians at the Cotton Club support another view. Sonny Greer, the drummer in the Duke Ellington band, noted that Owney Madden was a good man to have on your side. Describing a scene in Duke Ellington's dressing room, he said, "So this cat Petrillo [the Musicians' Union boss James Petrillo] was standing up there, man, and these guys were his bodyguards. He was standing up there, talking to Duke, pointing his finger, 'You can't do this, you can't do that.' So I say to Duke, 'What's the matter, man?' He say, 'This guy's trying to give me a hard time.' They don't know Owney Madden is our boss. I say, 'Get on the phone, call this number.' We had to get a private number. So Petrillo say, 'Who are you calling?' I say, 'The man who owns our band.' And he knew, he knew the number. So Owney answered; said, 'Put him on.' What he said—no more trouble."[20]

Duke Ellington appreciated the fact that when he played at the Cotton Club it was more like playing in a theater in terms of the decorum of the listeners. He said, "The great thing about it was when the show was on—they did have a wonderful show—no one was allowed to talk during the shows. I'll never forget, some guy would be juiced, and talking, and the waiter would come around, 'Sir would you please . . . ' and the next thing the captain would come over, 'Sir,' and so forth, and the next thing the head waiter would come and then next thing, the guy would just disappear!"[21]

It is a commonplace to speak of the Cotton Club's whites-only policy when it came to clientele. Indeed, the Cotton Club aspired to and succeeded in attracting a high-tone crowd of celebrities. The club was patronized on occasion by members of the English nobility, Lady Mountbatten for one. Customers also included a fair share of elected officials, such as Mayor Jimmy Walker of New York and Mayor Zimmerman of Buffalo. Musicians Paul Whiteman, Ferde Grofé, Irving Berlin, and Eddie Duchin went to hear musical sounds they heard nowhere else. Celebrity entertainers such as Jimmy Durante went to the Cotton Club to be entertained. The Cotton Club was a good place to see and be seen. A typical gossip column read, "In the Cotton Club. . . . Listening to Duke Ellington and his dance-compelling orchestra. . . . It seems the stage and screen celebrities have made this their pet Harlem haunt! Here is good, old William S. Hart ringsided. . . . And here is Broadway's clown prince, Jack White, who's been basking in the limelight via George White's *Scandals* and doubling at the elite Chateau Madrid. . . . Here's Helen Kane with a party . . ."[22]

The policy of whites-only customers was somewhat flexible—a matter of perceived practicality rather than ideology. It also developed and altered over time. Abel Green's review of the Cotton Club show of December 7, 1927, noted that "the almost Caucasian-hued high yaller gals look swell and uncork the meanest kind of cooching ever exhibited to a *conglomerate mixed audience*." Green also suggests that the black service staff was far from servile in its behavior toward white clientele. "A trend at the club that [manager Harry] Block should curb is the psychological reaction of the service corps to the ofay invaders who, not content to dictate to the blacks downtown, enter the very heart of the so-called Black Belt. . . . The staff seems to take the attitude that for once it can assert itself in native territory with the morale and service dubious at times."[23]

Perhaps of greater interest is the degree of racial separation or commingling between the creative staff and the performing staff. The standard version of the story is that the creative team at the Cotton Club—the songwriters, costume and decor designers—were white, and the performers were black. Jimmy McHugh wrote for the Cotton Club from near the time it opened until 1930 when he left New York for Hollywood—nine years by his count. He said, "I was very fortunate, though: somebody offered me a job in Harlem, to write for the Cotton Club. I said, 'Well that sounds wonderful.' At that time I would have done anything."[24] Before he teamed up with Dorothy Fields, McHugh had worked with several lyricists at the Cotton Club, most notably Al Dubin. When he invited Dorothy to write lyrics for his Cotton Club songs, her initial reaction seemed to echo his. She stated, "McHugh said, 'Would you like to do some songs for the Cotton Club in Harlem?' And I said, 'I would write for the Westchester Kennel Club. I don't care what it is!' So we did a few shows there."[25] Clearly, a chance to write songs that an audience would hear—even if not on Broadway—was an opportunity not to be missed.

According to Lew Fields's biographers, Lew and Rose had misgivings about Dorothy's associating herself with a place like the Cotton Club. " 'Ladies don't write lyrics!' Lew proclaimed. Dorothy supposedly responded by paraphrasing her father's most famous line: 'I'm not a lady, I'm your daughter.' The response seems too cute not to be apocryphal, but then, clever lines were her business."[26] Moreover, bandying gag lines about the house was a family sport, and this was a particularly good setup for the punch line. Dorothy enjoyed her time working at the Cotton Club; it seemed to her neither sinister nor threatening. She reminisced, "I must say all the boys were simply wonderful. I was the little sister. They were very solicitous of me, very careful not to say anything wrong in front of me, and they got furious if anyone used improper language in my presence. No one was allowed to say 'Darn.' During the afternoon rehearsals, they'd go into the kitchen and bring out cookies and tea."[27] That Dorothy felt like the little sister suggests that she felt right at home, since that was the role she played in the family script.

Jimmy McHugh seconded her opinion. He recalled, "Owney Madden was one of the nicest fellows that you could ever meet. He was a real sweet fellow, and he was always nice to me."[28] Financial arrangements could be somewhat informal at the Cotton Club. McHugh reported a conversation he had with Ben Martin, one of the managers of the Cotton Club at an early stage in his employ. Martin said, "'What's the matter kid? Isn't everything all right with you? You're getting well paid here.' I said, 'I'm not getting a quarter from this place. I'm just doing the songs for nothing, and I'm writing my head off and hanging around here—.' He said, 'Well this shouldn't be. Are you sure?' I said, 'Yes, I don't get a quarter.' He said, 'Well, how would $250 a week be for you?' I said, 'How will it be? Well, as they say in our business, leave us not discuss anything further.'"[29]

The first show McHugh and Fields wrote for the Cotton Club opened on December 4, 1927. Dorothy told the story of that opening night many times. "The night that our show, our first, was to open, they also had Duke Ellington and his orchestra—first time he appeared in New York. We'd rehearsed with a woman—let's not mention her name. We'd rehearsed her in some nice songs. Opening night, Walter Winchell was there because he was a good friend of my father's. Huge family table—my mother, my father, my first husband, Joe and his wife, and Herbert. And she came out after intermission, and she sang three of the dirtiest songs you ever heard in your life. 'Easy Rider' was mild compared to these songs. My father looked at me and asked, 'Did you write these lyrics?' And I was green. I said, 'Of course I didn't.' So Winchell said, 'You'd better do something about it, Lew.' So Pop went to the owner, a man named Block—he was partners with a gangster named Owney Madden. He said, 'If you don't make an announcement that my daughter Dorothy didn't write those lyrics I'm going to punch you right on the floor.' So they made an announcement: 'These lyrics of Miss Blank were not written by Dorothy Fields. The music was not written by Jimmy McHugh.' That was my first experience in the theatre."[30]

In Dorothy's narratives of the start of her career, she begins by talking about her first Cotton Club show. She either ignores the *Delmar's Revels* or says they came after the Cotton Club, though *Delmar's Revels* in fact opened six days earlier. In another account of the story of her Cotton Club debut, Dorothy remembers the family table slightly differently—this recital does not mention her first husband being there but includes her sister.[31] In yet another version her outraged father exclaims, "You didn't learn those words at home," and she ripostes "I didn't write those words."[32] In none of her versions of the story did Dorothy name the singer.

There are several candidates for the singer whose name Dorothy chose to forget. Haskins, in his book on the Cotton Club, thinks it was probably Edith Wilson. Born in 1896, Wilson had a singing and acting career that extended from 1921 until shortly before her death in 1981. She appeared in a number of shows produced by Lew Leslie—*The Plantation Revue* (1922), *From Dover to Dixie* (1923), *Dixie to Broadway* (1924), and *Blackbirds of 1926*—often with Florence Mills. She started singing at the Cotton Club in 1924 with the entertainer Doc Straine. Abel Green's review of the December 7 Cotton Club show states that "Edith Wilson and Jimmy Ferguson were liked in a comedy skit." He does not mention that she sang at all.

L. Marc and Armond Fields and Deborah Winer claim the singer was Aida Ward.[33] In Abel Green's review of this show he lists Aida Ward as the principal chanteuse. "Aida Ward, who reminds of a Florence Mills in her song delivery, is a charming song saleswoman and the particular luminary of the proceedings. Miss Ward seems to be the nearest approach to the sainted blackbird-looking-for-a-bluebird. Her own 'Broken Hearted Black Bird' will become a standard for Miss Ward like other ditties did for Miss Mills."[34] It is hard to imagine that someone singing raunchy "adult" songs would be described as "a charming song saleswoman." The comparison with Florence Mills, a revered, recently deceased singer, also seems to suggest that Aida Ward did not sing salacious lyrics at that performance. The description of Aida Ward at this time by Barney Bigard, clarinet and tenor sax player in Ellington's band, likewise does not correspond to one's image of a singer of off-colored songs. "This prima donna, Aida Ward was her name, the prima donna of the show, and she was trying to get the band fired because the band they had before, she was going with one of the guys in the band. So Duke had to hire a fiddle player to lead her tunes. . . . So her part, she come out, she's got to have a big obbligato in front, you know, just she and the fiddle . . . So just before show time the guy left the fiddle on the piano, Otto Hardwick got some soap and dampened it and soaped the bow, you know, and soaped the bow up good. So when she came out to sing and starts that falsetto and the fiddle player's supposed to back her up with some little obbligato, there ain't nothing coming out. And she sings, and he's just going like mad and he can't get a thing, and she's looking back to see what's happening and we're just sitting there laughing like mad until she got so that she had to walk off the stage crying."[35] Aida Ward continued to sing at the Cotton Club through the 1930s. She introduced Harold Arlen's "Between the Devil and the Deep Blue Sea" there in 1931 and "I've Got the World on a String" in 1932.

Jimmy McHugh, reminiscing three decades later, claimed the singer was Lethia Hill and one of the off-color songs was called "Flat Tire Papa, Don't You Try to Retread Me."[36] Hill was billed as "Queen of the Blues" in later Cotton Club programs.[37] Haskins describes Lethia Hill as "the torch singer in residence at the club at that time [the 1930s] . . . For her, Arlen and Koehler produced such songs as 'Pool Room Papa,' 'My Military Man' and 'High Flyin' Man.' None of these songs bears Arlen's name. They were the sort of shocking songs that could be found only on 'race records.'"[38] The case for Lethia Hill being the singer whose name Dorothy chose to forget would be stronger if there were evidence that she performed in that particular Cotton Club show. She is not mentioned in Abel Green's December 7 review of the show but does this mean that she was not in this show or that he did not review that part of the show?

It is very curious that while Dorothy remembers her father insisting that an announcement be made that she did not pen the lyrics, Abel Green states that it was necessary that an announcement be made that she did write lyrics. "Jimmy McHugh is the solely programmed-credited for the restricted music, but Dorothy Fields, daughter of Lew Fields, was orally introduced as the authoress of the lyrics. Miss Fields, like her brother Herb, who is now an established musical comedy book author, is turning to the stage for her creative outlet. Even in a night club revue her words to music are impressive."[39] Perhaps the noise level at the club was such that one could not tell if the announcer was saying that the lyrics were by Dorothy or were not by Dorothy.

What is most puzzling about Dorothy's account about her opening night at the Cotton Club is her seeming naiveté. Did she not know that at some point in the show—even if not at the point when she expected to hear her own lyrics—songs with lyrics that would be offensive to her parents would be sung? She reported that none of the gangsters used foul language in her presence. But it was perfectly well known that "adult" songs were a standard part of Cotton Club shows. An advertisement for the Cotton Club in 1928 stated that there were two shows nightly. Were the "adult" songs reserved for a later show? Had Dorothy ever seen a Cotton Club show before the one in which her own lyrics were to be sung? There could not have been a full rehearsal of the December 4 show before it opened because up until that very morning Duke Ellington and his band were still working in Philadelphia. If Dorothy had not seen a previous Cotton Club show, what models was she using for her own lyrics? Her models for more sophisticated songs (Dorothy called them "smarty" songs) such as "Collegiana" could have been Lorenz Hart or Ira Gershwin, or P. G. Wodehouse. What were her models for Cotton Club lyrics? Or, was the very fact that she had no intimidating models for lyrics for her Cotton Club songs precisely what allowed her to flourish?

McHugh no doubt supplied Dorothy with samples, published or unpublished, of songs taken from the stock of the Mills Publishing company, where he had worked. It is certainly possible that McHugh showed Dorothy songs he and Al Dubin had written for previous Cotton Club shows. McHugh had written with Dubin "numbers like 'My Dream of the Big Parade,' 'The Lonesomest Girl in Town,' 'I Don't Care What You Used to Be, I Know What You are Today,'—all the real broken-down ballads that you can think of, of the women of the streets and of the houses Mr. Dubin used to frequent." He remembered, "I continued to write these knock-down and drag-out ballads, as we called them, with Dubin, but I wanted to write pretty songs."[40] We do not know if McHugh wrote any "knock-down and drag-out" ballads with Dorothy Fields. The front page of the program for the 1929 Cotton Club show *Spring Birds* announces "special restricted music by Jimmy McHugh and Dorothy Fields," so probably he did. However, it is not clear exactly what songs McHugh and Fields wrote for the various Cotton Club shows they worked on.

It was the pattern at the Cotton Club to put on new shows in the spring and in the fall. The next shows that McHugh and Fields produced songs for were *The Cotton Club Show Boat*, which opened April 1, 1928; *Hot Chocolates*, which opened October 7, 1928; *Spring Birds*, which opened March 31, 1929; and *Blackberries*, which opened September 29, 1929. There is some confusion regarding the names of the shows. Dorothy Fields recalled that the name of the first show (not the third) that she wrote was *Hot Chocolates*. Ken Bloom states there was a show called *Cotton Club Parade* in 1929, but "Parade" began to be attached to the Cotton Club shows of the 1930s, for which Harold Arlen and Ted Koehler wrote the songs. Acknowledging that the McHugh-Fields songs were only a small part of a show that included specialty dance acts, a chorus line of beautiful, interestingly clad women, comedy acts, and other diversions, one might expect a body of twenty or twenty-five songs to have emerged from this period. But one has scant idea of which songs were heard in which shows. The shows for which programs still exist list the order of performers, but not the music they performed. Judging by titles and dates of composition, songs that were likely written for Cotton Club shows include "I'm a Broken Hearted Blackbird" (mentioned in Abel Green's review), "Hot Chocolate," "Topsy and Eva," and "Harlem at Its Best." Evidence for the Cotton Club provenance of several others is the fact that they were recorded by Ellington; these include "Harlem River Quiver," "Hottentot Tot," "Freeze an' Melt," "Arabian Lover," "Hot Feet," "Red Hot Band," and "Harlemania." None of these songs became standards, but they prepared the way for one of the biggest Broadway hits of the 1920s: *Blackbirds of 1928*, a show with an all-black cast. The show's score would be written by Fields and McHugh, and it would be the big break that gave them entrée on Broadway.

GIVE MY REFRAINS TO BROADWAY

• • •

Jimmy McHugh's ambitions went beyond writing songs for the Cotton Club, just as they went beyond being a professional manager at Mills Music. Dorothy Fields was part of his ambitious plan. He stated, "I was looking at all times for somebody who had the flair, the charming lyrics, sort of a Larry Hart technique, and good vocabulary." He went on, "I wanted to do shows. That was my ambition."[1] Doubtless it did not escape McHugh's attention that Dorothy's father was an important Broadway producer. But as it turned out, the person who launched McHugh and Fields on Broadway was not Lew Fields but rather Lew Leslie, who hired them to write the score for *Blackbirds of 1928*.

Lew Leslie (né Lewis Lessinsky) was born in 1886 in Orangeburg, New York. He started out onstage doing imitations of comic actors including David Warfield and Sam Bernard (both of whom performed regularly at the Weber and Fields music hall). There is a certain aptness to the fact that Leslie, who built his career as a producer on his ability to assimilate and bring to a white audience African American musical talent and culture, started out as an entertainer who imitated Jewish American comics. Both as an impressionist and as a producer, Leslie showed an uncanny eye and ear for the talent of others.

Leslie's first coup as a producer came when he contrived to hire Florence Mills away from the cast of *Shuffle Along*, the first successful Broadway musical written, directed, and performed by African Americans. Its book was by Flournoy Miller and Aubrey Lyles and its songs were by Noble Sissle and Eubie Blake. Leslie offered to pay Mills three times the salary she was receiving and said he would build a show around her and accept her husband, dancer U. S. "Slow Kid" Thompson, as part of a package deal. Under Leslie's sponsorship, Mills starred in *The Plantation Revue* (1922), first at the nightclub Café de Paris, then on Broadway. She went on to conquer London and Paris in the revue *From Dover to Dixie*, then returned to New York to star in *Dixie to Broadway* in 1924.

Mills died young because of a failed appendectomy. Though her career lasted less than a decade, she came to be hailed as "the world's greatest colored entertainer." She excelled as a singer, dancer, and comedienne, seeming to surprise and delight not only her audience but herself with her spontaneity. She told an interviewer, "It all depends on the audience. I never know what I'm doing. . . . I just go crazy when the music starts, and I like to give the audience all it craves. I make up the dances to the songs beforehand, but then something happens, like one of the orchestra talking to me, and I answer back and watch the audience without appearing to do so. It's great fun. Something different at each performance. It keeps me fresh. . . . I'm the despair of stage managers who want a player to act in a groove. No grooves for me."[2] Her voice, it was reported, could soar to coloratura regions; unfortunately, her talent was never recorded on film or disk.

Mills saw her association with Leslie as beneficial both to her and her people. She said "I felt . . . that since [Bert] Williams established the Colored performer in association with a well-known revue [the *Ziegfeld Follies*] that I could best serve the Colored actor by accepting Mr. Leslie's offer, since he had promised to make his revue as sumptuous and gorgeous in production and costume as Ziegfeld's *Follies*, George White's *Scandals*, or *The Greenwich Village Follies*, at the same time using an all-colored cast. I felt that if this revue turned out successfully, a permanent institution would have been created for the Colored artists and an opportunity created for the glorification of the American High-Browns."[3]

In 1926, Leslie presented a new show starring Mills, *Blackbirds*. The show's title was probably a nod to one of Mills's most popular songs, "I'm a Little Blackbird Looking for a Bluebird," lyric by Grant Clarke and Roy Turk, music by George W. Meyer and Arthur Johnston, which she had performed in *Dixie to Broadway*. *Blackbirds* was a great success and toured the Continent. The company returned to New York in September 1927. When, on November 1, 1927, Florence Mills died, the outpouring of grief was enormous. Thousands of people filed past her coffin at the funeral chapel of A. Adolph Howell, and tens of thousands lined the streets for her funeral procession. Telegrams of condolence were sent to her family by Lee Shubert, Paul Whiteman, David Belasco, Governor Al Smith, and Mayor Jimmy Walker among many others. There was a $100,000 floral tribute at her funeral including "a tower of red roses four feet wide and eight feet high; the card was signed 'From a Friend.'"[4] The friend may have been the prince of Wales, who attended many of Mills's performances in London.

Leslie had successfully transferred his European hit *From Dover to Dixie* to New York, reshaping it and renaming it *Dixie to Broadway*, in 1924. He doubtless had planned a similar transformation of *Blackbirds* following its successful European tour. After the death of its star, Florence Mills, his revision of *Blackbirds* was radical. He not only hired a new cast of performers, he also hired a new songwriting team: Jimmy McHugh and Dorothy Fields. McHugh's connection with Leslie went back as far as 1923, when they were both working for the Cotton Club. He had seen *From Dover to Dixie* in London in 1924. He recollected, "I called Leslie, 'I have a wonderful lyric writer in the states, and when you come back, I'd like you to come up to the Cotton Club and listen to the show and hear her lyrics.' He said, 'All right.'"[5] McHugh's memory cannot be completely accurate on this. If his meeting with Leslie in London was in 1924, as he claimed, that was several years before he started to write Cotton Club shows with Dorothy Fields; the first McHugh-Fields Cotton Club opened a month after Florence Mills's death. With or without an invitation from McHugh, Leslie was surely on an active talent search at that time.

McHugh and Fields's work at the Cotton Club turned out to be excellent preparation for writing the score for *Blackbirds of 1928* in two respects. First and more obvious, McHugh and Fields were steeped in material that white audiences wanted to hear from black performers. Second, there was a close relation between nightclub shows, whether in Harlem or midtown, and Broadway revues. Indeed, *Blackbirds of 1928* started its life as a nightclub floor show, not at the Cotton Club but at Les Ambassadeurs. Dorothy recalled, "Lew Leslie hired us to do a show called *Blackbirds of 1928*. First, we'd written songs for a show of his in a club called Les Ambassadeurs, on 57th Street, where we had Roger Wolfe Kahn—he was Otto Kahn's son—and his orchestra, and a lovely lady named Adelaide Hall, who sang."[6] McHugh recalled, "I knew about Roger [Wolfe Kahn] wanting to close the café, and I told Leslie, and Lew went up and made arrangements to take it over. This was the start, the first half, of a show called *Blackbirds of 1928*." He said, "There was a little trouble between Leslie and the Cotton Club group, because Mr. Leslie took some of the people out of the show up there, and there was sort of a threat to burn the place the night before the opening." He continued, "Leslie opened this Ambassador's Restaurant with the first half of the show." The show was a great hit. McHugh went on: "From there we wrote a second half, and we took the show to Atlantic City."[7]

Blackbirds of 1928 was a milestone in the careers of Dorothy Fields and Jimmy McHugh—the realization of a dream McHugh had cherished since coming to New York in 1921. The first Broadway show for which they wrote the complete score, *Blackbirds of 1928*, put them on the map. It was one of the most successful shows they were ever connected with, the team's trademark for the next several years. Advertisements for their subsequent Cotton Club shows would proclaim "music by Jimmie McHugh; lyrics by Dorothy Fields—authors of *Blackbirds*."

Lew Leslie hired Aida Ward and Adelaide Hall to replace Florence Mills. Both women had worked with Mills in earlier shows. Hall and Mills had both started out in the chorus of *Shuffle Along* (1921). Hall then appeared in shows in the United States (*Runnin' Wild*, 1923) and in Europe (*Chocolate Kiddies*, 1925). The recording she made in 1927 of Duke Ellington's "Creole Love Song" is a classic. Aida Ward had appeared with Mills in *Plantation Days* (1923) and in *Blackbirds* in London and Paris. An important addition to the cast was made just two weeks before the Broadway opening. During the show's out-of-town tryouts in Atlantic City, dancer Bill "Bojangles" Robinson, who had been getting vaudeville bookings, was brought in to enliven the second act.

As was normal for a revue, *Blackbirds of 1928* alternated musical numbers and comedy sketches. The sketches followed certain familiar formulas. There was a card-playing scene ("Brother, if you lay your hand on those chips, the next time you buy gloves, just ask for one"); a graveyard scene ("You know a dead man can't hurt you." "Maybe not, but they kin make you hurt yourself!"); and two wedding scenes—"Magnolia's Wedding Day" and "Getting Married in Harlem."

The musical numbers also clustered around certain predictable tropes. One of the functions of these formulas and tropes was to emphasize difference—a distancing technique. Hence there was a "jungle" number, the refrain "Diga, diga, doo" sung by a "Zulu man" living in "Samoa by the sea." To be sure, there was no value placed on geographical or historical accuracy. A generalized exoticism sufficed. Moreover, many of the performers had American ancestry going back several generations further than many white members of the audience. Josephine Baker had been playing the same "jungle" card to enormous success in Paris. What is most interesting about "Diga, Diga, Doo" is the demonstration it gives us of Dorothy's playfulness and willingness to sound silly. This was not a lyric one would expect from the pen of Larry Hart or Ira Gershwin. Dorothy was perfectly willing to learn from Hart, Gershwin, or anyone else. But for the lyrics she wrote for the Cotton Club and for *Blackbirds of 1928*, she needed other sources—her own internal resources.

Another genre of songs recalls putative happy days on the plantation—presenting the plantation as one more place where Negroes can sing and dance. These songs once again emphasize difference—a different kind of exoticism—while offering false reassurance to the white audience. In Lew Leslie's *Dixie to Broadway* (1924), there were several such numbers—"Put Your Old Bandana On," "Dixie Dreams," and the hybrid "Jungle Nights in

Dixieland." There was only one such number in *Blackbirds of 1928*, "Bandana Babies," reflecting the increasing urbanization of black revues later in the decade. There is a certain amount of self-promotion in "Bandana Babies." The audience is lured with the promise, "You're gonna get an eyeful" and "You're in danger of losing all your cares."

A different slice of southern black life is offered in the song "Porgy." Dorothy Heyward and DuBose Heyward based their play *Porgy* on DuBose's eponymous novel of 1925. The Theatre Guild produced the play, which opened on Broadway in October 1927, just a few months before Dorothy Fields's first songs were heard in the Cotton Club. She may well have seen *Porgy* as part of her research into black turns of speech. Jerome Kern and Oscar Hammerstein II, following their success with *Show Boat*, had considered writing a musical version of *Porgy*, which would have had Al Jolson as its star, but they did not follow through with this plan. George Gershwin's *Porgy and Bess* opened in 1935, seven years after McHugh and Fields wrote the song "Porgy." A second engagement of the play *Porgy* opened at the Republic Theater on May 28, 1928, less than two weeks after *Blackbirds of 1928* had opened. Dorothy's lyrics, "He ain't much for to look and see / Lazy and no' count as he can be" are similar to the opening of "She's Funny That Way," written by Richard Whiting in the same year. The line "I'm changin' my style and this ol' way of livin'" may reflect the 1921 song "There'll Be Some Changes Made," by Billy Higgins and W. Benton Overstreet, a favorite with both Ethel Waters and Sophie Tucker. The organization of the lines of the chorus in groups of three is suggestive of blues construction.

There are several blues numbers or torch songs in *Blackbirds of 1928*. In these songs, the woman is allowed to sing of her unhappiness, but this unhappiness is personal, not sociological. That is, within the context of the show, life as a slave on the plantation was a happy life, whereas life as a free, modern, individual black is an unhappy one, but there is careful avoidance of any examination of why this should (or should not) be so. Despite all this, it is in these more personal songs that Dorothy comes into her own expressively.

The verse of "I Must Have That Man" begins as directly as can be, declaring the singer's unhappiness over being alone. She complains her lover is "not so strong for me, " and this sounds natural, but it might be a colloquialism invented for the sake of the rhyming pair "long for" and "strong for." The line in which the singer talks about the imperfections of the loved one makes the listener think the lyric will go in the direction of "Bill" which was first heard in *Show Boat* a year earlier. Then again, that kind of complaint may be the essence of any torch song, as for example "Can't Help Lovin' Dat Man" from

Show Boat. "I want to be his way" sounds simple but is slightly obscure. Does it mean she wants to be like him? More likely, she wants to be whatever way he wants her to be if that will make him love her. Or does the line suggest she wants to be in his way, almost as if he could not avoid stumbling over her? In the chorus, the word "mammy" is perhaps the only thing (apart from the dialect) that reveals the singer to be Negro. The singer comparing herself to an "oven that's cryin' for heat" is as sexy a line then written for Broadway, but not for the Cotton Club. Could Dorothy have written such a line had she not had her year's apprenticeship at the Cotton Club? The next line may contain another nod to black language by referring to her lover as a boy rather than a man. Or did Dorothy just want to avoid the redundancy of having the word "man" repeated in two consecutive lines? The heat imagery is maintained in the release with a reference to Hades. The release has lots of rhyming pairs, Hades and lady's; cooled off and ruled off; kissed, list, and missed. The end rhymes are simple, but the internal rhymes are more sophisticated.[8]

In "Baby," another torch song, the verse uses the conceit of rejecting high-flown descriptions of love but explaining the feeling of love in less romantic, more down-to-earth language, "I need him more than I need my meals." This line is more direct, if less witty, than "I need that person much wors'n just bad" in "I Must Have That Man." "I crave the touch of him" seems like fancy diction, but it rhymes with the more down-to-earth "Can't get too much of him."[9]

The show also has some dance numbers. Dancing, particularly fast dancing, had a place of pride in black revues and could be counted on to get praise from reviewers. It may be remembered that the Charleston, the dance that symbolizes the Roaring Twenties, came out of the black revue *Shuffle Along.* "Doin' the New Low Down" was written expressly for Bill Robinson; it was the only number he performed in *Blackbirds of 1928.* But for many critics, his turn was the high point of the show.

Blackbirds of 1928 was not an unequivocal success from the start. Many reviews were enthusiastic about the performers; some were lukewarm about the comedy sketches. Dorothy, with her preference for autobiographical stories about overcoming adversity, suggested that the show in general and "I Can't Give You Anything but Love" in particular were dreadful flops at first. "Horrible reviews for *Blackbirds.* Panned. Everybody loathed it. Gilbert Gabriel, who later became a close friend of mine, wrote, 'And then there was a sickly, puerile song called 'I Can't Give You Anything But Love.' "[10] She ignored, or forgot, that Gabriel also wrote, "One thing catches the ear extremely well, though; Dorothy Fields' lyrics. . . . Her jinglings are far and away the warmer and wittier part of every song."[11] Dorothy also suggested that what turned the show into a success was the establishment of midnight performances on Thursday. "We waived royalties and the show limped along until Leslie got the idea to do midnight shows on Thursdays. And that became the rage of New York. Everybody went to *Blackbirds* on Thursday midnights. Woolcott re-reviewed it, Gabriel, everybody re-reviewed it, and it ran for two years! Ran in Paris, ran in Chicago, everywhere."[12]

Dorothy's version has it that the midnight shows on Thursday were conceived as a rescue operation when *Blackbirds of 1928* was not doing as well as the producer had hoped. However, both the opening-night program and the opening-night advertisement in the *New York Times* make clear that Thursday midnight shows were part of the original conception of the run of the show. *Blackbirds of 1928* opened on Wednesday, May 9, and there was a midnight show the next night. The idea that people will come to a show to watch more famous people watching the show had been well tested at the Cotton Club, and Lew Leslie was hoping it would work for *Blackbirds of 1928*. It did.

By the fall of 1928, it was clear that *Blackbirds* had a long run ahead of it. Indeed, its run of 518 performances made it one of the ten longest-running shows of the decade. Touring companies hit the road. When *Blackbirds* played the Tremont Theatre in Boston in November 1928, it was publicized as having "an All-Star Cast of 100 Colored Artists," including Harriett Calloway, Hamtree Harrington, Beebee Joyner, Clarence Foster, Emmett Anthony, Jessica Zackey, and Cecil Mack's Blackbird Choir.

Speaking of this period in her career from the perspective of more than four decades later, Dorothy Fields remarked that she "seemed destined to write revues. It's tough. You start from scratch twelve or fourteen times. And maybe that's good. If you can write extraneous songs, writing for a book show would be heaven. I wasn't to get to heaven for a little while yet."[13] But in saying this, Dorothy ignores her first book musical. The aptly titled *Hello Daddy* was a family affair, produced by Lew Fields with a book by Herbert Fields and lyrics by Dorothy Fields. The music was by Jimmy McHugh, who was to remain Dorothy's sole songwriting partner for about five years. For Lew and Herbert, *Hello Daddy* was a retrenchment, a step back from the daring, novelty, and innovation that had served them well in *Peggy-Ann* and *A Connecticut Yankee* but that had taken them past the public's and critics' acceptance in *Chee-Chee* (1928). *Chee-Chee* ran for only four weeks and brought to a screeching halt the string of successes that Richard Rodgers, Lorenz Hart, and Herbert Fields had been enjoying as a team. After its failure, Rodgers and Hart moved on to other collaborators. In statements that perhaps protest too much, Rodgers explained, "Despite rumors at the time, the failure of *Chee-Chee* was not the reason for the breakup of the Fields, Rodgers and Hart partnership. As a matter of fact, there never really was any breakup, because Larry and I later worked with Herb again on two shows and three movies. But after *Chee-Chee*, Herb was getting other offers, and so were Larry and I, and it was perfectly understandable that we take advantage of the best available opportunities"[14]

The antecedent for *Hello Daddy* was *The High Cost of Loving*, a farce adapted from a German source by Frank Mandel, in which Lew Fields had starred in 1914. The play was brought up to date by Herbert Fields, who minimized some of the ethnic components and made room for more romantic and musical scenes. The story presented Lew Fields as one of three men who, for the preceding twenty years, have been blackmailed into providing support for a nonexistent illegitimate son. The legitimate children and their friends provide the young-love pairs and do most of the singing and the dancing.

Dorothy and Jimmy adorned the play with ten numbers—seven in the first act and three in the second act. There are no solo numbers, but two duets, "I Want Plenty of You" and "Let's Sit and Talk about You," were singled out by critics as likely hits. The most popular number on opening night was "In a Great Big Way," performed by Betty Starbuck and Billy Taylor. For the most part, the music was presented with large ensembles going through the paces designed by Busby Berkeley. One of these numbers, "Futuristic Rhythm," is perhaps a nod to the Gershwins' "Fascinating Rhythm" written in 1924. "Futuristic Rhythm," "Let's Sit and Talk about You," and "In a Great Big Way" were recorded as instrumentals by both Jimmy McHugh leading the Bostonians (an ensemble) and by Ben Pollack conducting the orchestra of the original production.

The reviewers had good things to say about the songs for *Hello Daddy*. Robert Garland wrote that "the tunes give promise of popularity," and Burns Mantle predicted "it is probably the songs that will do the most for *Hello Daddy*." Paul Milton opined that "Dorothy Fields' lyrics are well-rhymed, emphasis being laid on the Larry Hart type of stuff," and Walter Winchell claimed that "Dorothy's lyrics (the typically intelligent and believable sort) fit snugly into Jimmy McHugh's contagious melodies." Several critics complained that the songs were not well sung. Herbert Miller stated, "Dorothy Fields' lyrics are intelligent but often garbled by those who use them." Burns Mantle lamented, "It is rather a pity that there is no one in the cast to sing the songs as they should be sung. The Giersdorf sisters swallow them harmoniously, and everybody dances them beautifully. But no one can sing them."[15] None of the songs from *Hello Daddy* became a standard. *Hello Daddy* ran for 198 performances in three different theaters. It opened in Lew Fields's Mansfield Theater, then moved to George M. Cohan's Theatre, which had a better location. When George M. Cohan's Theatre was needed for a summer schedule of motion pictures, *Hello Daddy* moved to the Erlanger.

Blackbirds of 1928 was running when *Hello Daddy* opened on December 26, 1928, and was still running when *Hello Daddy* closed in mid-June. Flush with success, Lew Leslie decided to try something new for him—a revue that made no use of African American performers. With no lack of hubris, the man who claimed he understood African American performers better than they understood themselves decided to take on the world. He invested $200,000 in *Lew Leslie's International Revue*. From England, he hired Gertrude Lawrence, who was in fact well known to American audiences from her much applauded appearances in *Andre Charlot's Revue of 1924*, costarring Beatrice Lillie, and in the Gershwins' *Oh, Kay*, in which she starred in 1926. From Ireland by way of the Ballet Russe, Leslie brought Anton Dolin to do an Apache dance on an elaborate set showing a street in Montmartre. He also had the prodigy Robert Conche to conduct and play violin and concertina. As a gamble, he hired, sight unseen, the Spanish dancer Argentinita. American talent was not neglected in this enterprise—Harry Richman had made his mark on stage, in radio, and in film, and Jack Pearl was famous for his radio character Baron Munchausen.

Leslie did hedge his bets, though. He hired performers he had never worked with, but for the songs he returned to the team that had helped make *Blackbirds of 1928* the hit it was, Jimmy McHugh and Dorothy Fields. They wrote a dozen new songs for him. As a nod to current financial events, Jack Pearl sang "The Margineers," which began with a comparison of Wall Street and the Wailing Wall and ended, "We'll be in the American Can in the morning. Three cheers for the poor margineers." Dorothy later commented that the song "got a lot of bitter laughs from the audience."[16] Her father would have been an excellent tutor for wringing some kind of laugh out of nearly any situation.

The two songs that had the greatest success—"On the Sunny Side of the Street" and "Exactly Like You"—were both sung by Harry Richman and Gertrude Lawrence. "On the Sunny Side of the Street" was an optimistic counterweight to "The Margineers." Stephen Sondheim has remarked, "What I like best about Dorothy Fields is her use of colloquialism and her effortlessness as in 'Sunny Side of the Street,' which is just perfect as a lyric."[17] I have been told that this song became a code anthem for African Americans passing as white, but I doubt this was Dorothy's first thought. Indeed, I believe the source for the title is an advertisement that appeared in a program booklet for *Hello Daddy*. A notice from the New York Tuberculosis and Health Association exhorts sufferers, "One can walk on the sunny side of the street." Like many of the best lyricists, Dorothy had the ability to see a passing turn-of-phrase as an opportunity and a gift.[18]

The other hit song of *International Revue* was "Exactly Like You."[19] In his analysis of this song, Alec Wilder remarks, "McHugh was a very fortunate man to have a such a talented lyricist as Dorothy Fields to work with. Her lyrics often swung, and their deceptive ease gave a special luster to McHugh's music."[20] Gertrude Lawrence and Harry Richman recorded "On the Sunny Side of the Street" and "Exactly Like You." These two songs were published, along with five others, by Shapiro, Bernstein and Co. One must assume that McHugh's break with Mills Music was complete by this time. The other published songs were "International Rhythm," a kind of successor to *Hello Daddy*'s "Futuristic Rhythm," "Keys to Your Heart," "Cinderella Brown," "I've Got a Bug in My Head," and "I'm Feelin' Blue ('Cause I've Got Nobody)."

Lew Leslie's International Revue opened on February 25, 1930, at the Majestic, and closed only twelve weeks later. Despite the extravagant sets and costumes and despite the huge compendium of talent, the show did not please the critics and did not draw an audience. Leslie's guiding hand faltered. The talent was too diverse and mismatched; the sketches, which he wrote with Nat Dorfman, failed to amuse. Leslie had, in the past, prided himself on the rapid pacing of his shows, but *International Revue* was very long and felt even longer. Argentinita did not even begin her act, which lasted more than thirty minutes, until past eleven, by which time many of the first-night critics had already left. Lew Leslie went so far as to pay Argentinita an additional $10,000 to leave the show after the first week. But, of course, the problem with the show was more substantial than one weak act. Many decades later, Gerald Bordman wrote in *American Musical Theatre*: "Because most of the *International Revue*'s material was not up to its music, the excellent cast seemed at times empty-handed. . . . The *World* called it 'long and dirty and dull,' while the more tactful *Times* complained 'the humor is anatomical.'"[21]

After the failure of the *International Revue*, Lew Leslie went back to Blackbirds revues. He produced one in 1930, one in 1933, and one in 1939. *Blackbirds of 1930* had songs by Eubie Blake and Andy Razaf; it was one of the few shows for which Lew Leslie employed African American talent behind the scenes. The show starred Ethel Waters, Flournoy Miller, the Berry Brothers, and Buck and Bubbles, but for all that it closed in the red. *Rhapsody in Black*, also starring Ethel Waters, ran for three months in New York, starting in May 1931. *Blackbirds of 1933* did not fare any better than *Blackbirds of 1930*, despite a cast that included Bill Robinson and Edith Wilson. As Allen Woll stated, "Most critics observed the 'lack of any spark of originality' [according to the *Sun*]—Leslie's enslavement to earlier versions of his show seemed to preclude any experimentation. Therefore, if one had seen an earlier, and no doubt better *Blackbirds*, there seemed to be almost no reason to visit [this one]."[22] The last hurrah was *Blackbirds of 1939*, which starred Lena Horne. It ran for only nine performances. In Leslie's obituary in the *New York Times*, his claim to fame is as the producer of *Blackbirds of 1928*.

Between 1928 and 1930, McHugh and Fields supplied songs for several other revues. Ziegfeld's *Midnite Frolic* had "stars from the Ziegfeld shows and Paul Whiteman and his entire orchestra," according to one advertisement. Ben Marden's *Palais Royale Revue* starred Ethel Waters. They also wrote for a revue for Ben Marden's *Riviera*. None of the songs for these revues became standards. Nevertheless, McHugh and Fields became a songwriting team to reckon with. Louis Sobol observed in one of his "Voice of Broadway" columns, "An index of song-writers compiled and submitted by Ed Weiner lists some of the outstanding gentlemen [sic] of the profession as follows: Irving Berlin, most quiet; Billy Rose, most formidable; Gene Buck, most oratorical; Charley Tobias, most methodical; Harry Tobias, most dreamy; George M. Cohan, most versatile; Ray Henderson, most unassuming; Dorothy Fields, most sophisticated; Jimmy McHugh, most affable; Jerome Kern, most erudite; Sigmund Romberg, most Bohemian; Al von Tilzer, most polite; Dick Rodgers, most elite; Lew Brown, most excitable; George Gershwin, most pianistic; Sammy Fain, most boyish."[23]

With the onset of the Great Depression in 1930, the economy brought about a sea change in the theater business. There were more than fifty vacant stores on Broadway and two bread lines in Times Square. Whereas there had been 233 productions on Broadway during the 1929–30 season, in the 1930–31 season there were only 187. By the fall of 1930, a great many theaters on and around Broadway were standing empty.

The Vanderbilt Theatre was among them. *A Connecticut Yankee*'s long run had come to an end on October 27, 1928. Despite the economy, Lew Fields and Lyle Andrews thought the Vanderbilt could be the site for a new revue. But the revue they produced was the biggest flop of Lew Fields's producing career. At a time when both taste and economics favored a revue that was small and simple or that was unified by some theme, *The Vanderbilt Revue* was a hypertrophied, sprawling mess. It had not only the two producers (Fields and Andrews), two directors (Lew Fields and Theodore J. Hammerstein), two choreographers (John E. Lonergan and Jack Haskell), five lyricists (Dorothy Fields, Yip Harburg, Ben Black, David Sidney, and Edward Eliscu), five composers (Jimmy McHugh, Mario Braggiotti, Jacques Fray, Edward Horan, and Ben Black), and eight sketch writers (Joseph Fields, Kenyon Nicholson, Ellis Jones, Sig Herzig, Edwin Gilbert, Arthur Burns, James Coghlan, and E. North). And that was just the behind-the-scenes talent. On stage were Joe Penner, Evelyn Hoey, Lulu McConnell, Teddy Walters, and M. Dalsky's Russian

Choir. The critics were not kind. Lew Fields's biographers write: "In a sign of the times, several critics complained about a risqué song sketch about a gigolo, while *Variety's* reviewer cited the fact that there was 'no nudity and little spice' as a liability."[24] The show went out not with a bang but a whimper. *The Vanderbilt Revue* ran for only two weeks, from November 5 to November 18, 1930.

Dorothy Fields and Jimmy McHugh provided four songs for *The Vanderbilt Revue*: "Blue Again," "Button Up Your Heart," "Cut In," and "You're the Better Half of Me." None of these achieved the popularity of, for example, "On the Sunny Side of the Street." But "Blue Again" must have had a certain place of affection in Dorothy's mind. She sang it in the Ninety-second Street YMHA retrospective of her work.[25]

Had *The Vanderbilt Revue* opened a few years earlier, perhaps it would have run longer. But by late 1930, circumstances were dire for Broadway shows. Many show people, unable to find work in New York, were leaving for California, which offered profitable work in the film industry. Indeed, Dorothy Fields and Jimmy McHugh had already tested the waters in Hollywood before *The Vanderbilt Revue* opened.

HELLO TO HOLLYWOOD

• • •

Historians ponder the sudden efflorescence of artistic activity in a given time and place—the outburst of visual art in fin de siècle Paris, or the welling up of music and art in Vienna at the same time. In the 1920s, Berlin and Blooms-bury were loci of innovation in literature and the visual arts. Likewise, one must view with astonishment the rain forest–like richness and diversity of artistic talents that populated Hollywood in the 1930s. A tennis game between George Gershwin and Arnold Schoenberg was not a genre-jarring fantasy but rather a regular occurrence. In a flight of whimsy, one can wonder what might be said in conversations between writers known to be simulta-neously present there—Thomas Mann and Tennessee Williams, or William Faulkner and Lorenz Hart, or Dorothy Parker and Bertolt Brecht. These peo-ple probably did meet one another at some Hollywood party or event.

Hollywood in the 1930s was a kind of glorious, golden refugee camp. It was full of people who were leaving behind a life that had turned unexpect-edly bad. There was an influx of people who had worked on Broadway in the boom years of the 1920s but had recently gone without work as more and more theaters were darkened by the Depression. Another emigrant group comprised musicians, authors, actors, and directors from Europe who were fleeing Nazism.

Southern California seemed wide open to talent. In 1926, Herman Mankie-wicz wrote to the journalist, novelist, and playwright Ben Hecht, "Will you accept three hundred per week to work for Paramount Pictures? All expenses paid. The three hundred is peanuts, millions are to be grabbed out here and your only competition is idiots."[1] By 1930, the talent pool had grown considerably.

The services of many of the newcomers to Hollywood were actively sought by the immigrants who had gotten there ten or twenty years earlier—former salesmen of fur or buttons or businessmen on the fringes of the entertain-ment industry—who were now the heads of studios or studio departments. The chief studios at the end of the 1920s were Metro-Goldwyn-Mayer, Warner Brothers, Paramount, Twentieth-Century Fox, and Radio-Keith-Orpheum, the big five. Also important were Universal, Columbia, and United Artists. Their prosperity reflected their successful response to the challenges of adapting movies to sound. These challenges were in part technical—getting equipment to record sound on film and to play the talking films in movie theaters. There were also artistic challenges: the studios now needed actors who had pleasing voices, writers who could produce convincing dialogue, singers who could sing, and songwriters who could write hits. Not all Hollywood stars of the silent era successfully made the transition from silent to talking films. The careers of John Gilbert, Vilma Banky, and Pola Negri crashed, but those of Richard Barthelmess, Wallace Beery, Joan Crawford, Ronald Colman, Gary Cooper, and many others continued to flourish.

A goodly cohort of screenwriters made the transition to sound comfortably, in part perhaps because they could turn to one another for help. Preston Sturges reported that screenwriters tended to work in teams "like piano movers. . . . Four writers were considered the rock bottom minimum required. Six writers, with the sixth member a woman to puff up the lighter parts was considered ideal."[2] In fact, a large number of women had established writing careers in Hollywood in the 1920s or earlier and continued them into the 1930s and beyond. Among these were Frances Marion, Anita Loos, Bess Meredyth, Jeanie Macpherson, and Sonya Levien, who did a great deal more than "puff up the lighter parts."

When it came to songwriters, the Hollywood studios began to fish very heavily in Tin Pan Alley's ponds. Composers and lyricists were needed to provide songs for musicals as well as promotional theme songs for films that were not musicals, and the studios used enticing financial lures. For some songwriters, the transition from Tin Pan Alley to Hollywood became both natural and necessary after Hollywood studios bought up the music publishing houses they had been working for. For example, when Warner Brothers bought the music publishers Remick, Harms, and Witmark, they gained not only a body of already published songs but the services of composer Harry Warren and lyricist Al Dubin, who went on to write the Academy Award–winning song "Lullaby of Broadway" and dozens of other songs.

Dorothy Fields and Jimmy McHugh first explored Hollywood together in 1929 after the transition to talkies had begun but before the stock market crashed. It is not clear if the first impulse to see what Hollywood had to offer came from Dorothy or from Jimmy. In 1925, while still in New York, McHugh had written the song "My Dream of the Big Parade," with Al Dubin, to help promote the movie *The Big Parade*. The film, starring John Gilbert, fared much better than the song.

Dorothy and Herbert Fields had traveled to California together in the summer of 1928. On their way back to New York they stopped off at Colorado Springs to visit Richard Rodgers. Rodgers remarked tartly in a letter to his future wife, Dorothy Feiner, "Herb and sister arrive tonight from the Coast, but they'll probably spend all their time on horseback."[3] A small article in the *Colorado Springs Evening Telegraph* that appeared under the headline "Writers of Musical Comedy Successes Are Visitors Here" said that "Mr. Fields has been in California in the interest of staging 'Present Arms.'" *Present Arms* ran for 155 performances in New York, from April 26, 1928, to September 1. It is certainly possible that Herb and Dorothy were looking into other employment possibilities in Hollywood as well.

McHugh and Fields went to Hollywood as a songwriting team, like Rodgers and Hart, or George and Ira Gershwin. There were other models of how to write a song in Hollywood, of course. Irving Berlin and Cole Porter were one-man teams, writing both words and music for their songs. Some composers and lyricists joined forces at the direction of the studio where they were under contract. For example, Harry Warren worked with Al Dubin and Johnny Mercer at Warner Brothers. At Twentieth-Century Fox, he worked with Mack Gordon. At MGM, he worked with Arthur Freed, Johnny Mercer, Ralph Blane, and Ira Gershwin. At Paramount, he worked with Leo Robin, Jack Brooks, Harold Adamson, and Leo McCarey.

Dorothy Fields and Jimmy McHugh signed their first contract with MGM studios on October 3, 1929, just a few weeks before the stock market crash. This suggests that their decision to go to Hollywood was not driven by anxiety, fear, or despair, but rather by a spirit of adventure. It is true that none of their Broadway shows in the past year had had the success of their first show, *Blackbirds of 1928*. Still, McHugh and Fields had no reason to believe that Broadway had become a barren field when they went to Hollywood; the grass simply must have looked greener farther west.

They did not sign long-term deals with MGM. Instead, their contracts were for a total of six months, broken up into two three-month periods, each to begin at a time specified by MGM; the studio agreed to give the songwriters four weeks' notice before they were expected to start writing. This arrangement suited the studio because at this time songs were generally added to a movie after it was shot; songs were a part of post-production. In 1930, movies were typically shot in about a month's time. Thus, when a film started into production, songwriters could be notified that they would be needed a month later.

The arrangement, although designed for the studio's convenience, suited Dorothy Fields well since it was not her intention to sever ties with her family, friends, and working associates in New York. For a few years, she and

McHugh had bicoastal careers. In 1930, they contributed four songs for MGM's *Love in the Rough*; back in New York, they wrote fourteen songs for the *International Revue* and four songs for the *Vanderbilt Revue*. The next year, they added songs to *Cuban Love Song* and *Flying High* in Hollywood and to *Rhapsody in Black*, produced by Lew Leslie, *Shoot the Works*, and *Singin' the Blues* in New York.

At the end of 1932, Dorothy and Jimmy took part—both as songwriters and performers—in a historic show-business event in New York. Radio City Music Hall, with seats for more than six thousand people and a stage larger than some entire theatres, opened on December 27 with a very long and wildly eclectic program. Excerpts from *Carmen* rubbed shoulders with a salute to Francis Scott Key arranged by Ferde Grofé; the Wallenda family, a noted European aerial act, shared the program with the Tuskegee Choir; dancers ranged from Ray Bolger to the Berry Brothers to the Radio City Music Hall Ballet.

The opening also featured performances by Weber and Fields. As it turned out, these Radio City Music Hall performances were the last the comedy team gave in New York. Just three months before, they had been feted at a lavish fiftieth-anniversary Jubilee at the Hotel Astor. On opening night at Radio City Music Hall, the Weber and Fields act had been saved for a grand finale. But the show ran so long that they did not come on stage until past midnight, when much of the audience and most of the critics had already left. This gaffe was quickly rectified. On the program declaring "Happy New Year" across the top, Weber and Fields performed third.

In 1919, Lew Fields and Herbert Fields had appeared together in the play *A Lonely Romeo*. Now, thirteen years later, it was Dorothy's turn to share a stage with her father. In a scene called "Night Club Revels," Dorothy sang one of her new songs, "Hey! Young Fella!" Mining the vein she had exploited so well in "On the Sunny Side of the Street," "Hey! Young Fella!" gave voice to the optimistic sentiments in such short supply during the Depression. Atypically, but perhaps as a public service, the complete lyric was supplied in the program.[4] The program announced, "Miss Fields, daughter of Lew Fields, is making her first stage appearance." Critics decided she acquitted herself very well. During the next few years, Dorothy and Jimmy would occasionally perform their songs on the radio, but at this stage in her life—in contrast to her high school years—performing was a hobby rather than a career. Her creative enterprise was writing. The venue for her writing, for most of the 1930s, was Hollywood.

The first film that Dorothy and Jimmy provided songs for, *Love in the Rough* (1930), was the sort of cheery fare that would become typical of musicals produced during the Depression. *New York Times* reviewer Mordaunt Hall called it "a frothy, light affair, with melody, golf, and farcical antics."[5] Dorothy's memory of *Love in the Rough* had less to do with the frothiness of the plotline than with a specific constraint on it imposed by the film industry in those days:

> It was almost the beginning of musical pictures. In those days there was a theory that every time you did a song in a picture it had to be excused by either having a guitar or a banjo on the set. They refused just to do a song per se and have the music come from nowhere. They felt in those days that you could not, shall we say, square music in a picture unless you could see an instrument playing the music. This was 1929, and there hadn't been many musical pictures. I remember so well—there was a picture we did called *Love in the Rough* for Robert Montgomery and Dorothy Jordan. It was a golf story, and the caddies had little harmonicas, you see; and every time we did a song, the caddies would accompany this love song, behind the bushes, and then the music would creep in. But they held it imperative to have some kind of instrument on the set so the people would know where the music was coming from. Of course, later they gave all that up.[6]

The film was based on Vincent Lawrence's play *Spring Fever.* The screen version added four songs: "Go Home and Tell Your Mother," "I'm Learning a Lot from You," "I'm Doin' That Thing," and "One More Waltz." This was not really a musical comedy, then, but rather a comedy with music or a comedy with added songs. The *New York Times* review noted, "It is a moderately good entertainment with one especially catchy song, "Go Home and Tell Your Mother," rendered by Robert Montgomery and Dorothy Jordan in an acceptable fashion."[7]

Fields and McHugh were luckier than Rodgers and Hart with regard to golf films. Rodgers and Hart wrote four songs for a golf film, *Follow Thru,* based on the 1929 Broadway musical of the same name by DeSylva, Brown, and Henderson. By the time Paramount released it, at the same time as *Love in the Rough,* only one Rodgers and Hart song, "I'm Hard to Please," had survived. There is a nice symmetry to the fact that in Dorothy's first paid-for lyric she celebrated Ruth Elder's flight-to-be across the Atlantic, and the first film she wrote lyrics for was about another up-to-date and trendy fashion, golf.

The next year, Fields and McHugh were assigned some of the songs for *Cuban Love Song,* a vehicle for Lawrence Tibbett, costarring Lupe Velez, with Ernest Torrence and Jimmy Durante. Tibbett had made his debut at the Metropolitan Opera House in 1923 and scored a considerable success in the role of Ford in Verdi's *Falstaff* in 1925. MGM hired him in 1929 for *Rogue Song,* an adaptation of Franz Lehár's *Zigeunerliebe,* and he was nominated for an Academy Award for his performance. *Cuban Love Song* was his fourth and last movie for MGM.

The plot of *Cuban Love* song has points of contact with Puccini's *Madama Butterfly.* Tibbett plays a U.S. Marine who, during a brief stay in Cuba, falls in love with a local peanut vendor. After leaving Cuba he makes a more suitable marriage to an American ingénue. Ten years later he returns to Cuba to find the peanut vendor is no longer alive but has left behind their son, whom Tibbett brings back to the United States.

The film has a composite score. Tibbett sings the Marine Corps anthem, "From the Halls of Montezuma," and a popular song, "The Peanut Vendor," as well as two newly composed songs by McHugh and Fields, "Tramps at Sea" and "Cuban Love Song." Over time, Dorothy came to feel at least a little ambivalent about "The Cuban Love Song." In her 1972 retrospective talk at the Ninety-Second Street-Y she mocked the lyrics. " 'I love you. That's what my heart is saying.' Ridiculous! Your lips say the words. Your heart may dictate them, but hearts don't talk, they beat." She also gave credit to another lyricist for one of the rhymes. "Fashion and passion rhyme courtesy of Lorenz Hart."[8] She probably had in mind a little-known Rodgers and Hart song from 1921, "Something Like Me," in which the singer suggests one should choose a man "Of fashion, And passion, A thinker, No drinker."[9]

Cuban Love Song was McHugh and Fields's first opportunity to write a title song together. The use of title songs predated talking or singing movies (as, for example, McHugh's title song for the 1925 *The Big Parade*). Movies and title tunes had a commercially symbiotic relationship. A movie could provide a remarkably powerful plug for a song, introducing it to large audiences across the country in a short period of time. Title tunes, on the other hand, could be a kind of warm-up act or advertisement, heard on radio or phonograph, stimulating interest even before the film was released. Title tunes need not have lyrics. Max Steiner's "Tara" theme for *Gone With the Wind* did not require words to attach itself to people's memories. Sometimes the words were added after the movie was released. For example, David Raksin's "Laura" subsequently acquired a brilliant lyric by Johnny Mercer. However, the title tunes that McHugh and Fields wrote were songs from the start. They incorporated the title of the film in the text of the song, and the song was sung in the course of the film.

The next film Dorothy and Jimmy wrote a title song for (although not the next film they wrote songs for) was *Dancing Lady.* The picture starred Joan Crawford, Clark Gable, and Franchot Tone, all of whom achieved greater fame in later years in nonmusical films. Actually, neither Gable nor Tone is called upon to sing or dance in this film. They play rivals for the affection of Joan Crawford, who is more than ably partnered in her dance numbers by Fred Astaire.

Critic Mordaunt Hall noted in the *New York Times* (December 1, 1933): "Undaunted by the scathing remarks made against it, the backstage story rears its head more impudently than ever in the picture 'Dancing Lady.' . . . The closing interludes are given over to a lavishly staged spectacle which by some stroke of magic the leading male character is supposed to put on in an ordinary sized theatre. It looks as though it might be better suited to the Yale Bowl or Chicago's Soldier Field."[10]

Several composers and lyricists wrote songs for *Dancing Lady*. A musical score by committee was familiar to McHugh and Fields not only from previous films such as *The Cuban Love Song* but also Broadway revues such as *The Vanderbilt Revue*. Rodgers and Hart supplied the song used in the finale, "Rhythm of the Day." That Dorothy should find herself working on the same film as Rodgers and Hart, her buddies from her high school days, suggests some of the big town–small town atmosphere of the film colony in the 1930s. Rodgers noted in his autobiography that he had gone to public school with the producer of *Dancing Lady*, David O. Selznick. In his discussion of his life in Hollywood, Rodgers never mentions Dorothy Fields. This omission is puzzling considering both Dorothy's success and Rodgers's connections with several members of the Fields family. Rodgers and Hart also wrote a title song for *Dancing Lady*—two versions, in fact. On June 7, 1933, Rodgers wrote to his wife, "We've written the Crawford song, but it hasn't been officially accepted so far. It's called 'Dancing Lady' (the name of the picture) and I wouldn't be surprised if it reminded you of 'Ten Cents a Dance.' It isn't really bad."[11] It was common in Hollywood in the 1930s for several people or teams, unbeknownst to one another, to be assigned what amounted to options for the studio to choose from; it was a practice many writers found unnerving. In the end, the most popular song to come out of *Dancing Lady* was neither the title song by McHugh and Fields nor the song for the finale by Rodgers and Hart. The big hit was "Everything I Have Is Yours," written by twenty-one-year-old Burton Lane with lyricist Harold Adamson. Burton Lane and Dorothy Fields would collaborate on a television musical version of *Junior Miss* more than twenty years later.

Dorothy reconnected with another New York acquaintance while working on *Hooray for Love*, an RKO picture released in 1935, starring Gene Raymond, Ann Sothern, and Bill "Bojangles" Robinson. In *Hooray for Love*, Robinson plays himself: that is, he plays an entertainer called Bill whose dramatic role consists of performing. For some audiences, this definitely enhanced the appeal of the film. Robinson was by then quite famous; in 1935 he also made two films at Twentieth-Century Fox playing opposite Shirley Temple—*The Little Colonel* and *The Littlest Rebel*. A reporter for the *Chicago Defender* observed, "When Bill's Harlem scene flashed, the applause was deafening. It was as if Bill was on the stage in person, smiling in response to the welcome, as if he knew and understood that he was the asset necessary to the happiness of the audience."[12]

Another New Yorker performing in *Hooray for Love* was Fats Waller. If, as some have claimed, Waller believed that "I Can't Give You Anything but Love" was written by him and sold to McHugh for a small sum, one can only speculate on his feelings while working in a minor role in *Hooray for Love* (his name is not even mentioned in the *New York Times* review), the songs for which were written by the successful team of Fields and McHugh, whose first great hit was precisely that song. As it turned out, *Hooray for Love* did not give anybody's career a big boost.

Hooray for Love is yet another treatment of the theme of trying to put on a show. The *New York Times* reviewer commented, "Gene Raymond is a struggling producer of musical shows. . . . His show turns out to be a smash hit in the last three minutes of the picture, but this, although it might have been compensation enough for Mr. Raymond, was not enough for the audience." He went on, "Strictly speaking, the film is not a musical film at all. . . . Only in the night-club and broadcasting sequences at the start—the best ones in the picture—is there any attempt to fuse the music and the dramatic action."[13] This remark reminds us how blurry the boundaries are between films with songs and musicals. With Robinson in the cast, there was dancing as well as singing, although the reviewer in *Variety* complained of "the lack of any real production numbers." Certainly the number of songs alone does not determine if a film is perceived as a musical. *Hooray for Love* has six songs (or five, according to Ken Bloom). The *New York Times* reviewer liked the songs but complained about the musical arrangements. "Dorothy Fields and Jimmy McHugh have written several good songs, but the orchestral transcriptions are of the most banal nature and they are played without gayety [sic]." In contrast, *Top Hat*, also made at RKO in 1935, starring Fred Astaire and Ginger Rogers, with a score by Irving Berlin, has only five songs but it is the archetypal musical of the 1930s in part because these songs are so integral and essential to the film.

During this period of film work for Dorothy, her family was, in ones and twos, moving to California—first Herbert, then Joseph, then her parents. Herbert was in Hollywood by June 1930, working at Warner Brothers on the script for *The Hot Heiress* at about the same time Dorothy was busy with *Love in the Rough* for MGM. Herb too shuttled between New York and California during the '30s, depending on opportunities for work. Although he worked on projects with Rodgers and Hart in Hollywood, their collaboration did not continue at the same level of intensity that had resulted in eight shows on Broadway between 1925 and 1928, many produced by Lew Fields, and most of them hits. In the summer of 1930, Herb, Larry, and Dick worked together on *The Hot Heiress*, which was released in March 1931. But what had been a tight and then a loose triumvirate in the 1920s dissolved even further after that movie. In his autobiography, Rodgers speaks enthusiastically about working with Herb. "Though we enjoyed working with other writers, up to this time Larry and I had never had the kind of theatrical successes or creative stimulation that we'd enjoyed with Herb."[14]

Nevertheless, for a while in 1930, Rodgers seemed to need to put more distance between himself and Herb Fields. When he was working on a production of *Ever Green* in Glasgow, he wrote to his wife, "As you know now, we've told Herb [Fields] not to come. It would be awkward for all to have him in Glasgow."[15] Two weeks later, Rodgers wrote, "Herb's synopsis arrived and we have had the terrible ordeal of sending him a cable saying that we didn't like it. . . .. We both agreed entirely that it was terribly unoriginal and not the least promising. Our first objection to the locale [Hollywood] seems justified by the completed story. We feel strongly that satire is impossible in a scene that has been satirized to death already. . . . Success today is too difficult to allow us to do anything that isn't at least fresh in its inception."[16]

Rodgers and Hart's producer, Charles Cochran, settled on Benn W. Levy as book writer for *Ever Green*. Herb, meanwhile, went to work with Cole Porter on their second collaboration, *The New Yorkers*, which opened in New York on December 8, 1930. The first Cole Porter–Herbert Fields musical, *Fifty Million Frenchmen*, had opened on Broadway on November 27, 1929, and ran for 254 performances. *The New Yorkers* was not so fortunate. It ran for 168 performances. Porter biographer Stephen Citron observed, "With uniformly good reviews, it should have run for years but . . . three days after it opened the Bank of the United States failed, closing its sixty branches and wiping out the life savings of some 400,000 families."[17] Herb Fields and Cole Porter had intended to follow up *The New Yorkers* with a musical called *Star Dust*, but once again economic events beyond their control foiled them; this time, the principal backer withdrew.

If it is right to implicate the failure of the Bank of the United States in the shortened run of *The New Yorkers*, one should note one irony: this bank was headed by Herbert's in-laws, the Marcus family. Frances Fields, the oldest

Fields sibling, had married Charles Marcus in 1914, and for about a decade Frances was the most financially secure member of the Fields clan, although there were difficulties within the Marcus family. As early as 1916, Charles's younger brother Bernard began maneuvering him out of the bank's power structure. Charles left banking and, in partnership with Herbert Harris and Joseph Fields, went into the business of importing perfumes. Charles had always been a prudent and cautious businessman, and although no longer directly connected with the operations of the Bank of the United States, he had full confidence in the family enterprise. He was not aware that Bernard was engaged in shady business dealings. In less than twenty years, the Bank of the United States had grown to comprise fifty-nine branches with $302 million in deposits plus a real estate subsidiary called Bankus Corporation. When it all came crashing down, in December 1930, it was the largest bank collapse on record.

Charles had invested his financial assets in the Bank of the United States, and, under his insistent urgings, so had other members of the Fields family. After the bank's collapse, according to Fields family members, "he lost his business and brought ruin upon his wife and the kin whom he had patronized. Although there is no evidence that he had specific prior knowledge of Bernie's misdeeds, he blamed himself, and so did they. After the trauma of the bank failure came the public humiliation of a criminal trial that lasted for months. Bernard Marcus and three of his partners went to prison for seven years."[18] In some sense, the Marcus family never recovered from the precipitous plummeting of their fortunes. Charles went into an uncomfortable, curmudgeonly retirement. One of his and Frances's twins had a nervous collapse. Eventually Frances and Charles divorced.

For better or for worse, Lew Fields and his family were no strangers to financial ups and downs. Following his father's long-practiced example, Herbert Fields, with barely a glance backward at the wreckage of *Star Dust*, looked for the next show to work on. He reworked the libretto he had shown to Rodgers and Hart in July 1930, and this time they agreed it was worth a go. In his autobiography, Rodgers does not recall that he had once rejected Herb's libretto. "It occurred to the three of us that a show built around the crazy world of Hollywood would make a timely and amusing musical. Based in part on our own recent experience, we slapped together a piece about two kids who go to Hollywood, where the girl becomes a silent-screen star. With the sound revolution, it's the boy who makes good while the girl, as happened so often in real life, proves unable to maintain her success."[19] One could argue that "in real life," the careers of as many male actors were damaged by the coming of sound as that of females. But in *America's Sweetheart*, as later in *Singin' in the Rain*, it is the actress who is unacceptable when heard as well as seen.

The producers of *America's Sweetheart* were Laurence Schwab and Frank Mandel, whose successes on Broadway included *The Desert Song* (1926), *Good News* (1927), *The New Moon* (1928), and *Follow Thru* (1929). At Herbert Fields's suggestion, they hired as director Monty Woolley, with whom Herb had worked on *Fifty Million Frenchmen* and *The New Yorkers*. In an interview done a few months before *America's Sweetheart* opened, Lorenz Hart gave an interesting picture of Herbert Fields's pre-opening night jitters. "It's ghastly. Herb won't go into the theatre. When something goes wrong and he is badly needed I go crazy looking for him. He walks up and down in the alley outside or sits on a fire-escape smoking four packs of cigarettes, or hides in the men's room."[20] This is a classic case of the pot calling the kettle black. Hart complained of searching for Fields when he needed him. Meanwhile, Richard Rodgers continuously lamented the times that he wanted to work on a song, but Larry Hart could not be found. *America's Sweetheart* (the title alluding to Mary Pickford although she had no part in the show) opened at the Broadhurst Theater on February 10, 1931, a month after the birth of the Rodgerses' first daughter, Mary, and a month before *The Hot Heiress* was released. Reviews were mixed, and the show ran for 135 performances.

Herb and Larry, followed by Dick, returned to California. The contract that Rodgers and Hart had with Warner Brothers required two more pictures. But the bosses at Warner Brothers (and other studios) were disappointed with the box office draw of musicals in 1931. Warner Brothers bought out the contracts of Rodgers and Hart. The temporary decline of musicals was, for a while, harder on songwriters like Rodgers and Hart than on scriptwriters. Both Herbert and Joseph Fields wrote nonmusical comedies in the 1930s. Rodgers complained, "At first we hoped to continue the newly reactivated Fields, Rodgers and Hart trio, but Herb soon got an offer to write Hollywood scripts. Larry and I tried batting story ideas around, but nothing seemed to work. . . . Still, with Hollywood closed to us, we had no other alternative but to try to keep active and hope that something would turn up."[21] Hollywood was not closed to Rodgers and Hart for long. In 1932, their songs were sung by Maurice Chevalier and Jeanette MacDonald in *Love Me Tonight*. For the 1933 Al Jolson vehicle *Hallelujah, I'm a Bum*, Rodgers and Hart not only provided the songs but played cameo roles, Rodgers as a photographer and Hart as a bank teller. Rodgers, Hart, and Fields as a team were connected with only one other project in Hollywood in the 1930s: *Mississippi*, a Paramount picture starring Bing Crosby and W. C. Fields, released in 1935. The credits for the script demonstrate once again the film industry's penchant for recycling and work by committee: the screenplay by Francis Martin and Jack Cunningham was based on a adaptation by Herbert Fields and Claude Binyon of the play *Magnolia,* by Booth Tarkington, itself an adaptation of Tarkington's novel *The Fighting Coward.* There had already been two previous film versions of the play.

The friendship between Herb and Dick continued to be a warm one. On one occasion, Dick wrote to his wife about having long, serious conversations with Herb about the problems of working with Larry Hart. Another time, as Dick was getting ready to leave California and return to New York, he told his wife that Herb had helped pack the linens. Fortunately for both men, they could keep their friendship separate from their individual successes and failures in the business.

Richard Rodgers was happy to return to New York. Between 1935 and 1941 he worked on only two more films. The Fields family, in contrast, enjoyed a sun-filled lifestyle and productive work in Hollywood through the 1930s. Joseph and Herbert Fields continued to write film scripts. Dorothy's partnership with Jimmy McHugh was to run its course by the middle of the decade, and she then began to work with composers as different from one another as Oscar Levant, Fritz Kreisler, and Jerome Kern.

CHANGE PARTNERS AND WRITE

• • •

It was always a gamble. There was no way of knowing which film would be a success, which song would be a hit. It was hard to predict if this or that song would carry a movie over the financial finish line or if a movie could promote a song into a standard. If a film contained songs by several different writers, or if it was not a musical as such, a songwriter had to wait and see if his or her song would even be mentioned in the newspaper review. Dorothy Fields contributed songs to almost two dozen movies in the 1930s, but her name appears in *New York Times* reviews of these films only about half the time. Indeed, it was not in the hands of the songwriter to decide which—if any—of the songs he or she wrote for a film would be used. Not even the most highly esteemed songwriters—Irving Berlin, Cole Porter, Richard Rodgers, George Gershwin—escaped the humiliation of having their songs discarded from a film. On the other hand, once under contact they were always paid for their work, which in the 1930s was not a negligible benefit.

Sometimes a song would escape from its disadvantaged background and become a success. This was true for one of McHugh and Fields's best-loved songs, "Don't Blame Me," originally written for a show Lew Leslie put on in Chicago in 1933 called *Clowns in Clover*. MGM optioned the song for *Meet the Baron* (1933), but historians of popular song disagree on what happened to it. Ken Bloom claims it was used in the film, but Jack Burton and Roy Hemming do not list the song as appearing in this film.[1] Philip Furia and Jack Burton claim "Don't Blame Me" was used in the MGM movie *Dinner at Eight* (1933).[2] Alec Wilder calls the song "another winner, a standard if there ever was one. . . . The opening phrase in the music is as absorbing as a great first sentence in a story, though it consists of only three half notes, g, b-flat, and a."[3] It seems to me such an opening phrase presents a challenge to the lyric writer—three spondees, like Tennyson's "Break, break, break / On the cold grey shores, oh sea." "Ain't She Sweet" (1927, lyric by Jack Yellen, music by Milton Ager) starts with a rhythmically similar opening phrase, but in a perkier tempo. "Do, Do, Do," by George and Ira Gershwin, does not pause after the third word, but continues the musical and lyrical thought directly. In Cole Porter's "Night and Day," unlike the songs previously mentioned, it is the third note that falls on the downbeat of a measure.

Philip Furia sees in "Don't Blame Me" a "shift to a more languorously erotic style,"[4] but I see a certain bemused distance from passion. Several times the singer protests, "Don't blame me," laying the blame, instead, on the loved one's kiss and charms; in two lines the singer complains of his or her own helplessness. A more reluctant declaration of love is hard to imagine. Fields's handiness with colloquial speech is evident in the release of the song. The moon makes frequent appearances in love lyrics, be it a harvest moon, a blue moon, a desert moon, or an old devil moon. (In *Who Wrote That Song*, there are forty songs listed with moon or moonlight or some other moon-word in the title.)[5] Dorothy's lyric has "doggone moon," suggesting the singer's discomfort, almost irritation, with being in love.[6] One can speculate that as a woman lyricist, Dorothy was especially careful to avoid the overly sentimental or overly earnest love ballad. There is no chance of confusing her lyrics with those of, say, Dorothy Donnelly. Even the most urbane lyric writers, such as Cole Porter or Lorenz Hart, had their moments of purple prose, but Dorothy Fields seldom did.

The early 1930s produced two other McHugh-Fields hits. They appeared in the film *Every Night at Eight*, which was made at Paramount Studios, directed by Raoul Walsh, and released in 1935. This was one of the few films McHugh and Fields wrote for that was actually a musical, that is a film in which making music is central to the plot. The film stars Alice Faye, Frances Langford, and Patsy Kelly as a singing trio who, with the help of a bandleader played by George Raft, find success on the radio. Alice Faye and Frances Langford were both, in real life, protégées of Rudy Vallee, whose most successful venue was the radio. The *New York Times* review notes that the film "contains no emotional scenes and next to no love interest . . . The shyest of the girls falls in love with [the bandleader] but his only sign of affection is his announcement at the end that he is going to marry her. [The three females] are content with being themselves and do not try for any characterization to speak of." The reviewer evidently liked the film's approach: "It is simple, lighthearted and unpretentious . . . it moves at a smooth, pleasant clip."[7]

Every Night at Eight includes five songs by McHugh and Fields, two of which—"I Feel a Song Coming On" and "I'm in the Mood for Love"—became standards. The popularity of "I'm in the Mood for Love" shows, according to Allen Forte, that "the American public of the 1930s was not averse to erotic lyrics, as long as they were nice."[8] One reason that the eroticism of the lyric is acceptable in the movie is that it is not directed from one character to another character; instead it is sent out neutrally, over the air waves, sung to a radio audience in general but to no one in particular. The first stanza of the chorus shows there will be no words wasted. The first and fourth lines are identical and the second and third lines both end with "you're near me." Dorothy deals with the problem that there are so few words rhyming with "love" by having it simply rhyme with itself except for the last stanza where it rhymes with "cloud above."[9]

"I Feel a Song Coming On" is another of Fields's lyrics of unquenchable optimism and high spirits. Negative memories of "days of solitude" are banished to the verse. The joyousness of the chorus seems all the greater for requiring neither a reason nor a rationale. As in "I'm in the Mood for Love" Dorothy structures the chorus by placing the title in the first line of the first stanza, the last line of the last stanza, and somewhere in the second stanza.[10]

By 1936, despite their many songwriting successes, Fields and McHugh had ceased to be a team. After an eight-year partnership, they never wrote another song together. If there was acrimony in their breakup, McHugh was too much of a gentlemen and Fields too much of a lady to discuss these matters publicly. In his oral history interview for the Columbia University archives, McHugh spoke very warmly about the whole Fields family in general and Dorothy in particular. When asked why they stopped working together McHugh was evasive, but he tossed out many irrelevancies, hints, and innuendoes.

> INTERVIEWER: Could you tell us why you and Dorothy Fields stopped writing together?
>
> MCHUGH: Well, I don't think I should, because this is something of a personal nature. A lot of people have wanted to do life stories, and wanted to make of Dorothy Fields and Jimmy McHugh all kinds of stories, but I don't think that I would ever permit it to be done, and I know Dorothy would not want it, unless it was done in a very wholesome fashion. Dorothy was married to a very wonderful doctor who died of cancer. He was a dear friend of mine, and naturally Dorothy is, and I will always love her forever, I think, because she was just one of the greatest, and—
>
> INTERVIEWER: You're still friends then?
>
> MCHUGH: Oh yes, very delightful friends.[11]

Dorothy's description of her collaboration with McHugh is a good deal cooler. When Max Wilk asked her, more than thirty years after she and McHugh had stopped working together, what McHugh was like as a collaborator Dorothy replied in terse, clipped sentences, "Very facile. Taught me a lot. I sat beside him at the piano and wrote as he composed."[12]

Well-bred lady that she was, Dorothy seldom had an unkind word to say—at least in print—about anyone. Nevertheless, there are composers she speaks of very warmly—Jerome Kern, Harold Arlen, Arthur Schwartz, Cy Coleman, and Sigmund Romburg. Some collaborators she hardly speaks of at all—Max Steiner, Oscar Levant, and Albert Hague, for example. But although she talks about McHugh and has anecdotes about their work together, she does not speak about him with much warmth or humor. And yet he was the person with whom she wrote the most songs and had the longest and steadiest collaboration. Was there never much affection between them? Or does Dorothy's reticence mask unpleasant memories—like some people's reticence in discussing a failed marriage?

McHugh's biographer, Alyn Shipton, says that McHugh and Fields were, indeed, more than musical partners. "To the outside world, they were a close pair of professional songwriters, each married to someone else, but at the heart of their working relationship was a discreet love affair that was to last until the mid-1930s."[13] While it is not possible to disprove this assertion, there are reasons to be skeptical. The main support for the idea comes from McHugh's remarks, but all through his book Shipton points out that McHugh's narrations have only a casual relationship to factual truth. In an unpublished memoir from 1967 McHugh wrote, "Dorothy and I became very close—too close. I prayed to God to break it up." This sounds like a man enamored but conflicted. He continued, "Let us say merely that Dorothy Fields was the love of my life, *musically speaking*. Something happened to us both when we worked together. We outdid ourselves. Some merging of temperament and personality that allowed us to reach up and grab off a few great ones. I have not worked quite as well with anyone else."[14] Shipton buttresses his argument by saying, "The body language in photographs from that time is convincing evidence of their affair on the West Coast."[15] To me, it is in the eye of the beholder.

In any case, Dorothy's tone in talking about McHugh after they stopped working together is very different from the one she used while they were collaborating. In the 1920s, she speaks with enthusiasm about McHugh and credits him, rightly, with giving her her professional start. In a 1928 newspaper interview, Dorothy states, "I really never had the desire to write lyrics until I heard some of Jimmy McHugh's music. . . . I had wanted to be an actress. . . . Jimmy McHugh played some of his lyricless tunes for me. And then came the uncontrollable ambition to put his tunes to words."[16] Clearly, after they stopped working together there was some revision in her attitude.

The shared credit for some of the songs in the movie *Roberta*, in 1935, seems to suggest one area of conflict. The film marks the first time since she had become a professional that Dorothy supplied lyrics for music written by someone other than McHugh. At the request of the film's producer, Pandro Berman, she put words to a verse and a sixteen-measure refrain by Jerome Kern that became the song "Lovely to Look At." Dorothy spoke many times about this turning point in her career, and I will discuss it more fully in the next chapter. What is worth mentioning here is that the first several songs by Jerome Kern and Dorothy Fields—that is, "Lovely to Look At," "I Won't Dance," and "Jockey on the Carousel"—credit the lyrics to both Dorothy Fields and Jimmy McHugh.

To be sure, there are many anecdotes that suggest that unclear or mixed attribution of credit was a common occurrence in the world of songwriting. Film historian Gary Marmorstein tells about a time when Saul Chaplin, in his capacity as music arranger for the film *Cover Girl*, went to Ira Gershwin's house to get two more lines for a song by Jerome Kern. He found "seated around the living room producer Schwartz, Yip Harburg, Leo Robin, Johnny Mercer, Oscar Levant, and playwright Marc Connelly. Stuttering, Chaplin managed to explain to the entire group what he needed. Gershwin prevailed upon his pals to stay and help them. 'Lines started coming at me like buckshot,' Chaplin wrote. 'The biggest contributor was Yip Harburg. He sprouted couplets like a fountain. In the end, Gershwin came up with the two lines."[17] In another case, with the team of DeSylva, Brown, and Henderson, Lew Brown wrote words, Ray Henderson music, and Buddy DeSylva some of each. Their songs are published with the ambiguous credit, "Words and Music by DeSylva, Brown, and Henderson." However, with the exception of the first few songs, Dorothy Fields wrote with Jerome Kern, McHugh never claimed to be a lyricist. Was it a matter of copyright or contractual obligation? Could McHugh simply not envision Dorothy's name on a song without his?

If McHugh's claim to being co-lyricist was a source of irritation for Dorothy, she did not go off in a huff. After *Roberta* was released in March 1935, McHugh and Fields wrote songs together for two more films—*Hooray for Love*, released in July 1935 and *Every Night at Eight*, released in August 1935. But the breach had opened and continued to widen. Dorothy, it appears to me, was more eager to move on than was McHugh. She was ready to work with other composers and she was ready for a romantic relationship with film producer Felix Young. Young entered the Fields family's orbit in 1933. He was the associate producer for *Let's Fall in Love*, for which Herbert Fields wrote the story. Young was also producer for *Hooray for Love*, for which McHugh and Dorothy Fields wrote the songs, and later *Joy of Living*, which had songs by Dorothy Fields and Jerome Kern. Shipton wrote that McHugh "tended to push the line that 'Dorothy Fields decided that she liked Broadway better than

Hollywood and returned to New York.' This is a slight economy with the truth, as she was clearly already planning to remain in Hollywood to spend time with Young and to work with her new writing partner."[18] Later in 1935, McHugh joined his music to lyrics by Ted Koehler for the film *King of Burlesque*, and Dorothy provided words for composers Max Steiner, Oscar Levant, and Jerome Kern.

Dorothy wrote one song with Max Steiner in 1935. Steiner's importance to film music can be seen in epithets such as "the father of film composing" or "the emperor of studio film scoring."[19] He was one of six film composers honored with a 33-cent postage stamp. (The others were Dimitri Tiomkin, Bernard Herrmann, Franz Waxman, Alfred Newman, and Erich Wolfgang Korngold.)

Steiner was born in Vienna in 1888. His father and grandfather were the owners of the Theatre an der Wien, the site of the premieres of works by Beethoven, Schubert, Johann Strauss, Franz Lehar, and many others. Max's precocious talent for music was demonstrated when he graduated from the Vienna Imperial Academy of Music at thirteen. While still a teenager, he wrote an operetta, *The Beautiful Greek Girl*, which had a successful run at the Orpheum Theatre in Vienna, owned by one of his father's competitors. He toured London, Paris, Berlin, Moscow, and Johannesburg as a conductor of operettas and was working in London in 1914 when war broke out. To avoid being detained as an enemy alien, Steiner quickly emigrated to the United States.

In New York, Steiner was on the operetta circuit as a conductor and orchestrator, working for Florenz Ziegfeld. At this point, his career had certain parallels with Sigmund Romberg's, but with no musical shows composed for New York to his credit. He remained in New York for fifteen years, observing the development of American musical comedy in the works of Kern, Gershwin, Rodgers and Hart, Youmans, DeSylva, Brown, and Henderson, and many others.

In 1929 Steiner went to Hollywood and was on the scene at the start of an important American musical genre—the film score—but in this case, rather than being an observer, he was a primary shaper, the author of the first chapter. Steiner was hired by RKO as an orchestrator in 1929; soon he was head of the company's music department. In his long and frenetically active career as a film composer he produced about three hundred scores, starting with groundbreaking works for *Cimarron* (1931) and *King Kong* (1933). The film industry showed its appreciation of Steiner by awarding him three Academy Awards, nominating him eighteen times for Academy Awards, and, most important, by seeking his services continually for more than three decades.

Although Steiner's first musical experiences were in operetta and he had a gift for lush romantic melodies, he was not a songwriter as such. Indeed, his song output must be seen as an almost accidental by-product of his film scores. Oscar Levant spoke admiringly, or perhaps enviously, of Steiner's efficiency and productivity. But he noted that "with all his composing I doubt that he ever had the ten published songs necessary to get him into ASCAP. . . . Naturally it was a great source of irritation to him, one of the busiest composers in the country, to be excluded from this society."[20]

The music by Steiner for which Dorothy Fields provided a lyric was for the film *Alice Adams* (1935). Based on a 1921 novel by Booth Tarkington, produced by Pandro Berman and directed by George Stevens, *Alice Adams* was Katharine Hepburn's fourth film. She received an Academy Award nomination for her portrayal of a small-town girl, loyal to her family, who would like to be upwardly mobile but has more dreams than means. Oscar Levant speculated, "To return to Katharine Hepburn after scoring for mountains, monsters, armies, and jungles must have seemed rather piddling,"[21] but this overlooks the composer's great versatility. Steiner, with his great gift for not merely representing but almost creating a movie's characters with his musical themes, provides *Alice Adams* with a romantic waltz tune when the opening credits roll, when Alice dances with her Prince Charming (Arthur, played by Fred McMurray), and when, at several other moments in the story, their romance progresses. In one scene in the movie, the repetition of a song to produce a romantic effect is mocked; the members of a small ensemble in a restaurant where the couple are dining complain when Alice and Arthur request for them to play the same waltz over and over and pack up their instruments with a sigh of relief when Alice and Arthur finally kiss.

Dorothy's lyric "I Can't Waltz Alone" has a universal appeal, but is also particularly descriptive of Alice, who is the very opposite of the go-it-alone "tough broad" character of many movies of the '20s and '30s. As with other Steiner songs, "I Can't Waltz Alone" is not sung in the movie. It was meant to have a separate sheet music and radio life. Dorothy never spoke of actually working with Steiner.

She does speak of her collaboration with Fritz Kreisler, notable for its lack of personal contact between composer and lyricist. Kreisler is remembered primarily as a concert violinist. Although his reputation as a composer rests primarily on his compositions for violin, he also composed two successful operettas, *Apple Blossoms* (1919, in collaboration with Victor Jacobi) and *Sissy, the Rose of Bavaria* (1932). *Apple Blossoms* had a libretto by William Le Baron, who went on to become vice president in charge of production at RKO; the operetta also helped launch the Broadway careers of Fred and Adele

Astaire. Kreisler was near the end of a long line of musicians who were active both as violinists and as composers, including Corelli, Vivaldi, Paganini, Wieniawski, and Ysaÿe, among many others.

Kriesler, born in Vienna in 1875, was a child prodigy. He entered the Vienna Conservatory at the age of seven and won a gold medal there when he was ten. He then went to Paris and studied at the Conservatoire with Massart; he left the Conservatoire at age 12, his training as a violinist complete. He was a tireless performer. His biographer Louis Lochner described him as "a veritable glutton for making, composing, arranging, transcribing, and orchestrating music."[22] In 1909, he played thirty-two concerts in a thirty-one-day tour of Germany. "Sergei Rachmaninoff . . . once remarked jestingly, but with a justified undertone of seriousness, 'Fritz gives so many concerts that he doesn't need to practice.' "[23] Moreover, Kreisler, like the tenor Enrico Caruso, embraced early on the new recording technology, attaining celebrity status by reaching ever greater audiences.

Some of Kreisler's music came to the screen in 1936 in the movie *The King Steps Out,* made at Columbia Pictures. Columbia was not one of the Big Five studios in Hollywood, but it turned out many significant films. One of its first ventures into musicals, *One Night of Love,* made in 1934, was an overwhelming success, earning more money than MGM's *Merry Widow,* which was a top-of-the-line musical from a top-of-the-line studio. The plot of *One Night of Love* was described by film historian Richard Barrios as "a mix of Cinderella, Tosca, and Ruby Keeler—an American singer goes to Italy to study with a temperamental genius and finds love and stardom."[24]

One Night of Love starred Grace Moore, an American diva who, like Lawrence Tibbett, had a significant operatic career and inconsistent results in Hollywood. Moore made her movie debut in 1930 in *A Lady's Morals,* an MGM biopic about Jenny Lind. Her role in *One Night of Love* gained her an Academy Awards nomination. The film won Oscars for best sound recording and best score. Moreover, its profits were enough to start a brief trend of films built around operatic stars. Paramount hired Gladys Swarthout, RKO signed Lily Pons, and Warners brought in James Melton. MGM, having lost Grace Moore to Columbia, found consolation in the pairing of Jeanette MacDonald and Nelson Eddy.

Columbia made four more pictures starring Grace Moore, none as successful as *One Night of Love.* One of these was *The King Steps Out,* released in 1936. Pauline Kael wrote, "Those with merciful memories blocked this one out long ago. Josef von Sternberg [the director] asked that the film not be included in retrospectives of his works, but he really did make the damned thing. It's a monstrously overstaged version of Fritz Kreisler's operetta *Cissy,* with Grace Moore and Franchot Tone struggling through the scenery playing Princess Elizabeth of Bavaria and the young Emperor Franz Joseph."[25] (Actually, the screenplay, by Sidney Backman, is based on the operetta *Cissy* by Herbert and Ernst Marischka, not to be confused with Kreisler's own operetta, called *Sissy*.) There are four songs in *The King Steps Out*: "What Shall Remain," "Stars in My Eyes," "Learn How to Lose," and "The End Begins." Dorothy said that the extent of her actual contact with Kreisler was a note from him, after the release of the film, saying "Thank you, Miss Fields." Nevertheless, she had enough fondness for "Stars in My Eyes" to choose it as one of the songs sung at the Ninety-second Street Y's salute to her in its *Lyrics and Lyricists* series. Although this is not the sort of lyric she is best known for, it is interesting to see that when required to do so Dorothy could produce a lyric in the operetta style, replete with "eternal spring," "cheek . . . aglow," and "eager longing . . . laid to rest."[26]

Max Steiner and Fritz Kreisler were, in a sense, songwriters by default or by accident, their compositional capital being spent mostly on other musical projects. In that sense (and in many others as well), they stood in stark contrast to Jimmy McHugh. The songs that Dorothy made from their music (one can hardly speak of collaborations) attest to her professionalism and versatility. If asked to, she could pick up a lead sheet and produce a lyric, turning the tune into a song. During this period Dorothy wrote songs with another musician unlike McHugh—indeed, unlike anyone else: Oscar Levant.

An impossible character to pin down, Oscar Levant shuttled between New York and Los Angeles playing the roles of concert pianist, composer of art music, songwriter, composer of film scores, actor, celebrity, and hanger-on. Decades before Phil Donahue or Oprah Winfrey, Oscar Levant had made a popular spectator sport of public self-laceration. He was born in Pittsburgh on December 27, 1906. Hence he was the first composer Dorothy worked with professionally who was not a decade or more older than she. Levant was trained as a pianist and was a friend and important interpreter of the works of George Gershwin.

In the early years of talking films Levant wrote a spate of songs, most frequently with lyricist Sidney Clare, with whom he produced some twenty songs in six years for films made at RKO and at Twentieth Century-Fox studios. His best-known popular song, "Blame It on My Youth," was written in 1934 with lyricist Edward Heyman. The film for which Levant and Fields provided songs was called *In Person*, produced by Pandro Berman for RKO. Pandro Berman must be counted as one of Dorothy's great fans, for he was responsible for linking her up with Jerome Kern, Max Steiner, and Oscar Levant, all in 1935. Levant probably owed his assignment on the RKO film to Pandro Berman, who may have expected a more humble and grateful response from Levant. Levant related, "I left Hollywood for New York before the cutting was completed and didn't get to see *In Person* until a preview just before the opening. Later that evening I met Berman for dinner, and he started by asking me how I liked the picture. 'Frankly, Pan,' I said, 'I was disappointed.' He rose from the table in a rage, flung down his napkin and said, 'Who in hell are you to be disappointed?' The discussion of who had to be who to be disappointed took quite a long time."[27]

In Person opened in Radio City Music Hall on December 12, 1935. The film starred George Brent and Gingers Rogers—without Fred Astaire. Ginger Rogers and Fred Astaire first delighted audiences in the 1933 movie *Flying Down to Rio*. In *Roberta*, Astaire and Rogers were still a secondary couple—the stars of the film were Irene Dunne and Randolph Scott—but many critics found that the best parts of the movie came when Fred and Ginger were on screen. Despite their success together, each of them had reservations about being thought of as a team. Astaire's qualms came from being thought of as one of a pair while Rogers was hoping for recognition as a dramatic actress as well as a singer and dancer. She fulfilled this aspiration when she won an Academy Award in 1940 for her work in *Kitty Foyle*.

In Person finds Rogers cast as an actress trying to avoid encounters with her idolatrous fans. The film was not a critical success. *Variety* called it an "inept starring debut for Ginger Rogers . . . a very weak affair."[28] Nevertheless, the film was successful financially. Fields and Levant provided three songs for this movie—"Don't Mention Love to Me," "I Got a New Lease on Life," and "Out of Sight Out of Mind." "Don't Mention Love to Me"—another song with a negative in the title, like "Don't Blame Me"—seems to point to "Let's Not Talk About Love," a song Cole Porter wrote for the show *Let's Face It* (1941), with a book by Herbert and Dorothy Fields.

Dorothy never sank deep roots in the California soil, although in the course of the decade almost the entire Fields family moved west. Dorothy and Herb made up the avant-garde. Joe came a few years later, and Lew and Rose moved out in 1936. Dorothy and Herb rented four different houses in the 1930s, suggesting a kind of restlessness, a sojourner mentality. There was no property to be tied down to. (The songwriters who did invest in real estate, Jimmy McHugh and Yip Harburg among them, made substantial economic gains.) This is not to say the Fields family avoided the comforts and possessions that went along with the good life. There were cars—always at least four. The houses had patios and swimming pools—the site of nonstop gatherings of friends and colleagues. The bar was always well stocked, but the refrigerator was usually empty. Meals were not cooked—they were ordered in.

Like Dorothy, Herbert Fields worked both in New York and Los Angeles in the 1930s. Perhaps the most disappointing project he worked on in this period was *Pardon My English*, with songs by Ira and George Gershwin, including "Isn't It a Pity?" The play opened in New York at the Majestic Theatre on January 20, 1933, and closed forty-six performances later. It was one of the worst flops the Gershwins had ever endured; its failure marked the end of the producing partnership of Alex Aarons and Vinton Freedley.

In the course of his career on the Broadway stage, Herbert Fields had some enormous successes and some total failures. This suggests several possible explanations—a willingness to take daring risks and try out things that had not been done before or else an inability to gauge what audiences were ready for. When he worked with Rodgers and Hart, it was the best of times (*Connecticut Yankee* had 418 performances) and the worst of times (*Chee-Chee* closed after 31 performances). In *Chee-Chee*, the hero is under continuous threat of castration, and in *Pardon My English*, the protagonist is beset by psychological problems. Ira Gershwin complained, "I disliked enormously the central notion of the project—duo-personality or schizophrenia or whatever the protagonist's aberration was supposed to be."[29]

In Hollywood, Herbert Fields achieved neither the highs nor the lows he reached on Broadway. This is probably attributable, at least in part, to the checks-and-balances work-by-committee method of producing a script in Hollywood. The scripts Herbert wrote in Hollywood were mostly romantic comedies, some with songs, such as *The Hot Heiress* (1931), with songs by Rodgers and Hart, and *Let's Fall in Love* (1934), with songs by Harold Arlen and Ted Koehler; and some without songs, such as *People Will Talk* (1935) and *Love before Breakfast* (1936). The subject that seemed to engage Herb the most was rich people—whether on their own, as in *Love before Breakfast*, or colliding with the lives of the less well off, as in *The Hot Heiress*. Variations on his studies of social classes included poor people pretending to be rich, as in *Hands Across the Table* (1935), and rich people pretending to be poor, as in *The Luckiest Girl in the World* (1936). In *Down to Their Last Yacht* (1934), a film that would seem to adumbrate the television show *Gilligan's Island*, a group of wealthy people are stranded on a deserted island.

When Joseph Fields moved to California, he took up residence with his younger brother and sister. According to his cousins, "Joe had come to Hollywood as a $300-a-week writer of 'B' pictures for Republic, his fortune from the perfume business lost in the crash of the Bank of the United States. For a time, he was jokingly referred to as 'the family failure,' a cruel reminder that a few years earlier he had been the family's most conspicuous financial success."[30] Joe's scripts for Hollywood films show a wider range than Herb's.

He wrote $1,000 a Minute (1935), a comedy; *The Walking Dead* (1936), a horror film starring Boris Karloff; *Grand Jury* (1936), a seriocomic treatment of organized crime; and *Reported Missing* (1937), an aviation melodrama. Joe wrote a script for a comedy, *When Love Is Young* (1937), that had songs by Jimmy McHugh, who by then was working with lyricist Harold Adamson. Like Herb, Joe sometimes developed scripts from stories or plays by others and other times submitted the original idea for the script. One of Joe's better original stories was for the film *Annie Oakley* (1935), which starred Barbara Stanwyck. The character Annie Oakley would reappear when Herbert and Dorothy wrote the book for *Annie Get Your Gun*.

The change in the number of family members living together in Southern California was probably one of the reasons that Dorothy and Herb changed houses four times in less than ten years. The elder Fieldses came to Beverly Hills at the urging of their children. For Rose, the principal incentive for the move was having most of the family together again. For Lew, there was the added attraction of reviving his career by acting in films. And, indeed, Lew Fields did act in two movies after he moved to the West Coast. He played himself in *The Story of Vernon and Irene Castle* (1939) and in *The Lillian Russell Story* (1940). In 1939, he wrote to Dorothy, "Soon I'll be in front of a hot camera, I'm to play myself. . . . A few weeks ago they wanted me for a screen test. I was scared stiff, maybe I wouldn't look like Lew Fields, so I said to myself, so what?"[31] Lew Fields's career had a last hurrah in the movies. Dorothy Fields's career, and her personal life as well, was to go on to a fuller, richer phase in the next few years in Hollywood.

THE BEST OF HOLLYWOOD

• • •

Richard Rodgers remarked about his first meeting with Lorenz Hart, "I left Hart's house having acquired in one afternoon a career, a partner, a best friend, and a source of permanent irritation."[1] When Dorothy Fields began working with Jerome Kern, she gained not only a new collaborator but a second family and a new approach to integrating songs with dramatic works. Jimmy McHugh was a gifted musician, but Kern was a man of the theater. His Princess shows, some of which Dorothy saw when she was a girl, inspired many songwriters, including Rodgers and Hart and George Gershwin. With only a few exceptions, the team of McHugh and Fields had been writing for revues or for movies in which the songs were essentially decorative. Dorothy later complained that writing songs this way meant always starting from scratch. "It was a long time before I earned the luxury of writing for films or plays where there was a story line and characters to write for and songs to progress that story," she said.[2]

Dorothy's collaboration with Kern was a turning point in her life. Her father knew Kern; the first Jerome Kern song performed on Broadway came in a 1904 Weber and Fields revue, *An English Daisy*. Dorothy knew his songs but had never met him. On several different occasions, she told the story of beginning to work with him.[3] In a commemorative radio show soon after Kern's death, Dorothy related, "I wonder if you'd like to hear about the first song I wrote without Jerome Kern. It sounds strange, doesn't it, but actually I did write it without him. I was doing a picture at RKO [the film she refers to is probably *Hooray for Love*, which was released in July 1935] . . . At the same time on the lot they were doing a picture of *Roberta*."[4]

The movie *Roberta* was based on the Broadway musical by the same name, which itself was based on the novel *Gowns by Roberta* by Alice Duer Miller. The book and lyrics for the musical were by Otto Harbach. The story of an American football player who inherits his aunt's Parisian dress salon allowed for the creation of a hybrid of a book musical with elaborate, lavish costumes worthy of a Ziegfeld revue. The romantic triangle of the book—football player, his temperamental fiancée, and a salon assistant who turns out to be an émigré Russian princess—is supplemented by a secondary song-and-dance couple (Bob Hope and Lyda Roberti in the play, Fred Astaire and Ginger Rogers in the movie).

Roberta opened on Broadway on November 18, 1933, and closed 295 performances later, on July 21, 1934. A touring company performed the show until a week after the movie opened. Kern biographer Lee Davis writes that "not since *Show Boat* had Jerry composed a score of such uniformly high quality."[5] Four of the show's songs were kept for the film—"Smoke Gets in Your Eyes," whose popularity, some critics said, established the success of the show; "Yesterdays"; "Let's Begin"; and "I'll Be Hard to Handle," with a lyric by Bernard Dougall, a nephew of Otto Harbach's who was getting some theatrical experience. Two more songs, "The Touch of Your Hand" and "You're Devastating" are used as underscoring during the film's fashion show. Added to these was "I Won't Dance." This song, with words by Oscar Hammerstein II, had originally appeared in the musical *Three Sisters*, which ran for only seventy-two performances in London. Fred Astaire saw the show and asked RKO to buy the song for him to perform in *Roberta*.

Hammerstein's lyric refers to "dancing as an exercise" and suggests the complication that the dancing partner may be "too good to do good." Dorothy's substitute lyric is warmer, spicier, and sexier.[6] The use of the title line at the start and end of a song is a standard pattern. But here Dorothy has constructed the text so that the repetition at the end becomes a comic punch line. "I know that music leads the way to romance, So if I hold you in my arms I won't dance." One can compare this to Irving Berlin's song "Remember" (1925) in which, after listing many romantic aspects of the relationship, the singer chides, "But you forgot to remember." Wittier is Ira Gershwin's lyric "But Not for Me" (1930), which ends with the pun, "The climax of a plot should be the marriage knot, but there's no knot for me." Note also the self-referential in-joke citing "The Continental." Astaire and Rogers had danced to "The Continental," words by Herb Magidson and music by Con Conrad, in the 1934 movie *The Gay Divorcée*. Although Astaire and Rogers had danced together in two previous pictures, this was their first sung duet.

Credit for the lyrics for the screen version of "I Won't Dance" and "Lovely to Look At" is given to both Dorothy Fields and Jimmy McHugh. Although Dorothy speaks at length about the creation of the lyric for "Lovely to Look At," she never mentions McHugh. She said, "Of course, they had all the numbers. I was reworking some lyrically and doing a little extra dialogue."[7] The dialogue she is referring to is probably the comments about the gowns that Fred Astaire makes in his capacity as master of ceremonies of the fashion show. I've spoken before of the Hollywood version of the adage "Many hands make light work." In the 1940s, Dorothy, with her brother Herbert, wrote the books for several Broadway musicals by Cole Porter and one by Irving Berlin. But from this remark we see she wrote dialogue, distinct from lyrics, in Hollywood as well.

Dorothy continued, "There was one number of Jerome Kern's, one melody that didn't have a lyric, but they owned the melody, and they wanted to use it because it was very lovely. So Pandro Berman, who produced the picture, called me in one day, and he said, 'We need something for the fashion show. You've rewritten the fashion show for Freddy Astaire but we need something for Irene Dunne to sing because we are expecting to put her in a costume that costs about $8,000, and she really should sing something in anything as expensive as that.' So he said, 'I'd like it to be a song that could be used both as something to show off the clothes in a fashion show and that could be one of the love songs in the picture.' It was a kind of a tall order. And he played the melody, which I loved, and he said, 'Do you suppose you could have this by like tomorrow morning?' . . . I said, 'Well, does Mr. Kern know I'm supposed to do this?' and he said, 'No, but let's see how it is first.' . . . The title I luckily got was 'Lovely to Look At.' And Pandro was excited about it, and Irene Dunne loved it, and they decided to go ahead and produce it."[8] The film sequence in which this song is embedded lasts about thirteen minutes.[9]

Dorothy related, "All this time, Jerry Kern was in the east and didn't know much about what was going on at RKO; but nevertheless Irene Dunne appeared in this beautiful $8,000 costume, and they built a set and did a wonderful orchestration and had a fashion show, and the whole thing was what they called 'in the can,' which meant it had been shot and produced, and then they sent Mr. Kern a record. Well, nobody on the lot at RKO slept for two or three nights because you can imagine what would happen if it turned out that Jerry Kern didn't like it. Well, he did like it."[10]

Critics liked *Roberta* as well. Roy Hemming writes, "*Roberta* is arguably the first movie adaptation of a Broadway musical that turned out better than the original."[11] *Variety* called the film "musical picture-making at its best—fast, smart, good-looking, and tuneful."[12] *New York Times* reviewer Andre Sennwald called it "a model for urbanity in the musical films" and "a model for lavishness, grace and humor in the musical film." Sennwald specifically praised the songs: "Jerome Kern's songs, some of them borrowed from the stage edition and others composed for the occasion, are distinguished both for their literacy and their romantic wit." Regarding the fashion show at the end, he commented, "The finale . . . blossoms out with a ravishing fashion show. Doubtless this was originally intended to ensnare the enthusiasms of the ladies. But since Mr. Kern has put it gaily to music and Mr. Astaire has been persuaded to act as master of ceremonies, the gentlemen may be pardoned for enjoying it enormously."[13] "Lovely to Look At" received an Academy Award nomination (the first for both Kern and Fields) but lost to "Lullaby of Broadway" by Harry Warren and Al Dubin. The other also-ran song that year was Irving Berlin's "Cheek to Cheek."

Considering the cavalier treatment many songwriters' works received in Hollywood, the great concern for whether or not Kern would like the way his melody was treated indicates his special position in Hollywood, a special position which had three sources. One was Kern's high standing among his peers. Songwriter and scholar Alec Wilder noted that his colleagues considered Kern "the first great native master of this genre. Without exception they consider his songs a greater inspiration than those of any other composer, and his music to be the first that was truly American in the theater. . . . He was, in the opinion of all the great surviving theater composers, the first to find a new form of melodic writing unlike that of his predecessors or contemporaries."[14]

Studio executives, who were seldom intimidated by talent, would more likely be impressed by Kern's financial acumen. In the 1930s, Kern owned 25 percent of the stock of T. B. Harms, the most prestigious publisher of popular songs of the time and, naturally, the publisher of Kern's songs. And they may well have been in awe of Kern's ability to bring together culture and commerce through his collection of rare books. Kern had been collecting first editions and books with authors' annotations for about two decades when he decided to sell his collection in January 1929. The sale, handled by Anderson Galleries, brought Kern $1.73 million. Nor was it irrelevant that Kern was the composer of *Show Boat*, the most important and successful Broadway musical of the 1920s.

A third reason producers had to worry about Kern's reaction to the treatment his music received was Kern's personality. Kern did not mind a fight; indeed, he seemed to enjoy a good argument and often sought one out. There was something puckish and provocative about Kern, something of the trickster archetype. Kern's orchestrator, Robert Russell Bennett, said, "It was a different stunt every day. He'd wake up and say, 'How'm I going to shock them today?' "[15] Moreover, Kern was fiercely protective of his music. His collaborator P. G. Wodehouse related that at the very start of his career Kern "had managed to sell a song to one of the Charles Dillingham shows. He attended an orchestra rehearsal and frowned a dark frown. 'Is that the way you're going to play my song?' he asked. He was assured that it was. He immediately collected all the orchestra parts and walked out with them. . . . He was a perfectionist, and was prepared to starve in the gutter rather than have his stuff done wrong."[16]

Although all of Kern's lyricists had the highest esteem for his music, many acknowledged he was not an easy person to work with. Ira Gershwin's working relationship with Kern exemplifies the kind of ambivalence a lyricist could feel. He said, "One reason I did my first work after George died with Kern was that it took me back to when we started in the theatre, when Kern was our musical god."[17] Nevertheless, Gershwin said, "Kern was so impatient when I had trouble coming up with a satisfactory, at least to me, setting of the melody that became 'Long Ago (and Far Away)' that he sent me his own dummy lyric. It began 'watching Little Nelly P.' "[18] When Leo Robin worked with Kern, in 1945, he was a seasoned veteran with four Academy Award–nominated songs to his credit. He also found collaboration with Kern difficult. He said, "I was completely in awe of Kern from the minute we got together and it cramped my style a little bit. . . . After we got started he used to call me up every day, bugging me—'You got anything yet?' I wanted so much to please him and to measure up to his high standards that I don't think I did my best work."[19]

Dorothy Fields's relationship with Jerome Kern was a special one that gave her pride and pleasure. After *Roberta*, Kern chose Dorothy to work with him on the next film project for RKO, *I Dream Too Much*. She said, "[Kern] came out to California a few weeks after [*Roberta* was completed], and he wanted to meet me because he was to do another picture, for Lily Pons and Henry Fonda, and he said, 'I think I'd like Dorothy Fields to do the lyrics.' . . . When I met him, I walked into the room kind of shaking a bit; he left the piano and came up and kissed me. Well, that was the start of a very wonderful association with Jerome Kern."[20]

Women songwriters had already been part of Kern's real-life and fictional worlds. He had worked with lyricist and librettist Anne Caldwell on eight shows between 1919 and 1926.[21] Moreover, the heroine of Kern's musical *The Cat and the Fiddle* is a songwriter. If Fields did worry about being anomalous as a lady-songwriter, she would at least have known that she was not Kern's first female songwriting partner. And, despite her description of being nervous about meeting Kern for the first time, she was an esteemed and financially successful practitioner in her own right with little need to be overawed by Kern's superstar status. After all, she had lived with a superstar, her father, all her life. One of the advantages of that for her was an ability not to be intimidated by famous figures.

Kern and Fields were, in many ways, a study in opposites, but they were complementary opposites. Dorothy had a more contemporary lifestyle than did Kern. When traveling from coast to coast, he would take the train; if she was in a hurry, she would fly. Dorothy enjoyed driving a car, an accomplishment that eluded Kern although he did not hesitate to pass judgment on the stylishness of the cars she bought. Kern was twenty-one years older than Dorothy—old enough to be her father. But Kern was younger than her father, full of admiration and respect for him, and by the 1930s was more important in the entertainment industry than he. Dorothy, who often gave nicknames to her collaborators, called Kern "Junior," perhaps because she was several inches taller than he, but perhaps because, on some level, he was a junior, more manageable version of her father. Dorothy was a warm friend not only to Jerome Kern but also to his wife, Eva, and their daughter, Betty. Dorothy's description was, "I was a part of that family, and they were part of my family, and it wasn't a question of any formality. I would run over in the morning, and Jerry would be out doing something—some bit of business like going to the farmer's market or looking for an antique, and I'd have coffee with Eva in the breakfast room. And he would come in, and we would sit down and start to work, and then he'd think of something else he wanted to do, like finding out from the bookie what horses were good in the third race at Santa Anita, so we'd knock off work to do that for a little while."[22] It should be remembered that Lew Fields's fondness for gambling was a great source of conflict in the Fields household while his children were growing up. Kern's enjoyment in playing the horses—an enthusiasm shared by many members of the film community—must have seemed a safer and more playful version of her father's love of gambling.

"And every night, I think, for two years when the game Monopoly first came out, we used to play every single night," Dorothy said. "Eva Kern, Jerry Kern, Betty Kern, and Johnny or Dick Green who were around the house at the time and myself. And we'd play until two or three in the morning. And there was always a—I don't know—a kind of family feeling about my association with the Kerns."[23] The baby of the Fields family, Dorothy probably enjoyed playing big sister to Betty Kern. At this time, Betty Kern, an only child, might have been happy for some sisterly advice. She had gotten engaged to Richard Green, younger brother of songwriter Johnny Green; she knew that it was probably a mistake but did not know how to break things off. Dorothy, whose own marriage to Jack Wiener she seemed to recognize as a mistake from the start, must have been a sympathetic listener every step of the way. Betty Kern married Richard Green, divorced him, and married Artie Shaw, with whom she had a son, Steven Kern Shaw. She later divorced Artie Shaw and married Jack Cummings.

Dorothy Fields's first full-fledged collaboration with Jerome Kern, *I Dream Too Much*, was intended as the vehicle for the screen debut of Lily Pons. In the rush to find photogenic opera stars after the success of *One Night of Love*, the signing of Lily Pons by RKO must have seemed like a particular coup. She had an established operatic career and was unusually attractive. Moreover, through recordings, radio broadcasts of the Metropolitan Opera, and concert tours through the United States, the French-born Pons had already won a large and enthusiastic American following. Indeed, in her desire to reach a wider American audience, Lily Pons had approached Dorothy Fields and Jimmy McHugh for songs to use on tour. A reporter explained she had "always liked American dance music, which she considers very 'melodious,' but because she could not understand English very well she did not include any selections of it in concerts. Now she knows English and therefore will be able to 'put herself into' what she in singing."[24] At a publicity gathering in Pons's Central Park West apartment, several McHugh-Fields songs, including "I Can't Give You Anything but Love" and a newly composed "Will You Remember, Will You Forget" "were sung by Miss Fields accompanied at the piano by Mr. McHugh, while the operatic stars observed the method of presentation." One photo accompanying the news story shows Pons seated on the piano bench alongside McHugh; another photo shows her perched atop the piano, à la Helen Morgan.

In *I Dream Too Much*, Pons was given six opportunities to show her vocal prowess. No other character in the film sings. She sings part of "Caro Nome" from *Rigoletto* in a vocal lesson and a fully staged version of the Bell Song from *Lakme*. Jerome Kern provided four new songs designed to demonstrate her versatility—and his. There are two songs in operetta style, "I Am the Echo, You Are the Song" and "I Dream Too Much." "The Jockey on the Carousel" is a lighthearted story song, whereas "I Got Love" simulates a swinging, hot jazz number. Of these four, "Jockey on the Carousel" has the least typical Fields lyric.

The film was only a moderate success. Some were left cold by Pons's singing. One critic dubbed the movie "I Scream Too Much," and a distributor complained that the audience was being high-C'ed to death. To my ear, the problem lies not so much with her tones but with her text. When she sings, the words are hard to distinguish, and when she speaks her tone is grating. The enticing French accent and Gallic charm that served Maurice Chevalier so splendidly did not wear as well for Lily Pons.

A greater problem for the film, though, is the script. *I Dream Too Much* was the first film with songs by Jerome Kern that was not based on a preexisting stage work. Kern had previously been involved in two failed attempts at an original screen musical. He had worked with Otto Harbach on a score for a film first called *Stolen Dreams* but released in 1931, stripped of all its songs, as *Men of the Sky*. A proposed film for MGM called *Champagne and Orchids*, which Kern and Hammerstein worked on in the first months of 1935, never got made. In *I Dream Too Much*, almost all of the characters, major and minor, are unsympathetic in one way or another. The tyrannical singing teacher we see at the beginning of the film is a simple stereotype. The small roles of an American family of tourists in Paris (the daughter played by Lucille Ball) are also subject to sour-tempered satire. The composer-hero (Jonathan Street), played by Henry Fonda, is entirely self-absorbed; he gets married to the heroine when he is too drunk to remember what happened, and he is jealous of his adoring wife's success. One need not be a radical feminist to be distressed at the lack of respect and appreciation for her own talent shown by the Lily Pons character (Annette Monard). At the beginning of the film, she says to her overly demanding voice teacher, "I want something besides singing. I want to have some fun." The first time her singing brings her into conflict with her husband, she declares, "I wish you'd forget about my voice. I don't want to be an opera singer. I want to be your wife." She makes several similar declarations in the course of the film. To give her character credit for consistency, toward the end of the film, at the height of her success, she maintains, "What do I care about singing? I never wanted to be a singer. I just wanted to be your wife, but you won't let me." To audience members not overburdened with talent or opportunity, this may seem both ungrateful and unenlightened.

What Dorothy Fields (or Lily Pons herself) must have thought of such a character we can only guess. Nevertheless, Annette Monard's lyrics, whether sung as herself or as a player in her husband's opera, are all consistently in character. She sings "The Jockey on the Carousel" to a crying child, partly to distract him from the fact that she has eaten his macaroons. She tells him the song is a lullaby her mother used to sing to her. In "I'm the Echo, You're the Song That I Sing," the song she performs for a potential producer of her husband's opera, the lyric asserts that without him she is "a pitiful thing." "I Got Love" is a little less abject, even though the singer cheerfully enumerates all the things she does not need because she's got love.

The climax of the movie is the presentation of Jonathan Street's work, formerly an opera called *Echo and Narcissus*, transformed into a musical, *I Dream Too Much*. In a rehearsal scene, we see Lily Pons urging on the chorus line, dancing to "I'm the Echo" played by a rehearsal pianist. "Faster, it must go faster," she tells them. "This is not grand opera. This is musical comedy." But the dance we see, performed to "I Dream Too Much" is something between ballet and the ballroom style of Irene and Vernon Castle, full of waving arms and arching backs. It is not Hermes Pan's shining choreographic moment. The model for the finale of *I Dream Too Much* is clearly the fashion show at the end of *Roberta*. Instead of Irene Dunne, it is Lily Pons who appears above the stage level, gorgeously clad in a dress that would not be out of place in *La Traviata*, to sing the title song. The song is sung twice, repeated wordlessly twice for a fashion show and twice more for a dance routine, then is sung once more, up-tempo, with a slow coda. *New York Times* reviewer Andre Sennewald commented, "The film introduces a musical comedy production number—on the occasion of the young composer's triumph—that looks like something Pandro S. Berman had left over from his Fred Astaire films."[25] The issue of "high art" versus popular entertainment, which haunts many movies of this time and many of Kern's stage musicals as well, rears its head at the end of the film. Backstage after the successful premier, a woman declares Street's melodies are like Schubert's. With uncharacteristic modesty, he declares it is "nothing at all. I just try to write the music people want—tunes people can whistle." At the end of the film, he modifies this to "tunes that twenty million people whistle." Lily Pons went on to make two more movies for RKO. *I Dream Too Much* was a modest financial success. *That Girl from Paris* (1936) and *It Never Happened Before* (1937) did less well.

Dorothy Fields worked with Jerome Kern on five films. *Swing Time* was the best of them. Dorothy felt it was their most successful collaboration. *Swing Time* was the sixth picture in which Fred Astaire and Ginger Rogers appear together. They were a secondary couple in *Flying Down to Rio* (1933), *Roberta* (1935), and *Follow the Fleet* (1936); in *The Gay Divorcée* (1934), *Top Hat* (1935) and *Swing Time* (1936) they did not share the plot with another romantic couple—they were the stars.

If we do not pay much attention, we can think of the Astaire and Rogers pictures as consisting of Fred and Ginger dancing together and singing together. Perhaps that is what we all wait for, just as some opera fans wait for singers' high notes. But the musical numbers in these films offer a balance of singing alone, singing together, dancing alone, and dancing together. Sung duets are relatively rare occurrences in the Fred-and-Ginger pictures. And in the sung duets, Fred and Ginger do not actually sing together; that is, they do not sing in unison. In "Pick Yourself Up," the first number in *Swing Time*, Fred and Ginger both sing, but they do not sing the same words nor do they sing the same music. In the film, in a masterstroke of irony, the Astaire character presents himself to the Rogers character as someone in need of dancing lessons. He sings to her, in the verse, that he is "awkward as a camel." Rogers encourages him, in the chorus, to try—even resorting to quoting Rudyard Kipling's poem "If," telling him "you'll be a man, my son!" In the next verse, Astaire exhorts Rogers not to give up on him, and Rogers repeats the "Pick yourself up" chorus.[26]

According to Fields, "Pick Yourself Up" and "A Fine Romance" were among the very few songs she worked on with Kern that began with a lyric and then had music added to it. We do not know why Kern and Fields worked in that manner on these songs. It may be that Kern was having a little trouble getting his muse in gear for this film; he and Astaire were working at cross-purposes. Astaire wanted at least two dance numbers in a jazzy, swingy style, a style antithetical to Kern's musical strengths. Dance scholar John Mueller recounted Dorothy Fields's recollection: "Fred took me aside. 'My God can we ever get a tune that I can dance to? Syncopated.' and the two of us sat with Jerry and Fred hoofed all over the room and gave him ideas . . . and finally Jerry came up with a very good tune, 'Bojangles of Harlem.' "[27]

Of course Dorothy was in familiar territory writing a Bojangles text. Bill Robinson was the last-minute star of *Blackbirds of 1928*, singing and dancing to the Fields-McHugh song "Doin' the New Low Down." In 1935, Fields and McHugh provided songs for *Hooray for Love*, which featured Bill Robinson. (McHugh also composed for the 1936 film *Dimples* with Shirley Temple and Bill Robinson, but by that time McHugh and Fields were no longer working together.)

The Bojangles number is in some ways perplexing. It has no connection with anything that has happened in the film until then, unlike, for example, the fashion show finale in *Roberta* or even the "Top Hat" number in *Top Hat*. Moreover, Fred Astaire's style of dancing has few points of contact with that of Bill Robinson, so one wonders why the big dance solo for Fred Astaire turned out to be a tribute to Bill Robinson. According to dance historian John Mueller, Dorothy may have prepared an extensive scenario for this number with scenes set in the jungle, Harlem, and heaven. None of this material was used.[28]

"Waltz in Swing Time" also gave Kern some troubles and uncharacteristically, he turned a portion of the composition (he may have thought of it simply as arranging) over to Robert Russell Bennett. Kern's biographer, Gerald Bordman, said that Bennett told him that "Kern provided some basic themes and then told him to put them together in any way that would satisfy Astaire."[29] Hal Borne, the piano accompanist for Fred Astaire and Hermes Pan, also claimed to have a hand in the composition of both "Bojangles" and "Waltz in Swing Time." The latter does not have a lyric.

"A Fine Romance," the other song in *Swing Time* born lyrics-first was composed last. It was completed only a short time before the film went into production. Perhaps the score of *Swing Time* indicates how little it matters, with respect to a song's quality, whether the melody or the lyric is written first.[30] In some ways the lyric is reminiscent of Cole Porter—a list song with lots of references to current events and products (such as "Seidlitz powder" or the "March of Time"), some of which by now have become obscure, but that does not hurt the popularity of the song.

In the most successful Kern-Fields collaboration, *Swing Time*, the most successful song is "The Way You Look Tonight." There are no anecdotal suggestions that this song gave Kern any trouble. It is Kern at his truest and best. Dorothy often told this story about "The Way You Look Tonight": "The first time Jerry played that melody for me I had to leave the room because I started to cry. The release absolutely killed me. I couldn't stop, it was so beautiful."[31] "The Way You Look Tonight" won Jerome Kern his first and Dorothy Fields her only Academy Award.[32]

The last danced duet in the movie, "Never Gonna Dance," is unusually dark in tone and sentiment.[33] It has points of contact with Irving Berlin's "Let's Face the Music and Dance," which Astaire and Rogers performed in *Follow the Fleet* (1936). But that song is presented as a play within a play. "Never Gonna Dance" is done in a completely empty room; there is no audience, as for "Waltz in Swing Time," not even three appreciative watchers as for "Pick Yourself Up." In the context of this enforced intimacy Astaire sings a song not of seduction, not of reconciliation, but of resignation. The declaration "Never gonna dance, . . . only gonna love you, never gonna dance" is the shadow side of Fields's lyric "if I hold you in my arms I won't dance," which Astaire sang in *Roberta*. "Let's Face the Music and Dance" is sung as a rejection of suicide. The last-will-and-testament list in "Never Gonna Dance," disposing of his shoes, rhythm, dinner clothes, cravat (which he leaves to Groucho Marx), and his shiny silk hat (which he leaves to Harpo), though sung with Astaire's customary insouciance, is chilling rather than charming. The first line, "Though I'm left without a penny," is of course, a pun on the name of the Ginger Rogers character, Penny Carroll. This trick is played again in the Rodgers and Hart song "My Funny Valentine" which is sung to a character named Valentine in the musical *Babes in Arms* (1937). The lines "the La Belle, La perfectly swell romance" refer back to lines spoken before Astaire and Rogers launch into "A Fine Romance." Dance critic Arlene Croce observed, "The two key songs, 'Never Gonna Dance' and 'A Fine Romance' were linked by the phrase 'la belle romance' which was also inserted in the dialogue because, as Miss Fields says, 'Kern always liked to work tidy.'"[34] The movie has an unusually large number of recurrent elements. At the beginning of the film, Astaire's marriage to the wrong person is thwarted when his dress pants are taken away to be altered. At the end of the film, the same trick is played on Roger's incorrect groom-to-be. At the end of the film many of the characters declare, "There isn't going to be any wedding," and earlier on it is declared, "There isn't going to be a dance." The dance step Rogers attempts to teach Astaire in their first dance number appears at the start of their first dance number, "Pick Yourself Up" but also in their two subsequent dance duets, "Waltz in Swing Time" and "Never Gonna Dance." It must have pleased Jerome Kern, who composed with a bust of Richard Wagner sitting on the piano, to have written a score for a movie so filled with leitmotifs.

END OF AN ERA

• • •

The year 1937 should have been particularly productive for Dorothy Fields. Her split with Jimmy McHugh would have to be accounted as a very successful break. She had, in 1936, provided lyrics for several other composers, including Max Steiner, Fritz Kreisler, Oscar Levant, and, most important, Jerome Kern. She had contacts at various studios: MGM, Paramount, RKO, and Columbia. Producers would have known that she could write high-tone or down-to-earth texts, suitable to be sung by operatic singers such as Lawrence Tibbett and Lily Pons or popular singers such as Alice Faye, Ginger Rogers, and Fred Astaire. After she and Kern received an Oscar for "The Way You Look Tonight," one would expect she would have been much in demand. But this was not the case; 1937 was a lull in Dorothy's career. Only one film with new lyrics by Dorothy Fields was released in 1937, *When You're in Love*, and that had only two new songs.

Movie musicals had already undergone more than one boom-and-bust cycle in the decade since *The Jazz Singer*. From 1927 to 1930, musicals were in great demand; by 1931, musicals were box-office poison. The 1933 musical *42nd Street* started a boomlet of backstagers (movies that were about people involved in the theater and their lives backstage). There was a brief fad for operatic voices after Grace Moore's success in *One Night of Love* (1934). Most Hollywood songwriters' careers had ups and downs with respect to both quantity and quality. (Perhaps the most important exception to this general pattern was the consistently productive career of Harry Warren.)

Quite separate from the business cycles, however, toward the end of the 1930s, for many members of the Hollywood community the champagne went flat, balloons deflated, and many lives took a turn for the worse. The illnesses and deaths of a number of uniquely talented and much-loved people, many at the height of their careers, cast a long shadow on sunny Hollywood.

On September 14, 1936, Irving Thalberg died of pneumonia at the age of thirty-seven. For a dozen years, from 1924 to 1936, Thalberg had been in charge of production at MGM. He had a special talent for overseeing movies that were both prestigious and profitable. Thalberg's ability to help shape a script was particularly admired by writers, and many felt that after Thalberg's death the overall level of script writing in Hollywood went down. Thalberg is thought to be the model for Monroe Stahr, the hero of F. Scott Fitzgerald's *The Last Tycoon.*

Thalberg's health had never been robust; he had suffered since his youth from a rheumatic heart. His death was lamentable but not shocking. The near-incomprehensible death was that of George Gershwin, who succumbed to a brain tumor on July 11, 1937, at the age of thirty-eight. Playwright George S. Kaufman wrote, "His death seems to me the most tragic thing that I have ever known."[1] Gershwin had always been the picture of vigorous good health. He swam, jogged, played tennis and golf. Sam Behrman described him as one who "lived all his life in youth."[2] Gershwin had written music for only four films, none of which were tremendous moneymakers at the time. Nevertheless, he was the heart of a creative community in Hollywood. As was the case in New York, around the Gershwins assembled a throng of talented, fun-loving people. A memorial concert for Gershwin, given at the Hollywood Bowl on September 8, 1937, was a colossal if sorrowful event with a symphony orchestra and several singers and pianists; CBS radio transmitted the event live. For his friend and interpreter Oscar Levant and for his brother Ira Gershwin, George's death produced an unhealable wound, a permanent trauma. For many other people, even those less close to George, the extinguishing of his light made their lives inescapably colder and darker.

Two other songwriters suffered reverses of health at about this time. On March 21, 1937, Jerome Kern suffered a severe heart attack; in the next few weeks, complications—from either a stroke or an embolism—set in. In time, Kern returned to more or less complete health, but his convalescence was protracted and accompanied by periods of despondency. He wrote to a friend, "I have had periodic drops into the indigo that make Hamlet a giggling, buoyant acrobat."[3] News of Gershwin's death was kept from Kern for fear of setting back his recovery. As Kern regained his health, news about Gershwin was given to him in small doses. First, Kern was told only that Gershwin was sick. Kern's biographer relates, "Kern immediately wrote Gershwin a get-well note, which makes for eerie reading considering it was written after Gershwin had already died. 'They have been keeping me in cellophane and absorbent cotton, and shielding me from all distressing news. So it was only yesterday that I heard of your trouble. I hasten to send you my best wishes for the speediest and completest recovery.'"[4]

Cole Porter, who practiced the art of fine living at the very highest level, had his life changed irrevocably for the worse at about this time. In October

1937, his legs were crushed in a horse-riding accident on Long Island. He sustained compound fractures of both legs, and eventually osteomyelitis set in. The first doctor treating him recommended the amputation of both legs. This grim fate was postponed (Porter's right leg was amputated in 1958), but Porter underwent numerous operations on his legs and was in almost continuous pain from that time forward.

At the Fields home, Dorothy's brother Herbert had a bout of ill health. Herbert's cousins wrote he had "two difficult years recovering from a heart attack and depression brought on by the death of Gershwin."[5] In good times and in bad, Dorothy continued to write. In the last few years of the 1930s, she worked with Jerome Kern on songs that appeared in three more films—*When You're in Love* (1937), *The Joy of Living* (1938), and *One Night in the Tropics* (1940).

When You're in Love was Columbia's penultimate attempt to keep Grace Moore's stardom afloat. Perhaps as a talisman, they changed the title of the film from *Interlude* to one that sounded more like Moore's greatest success, *One Night of Love*. More practically, they cast her opposite Cary Grant, who seemed to bring out the best in his leading ladies. Grant first appeared in films in 1932. In 1933, he played opposite Mae West in *She Done Him Wrong* and *I'm No Angel*. He made a number of films with Katharine Hepburn, starting with *Sylvia Scarlett* in 1936. The studios were avid trend-watchers, and Columbia hired Kern and Fields to write a score for Grace Moore similar to the one they had written for Lily Pons. But this plan gave way to one that would demonstrate Moore's all-things-to-all-people versatility by having her sing "Minnie the Moocher," "Siboney," "In the Gloaming," Schubert's "Serenade," and arias from *Tosca* and *Madama Butterfly* in addition to two songs by Kern and Fields.

Writing idiomatic American lyrics to be sung by opera stars was familiar territory to Dorothy Fields by now. The story of *When You're in Love* concerns an Australian opera singer (Moore) who marries an American (Grant) to gain entry to the United States to perform; predictably, by the end of the film, love replaces convenience in their union. The two new songs, both waltzes, are "The Whistling Boy" and "Our Song." "The Whistling Boy" is sung to a group of children. It must have been thought that as in *I Dream Too Much*, in which Lily Pons sings to a child on a carousel, an operatic voice could be humanized by having it addressed to youngsters. The romantic ballad "Our Song" is more successful, but not quite top-drawer Kern.

With the exception of his marriage, Jerome Kern avoided exclusive commitments. When he was in Hollywood, he had contracts at one time or another with almost every major studio—Universal, Warner Brothers, MGM, RKO, Paramount, and Columbia. Similarly, Kern did not team up with only one lyricist. In 1937, the same year he collaborated with Dorothy Fields on *When You're in Love*, Kern also worked with Oscar Hammerstein II on *High, Wide and Handsome*.

Set in Pennsylvania in 1859, *High, Wide and Handsome* stars Irene Dunne as a member of a traveling medicine show, Randolph Scott as a farmer who discovers oil on his property, Alan Hale as a villainous railroad man, and Dorothy Lamour as a singer and temptress. The director, Rouben Mamoulian, had a notable career on stage and screen with both musicals and dramas. The film contains six new songs by Kern and Hammerstein. In spirit, *High, Wide and Handsome* seems to be both a successor of Kern and Hammerstein's *Show Boat* and a predecessor of Rodgers and Hammerstein's *Oklahoma!* It also has points of contact with a distinctly Hollywood phenomenon: the horse opera. Cowboys had been singing in films as early as 1930; Gene Autry made his first film in 1934. Critical opinion about *High, Wide and Handsome* was radically divided when it opened. The *New York Times* reviewer thought it was better than *Show Boat*. The *Variety* reviewer complained about the script, the acting, and the direction. The film did not earn back the $1.9 million that had been spent on it.

The Joy of Living was the first film that Dorothy and Herbert Fields worked on together officially. Unofficial collaboration had long been a way of life for the Fields family. On and off, they lived together and ping-ponged ideas, jokes, and gag lines back and forth. But in the 1920s, there was only one official family collaboration (*Hello Daddy*, which opened in New York in late 1928) and in the '30s only one credited screen collaboration: *The Joy of Living*. Dorothy did the lyrics for the songs, and the screenplay was based on a story by Herbert and Dorothy Fields. *The Joy of Living* was made at RKO studios, where *Roberta* and *Swing Time* had been filmed. It reunited Jerome Kern with his preferred songstress, Irene Dunne. As in *Roberta*, Dunne's costar, in this case Douglas Fairbanks Jr., does not sing, but just looks on admiringly. Unlike *Roberta*, *The Joy of Living* did not have Ginger Rogers and Fred Astaire there to pick up the slack.

The story of *The Joy of Living* concerns a musical star, Margaret Garrett (Dunne), who is preyed upon by a dependent and manipulative family (mother, father, sister, brother-in-law, and twin nieces); besieged by her fans; and adored by a gallant Dan Brewster (Fairbanks) who has liberated himself from the responsibilities, but not the wealth, of his Boston banking family and who hopes to win her love by showing her that more freedom and happiness is available to her. (Herb and Dorothy certainly had plenty of experience with an extended family living together, but it seems unlikely that the very negative picture of family living given here is autobiographical.) Certain tropes from other movies Dorothy and Herb had been associated with appear here. *In Person* showed us an actress overwhelmed by enthusiastic fans; *I Dream Too Much* showed a singer worn out by her own success. Many of Herbert's movie plots show an interest in what the very rich do with their wealth. One critic found the movie "not quite zippy enough to make one forget its irritating archness, but socio-historically very interesting."[6] We are told that Margaret Garrett earns $10,000 a week, but half her earnings are dissipated by her spendthrift family, and half is taken by the government, so she is broke. Brewster owns an island in the Pacific where there are "no wars and no recessions," an interesting remark to make in 1938, when the United States was not yet involved in the war and when "recession" was surely too weak a word for the economic situation.

The *New York Times* reviewer, Frank S. Nugent, disliked the screenplay and the direction but wrote that "the saving grace is the Jerome Kern score."[7] The film contains four new songs, "You Couldn't Be Cuter," "Just Let Me Look at You," "What's Good about Good Night," and "A Heavenly Party." Kern's contract had called for six songs. These four had been completed before Kern's heart attack, and no more were forthcoming from him, even though Kern had recuperated by the time the film was completing production in 1938. A curious feature is that all of the songs are presented with some gag attached to them. One wonders if the success of "The Way You Look Tonight," a beautiful ballad presented in *Swing Time* with a sight gag at the end,[8] encouraged the director, Tay Garnett, to try a similar approach to all the songs in this film. Garnett also decided to show some source of the accompaniment for all of the songs. It is hard to tell if the presence of accompanying instruments for all the songs in *The Joy of Living* is a conservative feature or a kind of playful in-joke.

Irene Dunne as Maggie sings "You Couldn't Be Cuter" as a lullaby for her twin nieces, accompanying herself on a toy piano, but she falls asleep herself midway through a repetition of the chorus. In print, the song has a verse and a chorus, but in the film only the chorus is sung. Dunne first sings "Just Let Me Look at You" to an accompaniment played on a portable record player. When, in a courtroom, she is asked by the judge to sing this song, she coyly states, "Well, I'd love to sing for Your Honor, but I have no music." Dan Brewster, who is on trial for mashing, replies, "I anticipated that," and produces a concertina player. Dunne sings a bit more than half of the song in a disinterested mode but continues (accompanied by an invisible orchestra) more expressively and even seductively. She sings "What's Good about

Goodnight" as a radio broadcast. She had sung it at the very start of the film as a show-within-a-movie sequence. Here the gag is that between the first statement of the chorus and its repetition, she receives a message saying that Brewster is departing imminently. She races through the repetition of the chorus so quickly that the bandleader finds it impossible to keep up with her. Film critic Roy Hemming notes, "As the conductor, Franklin Pangborn is hilarious in what looks like a deliberately wicked takeoff on the then-popular (and often pretentious) Andre Kostelanetz."[9] "A Heavenly Party" is sung at a make-your-own record concession. The combination of calliope music and the barker outside the concession suggests that this scene takes place in an amusement park. After she sings, the piano accompanist comments, "Not bad girlie, not bad. But let me give you a load of how Maggie Garrett sings it." He then launches into the song in a jazzy, swinging version, unlike Dunne's style or, for that matter, Kern's. Dorothy had commented that "Jerry rarely had a feeling for a hot beat."[10] But it is also true that Kern rarely involved himself with his songs once he turned them over to the musical director or film director. We have no record of his reaction to the treatment of his songs in this film.

Toward the end of 1936 and the beginning of 1937, Kern and Dorothy also wrote songs for a film to be done by Universal Studios, to be called *Riviera*, but that film was shelved before it went into production. In 1940, when Universal was in financial difficulties, producer Leonard Spigelgass thought the unused songs might be used for *One Night in the Tropics*, a film based on the novel *Love Insurance* by Earl Derr Biggers. Spigelgass may not have realized that Kern (and now Fields, more and more) took pride in fitting the songs to specific characters and plot situations. When Spigelgass set up a meeting with Kern to ask permission to transfer the unused four-year-old songs into a new film, he was unprepared for Kern's reaction, which, according to his biographer Gerald Bordman, "he described as one of 'icy rage.' But before Kern could fully articulate his anger the phone rang. It was a message for Spigelgass, advising him his mother had been rushed to the hospital. Kern's rage melted abruptly. He became solicitous and concerned, offering to take the producer to the hospital in his own car. By the time discussions resumed, Kern was at least partially mollified, or else he had decided on the tack he would take. He agreed to authorize the use of the score for a substantial additional payment."[11]

One Night in the Tropics contains five songs by Jerome Kern. Four of them, "Back in My Shell," "Remind Me," "You and Your Kiss," and "Farandola" have lyrics by Dorothy Fields; one song, "Your Dream Is the Same as My Dream," taken from the musical *Gentlemen Unafraid*, has a lyric by Oscar

Hammerstein II. Each lyricist produced texts that are characteristic and typical of his or her work. Hammerstein's lines are sincere and earnest, with a touch of poetic yearning in a line such as "There's no sky too high for hearts like ours to fly to." Dorothy's are unabashedly artful, delighting in elements of surprise.

Dorothy Fields wrote the lyrics for the other romantic ballad in the film, "You and Your Kiss," and two anti-love lyrics, a genre she was making her own. When Allan Jones (the Gaylord Ravenal of the 1936 Universal Pictures version of *Show Boat*) sings "Back in My Shell," the woman to whom he sings it asks, "What kind of love song is that?" The singer seems to look forward to "No more love, no more grief . . . No more love, just relief." (Dorothy will revisit these sentiments, more than a decade later, in the song "There Must Be Somethin' Better Than Love.") "Back in My Shell" has a lazy, southern tone entirely incongruous with both the character and the setting. The music sounds as though it could have been written by Hoagy Carmichael or Johnny Mercer.[12]

Deborah Grace Winer declared "Remind Me," another ironic declaration of love, to be one of Dorothy Fields's best lyrics. "If you had to single out one song as the finest example of a Dorothy Fields lyric, the overwhelming temptation is 'Remind Me.' . . . As a popular song lyric, 'Remind Me' is not only perfect, it couldn't have been written by anybody else. . . . It is distinctly a woman's song, and probably the best argument for the case that Dorothy Fields's popular song lyrics are essentially feminine in viewpoint."[13] The lyric may not be obviously written by a woman, but it does need to be sung by a woman because of the second line of the chorus, "Remind me the world is full of men." Songwriters sometimes hope for a hit from a more versatile, gender-neutral song. But Dorothy Fields said that she did not try to write hit songs. She aimed at writing good songs that might become hits. "Remind Me" has both a verse and a chorus, but only the chorus is heard in the movie.[14]

The film ends with "Farandola," a big production number with scores of twirling dancers and long camera shots. This kind of final number was surely a cliché by this time. Con Conrad and Herb Magidson had won an Academy Award for the template of this kind of piece, "The Continental." Irving Berlin trumped "The Continental" when he wrote "The Picolino," which forms the finale of *Top Hat*. One suspects Dorothy did not expend a great deal of imagination on this song, which begins "Click, click the heel and tap, tap the toe/ Click . . . and tap . . . the gay Farandole."

Critical reception for *One Night in the Tropics* was lukewarm, and the film is most notable nowadays for having launched the film careers of Abbott and Costello. The film turned out to be the last active collaboration between Kern and Fields to reach the public—not that either of them knew that at the time. Dorothy would not work on another Hollywood film until the 1950s.

In 1938, Dorothy Fields returned to New York. With this move, she was not only changing place of residence and career orientation; she was also changing her marital status. On July 14, 1938, one day before her thirty-fourth birthday, Dorothy Fields married Eli Lahm. According to Stephen Sondheim, his father, Herbert Sondheim, was the matchmaker between Dorothy and Eli. Stephen Sondheim's biographer Meryle Secrest writes, "Sondheim said that his father introduced another of his close friends, Eli Lahm, to Dorothy Fields and 'made a *shiddach*,' i.e., a match. After they married and had children, Aunt Dorothy was at their apartment constantly, but [Stephen] Sondheim had no idea what she did until he became an adolescent."[15]

It is easy to imagine how and why Herbert Sondheim and Eli Lahm became friends. The two men were in the same business, clothing manufacture, and about the same age. Perhaps both had an interest in musical theater—certainly Sondheim had. He and another clothing manufacture buddy, Lloyd Weill, performed show tunes for charitable events—Sondheim at the piano and Weill singing. According to Secrest, "they became so well known that they were called 'the Rodgers and Hart of Seventh Avenue.'"[16]

But how and when did Dorothy become a friend of the Sondheims? She was living in California, and they were living in New York. Dorothy had been in New York on business several times in the 1930s—in 1932 for the inauguration of Radio City Music Hall, in 1933 when she and Jimmy McHugh were writing songs for *The International Revue*, in 1935 for a publicity shoot with Lily Pons and Tito Schipa. Had she and Eli met one of those times? Had they known one another for six or five or three years before they decided to marry?

There was a web of relationships that connected Dorothy Fields with Oscar and Dorothy Hammerstein and Herbert and Janet Fox ("Foxy") Sondheim. Dorothy Fields and Oscar Hammerstein II were both part of Jerome Kern's inner circle; they were among the Kerns' closest friends. But Dorothy Fields's association with Oscar Hammerstein II began long before she met Kern. Dorothy and Oscar were both second-generation show people. Hugh Fordin claims that Dorothy and Oscar were classmates at elementary school,[17] but since Oscar was nine years older than Dorothy, this cannot be true. Oscar was in the circle of friends that included Richard Rodgers, Lorenz Hart, and Herbert Fields (all three men had connections with Columbia University), and Dorothy probably knew him as early as her teenage years.

Oscar Hammerstein's second wife, Dorothy Blanchard Hammerstein, took up interior decorating as a career in California in the 1930s. She decorated the houses of Larry Schwab, Norma Talmadge, and Pandro Berman. She also decorated the house on Arden Drive in Beverly Hills in which the Fields family took up residence. When making friends, Dorothy Fields was able to wear more than one hat. She could be one of the boys with Jerome Kern or George Gershwin or Oscar Hammerstein II; she could also be one of the girls with Eva or Betty Kern or Dorothy Hammerstein.

After the Hammersteins moved back to New York from California, Dorothy Hammerstein made the acquaintance of Foxy Sondheim who, for reasons partly personal and partly commercial (given the Sondheims' involvement in manufacturing women's clothing), cultivated celebrities. The Hammersteins' son Jamie and the Sondheims' son Stephen—a year apart in age—were great friends, and in some ways the Hammersteins were more of a family for Stephen than his parents were. It would be convenient to think that the Hammersteins introduced Dorothy Fields to the Sondheims, who introduced her to Eli Lahm, but the timing does not work. Dorothy and Eli were already married before the Hammersteins came back to New York.

Beyond questions of where, when, and how Dorothy and Eli met, questions of a psychological nature take precedence. It took Dorothy only a few weeks in 1924 to realize that marriage, at least marriage to Dr. Jack Wiener, was not for her. Dorothy lived as a single woman for the next fourteen years. Her marriage to Eli Lahm produced two children and lasted until his death in 1958. It is tempting to say that the second time around, Dorothy was lucky enough or wise enough to find the right man for her. It would be nice to know what about Eli Lahm was so right for Dorothy, but information about him is scarce. The obituary notice for him in the *New York Times* is brief. "David Eli Lahm, a manufacturer of women's wear associated with Dove blouse, Inc. 1375 Broadway, died yesterday of a heart attack in his home, 12 East Sixty-ninth Street. He was sixty-six. Surviving are his widow, Dorothy Fields, lyricist and playwright; a son, David F.; a daughter, Eliza; and a brother, Mortimer."[18] Eli was twelve years older than Dorothy and one year older than his brother, Mortimer. Mortimer's life played out somewhat more in the public eye. He was the chairman and founder of the M. H. Lamston variety store chain and active in many charitable organizations, including the Jewish Board of Guardians, the Federation of Jewish Philanthropies, and the World Federation of Mental Health. In Mortimer's obituary, he is described as "a modest, quiet man."[19] This, from all I can gather from interviews, would seem to describe his brother, David Eli, as well.

There are very few extant photographs of Eli—no formal wedding pictures, no family portraits. Dorothy the lyricist was photographed a lot; Dorothy the mother appears in a few photos. The one photo of Dorothy and Eli that has been published shows them dressed up as Weber and Fields for a costume party, Dorothy in the guise of Joe Weber, and Eli as Dorothy's father, Lew.

Dorothy and Eli's wedding seems also to have been modest and quiet, or at least without press announcements. In this, Dorothy's second wedding resembles her first. I do not know who, if anyone, from Dorothy's family attended the wedding. Nor do I know Dorothy's family's reaction to her second marriage. It seems likely that Lew and Rose were happy to see Dorothy "settled" once more and that they were delighted to become grandparents once again. Dorothy's sister, Frances, and her brother Joe both made happy second marriages. The family member whose adjustment to Dorothy's wedded state may have been most difficult was Herb. Dorothy was the family member Herb was closest to; he confided in her—to a large extent she was his family—and 1938 was a time of illness and depression for Herb. It is hard to say how Dorothy's marriage played into his depression. But he may have felt as though he was in some sense losing—or at least sharing—his best friend, ally, and professional collaborator.

One must assume that Dorothy Fields was able to enter into a second marriage not only because she had found the right man for her but also because she herself had changed in important ways. When Dorothy married at age twenty, she must have known herself as a daughter and a sibling, as a person drawn to the stage, as a person with some talent for singing and for writing. When she married at age thirty-four, she was an esteemed lyricist, capable of entering into (and exiting from) successful working collaborations with composers, capable of supporting herself and others (she was at this time the best-paid member of the Fields family). From a position of greater independence and greater sense of self, she was able to begin a new stage of her life, one that would play out on Broadway and bring forth some of her most enduring successes.

11

HOLLYWOOD THROUGH A
BROADWAY LENS

• • •

The Broadway to which Dorothy Fields returned in 1939 had not yet bottomed out financially. Every year in that decade saw fewer productions on Broadway than did the year before.[1] Producers of shows in 1939 had hoped that with the increased number of visitors to New York to see the World's Fair, ticket sales on Broadway would go up, but in fact they went down. Nevertheless, many composers and lyricists who had tasted what Hollywood had to offer in the first half of the 1930s found themselves carried on a return current to New York.

Of course, there were a number of Hollywood songwriters who had little or no attachment to Broadway—Harry Warren, Ralph Rainger, Richard Whiting, and Hoagy Carmichael among them. Once they arrived in Hollywood, for the most part they stayed there. Others successfully adapted their talents to the demands of stage or screen. Chief among them were Irving Berlin and the seemingly imperturbable Cole Porter.

Other songwriters, such as Richard Rodgers, tested the waters on both coasts but found the Broadway stage definitely more congenial. In his autobiography, Rodgers refers to his first stay in Hollywood, two and a half years starting in 1931, as "the most unproductive period of my professional life."[2] Broadway was still in the doldrums when Rodgers and Hart returned to New York in 1934. Rodgers noted, "Between March and June not a single new musical opened on Broadway, and the prospects for the fall weren't encouraging."[3] Nevertheless, starting in 1935, Rodgers and Hart had an extraordinary run—ten productions and nine successes in seven years, including *Jumbo* (1935), *On Your Toes* (1936), *Babes in Arms* (1937), *I'd Rather Be Right* (1937), *I Married an Angel* (1938), and *The Boys from Syracuse* (1938).

For Dorothy, and indeed the entire Fields family, Hollywood had been a good place to be in the 1930s. Lew Fields's career did not have a resurgence in films, as he had hoped it might, but retirement in California was comfortable. Joseph Fields established himself as a screenwriter before he started writing books for Broadway shows. From 1935 to 1939 he wrote two or three scripts a year, for Republic Pictures, Warner Brothers, and RKO. Herbert Fields, a bit like Cole Porter, seemed able to ride the waves of success and failure in both New York and Hollywood. On Broadway, Herb provided the books for *Pardon My English* (1933), which flopped, and for *Du Barry Was a Lady* (1939), which was a great hit. A few of the scripts he wrote in Hollywood got panned by reviewers. The *New York Times* critic considered the story of *The Luckiest Girl in the World* "formularized" and that of *Love before Breakfast* "thin to the point of emaciation." Still, Herb seldom lacked for work. For the second half of the decade, only in 1937 did Herbert Fields not have a screenplay before an audience. For Dorothy Fields, as we have seen, the 1930s in Hollywood was a time of professional and personal blossoming. Nevertheless, in 1938 she moved back to New York and did not return to Hollywood for more than a decade.

The New York stage in the 1930s was undergoing both quantitative and qualitative changes. There were fewer productions each year, and, not surprisingly, many productions took on a darker, more satirical and socially relevant cast. The change was most noticeable in the musicals; in the 1930s, revues raised social and political issues to a degree unthinkable in the 1920s. *New Americana* (1932) was a multi-authored revue with songs by Harold Arlen, Burton Lane, Vernon Duke, and Johnny Mercer. It provided one of the Depression's anthems, "Brother, Can You Spare a Dime," by Jay Gorney and Yip Harburg. In Irving Berlin's *As Thousands Cheer* (1933), what should have been an impossible mixture (even in a revue) of comic and serious coexisted. In one part of the show, Ethel Waters sang the sizzling and sexy "Heat Wave," and in another the searing indictment of lynching, "Supper Time." Some shows were lighthearted, like Harold Rome's *Pins and Needles* (1937), a life-imitates-art revue in which a group of amateur players from the garment-manufacture trade created a show that unexpectedly became a long-running hit.

Europe had seen a golden age of satirical operetta in the second half of the nineteenth century, memorable for the works of Gilbert and Sullivan in England and Offenbach in France. In the United States in the 1930s, George and Ira Gershwin showed that musical comedy and political satire were not strange bedfellows with *Strike Up the Band* (1930), *Of Thee I Sing* (1931), and *Let Them Eat Cake* (1933). *Of Thee I Sing* even won a Pulitzer Prize in Drama for the authors of the book, George S. Kaufman and Morrie Ryskind. Kurt Weill, transplanted from Germany to the United States, made two important contributions to the genre, *Johnny Johnson*, set in the present, and *Knickerbocker Holiday*, set in seventeenth-century New Amsterdam. Some of the musical satires had an earnest, didactic tone, such as Harold Arlen and Yip Harburg's *Hooray for What!* (1937), and Marc Blitzstein's *The Cradle Will Rock* (1938).

Others were more playful, as when George M. Cohan portrayed Franklin D. Roosevelt in Rodgers and Hart's *I'd Rather Be Right* (1937). *I'd Rather Be Right* was very successful in its time, but it is likely that celebrity gawking—watching George M. Cohan impersonate FDR—rather than cutting satire accounted for much of its popularity.

Another rich target for satire on Broadway, both in musicals and nonmusicals, was the film industry. Talking pictures constituted serious competition for the entertainment dollar, but they were also fodder for comic plays throughout the '30s. George S. Kaufman and Moss Hart produced one of the first, and perhaps one of the best of these shows in 1930, *Once in a Lifetime*, in which some former vaudevillians become elocution experts for talking films. The foibles of Hollywood were revisited in 1935 in *Boy Meets Girl* by Sam and Bella Spewack. Insiders themselves, the Spewacks mocked actors, agents, and producers alike. The search for an actress to play Scarlett O'Hara in the movie *Gone with the Wind* gave Clare Boothe Luce the grist for her play *Kiss the Boys Goodbye* (1938).

The idea for a musical satire of Hollywood, *Stars in Your Eyes*, originated with the composer Arthur Schwartz. Schwartz had an impressive number of academic degrees, but none of them in music. He had a bachelor's degree from New York University, where he graduated Phi Beta Kappa with master's and law degrees from Columbia University. As a pianist and composer, however, Schwartz was essentially self-taught. He was born in Brooklyn in 1900 and became a lawyer under the insistent guidance of his lawyer father. His mother supported his love of music, which first found expression in low-profile activities such as playing piano for silent movies and collaborating on songs with Lorenz Hart at a summer camp where they were both on the staff. Hart found success some years later with Richard Rodgers, with songs for the *Garrick Gaieties,* and he never worked with another composer. It took Schwartz several more years to find the person who would be his longtime, but not exclusive, collaborator, Howard Dietz, a fellow Columbia alumnus. They were not classmates, Dietz being four years older, but Dietz had left behind him a reputation as a wit. Schwartz recalled, "Howard was a very funny man. You know, when he was at Columbia, they held a competition among all the students at the Journalists' School to see who could write the most sensational short headline. Howard won with 'Pope elopes.'"[4]

Schwartz first approached Dietz by letter in 1924. He wrote, "I'd love to work with you. . . . . I think you are the only man in town to be compared with Larry Hart, and from me that's quite a tribute, because I know almost every line Larry has written. I think that three or four tunes of mine will be riots in the *Grand Street Follies* this year IF they have lyrics such as only Larry and you can write. Don't be too amused at the fact that I speak of tune-writing under a lawyer's letterhead. I'm giving up the law in a few months to spend all my time at music."[5] Schwartz was rebuffed by Dietz initially, but they got together a few years later. Their first Broadway success, in 1929, was a revue called *The Little Show*. This was followed by *Three's a Crowd* (1930) and *The Bandwagon* (1931), which Stanley Green said "may well have been the most sophisticated, imaginative, and musically distinguished revue ever mounted on Broadway."[6]

Dietz's talent as a writer gave him careers as both a lyricist and as a publicist. For more than thirty years, he worked for Metro-Goldwyn-Mayer. He invented the company's trademark, Leo the Lion, and its slogan, *Ars Gratia Artis*. After 1937, for almost a decade, Dietz gave his attention entirely to his duties as a publicist for MGM, obliging Schwartz to find other lyricists. Schwartz turned first to Albert Stillman for songs for *Virginia* (1937) and then, for the *Stars in Your Eyes* project, to Dorothy Fields.

The book writer for *Stars in Your Eyes*, J. P. McEvoy, had a peripatetic writing career including stints as a journalist and a writer of greeting card messages. He also spent time as a writer in Hollywood. The first version of the libretto, then called *Swing to the Left*, was a satirical look at the clash between earnest propagandists trying to reveal social injustices in America and the commercial machine that drives picture making in Hollywood. Schwartz, Fields, and McEvoy brought their idea for a musical to Dwight Deere Wiman.

Wiman had produced Schwartz's first success, *The Little Show*, in 1929. In the 1930s, the most successful musicals he produced were *Gay Divorce* (1932), *On Your Toes* (1936), *Babes in Arms* (1937), and *I Married an Angel* (1938). Wiman was the heir to the John Deere farm machinery fortune. Richard Rodgers thought, "Wiman was a curious anomaly in the frequently rough-and-tumble world of Broadway. . . . Something about him made people take him for a dilettante. He was what my mother called a 'swell.' He had inherited wealth, plus the manners, accent and appearance to go with it. He may have lacked that certain drive and dedication associated with producers, yet he probably had more profitable attractions than most of the more aggressive members of the breed."[7]

Wiman brought in as director of the play one of his protégés, Joshua Logan, who had worked in various capacities both on Broadway and in Hollywood. The first two musicals he had directed were the very successful *I Married an Angel* (338 performances) and the less successful but well-esteemed *Knickerbocker Holiday* (168 performances). Logan recalled, "McEvoy's plot line for this show was based on a young boy genius, like Orson Welles or Pare Lorenz, going to Hollywood. Only this boy would be leftist, which was a popular theme then. . . . [Wiman] was on fire to have a big musical on Broadway in time for the upcoming 1939 World's Fair, and had already signed two supergreats, Ethel Merman and Jimmy Durante. He told me, 'If you don't like it the way it is change it; only make sure it's a hit.' 'All right,' I said. 'Let's throw all the unfunny Communist stuff out the window and just do a show about the crazy way Hollywood people mix sex and movies.'"[8] Since no one involved in the show had the socialist zeal of, say, Yip Harburg or Marc Blitzstein, Logan's attitude prevailed. The book was revised throughout rehearsals. When the show opened in Boston, it was about an hour too long, and a new round of cutting and rewriting began before the New York opening. Theater historian Ethan Mordden writes, "Out went the fifth-column jokes, the pointed songs, the carefully planned-out book. All that remained was the movie lot of Monotone Pictures and the cast, Ethel Merman as a temperamental movie star, Jimmy Durante as the studio troubleshooter, Richard Carlson as a roiled-up writer, Mildred Natwick as Dorothy Parker called something else, and Tamara Toumanova as (what else?) a ballerina."[9] The show still contains the character of an idealistic midwestern writer, but the satire is directed away from larger social issues and aimed more at empty-headedness and misuse of power in the film industry. More significant, the burden for the success of the show shifted away from the book and toward the ability of the star performers, Jimmy Durante and Ethel Merman, to delight the audience.

The paths of Jimmy Durante and Ethel Merman had intersected several times. One of Merman's earliest professional appearances, in 1930, was at Les Ambassadeurs, the same nightclub in which the team of Clayton, Jackson, and Durante were performing. Both Merman and Durante spent several years in Hollywood that were only mildly productive.

Merman made twenty-seven movies in Hollywood, but she seldom had a leading-lady role. The main exceptions were film versions of Broadway shows in which she had starred, such as *Anything Goes* and *Call Me Madam*. One writer theorized that it was her "oversized quality that confounded Hollywood. . . . It was her exultant presentation. No matter how Merman toned down her performance in front of the cameras, it was always too much for closeups."[10] On Broadway, she was sensational in her debut in *Girl Crazy* and was a large-magnitude star thereafter. Over the span of four decades, she gave definitive performances of songs by George Gershwin, Cole Porter, Arthur Schwartz, Irving Berlin, and Jule Styne. She and Durante had appeared together in Cole Porter's *Red, Hot, and Blue* (1936), notable to theater historians for the Solomonic solution to the problem of how to give top billing to both stars.

Jimmy Durante also had great talents which did not translate well to film. (There were more people in Hollywood who were able to spot talent than there were people who knew how to use that talent to good advantage.) Just as Merman's voice made its best effect when heard live and unamplified, Durante's type of humor was best suited to a setting that allowed for spontaneous, improvisatory wackiness—nightclubs and cabarets, his own radio or television programs, or even the New York stage if he was not too tightly reined in. Unlike, for example, the Marx Brothers, whose zaniness remained untamed on a Hollywood set, Durante obediently read the lines given to him by a succession of inferior script writers. Although he was well paid, being seen in one bad film after another was undermining his career. Durante and Dorothy Fields first met in 1930 when they were both novices in Hollywood. Durante appeared in *The Cuban Love Song*, which had two songs by Fields and McHugh. Dorothy very likely admired Durante's gift for mauling the English language, a gift he shared with her father.

After securing the services of Merman and Durante, Dwight Deere Wiman added one more signature touch to the casting; he hired Ballet Russe ballerina Tamara Toumanova. Wiman had had great success with Rodgers and Hart's *On Your Toes*, in which dance was not simply decorative but essential to the plot. Rodgers noted, "We made our main ballet an integral part of the action; without it, there was no conclusion to our story. During the dance, two gangsters enter a theater box intent on shooting the hero [a dancer on stage] at the conclusion of the ballet. Seeing their guns aimed at him, he beckons the conductor to continue the music so that he can keep on dancing to avoid being a target. Finally the police come, and the hero falls to the floor exhausted."[11] The main dancers in *On Your Toes* were Ray Bolger and Tamara Geva; the choreographer was George Balanchine. The next dance-centered show Wiman produced was *I Married an Angel*. Again the songwriters were Rodgers and Hart, and again the choreographer was George Balanchine, but this time the ballerina was Vera Zorina.

Tamara Toumanova had been under Balanchine's guidance from a very early age. (But unlike Geva and Zorina, she did not marry him.) An abundance of dancing talent supported Toumanova in *Stars*, including Dan Dailey, Alicia Alonso, Nora Kaye, and Jerome Robbins, all of whom went on to distinguished and diverse careers. The credited choreographer for *Stars in Your Eyes* was Carl Randall, but it is likely that Toumanova did much of the choreography for her own solos. There are two ballet scenes in *Stars in Your Eyes*, one in a night club and one a dream ballet. After *Oklahoma!*, the dream ballet sequence was a frequent feature in musicals, but *Stars* predates *Oklahoma!* by four years.

Stars in Your Eyes opened in New York on February 9, 1939, and closed 127 performances later. Critics were unanimous in lavishing extravagant praise on Ethel Merman and Jimmy Durante. Several reviewers admired Merman's acting and comedic skills as well as her singing. A few complained that Merman and Durante did not have a number together until the very end of the show but they also reported that this part of the show was its high point in hilarity. Likewise, Tamara Toumanova was almost universally praised, and some critics found her a charming actress as well as an admirable dancer. Also well liked were the supporting players, Richard Carlson and Mildred Natwick, and the imaginative sets of Jo Mielziner.

What did not go down well with about half the critics was the book. Some complained about the premise. In the *New Yorker*, Robert Benchley said, "It is not so much that we were all crazy mad to see another Hollywood satire."[12] In *Billboard*, Eugene Burr felt that the "idea of satirizing Hollywood [was] a pastime that should have—and to all intents and purposes did—end with *Once in a Lifetime*." Others disliked the realization. Richard Lockridge complained that "the book hobbles the fun during much of the first act," and Richard Watts suspected "the libretto of getting under the feet of the performers from time to time, but they wisely push it aside and go on with their more comforting songs and antics."

The score also received a mixed reception. John Mason Brown thought Schwartz's songs were inferior to the ones Cole Porter had previously composed for Merman. "The proof . . . of her skill as a singer is that while she is singing them, even Mr. Schwartz's songs at the Majestic seem to be almost as good as were such of her past masterpieces as 'Eadie Was a Lady,' 'Sam and Dalilah,' 'You're the Top,' and 'I Get a Kick Out of You.'[13] It is only when she has stopped that you realize how flat most of them are." Richard Watts felt Schwartz fell below his own normal high level in this show. "I have heard better scores from Arthur Schwartz, but his current contribution is a lively, tuneful and pleasing one." Some critics picked the numbers they liked best— almost all sung by Merman—or the ones they thought most likely to become hits. In fact, none of the songs in *Stars in Your Eyes* became a standard.

The reviewers who mentioned the lyrics did so admiringly. Brooks Atkinson noted there were "a number of good music hall songs for which Miss Fields has written salty lyrics." Kelcey Allen thought "the lyrics . . . are away above average . . . [and the music] is richly tuneful." George Ross thought "Miss Fields' words fit the music neatly and she has written a turbulent set of lyrics for Jimmy." Columnist Wilella Waldorff noted that Merman "will probably never have a number as rare as "Eadie Was a Lady" . . . but Arthur Schwartz's tunes are pleasant enough and Dorothy Fields has provided neat lyrics to match."

Irving Berlin once warned "You better not write a bad lyric for Merman, because people will hear it in the second balcony."[14] Berlin wrote very good lyrics for Merman in *Annie Get Your Gun* (1946) and *Call Me Madam* (1950). Dorothy Fields also wrote excellent lyrics for Merman. Excluding the finales, there are sixteen different musical numbers in *Stars in Your Eyes*. Two of them are ballets and five are ensemble or company numbers. Of the nine remaining numbers, five are sung by Ethel Merman—three as solos, one with ensemble backup, and one a duet with Jimmy Durante. All of the Merman songs except the duet were recorded in 1939. Of the three solos, "I'll Pay the Check" is a torch song; "A Lady Needs a Change" is an antisentimental song—a song that announces "I am not an ingénue"; and "Just a Little Bit More" is an uncharacteristic social relevance song, first conceived in the earlier, more political, phase of the show.

It is interesting to consider two lyrics on the same general theme, created for the same star by two equally resourceful writers. One of Cole Porter's classics of discontent, which Merman had sung in *Red, Hot, and Blue*, is "Down in the Depths." It makes a game of contrasting how well off the singer is financially and how bad off she is emotionally. The singer declares, "I'm deserted and depressed, in my regal eagle nest." Dorothy Fields's lyric for "I'll Pay the Check" also gives us a rich woman's love lament, but the sentiment and expression are more straightforward, simple, and direct. The singer recognizes disappointment and has the courage and the dignity to face up to it. It is the song of someone down but not out.[15]

"A Lady Needs a Change" is a sassy song, not disillusioned, but nevertheless without illusions. It is, incidentally, a song that meets Cole Porter on his own ground, a kind of a list song with both current (Havelock Ellis) and historical (Lucrezia Borgia) allusions, and it drips innuendos.[16] The lyric has a family resemblance to that of "A Fine Romance." Where the earlier song complained that the loved one "won't wrestle," the later one states that a lady needs a change "when there's no rough and tumble," or "when there's no thrill in fighting." This connection between loving and fighting brings to mind Lorenz Hart's "I Wish I Were in Love Again." The tomatoes/potatoes rhyme shows up in both "A Fine Romance" and "A Lady Needs a Change" (as it does in the Gershwin song "Let's Call the Whole Thing Off"). There are other food metaphors. "Clams in a dish of chowder," turns up in "A Fine Romance" and "love is just a warmed-up plate of hash" is on the menu in "A Lady Needs a Change." As a narration by an entirely unabashed character, this song also looks forward to a later Schwartz-Fields collaboration, "He Had Refinement" from *A Tree Grows in Brooklyn*.

"Just a Little Bit More" is a Depression lament, but a strange one. Unlike "Brother, Can You Spare a Dime," or the later "One Meatball," which speaks for the impoverished, "Just a Little Bit More" is a middle-class complaint. It is an unusual song, atypical of Fields's body of work and of the time when it was written. Indeed, the mood of the song seems closer to our own time in that it is about finding personal satisfaction. It acknowledges that if the problem is a sense of emptiness or malaise, the solution may be more internal than external. The verse begins by establishing that the singer is not politically oriented. In the chorus the minor mode melody modulating to the major at the end of the phrase gives the song just the right touch of pathos.[17]

At this time in her life, perhaps, a little bit less was a little bit more for Dorothy. She was living with just one other person now, her husband. The period of the entire Fields family being together—living under the same roof or, at least, having Sunday dinner together—had come to an end. Lew and Rose Fields were still in California; Dorothy and Herbert were now living in New York. Indeed, shortly after Ethel Merman stopped singing Dorothy's lyrics because *Stars in Your Eyes* closed, Herbert was putting words in her mouth—he wrote the libretto for Merman's next show, *Du Barry Was a Lady*, which opened in New York on December 6, 1939. In the next few years, the family would undergo changes more profound than geographic separation; these changes would involve death and births.

12

LIBRETTOS INSTEAD OF LYRICS

• • •

Changes in Dorothy Fields's personal life in the late 1930s and early 1940s were profound. Perhaps, for a while, she thought the changes in her life would require only minor adjustments. She was married, but her husband supported and encouraged her work. She was living in New York instead of Hollywood, but New York was the place her career had begun, and opportunities on Broadway were growing. As if to confirm this, Dorothy could note that she got married on July 14, 1938, and on February 9, 1939, *Stars in Your Eyes* opened on Broadway with her lyrics set to the music of a new collaborator, Arthur Schwartz.

After her marriage, the first major change in Dorothy's personal life was the birth of her son, David Lahm, born on December 12, 1940. David was given the same first name as his father, but since his father was regularly called by his middle name, Eli, there was no confusion. At thirty-six, Dorothy was slightly old to be a first-time mother. But she was strong and healthy, and the birth was without complications.

The next change in Dorothy's life, equal and opposite one might say, was the death of her father. Lew had been in physical decline during the late 1930s. To his great delight, his children were having a string of successes on Broadway. But Lew did not have the energy to travel back east to see *Stars in Your Eyes* or *Du Barry Was a Lady*, which opened in New York on December 6, 1939, starring Ethel Merman and Bert Lahr, with a score by Cole Porter and a book by Herbert Fields. Lew, who all his career staunchly upheld the ideal of good, clean family entertainment, might well have been shocked or offended by some of the text and lyrics of this show. Certainly, Bert Lahr was. He remarked, "When Cole got dirty, it was dirt without subtlety. Nothing I sang in burlesque was a risqué as his lyrics. It would never have been allowed on the burlesque stage."[1] *Du Barry Was a Lady* ran for 408 performances.

During the 1940–41 season, both of Lew's sons had long-running hits on Broadway. Herbert provided the book for another Cole Porter show starring Ethel Merman, *Panama Hattie*, which opened on October 30 and ran for 501 performances. Joseph's play, *My Sister Eileen*, followed soon after, opening on December 26. *My Sister Eileen* is a comedy, but not a musical. Written with Joseph's friend from Hollywood, Jerome Chodorov, the play was based on a series of *New Yorker* stories by Ruth McKenney. In an interview for the *New York Herald Tribune*, Joe complained, "The trouble with an adaptation . . . is that if it's good everyone says of course you had the characters and the situations made to order, and if it's bad they blame you for not getting the feel of the original."[2] He claimed he and Jerome Chodorov rewrote the last act of *My Sister Eileen* six times, although the second act finish—the experiences of the sisters with members of the Brazilian Navy—was the first idea for the show. *My Sister Eileen* starred Shirley Booth and was directed by George S. Kaufman. It had a spectacularly successful run of 866 performances, was made into a movie in 1942 (screen adaptation by Chodorov and Fields) and into a musical, *Wonderful Town*, in 1953.[3]

Lew Fields, in retirement, could enjoy his offspring's successes only by report. He and Rose had moved to California to join Herb, Joe, and Dorothy; but the children had all returned to New York. Even in the benign California climate, Lew Fields's lungs began to fail him. In July 1941 he developed a case of pneumonia that proved fatal. In the days before the widespread use of antibiotics (sulfa drugs were in use, but penicillin was not widely available), pneumonia was frequently deadly, and Lew's lungs may well have been compromised by a lifetime of smoking. The women of the Fields family—Rose, Frances, and Dorothy—were with him during his last days, as was Joe Weber. His sons were in New York. When Dorothy traveled from New York to California to be with her dying father, she was in the midst of preparations for her first Broadway show as a book writer; she and Herb were working together on the libretto for *Let's Face It*, with a score by Cole Porter.

Lew Fields died on Sunday, July 21, 1941. Only Rose, the children, and Joe Weber were present at the "intensely private" funeral. Lew was cremated, and his ashes brought back east for interment in the family vault in the Union Field Cemetery in Westchester—another indication that the family considered their stay in California a phase, a time of sojourning rather than a true relocation. There was a great outpouring of sorrow at the death of Lew Fields. His passing was marked in the *New York Times* by not only an obituary but an article on the editorial page. Many of the written tributes to him were draped in nostalgia. Perhaps some of the writers sensed how much more radically the world was about to change with much of Europe already engaged in war.

After *Stars in Your Eyes*, Dorothy wrote no new lyrics for more than five years. This is not to say she left show business in favor of domestic life. *Let's Face It* opened on Broadway on October 29, 1941, a few months after the death of her father. This was Dorothy's debut as a Broadway librettist, but not the first time she had worked with Herbert on a script. They had previously collaborated on the screenplay for the RKO film *Father Takes a Wife* (1941). In an interview, Dorothy stressed the family rather than the business aspect of her emergence as a librettist. "Herbert gets lonesome when he writes and he likes to have some one with him. . . . So he asked me to write a musical comedy book with him. . . . We work well together and we're going to keep on collaborating."[4] Early in his career, when he was part of a triumvirate with Rodgers and Hart, Herbert was the sole librettist. After he returned to New York from Hollywood, following a bout of ill health and depression, he never worked on a libretto without a collaborator. Almost all of the stage work Dorothy and Herbert did from the time of *Let's Face It* until his death in 1958 was done together. (Herbert did not work on *A Tree Grows in Brooklyn*, for which Dorothy wrote the lyrics but not the book.) A photo accompanying a *Life* magazine article titled "The Fabulous Fields Family" shows them working together.[5] In a comfortably appointed room with flowers on the table and scrapbooks on the floor, Herb sits at a typewriter table peering with intense concentration at what he has just written while Dorothy reclines on an easy chair peering with intense concentration at Herb. It is as if it has become clear to Dorothy, after her marriage and the death of her father, that her career and her family life were not in opposition

Dorothy also emphasized that *Let's Face It* was to some extent a continuation and perpetuation of Lew Fields's work.

> *Let's Face It* is really Pop's idea. . . . He wanted to make a musical out of "Cradle Snatchers" for years, but somehow he never got around to it. Herbert and I thought of it again last season and we pounced on it because we imagined there would be very little work to do. We remembered it as a funny farce which had played for more than a year back in the middle '20s. But when we read it over again, we were disillusioned. Most of the jokes were hopelessly dated and the dialogue was stuffed with references to "cake eaters," "finale hoppers," and "lounge lizards." . . . Outside of the original premise, that of three married women who hire a trio of escorts to make their philandering husbands jealous, we had to invent entirely new situations. . . . We had to make the women younger, of course, and as a topical note we changed the three college boys to Army draftees.[6]

The book-writing team of Dorothy and Herbert Fields suited Cole Porter well. He had complained in 1939, "My great professional tragedy is that I have to be a book hunter . . . Such scoundrels as Rodgers and Hart . . . know how to write their own books."[7] This statement has several ironic aspects.

One is that Rodgers and Hart wrote their own books as a kind of act of desperation, *faute de mieux*, and they were not very good at it. A second irony is that Herbert Fields had provided the books for most of Rodgers and Hart's successes in the 1920s before contributing to many of Porter's successes in the 1930s and 1940s. Porter appreciated the Fieldses' facility, which was aided, when necessary, by resort to materials their father had used. For example, a scene in *Let's Face It* has two characters who are not supposed to be away from their Army base pretending to be statues to avoid being discovered. The gag is based on a Weber and Fields act in which they whitened their bodies and posed as statues of gladiators.

Let's Face It was blessed with an abundance of talent. Danny Kaye got promoted from a supporting part as a fashion photographer in *Lady in the Dark* to a starring role as one of the soldiers in *Let's Face It*. His wife, Sylvia Fine, supplied him with some tailored-to-a-Kaye material such as "Melody in 4-F" and "Shootin' the Works," but perhaps his biggest hit in the show was Porter's duet "Let's Not Talk about Love" which Kaye sang with Eve Arden. Arden had other successes on stage and in film before she went on to fame in the 1950s television series *Our Miss Brooks*. Another of the bored wives in the play, Vivian Vance, likewise became a television icon as Ethel Mertz in *I Love Lucy*. One of the understudies in *Let's Face It* was Carol Channing, and one of the bit players was Nanette Fabray who, in 1950, starred in another Dorothy and Herbert Fields show, *Arms and the Girl*.

Discussing *Let's Face It*, theater historian Ethan Mordden noted, "As the story-telling improved, the songs had to keep up with the plot, work a little harder. Cole Porter's *Let's Face It* songs did include go-everywhere Cole Porter numbers. . . . [But] the bouncy, brilliant 'A Lady Needs a Rest,' a cross section of the daily routine of the worldly socialite . . . could only have been inspired by the show's central players: three bored, lonely, trendy, vital, satirically minded New York ladies."[8] Yet another source of inspiration for that song may have been a lyric Dorothy had written two years earlier, "A Lady Needs a Change," sung by one of Porter's preferred singers, Ethel Merman, in *Stars in Your Eyes*. Cole's lyric may well have been a friendly tribute to Dorothy's. While "A Lady Needs a Change" lists symptoms of a romance going sour, "A Lady Needs a Rest" expands a sense of ennui to an entire style of life. *Let's Face It* opened at the Imperial Theatre in New York on October 29, 1941, and ran for 547 performances.

The start of 1943 was a high-water period for the Fields family. What with old hits and new hits, Joseph, Herbert, and Dorothy collectively had five shows running on Broadway—*My Sister Eileen, Let's Face It, Junior Miss, The*

Doughgirls, and Herbert and Dorothy's new work with Cole Porter, *Something for the Boys*. The media began to emphasize the family aspect of their successes. Various newspapers ran articles with titles such as "Amazing Fields Family" or "Fabulous Fieldses Writing Plays and Coining Money" or "The Fields Family Has a Field Day on B'way."

In *Something for the Boys*, once again the stage is full of servicemen. The story, which the reviewer for *Variety* thought was "shrewdly geared to the times," concerns three cousins, previously strangers to one another, who inherit a rundown ranch in Texas near an Army Air Corps base. They convert it into a combination machine shop manufacturing small parts for planes and boardinghouse for wives and sweethearts of the men on the base. The most far-fetched part of the plot—the heroine prevents a plane from crashing by receiving radio signals through the carborundum fillings in her teeth—was inspired by a newspaper story. Wolcott Gibbs reported in the *New Yorker*, "Probably it all began when Dorothy and Herbert Fields picked up a newspaper and read about a man who could receive radio programs with his teeth. I forget now just how this miracle was accomplished, except there he would be, walking along, bothering nobody, when suddenly a wild private music would shower his molars, and thereafter his footsteps down the street would be syncopated and peculiar. Anyway, the Fields, Dorothy and Herbert, read this not necessarily bogus item and said with one voice, 'Now there's an idea for a musical comedy.'"[9]

Vinton Freedley, who had produced *Let's Face It*, had been part of the initial planning phase of *Something for the Boys*, but irreconcilable differences grew between Porter and the Fieldses on one side and Freedley on the other. The alterations that Freedley wanted all seemed to Porter and the Fieldses to be changes for the worse and Freedley left the team. Herbert and Dorothy had an opportunity for comic revenge on Freedley sometime later. A newspaper item reported, "It is common knowledge that Vinton Freedley turned down *Something for the Boys* by Herbert and Dorothy Fields, with songs by Cole Porter after commissioning them to write it. . . . Now comes the story that when 'Dancing in the Streets' revealed a million flaws in its Boston tryout Freedley appealed to Herbert and Dorothy to please look the property over and perhaps doctor it up. The brother and sister saw the musical and then, before proceeding to the Coast, sent Freedley several pages of suggestions which in their opinion might strengthen the show. . . . At the bottom of the page they wrote: 'If you use any one of these suggestions, darling—we will sue you for every nickel you've got!'"[10]

Replacing Vinton Freedley as producer of *Something for the Boys* was Michael Todd. Born Avrom Hirsch Goldbogen on June 22, 1907, in Minneapolis, "by the time he was nineteen," according to his son, "he had made and lost a million dollars in the construction business in Chicago."[11] His first theatrical hit was *The Hot Mikado* (1939), a retelling of the Gilbert and Sullivan operetta with an African American cast. He had another hit with the revue *Star and Garter* (1942). Todd told a reporter he considered himself "a streamlined P. T. Barnum" and indeed he was a master at manipulating public-relations machinery. On the other hand, in his willingness to spend lavish amounts on productions and his reliance on gags and girls to ensure the success of a show, he might be better compared to Florenz Ziegfeld.

Something for the Boys was the last of five shows that Cole Porter wrote for Ethel Merman. It was the sixth of seven shows he wrote with Herbert Fields. Ethan Mordden has asserted that "Porter's most sympathetic librettist was Herbert Fields, who wrote or co-wrote seven Porter scripts and who, in the 1920s, first edged musical-comedy librettos into the racy. Fields collaborated with B. G. DeSylva on *Panama Hattie* and with sister Dorothy Fields on *Something for the Boys*, but they are basically the same piece: Ethel defies the snobs to win over the hero in exotic locations with a strong wartime atmosphere in which she pulls off a stunt advantageous to the war effort."[12] Costarring with Ethel Merman in *Something for the Boys* was Paula Laurence, who had played in *Junior Miss* in Boston but was better known as a nightclub entertainer. Together they sang the closing duet of the show, "By the Mississinewah," which convulsed and delighted audience and critics alike. A later commentator finds this duet "so witless that one wonders what staging tricks director Hassard Short dreamed up for it, as it was hailed as the funniest musical number in Broadway history."[13] Later in the run, Merman got Laurence fired, claiming that Laurence had stolen some of her comic bits in the duet. Merman's other costars were Allen Jenkins playing the third inheriting cousin, Bill Johnson as Merman's romantic interest, and Betty Garrett as Merman's romantic competition.

Something for the Boys opened at the Alvin Theatre in New York on January 7, 1943, to enthusiastic reviews. The critics declared that "*Something for the Boys* is something to cheer about" and that "*Something for the Boys* is something for the box office." The 1942–43 season must have opened dully. Lewis Nichols thought the only good musical in the past six months had been Rodgers and Hart's *By Jupiter*. In the *New York Times* he declared "all season long the world has yearned hopefully for a big, fast, glittering musical comedy. It has it now." The *Time Magazine* reviewer agreed the show "gives Broadway the musical comedy it has been thirsting for since September." *Something for the Boys* played for 422 performances in New York and had a successful tour with Joan Blondell in the Ethel Merman role. Ten months into its New York run *Something for the Boys* was one of four shows—the others were *Oklahoma!*, *Life with Father*, and *Tomorrow the World*—to offer tickets for a special matinee performance as an inducement to buy war bonds. The endeavor raised $8.2 million.

Several critics noted with pleasure that Todd had somehow managed to get around the problem of wartime shortages to produce an extravagantly good-looking show, designed by Howard Bay. Todd later commented that he had spent more on curtain calls for *Something for the Boys* than *Oklahoma!* had spent on its whole production. The success of *Oklahoma!*, which opened on Broadway less than three months after *Something for the Boys*, was a watershed event. To some extent, *Oklahoma!* became the standard against which all later musicals were measured. Richard Rodgers's previous Broadway musical had been *By Jupiter*, the last and most successful show (421 performances) he had written with Lorenz Hart. As if to signal a shift in theatrical tides in 1943, the revival in November 1943 of a 1927 Rodgers and Hart hit, *A Connecticut Yankee*, ran for only 135 performances. The revival kept five of the older songs and added six new ones. The most popular of the new numbers, "To Keep My Love Alive," was written for Vivienne Segal. This was Lorenz Hart's swan song, the last lyric he wrote.

On November 22, 1943, Lorenz Hart succumbed to pneumonia at age forty-eight. Hart had been actively participating in his own destruction for many years, and his death was not as shocking as George Gershwin's had been. But the grief and sense of loss that people felt at the passing of this talented, generous, lovable, and unhappy man was no less profound. More than three hundred mourners were at the funeral service held at the Universal Funeral Chapel at Lexington Avenue and Fifty-second Street, including four Dorothys—Dorothy Parker, Dorothy Rodgers, Dorothy Hart, and Dorothy Fields. Friends on the West Coast, including Herbert Fields, Oscar Hammerstein II, and Jerome Kern, attended a memorial service held in Hollywood at the same time.

The final show that Herbert and Dorothy wrote with Cole Porter was *Mexican Hayride*, again produced by Mike Todd. Like their two previous musicals, *Mexican Hayride* was a financial success, chalking up 481 performances, but it seemed to be a hit despite itself. Porter himself thought the show was "lousy." Mordden commented, "*Oklahoma!* opened, and suddenly Porter's *Mexican Hayride* (1944) looked tacky, though it too was a smash."[14]

Todd followed the formula that had served him well in *Something for the Boys*. The production was lavish with a large cast and a delectable chorus line. One critic felt that the production itself was the star. The cast could not boast Ethel Merman, but it had the popular comedian Bobby Clark, June Havoc, and Edith Meiser. Clark had played the vaudeville circuit and in legitimate theaters, in the comedy team Clark and McCullough, starting in 1912. He had appeared in an earlier Todd show, *Star and Garter*, with June Havoc's sister, Gypsy Rose Lee. (Ethel Merman was to have one of her greatest roles in *Gypsy*, in which she played the mother of June Havoc and Gypsy Rose Lee.) June Havoc had performed with Gene Kelly and Vivienne Segal in *Pal Joey* (1940). Edith Meiser had played one of the wives in *Let's Face It*.

In *Mexican Hayride*, Clark played a crook hiding out in various locations in Mexico. No disguise was considered too ridiculous for the audience to swallow; Clark presented himself as a member of a Mariachi band and later as an Indian squaw. The squaw disguise may have been intended as an echo of the "By the Mississinewah" number in *Something for the Boys*. *Mexican Hayride* was enthusiastically received. Robert Garland in the *Journal-American* declared, "Broadway in general, and the drama critics in particular, can continue their custom of writing the word "fabulous" in front of the name of Mike Todd. For the truth is that last night the fabulous Todd produced a musical comedy so funny, so tuneful, so beautiful, that you could hardly believe your ears and eyes."[15]

After *Mexican Hayride* opened, newspapers reported plans for another Mike Todd production with Cole Porter, but this never materialized: Porter's next musical, *Seven Lively Arts* (1944), was produced by Billy Rose. Bobby Clark worked with Michael Todd again on *Michael Todd's Peep Show* (1950), but this time offstage, as writer and director. Dorothy and Herbert Fields worked with Todd on his next show, *Up in Central Park*.

Despite her recent successes, Dorothy was probably feeling some sense of frustration and dissatisfaction with working as a librettist but not a lyricist. The book of a musical was frequently underappreciated and undervalued both by critics and the audience. She remembered, "Whenever we'd get to Boston to try out one of our shows with [Cole Porter], we loved to go out into the theatre lobby on Saturday afternoons when all the Back Bay dowagers would come to the matinee. I think it was during the tryout of *Let's Face It*, which starred Danny Kaye. Cole and Herbie and I were standing and listening to all the stuff those old biddies were talking about. And right next to us was a very aristocratic old dame. She said, 'I don't know *how* these actors think up all those funny things to say!' Cole was delighted with her remark. He nudged us, and he said, 'You see? You Fieldses want to write *book*?'"[16]

It may have been that the routine damning with faint praise from the critics was even more irritating. Reviewing *Something for the Boys* for the *Christian Science Monitor*, Edwin Melvin remarked, "But the book, after all, is merely a device for introducing the songs and dances." The *Variety* review of the same show commented that the book "starts off with a wallop in a three-scened prolog, and a first scene which seemingly are without recent parallel for setting the key for a musical show. That it fizzles out by the end of the act, and remains thereafter something of a nuisance, by no means diminishes its value as a skeleton upon which to hang the show, for it's salted throughout with lusty dialog and good springboards for songs and specialties."[17] *Newsweek* said of the book, "At least it does not get in the way of the entertainers." Their next show, *Mexican Hayride*, brought similar comments from the press. The book "was one of the least substantial articles of its kind ever turned out as the basis of so gorgeous a production," remarked the critic of the *Boston Herald*. There was certainly dissonance between the high regard Dorothy and Herbert received within their professional community and the kind—or lack—of recognition coming from the critics and public at large. Recognition aside, Dorothy was probably getting impatient to reemploy her talents as a lyricist.

New Yorkers or visitors to New York were not the only people to enjoy the Porter-Fields collaborations. Films based on the musicals had national distribution. *Let's Face It*, which opened on Broadway in 1941, was redone by Paramount in 1943; *Something for the Boys*, which opened on Broadway in 1943, was redone by Twentieth-Century Fox in 1944; and *Mexican Hayride*, which opened on Broadway in 1944, was redone by Universal in 1948. These film versions were all radical reshapings, or one might say defacings. Cole Porter and Herbert Fields were old hands at turning shows over to Hollywood. *Gay Divorce, Anything Goes, Du Barry Was a Lady*, and *Panama Hattie* had all undergone this metamorphosis. The original creators accepted the reality that once a contract was signed, with the best economic deal one could make, it was wise to let go and not look back because one's work might be changed into something unrecognizable.

When transformed from plays to films, Porter's musicals were usually recast both literally and figuratively. Hollywood star power replaced the strengths of the play, such as the score and the book, as the chief element of marketability. *Let's Face It* was unusual in keeping one of the stage performers in the film version—Eve Arden. Danny Kaye, one of the stars of *Let's Face It* on Broadway, did not make his screen debut until 1944, when he won great success as a hypochondriacal soldier in *Up in Arms*. The stars of the movie *Let's Face It* were Bob Hope and Betty Hutton. The *New York Times* critic, who acknowledged that he did not much care for the musical on which the movie was based, described the film as "a rather feeble and outdated contraption. . . . No one can do more with poor material than Mr. Hope, but there are limits."[18] The screenplay for *Let's Face It*, by Harry Tugend, added a subplot in which

Bob Hope captures a German submarine, a defensible updating because by 1943 the United States was deeply enmeshed in WWII. Betty Hutton, who had been a featured player on Broadway in Cole Porter's *Panama Hattie*, sang Porter's "Let's Not Talk about Love" in the film.

After the successful Broadway opening of *Something for the Boys*, Twentieth-Century Fox, which had been a financial investor in the play, bought the screen rights as a vehicle for Betty Grable, who, in the end, did not appear in the film. The studio paid Porter and the Fieldses the unusually high fee of $305,000 for the rights. The stars of the film were Carmen Miranda (taking Ethel Merman's role), Vivian Blaine, Phil Silvers, and Perry Como. Once again, most of Cole Porter's songs were dropped; new songs by Harold Adamson and Dorothy's former songwriting partner, Jimmy McHugh, were added. McHugh had contributed songs to several Hollywood musicals featuring men and women in uniform, including *Seven Days Leave*, *True to the Army*, *Two Girls and a Sailor*, and *Four Jills in a Jeep*. The decision to replace a song was often made more on financial than aesthetic grounds. New songs, written by composers employed at the studios, allowed those studios to collect more royalties. Although the songs were changed, the story remained essentially the same. Bosley Crowther observed that the plot was "lifted rather neatly from the original stage show by Herb and Dorothy Fields."[19]

Clearly, the rewards for selling the film rights to a musical were more financial than artistic. And sometimes even the financial rewards were problematic. Porter's biographer reports, "Cole was hoping . . . that Mike Todd would fail in his efforts to arrange a picture deal for *Mexican Hayride*, as he felt that the sale would make him so much poorer, owing to taxes."[20] *Let's Face It* and *Something for the Boys* were turned into films just one or two years after their stage premieres. There were four years between the stage and the screen versions of *Mexican Hayride*. Originally conceived as a star vehicle for Bobby Clark, *Mexican Hayride* was converted into a star vehicle for Bud Abbott and Lou Costello. All of Porter's songs were dropped from the movie, which Bosley Crowther called "a conspicuously substandard film," and "an obvious and weary little farce bearing slight (if any) resemblance to the stage musical on which it is 'based.'"[21]

On January 7, 1944, exactly three weeks before the New York opening of *Mexican Hayride*, Eliza Lahm was born. Like her brother, Eliza was named after her father, David Eli Lahm. During this time, although Dorothy stayed involved with activities on Broadway, she also was more engaged in domestic matters. She was not a full-time mother—there was a governess to help rear the children—and she never was a cook. (Her daughter recalled her mother's baffled amazement, on an occasion when Eliza fixed a meal, that all the dishes could be made to come out at the same time.)[22] But she did add to her life activities appropriate to a Manhattan matron, such as philanthropic work. She worked at the USO canteen. A few years later, Ellin Mackay Berlin got Dorothy involved in one of her favorite organizations—the Girl Scouts. In Hollywood in the 1930s, Dorothy had shown great adeptness at smoothly moving between spheres—fitting into both a man's world and a woman's world. Now that she was a mother, her range expanded even further. For a part of the time that the children were growing up, the family tried out country living, in Stamford, Connecticut, and in Brewster, New York, and Dorothy became an enthusiastic gardener. More remarkably, she became a markswoman. She had an extraordinary skill in balancing the disparate, fulfilling aspects of her life.

13

UP IN CENTRAL PARK

• • •

After a hiatus of more than five years, Dorothy Fields returned to writing lyrics for a new musical, *Up in Central Park*, produced by Mike Todd. She and Herb wrote the libretto together, as they had for their previous three shows. The composer was an old friend but a new collaborator—Sigmund Romberg.

Sigmund Romberg was born in Nagykanizsa, Hungary, on July 29, 1887. Although he showed prodigious talent as a violinist and pianist, he trained as an engineer and did eighteen months of military service starting in 1907. At the same time, somehow, he found time to work as a coach, accompanist, and assistant stage manager at the Theater an der Wien and to study harmony and composition with Victor Heuberger. When he was twenty-two, he immigrated to the United States, where he quickly put his engineering training behind him and began to work as a musician, first as a café pianist and then as a staff composer for the Shubert brothers. He put in several years of journeyman work, adding songs to revues and adapting European operettas for American audiences. He had moderate success composing the score for *The Whirl of the World* (1914) and phenomenal success with *Maytime* (1917).

Romberg's first connection with the Fields family came in 1915, when he wrote some songs for Lew Fields's production of *Hands Up*. (Fields had also purchased songs from the young Cole Porter for this play.) In 1920, Lew Fields connected with Romberg once again. Lew had hired Rodgers and Hart to write the score for a new play he was producing, *Poor Little Ritz Girl*. After the Boston tryouts, Lew had second thoughts about the abilities of this relatively untried pair. Without consulting Rodgers or Hart, he called in Sigmund Romberg and Alex Gerber to add some songs. In his autobiography, Rodgers wrote that his discovery, on opening night, that half of his score had been replaced was "the bitterest blow of my life."[1] Dorothy was sixteen at this time and had already performed some Rodgers and Hart songs in a nonprofessional setting. She may have given a sympathetic ear to Rodgers's "grinding pain of bitter disappointment," although she may not have been receptive to criticism of her father. Rodgers himself grudgingly acknowledged later that "most of the changes were improvements. The Romberg tunes, though not especially original, were energetic and helpful to this sort of piece."[2] In any case, Dorothy did not hold Romberg's usurpation of Rodgers and Hart's score against him, and they became good friends when they were in Hollywood in the '30s.

Romberg's place in American music is a curious and complicated one. He is often ignored in books about Tin Pan Alley or popular song. Charles Hamm, in his magisterial study, *Yesterdays: Popular Song in America*, mentions Romberg only once. Alec Wilder's important book, *American Popular Song: The Great Innovators, 1900–1950*, does not discuss a single Romberg song and mentions the name only three times, twice coupled with Friml's. Indeed, one would be hard pressed to make a case for Romberg as an innovator. The operettas he wrote are treated by many historians of musical theater as so much irrelevancy; but it may be truer, given his success, to consider his work as a significant countercurrent. Romberg composed the scores of the book musicals that had the second- and fourth-longest runs in the decade of the teens—*Maytime* (1917; 492 performances) and *Blue Paradise* (1915; 356 performances). In the 1920s, when fast-paced comedies and spicy revues were drawing large audiences, the longest-running musical was *The Student Prince of Heidelberg* (1924; 608 performances). Both before and after *Show Boat*, Oscar Hammerstein II had several successful collaborations with Sigmund Romberg. They wrote some of their greatest hits together, including *The Desert Song* (1926) and *The New Moon* (1928). Several of Romberg's shows were made into movies—some several times. *The Student Prince* was released as a silent film in 1927 and received full-scale Technicolor treatment in 1954. *The Desert Song* (which had its source, in part, in silent films of Rudolph Valentino) was filmed in 1929, 1943, and 1953. Likewise, *Maytime* was made into a movie in 1937, and *The New Moon* in 1940.

Romberg is often viewed as a successor to Victor Herbert (1859–1934) and a colleague—or rival—of Rudolph Friml (1879–1972). But we should consider him more properly with Irving Berlin and Jerome Kern. Like Berlin, Romberg helped feed the craze for popular dances in the teens. Berlin and Romberg, as patriotic naturalized citizens, both served in the U.S. Army during World War I and entertained the troops during World War II. Romberg's works seem so much to belong to a bygone age that one is surprised to learn he was two years younger than Kern and just a year older than Berlin. Like Kern, Romberg had deep roots in nineteenth-century European traditions. It is not an accident that Kern and Romberg were Oscar Hammerstein's favorite collaborators in the 1920s and 1930s. Romberg also shared with Kern an atypical comfort with female lyricists and librettists. His collaborator for

Maytime was Rida Johnson Young (1869–1926), who had written *Naughty Marietta* with Victor Herbert. Dorothy Donnelly (1880–1928) was an even closer associate. With her, he wrote *Blossom Time* (1921) and *The Student Prince of Heidelberg* (1924) as well as two less successful shows, *My Maryland* (1927) and *My Princess* (1927). He deeply mourned her death (from nephritis and pneumonia) in 1928. Oscar Hammerstein II's biographer Hugh Fordin suggests that Hammerstein may have taken up *The New Moon* again "to provide occupational therapy not only for himself but for Romberg, who was badly shaken by the recent death of his old friend and collaborator, Dorothy Donnelly. Oscar spent hours listening to the melancholy composer pour out his unhappiness. He often had to force him gently to the piano or write the lyrics first in an effort to stimulate the usually prolific Romberg."[3]

Romberg was not on the cutting edge of popular music, but his music was enormously popular for decades. Theatre historian Gerald Mast observed that "the Golden Age of American operetta coincided with the Golden Age of the American revue."[4] Indeed, in May 1928, Dorothy Fields and Jimmy McHugh premiered their first big hit on Broadway, the forward-looking, jazzy revue *Blackbirds of 1928*, and in September 1928 the Romberg-Hammerstein operetta *The New Moon* opened. *Blackbirds of 1928* ran for 518 performances, and *The New Moon* ran for 509.

In the 1930s, Romberg, Kern, Hammerstein, and Dorothy Fields were all in Hollywood, along with many other people who had been displaced from work on Broadway. They were not only colleagues but friends, participating in a range of social activities. Kern's biographer Gerald Bordman relates, "The Kerns often met Dorothy Fields and Sigmund Romberg at parties where George Gershwin was also a guest. Time and again either Gershwin alone was asked to play, or if George usurped the piano, as was his wont, no one protested that Jerry or Romberg should be given their hour. Dorothy long afterward remembered driving home from such an affair with Jerry, and Jerry poignantly complaining that he and Romberg were never asked to play. He wondered out loud whether they no longer liked his songs, or thought he could not play well. Of course, neither Kern nor Romberg was the pyrotechnical pianist that Gershwin or Rudolf Friml was, but both clearly deserved more courteous treatment."[5]

Up in Central Park was Romberg's first Broadway hit in almost two decades. Only one show with new music by Romberg had appeared on Broadway in the 1930s, *May Wine*, with lyrics by Oscar Hammerstein II. Romberg's *Sunny River* opened on December 4, 1941, and closed after only thirty-six performances. *Up in Central Park* was also Dorothy Fields's return as a lyricist after several years of writing books with her brother for Cole Porter shows.

The generating idea for *Up in Central Park* was, appropriately enough, an idea of the place itself. When work on the musical was well under way, a news article reported that the producer, Michael Todd, had "wanted to do a show about old New York for some time and thought that the park would readily lend itself to such an enterprise."[6] Todd brought his idea to Herbert and Dorothy Fields, quite naturally, since they had worked with him on his previous success, *Mexican Hayride*. The choice of composer may have been more problematic. It must have seemed apparent to Todd that the kind of show he had in mind would not have been Cole Porter's cup of tea. Perhaps Porter thought otherwise. His biographer William McBrien reported, "Porter was also waiting with some eagerness to see a story set in the 1890s which Herbert and Dorothy Fields had plans to send him."[7] Porter's next projects after *Mexican Hayride* were *Seven Lively Arts* (1944), produced by Todd's rival Billy Rose, and the turn-of-the-century story *Around the World in Eighty Days* (1946) produced by Orson Welles. Jerome Kern had already written, with Oscar Hammerstein II, a musical set in old Hoboken, *Sweet Adeline* (1929), with a score based on melodies of the period. Moreover, he was busy in Hollywood, enjoying life as a grandfather and writing the score for *Can't Help Singing*. One way or another, Romberg was chosen for the job.

Herb and Dorothy claimed they chose the time period for the show, around 1870, after seeing some Currier and Ives prints of Central Park at that time in the prestigious bookstore Brentanos. Perhaps other factors entered in as well. The 1870s was the time of Lew Fields's childhood. Of course, Central Park was a long way from the Bowery where Fields spent his youth, and the characters who populate the musical are Anglo-Saxon and Irish rather than Jewish immigrants. But interviews with Dorothy and Herbert from around this time suggest that their late father was much on their minds. In a less personal vein, the success of *Oklahoma!* demonstrated, among other things, that the New York public, during wartime, was receptive to stories of America's past, stories to inspire national pride. One possible view of theatrical trends, decade by decade, is that in the 1920s, Broadway audiences were swept away with the joys of being young and in the moment, whereas in the 1930s they were concerned with the immediate economic, political, and social worries of young and old alike. In the 1940s, the Broadway audience was not so fixated on its present—it wanted to consider its past as well.

Up in Central Park is a mixture of fact and fiction. Similar to stage and screen biographies—musical or otherwise—its story was essentially fiction with an anchor in history. In this it differs from *Oklahoma!* or *Carousel*, which are also set in the past, but without characters who had actually made news in their time. Two earlier shows with scores by Romberg that show historical characters doing things they never actually did are *Blossom Time* (1921), a pseudo-biography of Franz Schubert, and *My Maryland* (1927), which features Stonewall Jackson and Barbara Frietschie.

Before *Up in Central Park*, Dorothy Fields's reputation as a lyricist and librettist had been based on up-to-the-minute shows and films making contemporary references and using contemporary slang. *Stars in Your Eyes*, for example, satirized the Hollywood dream factory, which both Dorothy and composer Arthur Schwartz knew all too well. Even if the play that served as a source for a musical was a comedy ten or twenty years old (as was the case, for example, with *Let's Face It*) the language was altered, and the situations were brought up to date. Starting with *Up in Central Park*, the Broadway musicals Dorothy worked on for more than a decade all ignored the twentieth century.

Time and place being settled, characters and plot came next. The characters drawn from history are William Marcy "Boss" Tweed, the Tammany leader who functions as a comic villain, and Thomas Nast, who drew scathing cartoons of Tweed for *Vanity Fair*. In the musical, Nast is a friend of the romantic hero. There are two pairs of lovers, one pair more serious and one more comic. This practice has roots that go as far back as eighteenth-century Italian opera. The main romantic pair, Rosie Moore and John Matthews, disagree about politics; he is a reporter for the *New York Times*, crusading against Boss Tweed, and she is the daughter of a Tweed employee. The secondary pair, Bessie O'Cahane and Joe Steward, are primarily dancers; they are less important to the plot but contribute to the entertainment. Rosie and Bessie both have Irish fathers. The stereotype of the jovial Irishman equipped with colorful language and a humorous take on life appeared in plays and movies for decades. The earliest comic duos on the American stage, such as Harrigan and Hart, were Irish; before Weber and Fields invented the "Dutch" characters Mike and Meyer, they impersonated Irish characters.

There is another sociological element. The heroine is ambitious—she wants to achieve fame as a singer. As ambitions go, this is a fairly typical one in a musical. In contrast, *Bloomer Girl*, a musical set in 1861, which premiered in 1944 and was still running when *Up in Central Park* opened, has a more serious feminist heroine. Neither Rosie Moore in *Up in Central Park* nor Evaline and her aunt Dolly Bloomer in *Bloomer Girl* expect their happiness in life to be delivered to them by men. Both Rosie and Evaline have political disagreements with the men they are attracted to. But Evaline's and Dolly's ambitions have a large, generalized scope: women should have the right to wear comfortable clothing, and blacks should be free. Rosie's ambitions are purely personal: she wants to sing on stage. This story is not autobiographical, of course, but both Dorothy and Herbert could have drawn on their own memory banks for the feeling of wanting to achieve success as performers.

The librettists' research supplied not only some of the characters but also some of the language. They commented in the souvenir program book, "By the middle of last summer we were knee deep in Victorian slang."[8] The very first number, "Up from the Gutter" shows some of the results of this research. The lyric contains abundant linguistic markers to establish time and place. Bessie sings about putting on "rubber-bosom pads" and a "myrtle green polonaise." The millionaire Bessie dreams of snaring will have "Dundrearie whiskers" and a "Prince Albert coat." She imagines when she has entered society she will hobnob with Henry Irving and Horace Greeley. This careful depiction of details of the daily life of the time recalls Hammerstein's description of "The Surrey with the Fringe on Top," which has "isenglass curtains y' can roll right down in case there's a change in the weather."

Herbert and Dorothy wrote that before they had worked out the plot they "had a very strong determination that we would end the play with a big orchestra on the band-stand in the Mall."[9] The second act is weaker than the first with regard to plot. This may be in part because the end of the play is concerned less with action than with ambience. The Fieldses were supported in their view of the play by Mike Todd. According to his son, "Todd's conceptions were primarily visual, not verbal or musical."[10] Early in the course of writing the libretto, another shaping visual idea occurred to the book writers—an ice-skating scene suggested by a Currier and Ives print. Herbert and Dorothy may also have been aware of a successful ice-skating ballet, *Les Patineurs*, choreographed by Frederick Ashton and set to the music of Giacomo Meyerbeer, which had premiered in London in 1937. An ice-skating dance was similarly effective in *Up in Central Park*.

Dance had not been a major component in the three shows that Dorothy and Herbert had done with Cole Porter. For musicals set in the present, in which the major stars were singers, like Ethel Merman, or comics, like Danny Kaye, there was little purpose in a major ballet. *Mexican Hayride*, which had a more decorative slant than *Let's Face It* or *Something for the Boys*, had ballet sequences choreographed by Paul Haakon, but hopes for the success of the show hung on the comic business provided by Bobby Clark.

Up in Central Park had no big stars in the cast, but it had spectacular ballet scenes. One of the ripple effects of the success of *Oklahoma!* was that ballets, preferably dream ballets, became *de rigueur*. Indeed, more than one reviewer thought it worth pointing out that *Up in Central Park* had no dream ballet. *Variety* reported, "Give credit to Todd and his lieutenants also for keeping ballet in its place. There are plenty of dances and some fine ones, but the ballet effects are not allowed to sprawl all over the stage and interrupt the legitimate action, as has been perhaps too frequent in recent tryouts." Helen Tamaris, the choreographer for *Up in Central Park*, had won renown for incorporating jazz and Negro spirituals into dances she had created for her own company. The *Billboard* reviewer praised the dance performances especially: "If only for the ice-skating ballet for the Currier and Ives songs, it's worth the while sitting through the entire production. Also on the plus side is the Maypole Dance and the concert in the park finale with the pit band up on the stage."

The use of different musical tableaux to mark different seasons of the year brings to mind an immensely successful movie musical that had opened a few months earlier, *Meet Me in St. Louis*. The movie is set three decades later (1903–4) and in one scene presents the possibility of moving from St. Louis to New York as a potentially dreadful fate. Nevertheless, both *Up in Central Park* and *Meet Me in St. Louis* are deeply dipped in nostalgia for a more innocent and more colorful America.

Dorothy Fields and Sigmund Romberg worked together on only this one show, but they seem to have enjoyed their collaboration. (A few years later, Romberg collaborated with Dorothy's brother Joseph on *The Girl in Pink Tights*, but Romberg died before the show reached Broadway.) Romberg reported about Dorothy, "She's very clever with lyrics; she draws something out of you."[11] Romberg did not have a reputation for being sensitive to the meaning and nuance of words—quite the contrary. When he arrived in New York, he had very little knowledge of English, and even decades later his spoken English was highly idiosyncratic. Oscar Hammerstein II coined the term "Rommyisms" to denote Romberg's malapropisms. Romberg carried a carefree attitude toward language into his work as well. "In 1932 he went to Paris to write an original French operetta, *Rose de France*, although he didn't know a word of French."[12] An often repeated anecdote illustrating Romberg's disregard for texts has its setting at a game of bridge. "When Romberg could not figure out how many trump cards Jerry [Kern] held, Jerry began to whistle Romberg's 'One Alone.' Romberg failed to catch the hint, advising Kern after the hand, 'Who knows from lyrics?' "[13]

Romberg's preference was to compose the music first, then hand the melody over to the lyricist. Perhaps after that he lost interest. Dorothy was flexible in her collaborations with composers. She received melodies from Romberg and Fritz Kreisler and then set words to them without further consultation. That is also how she wrote the lyric for "Lovely to Look At," although once she had met Kern, Dorothy preferred to work side by side with him. For some songs she did with Cy Coleman, the lyrics came first. It was part of her polished professionalism that she could create as the circumstances demanded.

Up in Central Park opened in New York on January 27, 1945, three months after *Bloomer Girl* and three months before *Carousel*. Mike Todd put a lot of his abilities at promotion (some might say hucksterism) into ensuring its success. For example, he arranged for a post-premiere dinner party at the Tavern-on-the-Green in Central Park for selected guests, including much of the New York press, with everyone transported from the theater to the restaurant in horse-drawn carriages. *New York Post* columnist Earl Wilson, who reported on the party but not on the play, noted that among the six hundred guests were Orson Welles, Ethel Merman, Jeanette MacDonald, and Herbert Bayard Swope. Todd's son relates, "The party was still going on at dawn. Sunday afternoon it was difficult to remember when the show stopped and the party began, but both the show and the party were widely acclaimed by the press."[14]

Up in Central Park ran for 504 performances in New York before going out on tour, making it even more successful than *Something for the Boys* and *Mexican Hayride*. All of the critics liked the look of the show and praised the lighting design and sets of Howard Bay and the costumes of Grace Houston and Ernest Schraps. Kronenberger wrote that Bay was "the real hero of the evening." Bay's "stylish, glossy, and amusing sets evoke an era." Burton Rascoe wrote that "a snowfall for the musical number 'April Snow' is one of the most enchanting scenes ever devised for the stage." The music was also praised, sometimes faintly but more often enthusiastically. In general, the reviewers found that the score was just what one expected of Sigmund Romberg, but they split on whether this was a good thing or not. According to Kronenberger, "Sigmund Romberg's rather pretty but dated and undiversified score has a slightly sedative effect." Rascoe said that "most of Romberg's music is lush and singable and full of romantic schmaltz. . . . But Romberg has a gift for knowing just when two-step and waltz time need relief; and so he breaks the time and mood into fast comedic pieces such as 'Rip Van Winkle,' 'The Fireman's Bride' and 'The Birds and the Bees.'" Maurie Orodenker, reporting on the Philadelphia tryout, thought that the score was the strongest aspect of the show. He suggested that, "following the operetta pattern, much of the music promises to live on."

Indeed, several reviewers wanted to label *Up in Central Park* an operetta. Lines between genres such as operetta, musical comedy, and musical can easily blur, especially if one of the genres is disintegrating. One might ask if *Up in Central Park* belongs more in the category of operetta than, say, *Oklahoma!* or *Bloomer Girl*. It was booked into the New Century Theatre, a house that had been used for other operettas and was uptown from the theater district hub. To some extent, Romberg's name was synonymous with operetta but his writing for *Up in Central Park* has a more contemporary sound than, for example, *The Student Prince*, and Dorothy Fields's lyrics, for all her research into historical language, give the songs a resonance with the present. One might agree with Ethan Mordden that "operetta was over, because the musical play had absorbed it: *Up in Central Park, Carousel, The Firebrand of Florence, Kiss Me, Kate.* If musical comedy can sound like Puccini, who needs operetta?"[15]

The most critically disputed aspect of the production was the book. The most negative reviews found it too long, dull, and lacking in humor. The reviewer at the *New Yorker* thought that "its book . . . is one of those self-consciously quaint jobs that are apt to enchant the admirers of beer-hall melodrama while plunging others into an emotional vacuum not unlike death." But the book also had its supporters. The critic reporting on the Philadelphia opening for *Variety* said, "The real news is the book by Herbert and Dorothy Fields. This is really an exception to the old familiar adage about the book being the invariable weak link. . . . The story of 'Central Park' is adult, authentic, nostalgic and always believable; and it doesn't keep the audience waiting impatiently for song or dance numbers to interrupt the story development." In a thoughtful and balanced review, John Chapman noted, "Mr. Todd, Mr. Romberg, Mr. Bay and the authors, Herbert and Dorothy Fields, have given care and affection to 'Up in Central Park.' They have wanted, I think, to shift into a lower gear—to make a musical which is warm, gentle and affectionate instead of one which is brash, fast and smart-smarty. On the whole they have succeeded."

Mike Todd's gamble on a little-known cast paid off. All of the performers were praised by reviewers. The role of Rosie Moore had been played at the Philadelphia tryout by Rose Inghram, but she was replaced for the New York opening by Maureen Cannon, whom reviewers liked very well. Robert Garland seemed entirely captivated. "Frankly, I've no adequate words with which to praise the little lady who pretends to be Rosie Moore," he wrote. "She's got everything! She's got good looks, added to which is piquancy. She's got charm, added to which is sincerity. She's got a voice, added to which is the ability to make the most of it." Betty Bruce, as Rosie's best friend, Bessie, was also praised, especially for her dancing and for her rendition of "The Birds and the Bees," which she sang with Maureen Cannon. Wilbur Evans, in the role of John Matthews, was thought to resemble Ronald Colman by one reviewer and Thomas Dewey by another. Several critics felt that his singing was better than his acting. Many critics praised Noah Beery as Boss Tweed. John Chapman declared, "He has the paunch, the arrogance and the punch to fit the character and his part in the singing of 'Boss Tweed' is one of the high spots of the evening." Otis L. Guernsey Jr. also praised Beery. "The only matter for regret in the show," he wrote, "is that Herbert and Dorothy Fields haven't made the Boss and his satellites a more important part of the story."

The sabbatical Dorothy had taken from the writing of lyrics had a beneficial effect. The lyrics she wrote for *Up in Central Park* received, deservedly, high praise from reviewers. The critic in *Variety* found the lyrics "almost priceless, both the comedy and the serious ones." Ward Morehouse noted, "Dorothy Fields, besides serving as co-author of the book, has done the lyric-writing job and it's one of her best." Entering another time and place and doing research on language had fueled her creativity and was a useful strategy for many of her later works.

"Close as Pages in a Book" was praised by almost every reviewer, and went on to become a standard. It is a duet in the play, but is now frequently sung as a solo. Bing Crosby had a hit record of the song in the 1940s, and Vic Damone in the 1950s; in 1993, Barbara Cook recorded it on a CD dedicated to the lyrics of Dorothy Fields.[16]

"It Doesn't Cost You Anything to Dream," another duet, was cited almost as often by reviewers, but it did not become a hit away from the show. The acknowledgment by someone in love that his or her hopes and ambitions outstrip his or her financial means, is one which Dorothy explored several times. Her earliest big hit, "I Can't Give You Anything but Love," treats the subject playfully. "I'll Buy You a Star," sung by the romantic lead in *A Tree Grows in Brooklyn*, is a more fervently romantic take on the subject. "It Doesn't Cost You Anything to Dream" recalls to me the final couplet of Sonnet 87 by Shakespeare, "Thus have I had thee, as a dream doth flatter, In sleep a king, but, waking, no such matter." Interestingly, the dreams John and Rosie sing about in this duet have to do with their individual ambitions—John wants to "write the truth and not be disciplined"; Rosie wants to "sing like Jenny Lind." At this point in the musical, they do not seem to be dreaming of a life with one another.[17]

Two comic numbers are songs that tell stories—"Rip Van Winkle," sung by Boss Tweed, and "The Fireman's Bride," sung by Rosie. The song that tells a story has a long history both in Europe and America in opera, art song, and in popular song. In opera, the song that tells a story can be used to fill in events that occurred before the opera began. Think, for example, of the start of *Il Trovatore*, in which Ferrando, the captain of the Count di Luna's guards, tells of an old gypsy burned at the stake for witchcraft. Freestanding story songs or ballads could exist for sheer entertainment or for moral instruction. Some very popular songs from a period slightly later than the one in which

Up in Central Park is set, such as "After the Ball" (1892) or "A Bird in a Gilded Cage" (1900), strive for both entertainment and edification. The tale of "Rip Van Winkle" is told playfully, with rapid-fire rhyming heightening the comic effect. For example, we are told that his shrewish wife would "nag him . . . tag him . . . drag him . . . [and] gag him." "The Fireman's Bride" starts out like a set piece, a show-within-a-show, but in fact John is so offended by Rosie's singing the song in public that he argues with her and breaks off their relationship at the end of the first act.

Although Dorothy Fields did not work with Sigmund Romberg or Michael Todd again, some of the paths she explored in *Up in Central Park* were followed in her next five works for the stage.

Lew Fields (left) and Joe Weber dressed as Mike and Meyer.
Weber and Fields used these personae to entertain audiences for decades.
(Library of Congress)

*The Fields family in front of their home on Riverside Drive in 1910:
from left, Dorothy (age six), Lew (forty-three), Frances (sixteen),
Rose (thirty-five), Herbert (thirteen), and Joseph (fifteen).
(New York Public Library, Billy Rose Theatre Collection)*

Dorothy Fields (left) playing François Villon, opposite Miriam Rosenwasser, in "If I Were King" by Richard Rodgers and Lorenz Hart, performed in March 1923. (New York Public Library, Music Division, Richard Rodgers Scrapbooks)

Dorothy Fields in 1930. By twenty-six, she had married and separated from Dr. Jack Wiener and had seen her songs performed at the Cotton Club and on Broadway. (Photofest)

Dorothy Fields and Jimmy McHugh wrote songs together for almost a decade, both in New York and in Hollywood. They also performed together on stage and on radio. (Photofest)

Dorothy started writing songs for films in 1930. Over the next decade she worked with Jimmy McHugh, Oscar Levant, Jerome Kern, and others. (Courtesy of Eliza Lahm Brewster)

Dorothy Fields and Jerome Kern worked side by side at the piano, inspired— or not—by the bust of Richard Wagner. (Library of Congress)

Ginger Rogers and Fred Astaire, almost airborne, in the "Pick Yourself Up" number from "Swing Time." It was neither "Pick Yourself Up" nor "A Fine Romance" but rather "The Way You Look Tonight" from this same film that won Jerome Kern and Dorothy Fields an Academy Award in 1936. (Photofest)

In Hollywood Dorothy found not only new collaborators but also a large circle of friends. At this festive event are (from left) George Gershwin, Doris Wagner, Ira Gershwin, Dorothy Fields, and Jerome Kern. (Photofest)

The Fields family (clockwise from left): Frances Rose, Herbert,
Dorothy, Lew, and Joseph. Notice the portrait of Dorothy on the wall.
(Courtesy of Eliza Lahm Brewster)

Dorothy Fields congratulates Ethel Merman on her performance in "Stars in Your Eyes," 1939. (Getty Images)

Herbert Fields, Danny Kaye, and Dorothy Fields in a rehearsal conference for "Let's Face It," 1941. (Photofest)

Dorothy and Herbert Fields at work together on a script, 1942. Note the dictionary and notebook on the floor, the flowers on the table, the cigarettes in their hands. (Getty Images)

Dorothy Fields's husband, Eli Lahm, and their son, David Lahm. (Courtesy of Eliza Lahm Brewster)

At a rehearsal for "Up in Central Park," 1945. In the front row are Sigmund Romberg and Mike Todd; in the middle row, Dorothy Fields, Herbert Fields, and Helen Tamaris; in the third row, an unnamed manager and secretary. (Photofest)

The stars of "Annie Get Your Gun" with the creative and production team, 1946. In front, Ray Middleton and Ethel Merman; standing in back, Josh Logan, Irving Berlin, Richard Rodgers, Oscar Hammerstein II, Dorothy Fields, and Herbert Fields. (Photofest)

Arthur Schwartz and Dorothy Fields at work on
"A Tree Grows in Brooklyn," 1951. (Library of Congress)

Dorothy Fields had a great gift for fitting comfortably in a "man's world" or a "woman's world." Here, she is chairman of the "Festival of Song" luncheon for the Federation of Jewish Philanthropies. On the left is Dorothy Rodgers, an honorary chairman, and in the middle, Mary Martin, a guest of honor. (Photofest)

Dorothy Fields in 1953. She was one of the plaintiffs in an antitrust suit that the Songwriters of America brought against the broadcasting companies. (Photofest)

Joseph Fields and Dorothy Fields, 1959. (Photofest)

*Bob Fosse, Shirley MacLaine, and Gwen Verdon on the
movie set of "Sweet Charity." (Photofest)*

*Even in her sixties Dorothy was able to put over a song.
At the piano is Cy Coleman. (Photofest)*

ANNIE GET YOUR GUN

• • •

Annie Get Your Gun, for which Herbert and Dorothy Fields wrote the book, was the most popular and successful stage work Dorothy ever worked on. A number of famous people associated with the show have, in interviews, disclosed their own point of view on the making and meaning of this musical. This chapter, more than the others, is larded with quotations, not all taken at face value, in an attempt to get a multidimensional view of the work.

One story Dorothy Fields told about the genesis of *Annie Get Your Gun* goes like this. "Sometimes an idea for a show drops down from God's hands into yours. In 1945, I was working at the Stage Door Canteen, and I met a charming lady who was the head of Traveler's Aid. And she was telling me a story of a young sergeant who had been to Coney Island and had come in stoned, with kewpie dolls and lamps and cigars and candy, and across his tunic he had a row of sharpshooter's medals. And when I heard 'sharpshooter,' the idea struck: Wouldn't it be marvelous to have Ethel Merman as Annie Oakley?"[1]

The Stage Door Canteen operated in New York from March 2, 1942, to October 28, 1945. Irving Berlin saluted its work in his ballad "I Left My Heart at the Stage Door Canteen," written for his show *This Is the Army*. It is thought that the several Stage Door Canteens in the United States and Europe served more than eleven million people in uniform. *Variety* estimated that the hostesses at the Stage Door Canteens had danced ten million miles by the time they closed. Dorothy was proud of the work she did there and preserved in her scrapbook a photo of her standing next to Catherine Cornell as they serve food in a cafeteria line. This photo is a still from a movie called *Stage Door Canteen*, made in 1943, with dozens of stars in cameo appearances, among them Judith Anderson, Tallulah Bankhead, Ray Bolger, Helen Hayes, Katharine Hepburn, Gypsy Rose Lee, Ethel Merman, Harpo Marx, Paul Muni, George Raft, George Jessel, Yehudi Menuhin, Ethel Waters, and Ed Wynn.

Dorothy told the same general story, but with an important variant to Max Wilk. "During the war, my late husband did volunteer work down at

Penn Station, for Traveler's Aid, from midnight to seven A.M. And one of the ladies told him one night about a kid who'd just come in, a young soldier. Very drunk, he'd been to Coney Island and had kewpie dolls and lamps and every piece of junk you could possibly win. How come? Across his chest he had a row of sharpshooter's medals. And as if out of the sky, from Heaven, comes this idea. Because my brother and I had a commitment to write another show for Mike Todd. Annie Oakley—the sharpshooter! With Ethel Merman to play her!"[2] This version of the anecdote is one of the very few times Dorothy talks publicly about her husband, in any context.

The seed of the idea of a musical about Annie Oakley fell on ground that had been fertilized by Dorothy's family. During his teen years, Lew Fields actually ran into the Buffalo Bill Wild West Show, in which Annie Oakley later performed. The company with which Weber and Fields was touring intersected the Buffalo Bill Wild West Show in Paterson, New Jersey, and competed for lodging there. (The difficulties of getting the proprietor of a hotel to take in a company of performers turns up as a theme in the opening of *Annie Get Your Gun*.) Lew told anecdotes about his encounters with the show to the press, and presumably to his family as well.

Moreover, Dorothy was not the first member of the Fields family to explore the entertainment value of a story about Annie Oakley. A decade earlier, Joseph Fields had provided the story for the movie *Annie Oakley*, a 1935 RKO film directed by George Stevens, starring Barbara Stanwyck.[3] Annie Oakley and her husband, Frank Butler, both died in 1926; this movie appeared less than a decade after their deaths. Several elements from the film reappear in the musical. The historical characters who show up in both the film and the musical, in addition to Annie Oakley herself, are Buffalo Bill and Sitting Bull. The sharpshooter Annie falls in love with is renamed Toby Walker in the film; the musical uses the real name of the marksman Annie competed with and married, Frank Butler. In the movie, Annie's family consists of a mother and a younger brother and sister; in the musical she seems to no longer have parents, which increases the importance of her show-business mentors, but she has many younger brothers and sisters. In both the film and the musical, Sitting Bull is an important agent in bringing Annie and the man she loves together. In the film, this bringing together is a physical act. Sitting Bull spots the elusive Toby Walker, who has left Buffalo Bill's show, and drives Annie to him for a reconciliation that ends the film. In the musical, Sitting Bull is a mentor and counselor for Annie, adopting her as an honorary Indian and giving her important advice along the way.

An important prop in both the film and the musical is an advertising poster. At the start of the film, Annie falls in love with Toby Walker the moment she sees his image on an advertising poster—a bit like Tamino falling in love with Pamina the moment he sees her image in *The Magic Flute*. In the musical, the poster image that causes a psychic shift in Annie is of herself. Theater historian Andrea Most observed, "In a pivotal scene of the play, the newly minted star Annie Oakley discovers an enormous poster with her picture on it. She 'walks up to the picture slowly' and exclaims in wonder: 'It's me! Was I up there all the time?' . . . After gazing at her picture on the billboard for a moment, Annie sings a verse of 'There's No Business Like Show Business' in which she recognizes—and even pays tribute to—the confusing relationship between the 'real' Annie and the 'theatrical' star."[4]

The film and the musical both show Annie Oakley deliberately losing a shooting contest. In the film, the shooting match between Annie and Toby comes about twenty minutes after the first scene. Annie's character in the film, from beginning to end, is strikingly docile and pliable.[5] When Annie's mother says, "I hope you ain't gonna be the cause of that young man losing his position," the smitten Annie needs no further provocation to miss the next shot. Moreover, losing the contest is of no great importance in the plot, since she is invited to join Buffalo Bill's show anyway. In the musical, the shooting match between Annie and Frank Butler is saved for the end of the second act. Annie's pride in her talent, her identification of herself with her talent, is much greater in the musical, and her acceptance of her loss of the second shooting match to Butler has much more emotional weight. Unlike the film's version, in which Annie's mother encourages her to miss the shot out of a kind of feminine courtesy and reticence, in the musical Sitting Bull advises Annie, "You do fine. Keep missing—you win." Perhaps Dorothy, as coauthor of the book, knew better than the screenwriters the different ways a talented woman could be strong when choosing to reveal or conceal abilities.

It is possible that the heavenly part of the idea, as far as Dorothy was concerned, was not especially a story about Annie Oakley, but rather Ethel Merman impersonating Annie Oakley. Annie was one of Merman's most notable roles, but far from a typical one. Before *Annie Get Your Gun*, Merman usually played a tough, urban broad. Part of that persona is transferred to Annie—the feistiness, fearlessness, and the awareness of her own talent. But Annie is a romantic innocent, inexperienced and vulnerable, and portraying this part of a woman's personality was uncharted territory for Merman. Ethan Mordden commented, "Her comically slackjawed look of infatuation in her meeting scene with her vis-à-vis, Frank Butler . . . established a new concept of Merman, all unknown to the ways of love."[6]

After their success with *Up in Central Park*, Herbert and Dorothy had thought that their next show would be produced by Mike Todd. They brought him their Annie Oakley idea, but he rejected it. "We went to see Mike, to try the idea out on him. And he said, 'Merman? That old—! She'll never work again!' We asked him if he'd do it anyway, and he said he wouldn't touch it."[7] Ethel Merman sometimes rubbed her colleagues the wrong way, but she had been a significant moneymaker for Todd in his hit, *Something for the Boys*. Merman had withdrawn from a production of *Sadie Thompson* (produced by A. P. Waxman) in 1944, ostensibly because of a disagreement over some lyrics. Was it for that reason that Todd thought she would not work again? Hugh Fordin tells the story slightly differently. Dorothy "and Herb went to see Mike Todd, with whom they had a commitment for a show with Merman. Dorothy feverishly told him of their idea and the great show they could do. 'A show about a dame who knows from nothing but guns? I wouldn't touch it,' replied Todd. . . .'Are we out of our commitment, Mike?' she asked, 'because we want to do the show.' 'You got it—yes. I don't want any part of it!' "[8] Todd's ability to predict what the public wanted was far from infallible; famously, he had predicted that *Oklahoma!* would flop. After he saw the New Haven tryout he prognosticated, "No gags, no girls, no chance."[9] It is also possible that Todd much preferred to set into motion ideas that he had come up with himself.

Undeterred, Dorothy and Herbert took their idea to Rodgers and Hammerstein. After the success of *Oklahoma!*, Rodgers and Hammerstein had established auxiliary enterprises. They became music publishers under the name Williamson Music. As songwriter-publishers, they were preceded by Irving Berlin and followed by Frank Loesser. In addition, Rodgers and Hammerstein became producers, a role that may have seemed natural enough, at least to Oscar Hammerstein II, though it is hard to say who actually came up with the idea. They had great success initially with nonmusical comedies, among them *I Remember Mama* (1944) by John Van Druten, *Happy Birthday* (1947) by Anita Loos, and *John Loves Mary* (1947) by Norman Krasna. The only musicals they produced were their own works, with one important exception: *Annie Get Your Gun*.

Dorothy related that after Todd turned their offer down, "Herbert said to me, 'Okay, we're going to go to somebody else.' Now, there happened to be a meeting at ASCAP after our meeting with Todd, and the first person I saw when I came in was Oscar Hammerstein. He and Dick Rodgers were producing shows then as well as writing them. I said, 'Ockie, what do you think of Ethel Merman as Annie Oakley?' He said, 'We'll do it.' That's all! And then he said, 'Talk to Dick after the meeting.' I talked to Dick, and Dick said the same thing—'We'll do it.'"[10] All accounts agree that Rodgers and Hammerstein were immediately enthusiastic about the idea of Ethel Merman as Annie Oakley. Dorothy remembers their encounter taking place at an ASCAP meeting. Fordin thought it occurred at a Writers' War Board committee meeting that Oscar was chairing.[11] Rodgers remembered, "One morning Dorothy Fields and her brother Herb came to see Oscar and me in our office and asked, 'What do you think of Ethel Merman in a show about Annie Oakley?' Without hesitation we answered, 'Go home and write it and we'll produce it. It was a one-sentence suggestion and a one-sentence acceptance."[12]

The Fieldses and Rodgers and Hammerstein may all have agreed that Ethel Merman would be perfect as Annie Oakley, but Merman herself had not yet been consulted. Rodgers and Hammerstein asked Dorothy, "Can you get up to see Ethel?" This may have been a time when Dorothy found it a distinct business advantage to be a woman. Dorothy related that Ethel had "just gone to the hospital to have a child, by Caesarean, and she was feeling awful. I had a hell of a time getting into the hospital, but I did."[13] Ethel Merman corroborates this story. She said Dorothy called her while she was in the hospital. "'I have to see you, Mermsy,' Dorothy said. She didn't say what about, so I told her, 'I'll call my obstetrician and ask him. After all, I'm in stitches, and not from laughing.' Naturally after an operation that serious, there was pain, so I called my obstetrician. 'She may see you for fifteen minutes,' he said. So she went up to Doctors Hospital and said hello to all the nurses on the floor. She knew them very well, having been there herself, and she told them, 'I've got to see Mrs. Levitt.' 'I don't think you can see her,' they said. 'She's not very comfortable.' 'Tell her Dorothy Fields is here,' Dorothy said."[14] Dorothy could have gone to Ethel's hospital room prepared to swap stories about pregnancies and deliveries. Ethel, at age thirty-six, had just had her second child, Robert. Her daughter, also named Ethel, had been delivered by Caesarean section in 1942. Dorothy was five years older than Ethel and, in 1945, the mother of a four-year-old son and a one-year-old daughter. She was in a good position to be a supportive, sisterly friend. Merman declared that Dorothy "was one of my oldest and closest friends. She was a woman of great warmth and wide experience. . . . Dorothy was a gal who took time for friendship. She was as extravagant of her emotions as of her money. When Mom or Pop had a birthday, Dorothy would send flowers and take them to dinner. Everyone was her friend."[15] With only fifteen minutes allowed for a visit, Dorothy got right to the point. "I went over to her bed and I leaned down and said, 'Merm, what would you think of yourself as Annie Oakley?' She looked up from her hospital bed, and blinked, and said, 'I'll do it.' It was as simple as that."[16] Actually, Merman remembered, "I was having postoperative gas pains and felt like anything but a lady sharpshooter. I asked Dorothy to give me time to get out of the hospital. Then I'd decide. She agreed."[17]

With producers, librettist, lyricist, and star lined up, the next essential was the composer. The first choice, for many reasons, was Jerome Kern. Both Dorothy and Oscar had worked with Kern—Dorothy on films, Oscar on films and Broadway musicals. They had the highest admiration for his music and the warmest personal affection for the man. Rodgers, too, was a great admirer of Kern's. Kern was not in the best of health—the heart attack in 1938 had taken a toll—but he was not in retirement. In 1945, he was providing songs for MGM's *Centennial Summer*. He was also involved, somewhat reluctantly, in MGM's biography of him, a film which would appear in 1946 with the title *Till the Clouds Roll By*.

Rodgers suggested that it was easy to bring Kern into the project. "We mailed him a script and I sent him a wire: It would be one of the greatest honors in my life if you would consent to write the music for this show. Soon afterward we received an enthusiastic response."[18] Fordin, on the other hand, wrote that Hammerstein had to apply considerable powers of persuasion to get Kern to agree to come to New York to write a new show. Kern's last Broadway show, *Very Warm for May* (1939), which he had written with Hammerstein, was not a success. "Oscar used the revival [of *Show Boat*] to try to persuade Jerry to write a show with Dorothy Fields which he and Dick would produce on Broadway. Jerry was interested but resistant. Referring to *Very Warm for May*, he said, 'I'm not going to go through that again.' Oscar told him that the revival would help him get the feel of the theater after all his movie years. 'I'm too old,' said Jerry. 'That's no excuse,' Oscar retorted. 'If you said you'd written enough, I'd be convinced. This would be your one hundred and seventh score, and I figure you're good for another forty-eight.' He reminded his friend of the telegram he had sent to [Oscar's son] Jimmy on the day of his birth, promising to do a show with him in 1947. Finally Jerry agreed to do it."[19] It is possible that Rodgers's effulgent telegram makes more sense in the context of trying to persuade a reluctant Kern.

Kern had voiced disillusionment and discouragement about working in Hollywood. His biographer noted, "Jerry was displeased with the way the musical numbers were being handled [in *Till the Clouds Roll By*]. He complained to [Harry] Warren about myriad infelicities, such as the way the orchestrations went from the verse into the chorus of 'Who?' Warren retorted that Jerry should protest, but Jerry replied he had all but given up fighting Hollywood's strange ideas and ways. He missed the authority Broadway granted him to impose his taste on his material. In fact, he missed Broadway."[20] New York beckoned with two offers: writing the Annie Oakley show and working on a revival of *Show Boat*. Before he left California, he told friends there that he might permanently resettle in New York.

Jerome and Eva Kern arrived in New York on November 2, 1945, and checked into the St. Regis Hotel. On Monday, November 5, Kern was scheduled to be at a chorus audition for *Show Boat* at 2 P.M., and Dorothy Fields was scheduled to have lunch with Eva. According to Fordin, Dorothy had called in the morning and gotten scolded by Kern. "'You know better than to call at this hour. Eva's asleep, but I'll leave her a message on the bathroom mirror where she's sure to see it.' He took a bar of soap and scribbled on the mirror, 'Meet the bitch at Pavillion at 1 o'clock! See you later and don't eat too much!'"[21] This anecdote does not ring true to me. For one thing, it seems a long message to write in soap. For another, given the impermanence of the medium, the only people who could have seen this message were Jerome, Eva, and the chambermaid who cleaned it up. So who passed it on? Even if Jerry had referred to Dorothy as "the bitch," it seems doubtful that Eva Kern would have repeated the message in that way. But it is also true that, many years later, both Harry Warren and Cy Coleman complained about Dorothy phoning too early in the morning.

Late that morning, Kern left the hotel to do some shopping for antiques. His biographer Gerald Bordman described his last conscious hour this way: "Stopping at the corner for a light, he suddenly collapsed on the street. Patrolman Joseph Cribben saw him fall and radioed for an ambulance. The composer, still unconscious, was taken by automobile and ferry to City Hospital on Welfare Island.[22] Authorities were disconcerted to discover the patient carried no clear-cut identification. But a card identified him as a member of ASCAP. Staff at ASCAP notified Hammerstein's office. Hammerstein's assistant, Leighton Brill, took the call and promptly phoned his boss at the Dramatists' Guild. Hammerstein summoned his physician, Dr. Harold Hyman, and the two rushed to Welfare Island."[23] The people closest to Kern were notified. Were Eva and Dorothy still at lunch when they found out, or had they gone their respective ways? Betty Kern was notified in California. Rodgers remembered that he was with Hammerstein when the news came in. "Someone at ASCAP had the presence of mind to get in touch with Oscar, who was then with me at a meeting of the Dramatists Guild at the St. Regis Hotel. When we were notified of what had happened, we got a cab and rushed over to the hospital."[24] Kern was moved to Doctor's Hospital (where Lorenz Hart had died two years earlier). Rooms in the hospital were provided for Eva, Betty, Oscar, and Dorothy Fields, so they could remain with Kern. Dorothy had remained at her father's deathbed in 1941. Now she was keeping the vigil again, for a man similarly dear to her. She recalled, "That was the worst week of my life. The worst week of everybody's life. Horrible."[25] Kern died November 11.

Soon after his death, several radio stations, including WQXR, WOR, and WNEW broadcast tribute programs of Kern's music. A one-hour coast-to-coast broadcast on CBS, arranged by ASCAP, included the reading of a telegram from President Truman: "I am among the grateful millions who have played and listened to the music of Jerome Kern, and I wish to be among those of his fellow Americans who pay him tribute today. His melodies will live in our voices and warm our hearts for many years to come, for they are the kind of simple, honest songs that belong to no time or fashion."

A small private funeral service was held at the Ferncliff Crematory in Ardsley-on-Hudson, New York, on November 12. Among the fifty people who attended, in addition to Kern's widow and daughter, were Dorothy Fields, her husband, her mother, her brother Herbert, and her brother Joseph and his wife, Marion. For all of them, but especially Dorothy, it was like losing a member of their own family. Also among the mourners were Irving and Ellin Berlin, Cole and Linda Porter, Oscar and Dorothy Hammerstein, Richard and Dorothy Rodgers, Otto and Eloise Harbach, Robert Russell and Louise Bennett, Andre Kostelanetz and Lily Pons, Edna Ferber, and Sigmund Romberg.

When Rodgers had agreed to produce a show about Annie Oakley, he thought, "With Dorothy and Herb writing it, with Merman playing the colorful sharpshooter, there was no way the show could fail."[26] But of course a good musical requires a good score. With the death of Kern, who had been everyone's first choice, a new composer had to be found. One might have thought that Rodgers himself, composer of *Oklahoma!* and *Carousel*, would be ideal to step in to the breach. Rodgers said, "The idea of our writing the score was never brought up because neither Oscar nor I thought we were the right ones for it. . . . Besides, since Dorothy Fields was a highly skilled lyricist, she naturally expected to collaborate on the score."[27] As things turned out, this was not to be. Of course, since Dorothy and Herb came up with the idea they did not intend to step aside and turn the writing of the book and lyrics over to Hammerstein. And Rodgers, who had collaborated with no one but Lorenz Hart from 1925 to 1941, had now decided he would write with no one but Hammerstein. Rodgers wanted a relationship that would be mutually exclusive, binding, monogamous. He wrote that after *Oklahoma!*, "one morning I heard that Oscar's lawyer, who by then was also my lawyer, was trying to line up a new musical for Oscar to write with Jerry Kern, another one of his clients. This so upset me that I went to see the lawyer and told him how I felt. That afternoon I had lunch with Oscar at Dinty Moore's and he brought up the matter. I told him of my conviction that it would be a serious mistake, except in an emergency, for either of us to do anything professional without the other. Oscar was in complete agreement. 'Then we can consider this a permanent partnership?' I said. 'As permanent as any partnership can be.' And it was, for the seventeen remaining years of Oscar's life."[28] Kern's death did not qualify, in Rodgers's mind, as enough of an emergency for him to write the music for the Annie Oakley project, working with Herbert and Dorothy Fields instead of Oscar Hammerstein II.

According to Rodgers, after the funeral, he and Hammerstein went into problem-solving mode. "Oscar and I were faced with the problem of finding a composer to replace [Kern] on the Annie Oakley musical. Having already chosen Kern, we felt it was extremely important to get another composer of equal stature, and this could only mean Irving Berlin."[29] It was an idea with interesting possibilities, but also with clear problems. It was Kern himself who had said, "Irving Berlin has no place in American music. He *is* American music."[30] Berlin had spent the war years tirelessly touring in the United States, Europe, and the Pacific to entertain the troops with his show, *This Is the Army*, giving more than two and a half million people a chance to forget their problems for a few hours. He returned to the United States in the spring of 1945 to work on the movie *Blue Skies* in Hollywood, went to Hawaii for the final performances of *This Is the Army*, and then returned to New York with some thoughts of doing another *Music Box Revue*.

One problem, if Berlin agreed to write the songs for the show, was that Dorothy Fields would have to give up writing the lyrics, since Irving Berlin, like Cole Porter, wrote both the lyrics and the music of his songs. When this problem was raised, Dorothy graciously agreed that she would simply work on the book and give up writing the lyrics. She recalled saying simply, "I have enough to do with the book. I don't care."[31]

The remaining problems had to do with persuading Berlin to join the project. Rodgers thought Berlin would never agree to do a show for which he was the second choice for composer, but Hammerstein wisely pointed out that they could not know this until they asked him. (Berlin's daughter Mary Ellin Barrett thought, contrariwise, that Berlin had some doubts about trying to replace a composer whom he admired as much as Kern.) Dorothy remembered that Berlin was concerned about the billing. "He said, 'Well, I don't know whether I'd want to do a show that isn't "Irving Berlin's whatsoever." So Herbert and I said, 'Irving, sorry, but this is our idea, our play, and it can't be "Irving Berlin's Annie Oakley." He said, 'Let me think about it over the weekend. And if I decide that I want to relinquish the billing that I've always had, then we'll talk about it.' He wouldn't read the first act we'd written—he wouldn't let that influence him. Monday he called up and said, 'Yes, I'd like to take a look at it.' He read the first act, and read the outline of the second act. And do you know that in the twelve days after he agreed to do the show, he wrote five songs?"[32]

Richard Rodgers remembered that Irving was concerned about writing a post-*Oklahoma!*-type musical. "As a result of *Oklahoma!*, everyone was upholding the importance of 'integration' in creating musicals, and he feared that sticking closely to the story line would inhibit him."[33] Although Berlin had integrated songs into several movies in the 1930s, on the Broadway stage he seemed to prefer revues. He had done only one book show per decade before the Annie Oakley project came up—*Watch Your Step* in 1914, *The Cocoanuts* in 1925, *Face the Music* in 1932, and *Louisiana Purchase* in 1940. Rodgers continued, "We argued that just the opposite would be true: a good libretto could offer tremendous help in stimulating ideas for songs and in showing exactly where they would be the most effective. Still, Berlin remained unconvinced. Finally I said, 'Irving, there's only one way to find out. Here's the script. Take it home, write a couple of numbers and then see how you feel about it.' That was on a Friday. On Monday morning Berlin came bounding into the office with a big grin on his face and handed over three songs."[34]

In Oscar Hammerstein II's biography by Hugh Fordin, Berlin's concern is reported to be the lyrics. " 'That hillbilly stuff, Oscar—it's not for me. I don't know the first thing about this kind of lyric.' 'That's ridiculous,' Oscar countered. 'All you have to do is drop the g's.' Berlin went home and reread the script. Then he sat down and, almost without effort, wrote 'Doin' What Comes Natur'lly' and 'They Say It's Wonderful.' A few days later he met with Oscar and Dick at their office. Still cautious, Irving said, 'Give me another week.' 'Why another week?' said Dick bluntly. 'Do you want to do it or don't you want to do it?' 'I want to do it,' said Berlin, and sheepishly pulled out his two songs. They concluded the business part of the arrangement in five minutes."[35] Berlin had a reputation for driving a hard financial bargain, but for *Annie Get Your Gun* he actually volunteered to take less money than was his due. Rodgers wrote, Berlin "was so grateful to Dorothy and Herb for the help their script had given him that he insisted that they receive part of his percentage of the show. Generosity such as this is an exceedingly rare commodity."[36] Typically, the creative team of a Broadway musical would split profits this way: one third for the librettists, one third for the lyricist, and one third for the composer. By such a formula Berlin would have received two-thirds, as lyricist and composer, and Herbert and Dorothy one-third. Instead, Berlin agreed that his due was half and that the Fieldses' was half.

It seems to me likely that all of these anecdotes have more than a grain of truth. It would be natural for Irving to discuss concerns about lyrics with Oscar, concerns about integrating the songs with the book with Dick, and concerns about billing with Dorothy and Herb. Conversely, it is possible that each of the people he spoke to interpreted Irving's concerns differently and looked for different ways to reassure him.

Once Berlin decided he was in, songs poured out of him at an astonishing rate—two or three songs in a weekend, five songs in twelve days, or ten songs in eighteen days. Berlin surprised everyone—perhaps even himself—with his fecundity on this project. Josh Logan, who had worked with Dorothy and Herb on *Stars in Your Eyes* and with Berlin on *This Is the Army*, was the director for *Annie Get Your Gun*. A few days before rehearsals began, he felt another song was needed for Annie and Frank. He recalled, "Berlin said, 'The only thing that I can possibly think is that if it's before a shooting contest, it has to be some sort of a challenge song. Okay, challenge song. Right?' At this point we were all exhausted, and we started to leave. My wife Nedda and I left Oscar's house and we took a cab. . . . As I was unlocking our door at the Lombardy, I heard the telephone ring, and I ran inside to get the phone. And Berlin, on the other end, said, 'Hello, Josh—this is Irving. What do you think of this?' And then he sang the whole damned first chorus of "Anything You Can Do, I Can Do Better"! Most amazing thing I ever experienced in my whole life! It couldn't have been more than, at most fifteen minutes from the time he'd first heard about it to the time he had me on the phone. He'd written the song—the entire first chorus. It was done like that."[37]

Two early typescripts of the libretto, preserved in the theater collection of the New York Public Library, show where the songs and ensembles were planned to be slotted in—thirteen in the first act, including one reprise, and six in the second act, including one reprise. At the time these librettos were typed, about half of the numbers were already written. They are represented in the script by titles, whereas the rest are indicated by the term "number" and the names of the characters who were to perform them. The first draft of the libretto, preserved in the Library of Congress, contains a few song titles supplied by Dorothy Fields when she thought Jerome Kern would compose the score. It is interesting that Irving Berlin did not disregard or reject these titles, but rather took them as among the gifts the book had to offer.[38]

Among the first songs completed are Annie's and Frank's initial responses to one another. "The Girl That I Marry" is a gentle waltz musically, but verbally it is a total rejection of Annie as she is. In "I Cain't Git a Man with a Gun," Annie in some sense takes on Frank's point of view and perhaps for the first time feels some dissatisfaction with herself. This stands in contrast with the attitude she had expressed in her previous song, "That Comes Naturally."[39] Other numbers finished early were two character pieces, "Moonshine Lullaby" and "I'm an Indian Too." Mary Ellin Barrett recalls, "In the family the saga of *Annie Get Your Gun* begins always with the sounds of 'I'm an Indian Too' from behind my father's closed door at 1 Gracie Square. Then the door is flung open and nine-year-old Elizabeth, Indian names fresh in her mind from school, invited in to help with the lyric. What resulted was one of the musical's comic high spots and, as it turned out, one of the most perishable."[40] Frank and Annie's duet, "They Tell Me It's Wonderful" and a second-act duet for Tommy and Winnie that was subsequently dropped, "With Music!" were also completed early on.

The rapid pace with which Berlin turned out his songs did not preclude tinkering with them and making small adjustments. The early typescripts of the libretto show that "You Can't Get a Man with a Gun" was once titled "You Can't Get a Feller with a Gun" and "I Cain't Git a Man with a Gun" before the two possibilities were combined. "They Say It's Wonderful" was first titled "They Tell Me It's Wonderful." Interestingly, the number that would become a show business anthem, "There's No Business Like Show Business," is indicated only as "Quartette—Annie, Frank, Charlie, Buffalo Bill." It is often related that "There's No Business Like Show Business" was one of the early numbers composed, but Berlin, disappointed by the reactions of Rodgers, Hammerstein, and Logan when he first played it for them, intended to drop it from the score. It was only after much subsequent pleading and reassurance that the rejected number was found and restored. The early typescript suggests that Berlin planned to put something in that spot, but he had not yet decided what. Another slight change is in the title of the musical itself. At the early stage of writing, the musical was simply called *Annie Oakley*. The new title seems to be a hybridization of *Annie Oakley* and *Jenny, Get Your Gun*, the discarded title for the hit musical *Something for the Boys*.

The cast of *Annie Get Your Gun* is very large. The piano-vocal score, published after the 1966 revival, lists thirty-seven characters plus "a full cast of singers and dancers." Of course, there was only one star in the show, Ethel Merman. But even she needed someone with whom to interact. In particular, the show required someone with whom Annie could believably fall in love at first sight and for whom she could pine until they are united at the end of the second act. The first man to create the role of Frank Butler was Ray Middleton, who had a successful career on Broadway for more than thirty years. Merman and Middleton were well matched in terms of Broadway experience. Her first notable role was in *Girl Crazy* in 1930; his was in *Roberta* in 1933. The romance in *Annie Get Your Gun* is not between an ingénue and a juvenile. Annie and Frank have both had life experiences, but not ones that would prepare them for an easy relationship with each other. And perhaps the real love affair for both of them is with show business.

Dorothy and Herbert were pleased with the book they created and were happy with the way their collaborators were treating it. They wrote that Irving Berlin "gave us a superb score, a score which never once deserts the mood or the story. The book didn't get in Irving's way. He strengthened it."[41] Jeffrey Magee, in his biography of Irving Berlin, has pointed out that there were some differences in Berlin's and the Fieldses' conceptions of the relationship of Annie and Frank, the Fieldses emphasizing competition and Berlin emphasizing collaboration. He also points to ways that Berlin's songs give Annie a softer side.[42] One can also note that Berlin allows himself flights of fantasy, whereas the book is more anchored in accuracy. For example, Annie first talks about her skill in shooting when she tries to persuade the owner of a boardinghouse to buy some of the birds she has shot. She says, "Look it over mister . . . look it over keerful. Lift up his wings. See? No buck-shot in that bird. Jes' one little hole in his head." In the song "You Can't Get a Man with a Gun," Annie complains, in a delightful triple rhyme, "You can't shoot a male in the tail like a quail." But, of course, Annie would never shoot a quail in the tail; she was deservedly proud of her ability to shoot a bird right through the eye. Berlin wisely allowed himself some poetic license.

The Fieldses also had high praise for director Josh Logan. "He has such great humor and such a sensitive quality that he has made scenes look and sound much better than they are. With Josh we were able to leave rehearsal for a cup of coffee and be absolutely certain when we came back we wouldn't have to say 'Annie' doesn't live here any more!"[43]

Rehearsals began in March, but there were a few bumps in the road before the Broadway opening. At the New Haven tryouts, it was decided that the orchestrations by Philip Lang were unacceptable. Jay Blackton, who conducted the premiere, later told Berlin's daughter Mary Ellin, "When Irving wrote a song and dictated it to Helmy Kresa, that piano part was sacred, that was the way Irving wanted the orchestra to play it, with his little answers between phrases and nothing else."[44] Richard Rodgers, who had hired Lang to do the orchestrations, acknowledged the problem and went about fixing it. "I telephoned Max Dreyfus. 'Max,' I said, 'I need Russell Bennett immediately.' Russell was out of town with another show, but the next morning, promptly at ten, he was at the Shubert Theatre in New Haven. He reorchestrated the entire score, [and] did his customary superlative job."[45] A few days before the scheduled New York opening, the Imperial Theatre began to fall apart—literally. A steel girder holding up the roof of the stage buckled, and a wall of scenery fell. Richard Rodgers was on stage when it happened and was protected from what could have been a serious injury by an alert stagehand who pushed him out of harm's way. The show went back on the road—this time to

Philadelphia—for two more weeks until repairs could be made on the Imperial.

Annie Get Your Gun opened at the Imperial Theatre on May 16, 1946. The reviews were generally excellent, although probably no one would have predicted after the first night that the show would run for 1,147 performances. The critics were unanimous in their praise for Ethel Merman both as a singer and as a comedienne. Reviews of Irving Berlin's music were initially more mixed. Louis Kronenberger of *P.M.* wrote, "Irving Berlin's score is musically not exciting—of the real songs only one or two are tuneful." Ward Morehouse of the *Sun* was a bit more complimentary: "Irving Berlin's score is not a notable one, but his tunes are singable and pleasant and his lyrics are particularly good." Vernon Rice of the *New York Post* had a very different impression of the music and its future: "Irving Berlin has outdone himself this time. No use trying to pick a hit tune, for all the tunes are hits."[46]

Rice was by far the most accurate forecaster. *Annie Get Your Gun* became a perennial in theaters throughout the United States and abroad. It ranks in the top five musicals licensed every year by the Rodgers and Hammerstein office (with *Oklahoma!*, *The Sound of Music*, *South Pacific*, and *The King and I*). The New York Public Library has in its collection more than one hundred programs for different performances of *Annie Get Your Gun* in the United States. Mary Martin made her mark on the role of Annie in the touring company; Dolores Gray played Annie for four years in London. One notable revival took place in Lincoln Center in New York in 1966. Irving Berlin composed a new number for it, "An Old Fashioned Wedding," and the role of Annie was resumed by Ethel Merman, indefatigable at age fifty-eight. The most recent Broadway revival, opening in 1999, had extensive and controversial alterations to the book by Peter Stone. This version won a Tony Award and Drama Desk Award for Best Revival of a Musical and a Grammy Award for Musical Show Album. Bernadette Peters, who played Annie, won a Tony and a Drama Desk Award; Tom Wopat, who played Frank Butler, was nominated for a Tony and a Drama Desk Award; and Reba McEntire, who replaced Bernadette Peters in 2001, won a Drama Desk Award Special Award. The revival ran for thirty-five previews and 1,045 performances.

MORE MOVIES

• • •

The Broadway musicals Dorothy and Herbert Fields worked on in the 1940s were all remade as films. The same year Universal released *Mexican Hayride*, it released *Up in Central Park*. As far as one can infer from the advertising trailer, the success of the stage version was the basis for marketing the film: after "over 1,000 performances," here was a "picture everybody can enjoy." In fact *Up in Central Park* played on Broadway for 504 performances; the "over 1,000" may have been standard Hollywood inflation, or perhaps it counted regional performances as well. Universal was also counting on the drawing power of two major singing stars and one super-suave villain. *Up in Central Park* was Deanna Durbin's penultimate film. She had begun her career as a teenage star in the 1930s—Universal's answer to MGM's Judy Garland. In 1938, she and Mickey Rooney received special Oscars for "setting a high standard of ability and achievement" for young adults. In 1945 and 1947, she was the highest paid female star in Hollywood. Her withdrawal from the public eye was abrupt; after 1948, she made no more films, choosing to retire at age twenty-seven. Dick Haymes, who played the *New York Times* reporter John Matthews in the film, was best known as a singer and was considered by some in the 1940s to be on a par with Frank Sinatra and Bing Crosby. His best screen role may have been in 1945 in Rodgers and Hammerstein's *State Fair*. (Two years before *Up in Central Park*, Haymes appeared in period costume in *The Shocking Miss Pilgrim*, set in 1870s Boston.) The role of Boss Tweed, played on Broadway by the earthy Noah Beery, went to the nonsinging, nondancing, smoothly sophisticated Vincent Price. Several of the secondary characters in the musical—who had the practical function of carrying some of the singing and dancing burden eight performances per week—were dropped from the film. The movie deletes Rosie's best friend, Bessie; Bessie's father and her boyfriend; and John's friend Thomas Nast, the cartoonist.

The screenplay, written by producer Karl Tunberg, shows a significant shift in tone. In the play there is a kind of good-natured, nostalgic glow, even when dealing with topics like political corruption and greed. The film is more earnestly patriotic. We first see Rosie Moore and her father on a boat arriving in New York. Various immigrants express their hopes for their future in America, and an official on board declares, "The thing that makes America such a miracle is the fine people who come here." Rosie sings a new song written for the movie by Sigmund Romberg and Dorothy Fields. "Oh Say Can You See" is another instance of Fields's ability to take a commonplace phrase—in this case, the first words of the "Star Spangled Banner"—and use it as a jumping off point for a lyric. She revisited the territory of a person from another country being delighted with what he experiences on American soil in *Arms and the Girl*, in which a Hessian soldier, Franz, sings "I Like It Here."

The hopeful immigrants immediately become dupes for the Tammany political machine. As soon as Rosie and her father set foot on land, they are taken off by a Tammany employee who persuades Mr. Moore to vote fraudulently in the mayoral election that day. The importance of literacy is an unexpected subsidiary theme in the film. Rosie's father goes back to school to learn to read, and his teacher, prompted by John Matthews, gives an impassioned speech denouncing people like Boss Tweed for ruining democracy.

Durbin plays a more aggressively materialistic and amoral character in the movie. She seems more in tune with Boss Tweed than with the idealistic reporter. The "rightness" of her ending up with Dick Haymes at the end of the film is undermined by the fact that they have sung only one number together, the lighthearted "Carousel in the Park," when they first meet. The more serious, emotionally warmer duets, "Close as Pages in a Book" and "It Doesn't Cost You Anything to Dream," were cut from the film, although oddly, in one scene between Deanna Durbin and Vincent Price, they speak briefly and wistfully of the contrast between dreams and real life, the subject of "It Doesn't Cost You Anything to Dream."

Dropping much or all of a score and changing the script was business as usual when Broadway musicals became Hollywood films. But that was not the way *Annie Get Your Gun* was treated. One reason for this was the growing popularity of original-cast recordings. People who had never seen the show on stage nevertheless knew all the songs and would expect to see them done on screen. In 1947, Decca had issued an album of songs from *Annie Get Your Gun* with Ethel Merman and Ray Middleton re-creating their Broadway roles and with Jay Blackton conducting. That same year, a medley from the London production starring Dolores Gray was available, and a set was put out by Victor with Al Goodman conducting. In 1950, the film soundtrack was released offering Betty Hutton, Howard Keel, Louis Calhern, and Keenan Wynn. It could be said, paradoxically, that in the case of *Annie Get Your Gun*, an original-cast recording was not so important precisely because the show had generated so many hit songs—at least nine.

Not to be overlooked as a factor for the respectful treatment that *Annie Get Your Gun* received in Hollywood was Irving Berlin himself. Always a careful bargainer, Berlin may have taken special pains over the contract for *Annie Get Your Gun* because Hollywood had turned his Broadway hit *Louisiana Purchase* (1940) into a flop. Berlin's biographer Laurence Bergreen noted that negotiations for screen rights "dragged on for the better part of a year; not until June 13, 1947, did Berlin, along with Herbert and Dorothy Fields, sign an agreement with MGM delivering the motion picture rights to the studio. [Producer Arthur] Freed was both exhausted and impressed by the way Berlin handled himself. 'It took longer to write one of Irving's contracts than it did the script,' the producer said, 'but after it was done, he forgot about the contract and gave you anything you wanted.' The amount of the sale—$650,000, payable in five annual installments—was a record for a musical."[1] Not only did the movie keep ten of the show's fifteen songs, the screenplay, by Sidney Sheldon, was quite faithful to the original book. The book was shortened by excising the subplot involving Frank's assistant, Dolly; her daughter, Winnie; and Winnie's boyfriend, Tommy. Dolly remains in the movie, in a reduced role, but with the dropping of Winnie and Tommy, their two duets, "I'll Share It All with You" and "Who Do You Love, I Hope," disappear.[2] The time saved goes to purely visual scenes, particularly those showing Buffalo Bill's Wild West Show. On the other hand, whole chunks of the book's dialogue are kept word for word, for example, Annie's monologue in which she imagines her reconciliation with Frank Butler, starting with "Shore I'll talk to him. I'll say: 'What do you want here, ye big swollen-headed stiff?'" and ending with "Then I guess I won't be able to stop myself from sayin: 'I love ye too!'"

Louis B. Mayer and Irving Berlin concurred that the role of Annie Oakley should go to Judy Garland. Filming began in earnest in October, after the show had closed on Broadway. In retrospect, one can see how badly the deck was stacked against Garland. At a time when her reserves of self-confidence were minimal, she was asked to take on a role that had already been filled by great stars—Ethel Merman on Broadway and Mary Martin on tour. And, utterly unlike the character she was asked to play, Garland had a phobic dread of guns and horses. Her health was in a downward spiral—her emotional problems were exacerbated by substance abuse, and vice versa. Her most manifest physical symptoms were insomnia, migraines, nausea, and hair loss. One of her doctors thought that a series of six electric-shock treatments might be useful, and she complied. Not surprisingly, she had trouble learning new material after the treatments. She reported, "I couldn't retain anything. I was just up there making strange noises. Here I was, in the middle of a million-dollar property, with a million-dollar wardrobe, with a million eyes on me, and I was in a complete daze."[3] Garland managed to record the entire score for the film; the serious problems began when the cameras started to roll.

To be sure, Garland's were not the only misfortunes plaguing the film. Charles Walters, the first choice for director, was dismissed because of a salary dispute. Inexplicably, producer Arthur Freed then hired Busby Berkeley to direct. Berkeley and Garland had not always gotten along, and Berkeley's first misstep was in directing a horse. Howard Keel, who played Frank Butler, was to make an entrance on a horse, and Berkeley wanted the horse to gallop. Either the ground surface was too smooth, or Berkeley shouted and spooked the horse. In any event, the horse slipped and rolled over on Keel, who suffered a broken ankle. If this were not misery enough, Frank Morgan, who was to play Buffalo Bill, died. Louis Calhern was called in to replace Frank Morgan; Betty Hutton replaced Judy Garland; George Sidney replaced Busby Berkeley; Howard Keel's ankle mended, and somehow the film was made.

Annie Get Your Gun triumphed as one of the most popular films of 1950. Although its production budget was enormous—around $3 million—it still made money for MGM. Its original release in 1950 and a re-release in 1956 combined to earn more than $8 million. The film received only one Academy Award, for musical direction, given to Adolph Deutsch and Roger Edens. Like the play, the movie was a good, solid, popular hit.

Starting in 1951, Dorothy Fields wrote lyrics for several films that were not remakes of Broadway plays. Hollywood had changed a great deal in the thirteen years since she had moved back to New York. Many of her family members, close friends, and associates were no longer there. Lew Fields, Lorenz Hart, George Gershwin, and Jerome Kern had died. Dorothy's mother, Rose, moved back to New York after Lew's death. Dorothy's family center, meaning not only her mother and siblings but also her husband and children, were all on the East Coast. And the dwindling of her circle of friends in Hollywood was not the only change: the city and the film industry had changed. In Dorothy's own words, "The subsequent trips to Hollywood, while they were all right, the business had changed, and the town of Beverly Hills had changed, and I must say I wasn't nearly as happy or as pleased to be working in pictures as I was in the old days. The period that I liked least was around 1950."[4] It is not surprising that the films from the period she liked least were relatively inconsequential works.

First came *Excuse My Dust*, for which she collaborated with Arthur Schwartz. *Excuse My Dust* is a typical MGM heartland musical. Set in Indiana in 1895, it celebrates American visionary inventiveness, both of automobiles and of jazz, and wholesome good-heartedness demonstrated at picnics, hayrides, and encounters on porches. The production is lavish—bright pastel costumes, crowd scenes, a six-song score, and an extended fantasy dance sequence—but one has the feeling of having seen and heard all of the elements before, each done slightly better.

The film stars Red Skelton as Joe Belden, earnestly attempting to create a functioning automobile (called a "gasomobile" in the film), and Sally Forrest as Liz Bullitt, the girl who loves him and believes in him. The obstacles the lovers face are both mechanical and human. Liz's father, played by William Demarest, owns a livery stable and fears the automobile will put him out of business; Skelton has a rival for Liz's affections in the Yale-educated son of the town banker, played by MacDonald Carey, and Liz's rival is played by Monica Lewis. But the antagonisms are all good-natured, and the car problems, including a barn burning down, a runaway car plunging into a lake, and Liz pitching herself from a moving automobile to lighten the load as it approaches the finish line of a race are all treated as comic violence. The climactic auto race, taking up the final eleven minutes, forty-two seconds of an eighty-two-minute film, is a hybrid of the *Ben-Hur* chariot race and a Keystone Cops chase.

Producer Jack Cummings assembled a fine artistic team for the film. Hermes Pan was the choreographer, creating a handsome if essentially superfluous four-minute dance sequence for Sally Forrest. Arthur Schwartz had two careers in Hollywood—as a producer and as a composer. Although he worked on films with some of Hollywood's best lyricists, including Frank Loesser, Sammy Cahn, Yip Harburg, Johnny Mercer, Leo Robin, Edward Heyman, and Dorothy Fields, few of Schwatrz's film songs became standards with the important exception of "That's Entertainment" (lyric by his old partner, Howard Dietz), which was added to the score of the film version of *The Band Wagon* (1953). Dorothy had worked with Schwartz on the 1939 Broadway show *Stars in Your Eyes*, and more recently on the musical *A Tree Grows in Brooklyn*, set in about the same time period as *Excuse My Dust*, but in New York rather than Indiana. (*A Tree Grows in Brooklyn* opened on April 19, 1951, and *Excuse My Dust* was released on June 27, 1951.)

Of the six songs heard in the film (three others were dropped) only one has some sense of intimacy, the duet "Spring Has Sprung." The rest are all emotionally generalized and publicly performed, frequently alfresco. "I'd Like to Take You Out Dreaming," sung by MacDonald Carey backed up by a male quintet, and "Lorelei Brown," a ballad about a "kind of spirit girl found in a bottle," sung by Monica Lewis and Guy Anderson, are presented as a contrasting pair of old-style and new-style songs. "That's For Children" has one set of lyrics in English and a second set sprinkled with French, including the phrase "Dites-moi, pourquoi" which must be Dorothy's crypto-tribute to Oscar Hammerstein II's lyric of the same title in *South Pacific*. "Goin' Steady" is sung by a chorus on a hayride, and "Get a Horse" is sung by a derisive chorus before a picnic.

In the same year, Dorothy wrote lyrics for another film starring Red Skelton, *Texas Carnival*. For this film, her song partner was Harry Warren. Born Salvatore Guadagno in Brooklyn in 1893 (his father changed the family name to Warren), he was at one and the same time a prototypical and an atypical Hollywood songwriter. His biography by Tony Thomas bears the title *The Hollywood Musical: The Saga of Songwriter Harry Warren*, and in some sense this equivalence between Warren's body of work and the Hollywood musical in general is justifiable. Warren worked for four major studios—Warner Brothers, Twentieth-Century Fox, MGM, and Paramount—and worked with many of the best lyricists, including Al Dubin, Johnny Mercer, Mack Gordon, Leo Robin, Ralph Blane, Ira Gershwin, and Arthur Freed. His work did not fail to get recognition; he was nominated for Academy Awards eleven times, and he won three: the first for "Lullaby of Broadway" (1935, lyric by Al Dubin), the second for "You'll Never Know" (1943, lyric by Mack Gordon), and the third for "On the Atchison, Topeka and the Santa Fe" (1945, lyric by Johnny Mercer). But Warren never had the cachet of composers who came to Hollywood after having achieved significant success on Broadway—composers such as Irving Berlin, George Gershwin, Richard Rodgers, and Cole Porter. And though the fraternity of popular songwriters was not an exclusively Jewish club (a few of the important exceptions were George M. Cohan, Vincent Youmans, Cole Porter, Jimmy McHugh, Hoagy Carmichael, Johnny Mercer, Nacio Herb Brown, and Richard Whiting), Harry Warren was, in his time, a rare Italian American composer. Many of the successful Hollywood songwriters were also successful socializers, and here too Warren was atypical. He reminisced with Max Wilk, "Maybe I should have gone and played piano at producers' parties. That's how you got attention out here. But the hell with that. I'm a family man. Always was. Most guys who got ahead in the picture business lived like single men, even if they were married. Played cards with the boss, went to the tracks, partied. But not me. I always came home. I didn't go out nights. You know, I've been living here since '32, forty years, and I never went to a Hollywood party."[5]

Warren's first important film, *42nd Street*, was made in 1932 and released in 1933. When he worked with Dorothy Fields in 1951, his career was winding down (although the hits "Affair to Remember" and "That's Amore" were still in the future). *Texas Carnival* had several elements in common with *Excuse My Dust*—same studio (MGM), same producer (Jack Cummings) same star (Red Skelton) and even a comic race toward the end, but this time it is a chuck-wagon race instead of early automobiles. Sharing the top billing with Red Skelton were three other MGM stars. Esther Williams was a swimming champion and model before she started playing in a series of MGM musicals featuring water ballets, with telling titles such as *Bathing Beauty*, *On an Island with You*, and *Neptune's Daughter*. Howard Keel, of the Frank Butler role in *Annie Get Your Gun*, had costarred with Esther Williams in another musical with songs by Harry Warren, *Pagan Love Song*. Ann Miller had tap-danced her way through more than two dozen musicals before *Texas Carnival*. Unfortunately, the film is something less than the sum of its parts; the stars have no significant way of interacting with one another's specialties. Howard Keel is not a swimmer, Esther Williams in not much of a singer, Red Skelton does not tap dance, and Ann Miller does not do slapstick comedy.

The film contains four songs, although Warren and Fields had written several more that were not used. "The Carnie's Pitch" is a rapid patter song sung by Red Skelton to the carnival crowd. "Whoa, Emma!" and "Young Folks Should Get Married" are both sung by Howard Keel—the first to his horse and the second to Esther Williams. "It's Dynamite" is sung and danced by Ann Miller with her typical explosive energy.

According to Thomas's biography, "of his MGM musicals, Harry Warren considers *Texas Carnival* the poorest of them."[6] Warren confided, "I didn't like it and it was an unhappy experience. This was the only time I worked with a lady lyricist—and she was the best—but we didn't have that rapport song-writing needs. She was a rather aggressive woman, and I'm kind of turned off by aggression. Dorothy would call me at all hours, even seven in the morning, to discuss lyrics, but what rankled most was her telling me I was wasting my time in Hollywood, and why didn't I go back and write for the New York theater? That was a thought I'd been trying to put behind me for years."[7] Dorothy's frankness and willingness to speak her mind sometimes unnerved her colleagues. In this case, she was discerning enough to zero in on a major conflict in Warren's life—the artistic insufficiency of his success in Hollywood—and not discerning enough to know how much she would upset Warren by trying to discuss it with him. Warren reminisced about the contradictions of working at MGM in the 1950s. "[Mayer] had a whole school of sopranos over there, all kinds of singers, vocal teachers, a stock company of singers and dancers. That lot was really jumping. I got the biggest salary of my life at Metro. Funny thing, though, the only song I ever scored with over there was in . . . *The Harvey Girls*, which I wrote with Johnny Mercer. Judy Garland sang it— 'On the Atchison, Topeka and the Santa Fe.'"[8]

Dorothy Fields's next film paired her with a new collaborator, but an old friend, Harold Arlen. Their professional lives had run on parallel tracks for decades. Both were singers in their teen years, before they turned to song-writing, and they continued to perform their own songs publicly in later years. Both found an important springboard for their careers at the Cotton Club; Arlen and lyricist Ted Koehler had written Cotton Club Revues from 1930 until 1934. Hence, some of Dorothy's and Harold's songs were premiered by the same African American singers—Bill Robinson, Adelaide Hall, and Aida Ward among them. None of the Fields-McHugh songs specifically written for the Cotton Club were big hits. In contrast, standards such as "Between the Devil and the Deep Blue Sea" and "I've Got the World on a String," are among the songs Arlen and Koehler introduced at the Cotton Club shows.

Both Fields and Arlen went to work for the film industry soon after the movies began to sing. Once again, she preceded him by a few years, but their tracks were parallel. Both traveled to Hollywood with their songwriting part-ners, but once there they found new collaborators. While Dorothy worked with Jerome Kern and other composers, Arlen worked with lyricists including Yip Harburg and Johnny Mercer. They were all in the same happy band of songwriters at that time. Arlen commented, "It was a great period! Maybe it was the accident of all of us working there because of the Depression. Practi-cally every talent you can name. So many. Jerry Kern, Harry Warren, the Gershwins, Dorothy Fields and Jimmy McHugh, Oscar Hammerstein—even Berlin, although he didn't stick around. All of us, writing pictures so well. We were all on the weekly radio Hit Parade. If we weren't first, we were second; if we weren't second, we were fourth. A sensational period. Lovely for me. I went to the studio when I damned well pleased, or when they called me. Got my check every week. And we were pouring it out! Oh sure, we all wrote picture scores that were bad. But people were having flops on Broadway, too, weren't they? It was a great life. Most of us played golf or tennis, or swam, and did our writing at the same time."[9] Dorothy also had fond recollections of Hollywood in the '30s. "Harold and Yip [Harburg] had Larry Tibbett's house in Beverly Hills, and we used to play tennis almost every afternoon at the Gershwins. Wonder-ful. That was the early period, the rosy period, as against the blue period."[10]

Most of the transplanted songwriters did not remain in Hollywood for the rest of their careers. Arlen returned to Broadway with the musical *Hooray for What!*, with lyrics by Harburg and a book by Lindsay and Crouse, which opened in 1937 and ran for two hundred performances. After Dorothy's return to Broadway for *Stars in Your Eyes* (1939), written with Arthur

Schwartz, she pretty much stayed on the East Coast through the 1940s, whereas Arlen had a more bicoastal career. For Broadway, he wrote *Bloomer Girl* (1944) with Harburg, and *St. Louis Woman* (1946) with Mercer. In Hollywood in 1939, Arlen and Harburg wrote the score for *The Wizard of Oz*. Arlen noted, "I always went back to Hollywood to the comforts of a home in Beverly Hills. Kept on writing pictures. Some good, some bad. Kept on wandering from one lyricist to another. I don't know what the reason for that was. I suppose I didn't want to be pinned down."[11]

For all the parallels in the course of their careers, Fields and Arlen had very different temperaments. Dorothy was "On the Sunny Side of the Street," whereas Arlen was "Stormy Weather" or "I've Got a Right to Sing the Blues." Yip Harburg described Arlen as "a very, very melancholy person. . . . Behind every song that Harold writes is great sadness and melancholy. Even his happy songs."[12] Frank Loesser, reporting to his wife about an ASCAP meeting in Hollywood, noted, "The meeting was the usual thing—Ira Gershwin fell asleep—Mack Gordon shouted louder than anybody, and Arthur Schwartz read a lot of legal stuff from a piece of paper. Arthur Freed raved about his own pictures, Johnny Mercer read a magazine, and Harold Arlen kept looking in the bar mirror, as if any minute his face would become bearable and then he'd start enjoying it."[13]

Arlen and Fields had a good working relationship and considerable affection for one another. Harold thought Dorothy was "a hell of a lyric writer."[14] According to Arlen's biographer, Dorothy thought Harold's songs "'were lyrically pure and in good taste, reflecting the man himself, a man full of love.' Only a year older than Arlen, Dorothy Fields recalled him with warmth and affection, almost maternally, calling him 'Schnitta,' a term of her own invention. Arlen, when not calling her Dotty, addressed her as 'The Red Arrow,' a tribute to her speedy way with a lyric."[15]

They joined forces first for *Mr. Imperium*. Another MGM musical, released in New York only two days after *Texas Carnival*, it was written by Edwin Knopf and Don Hartman, with Knopf also serving as producer and Hartman as director. The star was Ezio Pinza, who played opposite Lana Turner. Fields, as we have seen, had considerable experience writing for opera singers working in film. She wrote for Lawrence Tibbett in *Cuban Love Song* (1931), Lily Pons in *I Dream Too Much* (1935), and Grace Moore in *The King Steps Out* (1936). Arlen and Harburg wrote "Last Night when We Were Young" for Lawrence Tibbett, who recorded it but did not succeed in getting it interpolated into the film *Metropolis*.

Ezio Pinza had had an impressive, well-established international career as an operatic bass before he crossed over to star in musicals and movies. Born in Rome in 1892, he sang in the major Italian opera houses in the 1920s. Starting in 1926, he sang at the Metropolitan Opera House in New York every season for more than two decades. According to vocal scholar Desmond Shawe-Taylor, "Pinza was unquestionably the most richly gifted and most accomplished Italian bass of his day."[16]

At age fifty-seven, when he was cast in Rodgers and Hammerstein's *South Pacific*, he was seen by Rodgers as the "virile, mature Ezio Pinza," while his costar, Mary Martin, called him "Don Giovanni himself!" Singing beautifully was easy for Pinza. The more difficult adjustments for him were speaking English intelligibly and appearing in eight performances a week, week after week—tasks not normally required of an operatic star. Richard Rodgers complained, "All that marred the show's run was the frequency of Mr. Pinza's absences. He loved basking in the adulation bestowed on him as a middle-aged matinee idol, but he could never be counted on to show up for performances. He couldn't wait for his year-long contract to expire, and the minute it was up, he was on a plane for Hollywood—where he made two of the deadliest bombs ever released."[17]

Mr. Imperium was the first of these two "bombs" to be made, although it was released a few months after his other film effort, *Strictly Dishonorable*. In *Mr. Imperium*, Pinza plays a prince enamored of a showgirl who rises to the rank of movie star. The mantle of royalty hangs heavily on this prince's shoulders. He laments, "Beyond everything else in the world I wanted to be a singer." But he responds dutifully to the calls of country and family—once when his father dies and later to protect his son. The pairing of a prince and a commoner sounds like the material of operetta. However, the songs, though individually attractive, do not carry much dramatic weight. There are four—three by Arlen and Fields and one, "You Belong to My Heart," by Ray Gilbert and Agustin Lara, which had been previously used in the films *The Three Caballeros* and *The Gay Ranchero*. The first song, "My Love and My Mule," is sung by Lana Turner's character (dubbed by Trudi Irwin) in the first few minutes of the film. Since the song is presented as part of a nightclub act, presumably the text could have been on any subject, but this song highlights the Lana Turner character's American-ness, in contrast to Pinza's European-ness. Two earlier large-animal songs by Dorothy were "A Cow and a Plough and a Frau" in *Arms and the Girl* and "Whoa, Emma" in *Texas Carnival*.

The second song, "Let Me Look at You," is a beautiful ballad for Pinza. Alec Wilder describes the song as "a big-canvas, broad-lined song of great dignity, one not unlike Kern at his most independent."[18] It is possible that Dorothy was thinking of a Kern-Fields song, "Just Let Me Look at You," or even their Academy Award–winning song, "The Way You Look Tonight," when the title for this song came to her. We see in this lyric a mature ability to fit together in one text the playful springiness of multiple rhymes within a line—"Nonetheless you possess passionate tenderness"—and simple but urgent direct addresses, each one starting with the phrase "Let me."

The third song, "Andiamo," incorporates Italian words, particularly musical terms, in the text. As with the song "That's for Children" in *Excuse My Dust*, which has some text in French, Dorothy is allowing herself to be linguistically playful here. Its incorporation of solfège syllables into the text in some way adumbrates "Do-Re-Mi" from *The Sound of Music*. "Andiamo" is sung through once by Pinza; the Lana Turner character joins in a repetition, but the song is not truly a duet. Indeed, the problem of blending Pinza's voice with that of a popular female singer was never solved. When writing *South Pacific*, Richard Rodgers promised Mary Martin she would not have to combine her voice with Pinza's. In *Mr. Imperium*, Turner's character stops singing entirely after "Andiamo," and Pinza's sings only once more. *Mr. Imperium*, despite the presence of Pinza, is less a musical than a romance with a few songs added. Arlen's biographer, Edward Jablonski, says that six songs were written for this film, but only three were used. It is as if the placement of songs in the movie had everyone stumped.

In contrast, the other movie that Arlen and Fields worked on together, *The Farmer Takes a Wife*, overflows with musical numbers. Ken Bloom lists fifteen titles written for the film—enough to fill a Broadway musical.[19] The film uses only eight, but gives each a generous and lavish setting. There are full production numbers with a chorus of singers and dancers at the beginning, middle, and end of the film. In addition, there is a comic number sung by Eddie Foy Jr., one solo each for the leading lady, Betty Grable, and leading man, Dale Robertson, and two duets.

The film has the appearance of being an attempt by Twentieth-Century Fox to meet MGM on its own ground. The setting is rural upstate New York in the mid-nineteenth century; the brilliant blue sky and bright (though inappropriate) costumes are captured in scintillating Technicolor; there are dozens of apple-cheeked children; there is a fine score by Arlen and Fields, ably arranged by Lionel Newman. In addition, there are two good dance sequences—the first danced by vaudevillian Eddie Foy Jr., and the second by Betty Grable and Gwen Verdon. But somehow, as with *Texas Carnival*, the ingredients do not add up to as much as they should. Bosley Crowther, in his *New York Times* review, wrote that "the whole thing is just a bit too genteel, too quaintly and self-consciously costumed, too calculatedly folksy, too primly respectable."[20] Dorothy Fields reminisced with a little more bluntness. "When you have a girl like Betty Grable playing a cook on the Erie Canal, and she comes out in a pale pink organdy dress to work on a barge—and you try to write a very sincere story for a little comedienne who is completely unbelievable. Of course, that's where good stories go awry, often—in casting. I would say that this picture didn't ring."[21] The "sincere little story" first appeared in a novel, *Rome Haul*, by Walter D. Edmonds. It was turned into a stage play by Frank B. Elser and Marc Connelly. Then in 1936, it became a nonmusical film starring Janet Gaynor and Henry Fonda. The screenwriting team for the 1953 version consisted of Walter Bullock, Sally Benson, and Dorothy's brother Joe. Dorothy had worked much more frequently with her brother Herbert, with whom she was also closer personally. This time she worked with Joe and, given the Hollywood piecework method of putting together a film, it probably felt like much less of a collaboration than did her stage projects with Herbert.

Arlen's biographer felt that the score was better than the film deserved. However, none of the songs broke out as a hit. There is some continuing currency for "Today I Love Everybody," one of Dorothy's anthems of optimism, comparable to "On the Sunny Side of the Street" or "I Feel a Song Coming On," but simpler.[22] The lyrics for the songs for *The Farmer Takes a Wife* show Dorothy's professionalism—her ability to get the job done—but do not show her most characteristic gifts.

During this period, one more of the musicals Dorothy Fields was involved in underwent a makeover. This was not a stage musical moved to the screen, but a screen musical redone. In 1952, MGM decided to remake *Roberta*, the RKO film on which Dorothy had first worked with Jerome Kern in 1935. The new screenplay, by George Wells and Harry Ruby, had almost no point of contact with the old screenplay except for the inclusion of a lavish fashion show. However, many of the songs were kept, including the Kern-Harbach hits "Smoke Gets in Your Eyes," "Yesterdays," and "The Touch of Your Hand." Dorothy Fields added a lyric for "Lafayette" and revised the lyrics for "The Most Exciting Night," "You're Devastating," "I'll Be Hard to Handle," "Opening Night," and "I Won't Dance." And the lyric Dorothy wrote for the song in the earlier film's fashion show gave the title to the new film, *Lovely to Look At*. As she told her son more than once, "You can't copyright a title." Had Kern been alive, Hollywood convention would not have precluded asking the team to write some new material, but he was, alas, gone.

COLONIAL AMERICA AND BROOKLYN

• • •

When Dorothy Fields advised Harry Warren to go back east and write for Broadway, she was simply preaching what she practiced. Between 1950 and 1954, in addition to writing lyrics for four movies, she worked on three Broadway musicals. This burst of productivity was preceded by a relatively inactive period. Despite the great success of *Annie Get Your Gun*, in the years 1948 and 1949 no new theatrical project came to fruition. The end of the decade appeared to be another period of lying fallow for her. It was also a time of loss. On February 19, 1948, Rose Fields, the matriarch of the family, died at seventy-three. After the death of her husband, Rose had left California and returned to New York to be near her four children and four grandchildren. For a few years Rose and Dorothy had adjacent apartments at 171 West Fifty-seventh Street. In fact, the family had two residences at this time; Dorothy and Eli had bought a large house, on more than a hundred acres, near Brewster, New York, the year *Annie Get Your Gun* opened.

The three Broadway musicals Dorothy worked on in the first half of the 1950s—*Arms and the Girl* (1950), *A Tree Grows in Brooklyn* (1951), and *By the Beautiful Sea* (1954)—were all set between fifty and two hundred years in the past. That is, all of these musicals continue in the Americana tradition of the Fieldses' two previous musicals, *Up in Central Park* and *Annie Get Your Gun*. *Arms and the Girl*, like *Annie Get Your Gun*, features a weapon-toting heroine who finds her inner femininity, brings it to the surface, and wins her man.

The source play for *Arms and the Girl* was *The Pursuit of Happiness* by Lawrence Langner and his wife, Armina Marshall. It had had a moderately successful run on Broadway in 1933 and was made into a moderately successful movie starring Joan Bennett in 1934. Set in Connecticut in 1777–78, it tells of a young woman, daughter of an American officer in the Revolutionary War, who falls in love with a Hessian soldier who has deserted from the British army.

According to Rouben Mamoulian, who was to function as director and coauthor of the book of the show, he and the Langners had begun preparations to turn *The Pursuit of Happiness* into a musical in 1947. Harry Warren was approached about writing the music; he had just written the songs for two fine period movies, *The Harvey Girls* (1946) and *Summer Holiday* (1948). The latter film, based on Eugene O'Neill's play *Ah, Wilderness!* was directed by Mamoulian. Ever ambivalent about returning to New York, Warren did not sign on to the project.

Dorothy's first choice for a composer for *Arms and the Girl* was Burton Lane, but he too turned the project down. Burton and Dorothy had been friends for close to twenty years. When Fields and McHugh wrote the title song for the film *Dancing Lady* in 1933, Lane and lyricist Harold Adamson contributed what became the hit song of the film, "Everything I Have Is Yours." In 1947, Lane had an enormous success with *Finian's Rainbow* (lyrics by Yip Harburg), which ran for 725 performances.

According to Deborah Grace Winer, in 1949 "Burton Lane came in from California, and arrived at Dorothy and Eli's gracious country home in Brewster, New York. The idea was that in the country they would be able to relax and begin attacking the show in an informal setting. (Herb was also there, as it was where he and Dorothy did much of their work.) Dorothy, always an enthusiastic hostess, arranged dinner, and they sat around amiably until Lane, tired from the trip, excused himself to retire to his room. On his way up, Dorothy gave him a copy of the script, which he read before turning in. He later recalled that he woke up in the middle of the night with the realization that he had to find a way to get out of the project. His dilemma, obviously, was his affection for and close friendship with Dorothy. But he told them that he honestly thought the script was inadequate, and he left the project."[1] In 1957, Fields and Lane would collaborate on a musical written for television, *Junior Miss*.

It is not clear who suggested inviting Morton Gould to compose the score for *Arms and the Girl*. Gould was a remarkably versatile composer and conductor who wrote for stage, screen, concert hall, radio, and television. Born in 1913 in Richmond Hill, New York, Gould was musically precocious, and his first composition was published when he was six. While in high school, he studied at the New York Institute of Musical Art, the forerunner of the Juilliard School of Music and the same institution Richard Rodgers had attended a few years earlier. For a time, critical opinion positioned Gould with Aaron Copland and George Gershwin as a leading American composer on the border of classical and popular music. As a composer with a distinctive American voice who in addition had a substantial career as a conductor, he also shows some similarities with Leonard Bernstein. Throughout his professional life, but particularly during World War II, Gould composed several patently patriotic orchestral works such as *Cowboy Rhapsody* (1942), *Lincoln Legend* (1942), *American Concertette* (1943), *American Salute* (1947), and *Americana* (1950). He also wrote the scores for two documentary films produced by the U.S. Office of War Information, *Ring of Steel* and *San Francisco*. Unfortunately, Gould was relatively inexperienced as a composer of popular songs or stage works. He had written songs for one movie, *Delightfully Dangerous*, and had composed one ballet, *Fall River Legend* (1947), commissioned by Ballet Theater and choreographed by Agnes de Mille. *Billion Dollar Baby*, the one musical he had written before *Arms and the Girl*, with book and lyrics by Betty Comden and Adolph Green, had played for 219 performances in 1945.

The book for *Arms and the Girl* was coauthored by Rouben Mamoulian and Herbert Fields. Herbert had already written one book for a musical set in the American Revolution, *Dearest Enemy* (1925), the first successful book musical from the team of Herbert Fields, Richard Rodgers, and Lorenz Hart. The star of *Dearest Enemy*, Helen Ford, made the audience sit up and take notice when she made her first entrance wearing only a barrel. In *Arms and the Girl*, the correspondingly titillating scenes involve the colonial practice of bundling, in which an unmarried man and woman occupy the same bed but fully dressed. In the finales of both plays, George Washington functions as a deus ex machina setting everything right.

Mamoulian was an experienced director, having worked on *Porgy and Bess*, *Oklahoma!*, *Carousel*, and *Lost In the Stars*, but he was a novice playwright. Nevertheless, he had a clear concept of how a straight play should be adapted into a musical. "You must be unfaithful to the original form because if the original has been successful it has realized itself fully, and if you monkey around with something that is already good you will wind up spoiling the original. You don't just put a play to music—you don't paste songs and dancing on the play. No, you must change the entire form. You must make something new. What you try to do is be faithful to the spirit of the original—to find its kernel and out of that make an exciting musical evening, with new values of singing and dancing that enhance the original kernel and perhaps bring out new meanings in it."[2] Mamoulian also had strong feelings about the interaction between spoken text and song. "With me it's basic law that the music and dancing must extend the dialogue. If you say the same thing in a song you already have said in the speeches, it's without point. When emotion reaches an intense height, it can better be expressed in a song, in a dance, better than normal speech. Therefore, a song must lift the spoken scene to greater heights than it was before, or the song must be cut out no matter how beautiful is the melody. The song must not merely repeat in musical terms what has already been put across by the dialogue and actions."[3]

Lawrence Langner remarked on the changes Mamoulian made to the source play. "His conception of the characters was what was carried out. At times, I'll admit, I felt a little strange seeing the characters Armina and I'd invented doing and saying things we'd never dreamed of, but we hardly interfered."[4] It was primarily the female characters who were transformed. The mother in *Pursuit of Happiness* was eliminated entirely, and the heroine changed from a demure young woman into a fervent revolutionary. Tellingly, the name of the heroine went from Prudence to the more gender-neutral Jo.

The role of the servant is the most altered. In *Pursuit of Happiness*, there are two servants: Meg, who has difficulties keeping her flirtatiousness under control; and Mose, an escaped slave who is burdened with Negro stage stereotypes of the time, such as idiosyncratic grammar and exaggerated fearfulness. In *Arms and the Girl*, there is only one servant, a female escaped slave who takes on the name Connecticut. (She tells us, in her first appearance on stage, that she was formerly called Virginia.) Unlike Meg in *The Pursuit of Happiness*, Connecticut does not flirt with other characters; the 1950s attitudes about keeping color lines uncrossed were still felt in the north as well as in the south. Although the first scene finds Connecticut hiding in a barn, frightened by the sound of gunfire, she quickly leaves behind the stereotype of the fearful servant. Indeed, in the course of the musical she is revealed as a worldly philosopher and acts as an advisor and mentor to the heroine, a little in the mold of Sitting Bull in *Annie Get Your Gun*.

The stars of the production were Nanette Fabray as Jo Kirkland, Georges Guetary as Franz, the Hessian deserter with whom Jo falls in love, and Pearl Bailey as Connecticut. Fabray had been a child actress, on stage and in *Our Gang* movies. She had starred in *High Button Shoes* (1947) and before that had played a minor role in *Let's Face It*, a Cole Porter musical with a book by Herbert and Dorothy Fields. Georges Guetary was making his Broadway debut after having earned a substantial reputation in France.

Pearl Bailey made her Broadway debut in 1945 in *St. Louis Woman*, directed by Rouben Mamoulian. The two songs she sang in that show, "Legalize My Name" and "A Woman's Prerogative" (music by Harold Arlen, lyrics by Johnny Mercer) were showstoppers, and she received high praise from the critics. In *Arms and the Girl*, it was again Bailey's two numbers, "Nothin' for Nothin'" and "There Must Be Somethin' Better Than Love," that the critics enjoyed most. Two weeks after *Arms and the Girl* opened, Pearl Bailey threatened to quit because some members of the show had humiliated her with racial slurs. Earl Wilson reported in the *New York Post* Bailey's complaint that "members of the company call her 'Honey Chile,' pinch her cheek, and talk to her in Negro dialect or don't talk to her at all." Apologies were quickly issued by the

Theater Guild, feathers were unruffled, and Bailey stayed for the remainder of the show's run. Not one to hold a grudge, Pearl Bailey does not speak of this incident in her memoir, *The Raw Pearl*.

Arms and the Girl has thirteen musical numbers—three solos each for Fabray and Guetary, two duets for Fabray and Guetary, Bailey's two solos, one for John Conte as a Revolutionary colonel, and two numbers for chorus.[5] The song with which Jo introduces herself, "A Girl with a Flame," is interesting in several ways. One is the announcement that she is the person she is because her father shaped her that way. She declares, "Fifty times a day my father said: stick a gun in your belt." There is no suggestion of this in *The Pursuit of Happiness*; the source of the idea—Freudian or not—is Dorothy. The song also has echoes of "You Can't Get a Man with a Gun" from *Annie Get Your Gun* (for which, recall, Dorothy wrote the book but not the lyrics).

Jo's second number, "That's My Fella" is a comic characterization of love at first sight combined with a demonstration of Jo's feistiness and determination to get her man. Dorothy would treat the same topic more elegantly and more beautifully in her next musical, *A Tree Grows in Brooklyn*, in the song "Make the Man Love Me." Jo sings another song on a topic the lyricist will revisit—"I'll Never Learn." The self-deprecating sentiments of a woman who thinks that the failure of a romance is her fault emerge with great comic brio in *Seesaw* (1973) in the song "Nobody Does It Like Me."

Like Jo, Franz gets a song to introduce himself, "I Like It Here." A foreigner's fervent recognition of the gift of liberty might have played better ten years or even five years earlier. If one keeps in mind that in 1950 the excesses of the House Un-American Activities Committee and Senator Joseph McCarthy were on the horizon and about to gain force, the text now sounds unintentionally ironic. He sings, "There is no fear in this country anywhere! The right to be wrong over here is freedom!"

Franz's other paean to the good life in a new land, "A Cow and a Plough and a Frau," may also fail to win over some contemporary listeners, but for other reasons. Many of Dorothy Fields's most successful love lyrics have a certain air of amused detachment, in the style of Larry Hart or Cole Porter. The expression of heart-on-the-sleeve sincere sentiment combined with the pastoral or the bucolic, which Oscar Hammerstein could do so well, was not Dorothy's home territory.

The songs with the longest post-show life were the ones sung by Pearl Bailey, "Nothin' for Nothin'" and "There Must Be Somethin' Better Than Love." The verse of "Nothin' for Nothin'" opens by closely paraphrasing some lines in *The Pursuit of Happiness*. In the play, the mother warns her daughter, "Don't go turnin' your nose up too high, my gal: No bird ever found a worm by lookin' up in the air." The song begins, "No bird ever caught a worm by stickin' his nose in de air."

"There Must Be Somethin' Better Than Love" is the kind of lyric Dorothy Fields did so well. The stance is slightly cynical, eyes-wide-open, not failing to see the problems of being in love, but accepting them as part of the price one pays. The lyric has points of contact with Larry Hart's "I Wish I Were in Love Again," but the tone is quite different. Dorothy may also have kept in her ear the title of one of Cole Porter's songs from *Mexican Hayride*, "There Must Be Someone for Me."[6]

In the typescript of *Arms and the Girl* preserved in the New York Public Library, the lyrics that Connecticut sings are spelled so as to try to capture the sound of southern black dialect—the g's are consistently dropped, and th's are replaced by d's. (Recall the advice of Oscar Hammerstein II to Irving Berlin regarding writing "hillbilly" lyrics was that he should just drop the g's.) Interestingly enough, in the original cast recording, Bailey sings the text with standard northern U.S. pronunciation.

Arms and the Girl received mixed reviews and ran for only 134 performances. In general, critics admired Nanette Fabray, Georges Guetary, and Pearl Bailey but were not impressed by the book or the music. William Hawkins of the *World Telegram and Sun* summarized, "You can stash *Arms and the Girl* somewhere between the bottom of the top drawer and the top of the second."[7]

Dorothy's next musical was *A Tree Grows in Brooklyn*. Its starting point was a best-selling novel of the same name by Betty Smith. Smith was born Elizabeth Wehner in Brooklyn in 1896. Her formal education in Brooklyn went up to the eighth grade, after which she worked at clerical and factory jobs. After her marriage at age twenty-three to George Casper Smith, she studied literature and writing at the University of Michigan and at Yale Drama School. Although she is most famous for her debut novel, most of her professional energy was directed to the theater. In her lifetime, she wrote more than seventy plays; she also dabbled in acting.

A Tree Grows in Brooklyn appeared in 1943, when Betty Smith was forty-six. The critic of the *New Yorker* praised it as "a remarkably good first novel," the reviewer for *Yale Review* said it might be "the best novel of the year;" and the reviewer for *Book Week* rated it "one of the outstanding fiction works of the year—perhaps of many years." The book, somewhere between memoir and bildungsroman, tells the story of Francie Nolan growing up in the Williamsburg section of Brooklyn with her determined mother and her feckless father in the first two decades of the twentieth century. Seeking to understand herself, Francie also tries to understand her parents and grandparents, uncles and aunts. She pieces together their stories as best she can. Hence, the novel sprawls across three generations and deals with her mother, her mother's parents, her mother's sisters and their husbands, her father, her father's mother, his brothers, and his previous girlfriend. Also populating the novel are the people from the neighborhood and some of her teachers.

References to songs abound in the novel. This is not surprising because Francie's father, Johnny, works as a singing waiter and spontaneously bursts into song away from his job as well; song is an essential part of his nature. Songs are sometimes treated as prophetic. Shortly before he dies, Johnny sings the final verse of "Molly Malone," beginning "She died of a fever and no one could save her," which he had never sung before. Other times, the author reminds the reader that songs are not to be trusted. After Johnny's comically disastrous trip to Canarsie to go fishing with his children, the author concludes, "The songs of the sea had betrayed him." The local bartender loved hearing about places neither he nor Johnny had ever seen, but which Johnny knew of through songs. Johnny, through his songs, is a bringer of information or knowledge, but the information is not necessarily accurate, and the knowledge is dubious. At the start of her first menstrual period, Francie's memory of her father's songs leads her to an incorrect conclusion. "She had heard papa sing so many songs about the heart; the heart that was breaking— was aching—was dancing—was heavy laden—that leaped for joy—that was heavy in sorrow—that turned over—that stood still. She really believed the heart actually did those things. She was terrified thinking her heart had broken inside her . . . and that the blood was now leaving her heart and flowing from her body."[8]

In 1945, two years after the book first appeared, a movie version was released. Made at Twentieth-Century Fox, it marked the directorial debut of Elia Kazan. The film score was composed by Alfred Newman. The screenplay by Tess Slesinger and Frank Davis won an Academy Award nomination. Jamie Dunn, playing Johnny Nolan, received an Academy Award for best supporting actor, and Peggy Ann Garner, who played Francie, was granted a special Oscar for best child actress. The role of Francie's mother was played by Dorothy McGuire, and that of her Aunt Cissy by Joan Blondell.

Betty Smith did not work on the screenplay of *A Tree Grows in Brooklyn*. Nevertheless, the film is an unusually sensitive and faithful adaptation of the book. Not surprisingly, given the leisurely, ambling narrative of the book, the screen version cuts several characters and many incidents. In the movie, Katie has only one sister, Cissy, who borrows from Katie's other sister in the book, Evy, the detail that her husband is a milkman. Johnny's mother, brothers, and previous girlfriend are all deleted. The film is saturated in period music, and in this way too it is true to the book's frequent references to songs and occasional quotes of lyric.

The notion of turning *A Tree Grows in Brooklyn* into a musical began with a meeting between Smith's agent, Helen Strauss, producer Robert Fryer, and director George Abbott. Smith thought she would have no part in writing the libretto for the musical—she had had no part in writing the screenplay—but after speaking with Abbott, who was to produce, direct, and write the book for the show, she changed her mind. Actually, it is surprising she needed any coaxing: the first version of *A Tree Grows in Brooklyn* was a play written by Smith in 1930 called *Francie Nolan*.

Abbott's first choice of a composer for *A Tree Grows in Brooklyn* was Irving Berlin, with whom he had just collaborated on *Call Me Madam*, but Berlin was not ready to jump into another show right away. (One cannot help wondering if Berlin, had he accepted, would have used some of his own songs from the period. In the novel, Smith cites Berlin's song "Call Me Up Some Rainy Afternoon.") Abbott also considered Jule Styne, whose first Broadway hit, *High Button Shoes* (1947), was directed by Abbott and was set in about the same period as *A Tree Grows in Brooklyn*. Styne's next hit, *Gentlemen Prefer Blondes* (1949), is set in the 1920s and has a very different sensibility. At the time *A Tree Grows in Brooklyn* was being written, Jule Styne was venturing into producing. The next musical he was involved with as a composer was *Hazel Flagg* (1953). Abbott's third choice was Arthur Schwartz and Dorothy Fields.

Since there were already two people working on the libretto, Smith and Abbott, Dorothy was employed only as a lyricist, and Herbert was not involved in the show at all. This was the first time in more than a decade that Dorothy worked on a show without her brother. They both seem to have been entirely pragmatic regarding their involvement in shows. Recall that when it was decided that the best replacement for Jerome Kern would be Irving Berlin, Dorothy gave up writing the lyrics for *Annie Get Your Gun* and worked only on the libretto. Now, for *A Tree Grows in Brooklyn*, she did only lyrics and Herb sat this show out.

When the book was adapted as a musical, it once again supplied the characters, the setting, and elements of the plot. More surprisingly, perhaps, it was mined for material for the opening chorus.[9] The first numbers of the musical establish time and place, but also the socioeconomic status of the characters. They sing in "Payday" that "everybody's buying back something, from a plush sofa to a safety lock."

The suggestions for the lyrics of "Payday" and "Mine Till Monday" are in the novel. "Oh, what a wonderful day was Saturday in Brooklyn. . . . People were paid on Saturday and it was a holiday without the rigidness of Sunday.

People had money to go out and buy things. They ate well for once, got drunk, had dates, made love and stayed up until all hours; singing, playing music, fighting and dancing because the morrow was their own free day."[10] A few pages later, the author notes, "Women came in with bulky hock-shop bundles. The man's Sunday suit was home again. On Monday, it would go back to the pawnbroker's for another week. The hock-shop prospered on the weekly interest money and the suit benefited by being brushed and hung away in camphor where the moths couldn't get at it. In on Monday, out on Saturday. Ten cents' interest paid to Uncle Timmy. That was the cycle."[11] Dorothy's lyric is more spirited, more sprinkled with slang—one might say less ladylike. Smith's measured prose is replaced by springy rhythms and bouncy, frequent rhymes.

The focus of the first act of the musical is Francie's parents, Johnny and Katie Nolan. In the first act, they fall in love and get married. "Make the Man Love Me," sung first as a solo by Katie, then as a duet with Johnny, establishes, subtly, that she is the stronger character.[12] Katie, having fallen in love with Johnny, will make him hers and will see to it that their lives are joined, for better or for worse. Katie is the third in a series of female characters delineated in part by Fields's lyrics—starting with Annie in *Annie Get Your Gun* and continuing with Jo in *Arms and the Girl*—who fall quickly in love and then pursue their man until they get him. Regarding the lyrics for *A Tree Grows in Brooklyn*, Dorothy said, "The words for this show were made to be simple. No tricky lyrical tries. Our people from Brooklyn wouldn't conceivably sing the sophisticated Cole Porter things." Indeed, the verse for "Make the Man Love Me" reads almost like prose; there is only one end rhyme, "bold" and "told." Dorothy said that "the characters told me what I should write. I didn't tell them."[13]

A clear example of how perfectly she tailored a lyric to the character singing it can be seen by contrasting Johnny's act 1 song, "I'll Buy You a Star," with Dorothy's most famous words for a penniless lover, "I Can't Give You Anything but Love." In the earlier song, the singer's desires are concrete and grounded. "Gee, I'd like to see you looking swell, baby / diamond bracelets Woolworth doesn't sell, baby." Johnny, in contrast, is a dreamer and a poet. The jewelry he has in mind for Katie is "a fine silver chain, made from the rain of a summer afternoon." And while the earlier, anonymous singer admits to poverty, saying, "I can't give you anything but love," Johnny ignores troublesome reality, asserting, "I'll buy you a star."[14]

"I'll Buy You a Star" makes clear both why Katie would fall in love with Johnny and why their wedded life would be unlikely to prosper—not only because Johnny is not practical, but because his view of the world, revealed in his song, contrasts so strongly with Katie's down-to-earth view, revealed in her song. Ethan Mordden described George Abbott's stage direction this way. "His recipe for sound musical comedy structure was: get from A to B as directly as possible, from B to C even more directly, and so on. Psychology, atmosphere, realistic details, and yes, motivation would not slow him. So character was established in broad strokes, as in a comic strip. The stage picture was about movement, never about meaning."[15] Much of the meaning, character, psychology, and atmosphere of *A Tree Grows in Brooklyn* grow from and depend on Dorothy's lyrics.

The second act takes place about a decade later. Francie is on the brink of adolescence. Unfortunately, the actress chosen to play Francie, Nomi Mitty, could barely sing at all. She shares one number with Johnny, "Growing Pains," but this character, who is the center point of the book, does not get a chance to define herself through song in the musical. Even stranger, Katie, who is the backbone of the story in the book and the movie and who appeared to have the same function in the first act of the musical, has no new number in the second act and sings only in the finale, reprising part of "Make the Man Love Me." Johnny is given a chance for growth through music, shifting from a lover singing "I'll Buy You a Star" to a father singing "Growing Pains."

The musical spotlight shifts in the second act to Cissy, not to show the progress of her character or to move the plot forward, but because Shirley Booth, who played Cissy, was such a crowd pleaser. Indeed, no one listening to the cast recording of her renditions of "He Had Refinement" and "Is That My Prince?" would want to give up a second of her performance. But, unfortunately, the dramatic focus slips away. In some ways, Shirley Booth's position in *A Tree Grows in Brooklyn* is comparable with Pearl Bailey's in *Arms and the Girl*. Both were meant to be secondary characters, but they run away with the show by the force of their personalities. Dorothy is complicit in this problem. At age forty-six, she seemed to be more interested in and inspired to write lyrics for women who have seen something of the world rather than for ingénues. Indeed, in three of the four future musicals that she would write, *By the Beautiful Sea*, *Sweet Charity*, and *Seesaw*, the heroines are all older, experienced women; in *Redhead*, the heroine is virginal but on her way to spinsterhood.

Cissy has a solo and an ensemble number in the first act and two solos in the second act. In act 1, as Johnny and Katie are enjoying the optimistic first blush of love, Cissy presents herself as a more seasoned, worldly philosopher than they; she is able to see both the bitter and the sweet. On one hand, she says, "Love is the reason you was born." On the other, she calls love "a toothache in your heart." To the extent that this is a list song, it owes a debt to Cole Porter, but the song's stance or attitude is closer, once again, to Larry Hart's quasi-masochistic lyric "I Wish I Were in Love Again." Dorothy's lyric is a little more balanced regarding the pros and cons of love. For example, by claiming love as "a kick right in your pants" but also as "the aspirin you buy," she describes love as both a pain and a pain reliever.[16]

"He Had Refinement" is perhaps the cleverest character lyric that Fields ever wrote. While ostensibly describing someone else, Cissy is, of course, revealing much about herself. The lyric has points of contact with a list song, giving many examples of Harry's refinement, but in addition it has a dramatic shape both on a small and a large scale. Each stanza gives three examples of Harry's refinement, but the third example is always the most hilarious and ironic one, the punch line. The first stanza shows aspects of refinement that anyone could observe, even on casual contact. The next several stanzas have to do with Harry's gallantry specifically toward Cissy and, more specifically, their sexual relationship. Just as each stanza moves toward a punch line, the final stanza is the climax of the whole lyric, the most ironic example of Harry's refinement. Dorothy performed the song herself at the Lyrics and Lyricists series at the Ninety-second Street Y in 1972.[17]

Mark Steyn reports that "Betty Comden and Adolph Green, working on *Wonderful Town* (1953), were instructed by Rosalind Russell to write her a number that went: Da-da, da-da, da-da, *joke!* Da-da, da-da, da-da, *joke!* In its way, this is as good advice as any, distilling as it does the requirements of structure and momentum."[18] It is more than likely that Russell knew "He Had Refinement" and saw the structure exemplified there. Indeed, Dorothy's brother, Joseph, the author of the book for *Wonderful Town*, could have pointed it out to her.

When Cissy meets up with Harry again, she observes in the song "Is That My Prince?" that he has not aged well. As Cissy and Harry philosophize over this turn of events, their references to "blighted hope" and "vain regret" sound a bit like W. S. Gilbert. But their conclusion, "When love goes cool, You're foolish to warm it up" is more characteristic of the unsentimental stance of Dorothy Fields.

A Tree Grows in Brooklyn appeared on Broadway in the same season as several landmark works, including *Call Me Madam* (October 1950), *Guys and Dolls* (November 1950), and *The King and I* (March 1951). The musical that seems to have been more influential for *A Tree Grows in Brooklyn*, or at least shows a number of points of contact, is *Carousel* (1945). Johnny Nolan in *A Tree Grows in Brooklyn* is similar in many ways to Billy Bigelow in *Carousel*. (It should be noted, however, that Johnny's character is drawn from the novel, which appeared before *Carousel* reached Broadway.) The archetype of the charming but irresponsible man infuses many plays. To the extent that he is a man who remains a boy, Johnny's and Billy's literary ancestor is Peter Pan.[19] Sometimes, such a character is shown going on his carefree way, relatively unscathed or even untouched by the harsh realities of life. Not Billy Bigelow and Johnny Nolan: they both die young. One may speculate that in the time shortly after the Second World War, charming, irresponsible men were not allowed to get off so easy.

Johnny has five solo numbers and a duet in *A Tree Grows in Brooklyn*, more than anyone else. Johnny Johnston, who played Johnny Nolan, was relatively unknown to Broadway; the abundance of songs he is given must be attributed to the interest both Betty Smith and Dorothy Fields had in Nolan's character, first as a lover in act 1 and then as a father in act 2. When Dorothy wrote the words of advice and encouragement Johnny Nolan sings to his daughter, her own son was ten years old, and her daughter seven. Johnny sings "Growing Pains" seeming to hope that his daughter will have greater maturity than he had as a young man—if maturity is connected to being grounded in reality. In a sense, he is wishing that Francie will be more like her mother and less like her father, or he is reassuring her that if this happens it will be all right.[20]

Johnny's last lyrical utterance, "Don't Be Afraid," is also a song of encouragement for his daughter. A comparison of "Don't Be Afraid" with the more popular, anthem-like, "You'll Never Walk Alone" from *Carousel* is revealing. Although Johnny briefly slips into a Polonius-like stance with the lines "Be firm in your mind, / but soft when you speak," for the most part his diction is colloquial, and his similes and metaphors newly minted, such as "calm as a clam," or "a cast-iron chin" or "a ramrod of faith." This is a father talking to his daughter, not a speaker adjuring a graduating class to "Walk on through the wind, walk on through the rain, though your dreams be tossed and blown." Interestingly, although the *Carousel* song assures its listeners "You'll Never Walk Alone" (a sentiment reiterated by Stephen Sondheim in "No One Is Alone" in *Into the Woods*), Dorothy, a woman who prized her independence, sees it as a praiseworthy goal to stand alone and call one's soul one's own.

A Tree Grows in Brooklyn opened at the Alvin Theatre in New York on April 19, 1951. The critics were for the most part very positive. Shirley Booth received the most ecstatic comments. Her previous role in *Come Back, Little Sheba* had given no hint of her abilities as a comedian, singer, or dancer. Richard Watts Jr. called her "one of the wonders of the American stage, a superb actress, a magnificent comedienne, and an all-around performer of seemingly endless versatility. In a pinch, I suppose she could even play Juliet."[21] Upping the ante, John Chapman wrote, "She can do anything in the theatre and do it better than anybody else can. It wouldn't surprise me if she signed up at the Met for the female lead in *Tristan und Isolde*." Marcia Van Dyke and Johnny Johnston were both making their Broadway debuts (Van Dyke was a violinist, and Johnston a recording star), and they both acquitted themselves well. Another first-timer was Herbert Ross, who choreographed the nightmarish Halloween ballet—Johnny's fears and anxieties come to life. Brooks Atkinson commented, "They have been hard put to find a place for the customary ballet in this tenement fable. Herbert Ross' set-piece in the second act just about holds the franchise."[22] Ross later replaced both Peter Brook and George Balanchine to become the one-man choreographer-director of *House of Flowers* (1954).

A *Tree Grows in Brooklyn* ran for 270 performances, not quite long enough to make a profit for its investors, who included Betty Smith, Johnny Johnston, Leland Heyward, and Joshua Logan. Largely through the original-cast recording, the work has maintained a loyal following. Ethan Mordden wrote, "Schwartz and Fields wrote one of the decade's finest scores, romantic, comic, and streetwise to mirror the story's unusual blend of doomed love, . . . domestic farce, . . . and local color."[23] Ken Mandelbaum noted, "Few musicals that ran less than eight months, lost money in their original Broadway productions and have not received a major revival in almost forty years have maintained as strong a reputation as *A Tree Grows in Brooklyn*. . . . *Tree* was strong in all departments and deserved a greater success than it enjoyed."[24]

17
SOMETHING OLD, SOMETHING NEW
● ● ●

By the Beautiful Sea is in many ways a sequel to *A Tree Grows in Brooklyn*, and the fact that it was created at all is curious because the earlier work was not a financial success. Perhaps the people involved felt that *Tree* should have been a financial success and that if the same ingredients were blended slightly differently, the result would be a bigger box office hit. In any case, *A Tree Grows in Brooklyn* and *By the Beautiful Sea* have in common the same songwriting team and approximately the same setting. Perhaps most important, Shirley Booth, undeniably the star of *Tree*, moved from a supporting role to the person around whom the show was built. Robert Fryer was part of the production team for both *Tree* and *Sea*, Irene Sharaff did the costumes for both musicals, and Robert Russell Bennett the orchestrations. Originally, the two shows were not meant to be quite so similar. Before Arthur Schwartz was brought in for *By the Beautiful Sea*, the plan was for Burton Lane to compose. But, as with *Arms and the Girl*, Lane decided that this was not the show for him. Choreographer Helen Tamaris, who had contributed to the success of *Up in Central Park*, replaced Donald Saddler, who had staged the dances for *Wonderful Town* in 1953.

Up in Central Park is another important ancestor. The *Playbill* for *By the Beautiful Sea* says, "Coney Island has long been on the agenda of Herbert and Dorothy Fields as a frame for a musical comedy book." It does not say how long it had been on their agenda, but the way of thinking that starts out with a physical setting suggests *Up in Central Park*. The set designer for *Up in Central Park*, *A Tree Grows in Brooklyn*, and *By the Beautiful Sea* was Jo Mielziner. By 1954, after three decades of activity, Mielziner had designed more than 150 shows. For *By the Beautiful Sea*, he created sets for a theatrical boardinghouse and a vibrant boardwalk on Coney Island, complete with a tunnel-of-love-type ride. He also engineered the first-act finale, in which Shirley Booth appears to leap out of a hot-air balloon and parachute to the ground.

Other Fields shows contributed to *By the Beautiful Sea* in various ways. *Annie Get Your Gun* showed the value of having central characters who were performers—a variant of the backstage musical films of the 1930s. Pearl Bailey's success in *Arms and the Girl* suggested to the Fieldses that a musical could be beefed up by giving two show-stopper numbers to an African American female singer. In *By the Beautiful Sea* the singer was Mae Barnes. Probably, *By the Beautiful Sea* was very much the show Herbert and Dorothy wanted to write. It had limited success not because they could not do what they set out to do but rather because of a miscalculation regarding what would draw an audience in 1954.

In the musical, "By the Beautiful Sea" is the name of a theatrical boardinghouse in Coney Island owned by vaudevillian Lottie Gibson and her father. The house is populated by many colorful but essentially anonymous characters. Running the boardinghouse and keeping things and people (including her young son, Two Bits) in order is Ruby Monk (played by Mae Barnes), who is also Lottie's friend, confidante, and advisor. Lottie, at a mature age (Booth was forty-six when she took this role) has fallen in love with a Shakespearean actor, Dennis Emery, played by Wilbur Evans. Emery has an ex-wife and a teenage daughter who simultaneously turn up at Coney Island. Lottie struggles with the daughter's dislike of her and with the actor's need for financing before things are resolved at the final curtain.

The book revisits several themes from earlier musicals the Fieldses had worked on. A male lead with a daughter antagonistic to the female lead recalls *Panama Hattie*, for which Herbert had written the book in collaboration with Buddy DeSylva. The role of Ruby, the black outsider who gives practical, worldly advice to the heroine, is related to Connecticut in *Arms and the Girl* and Sitting Bull in *Annie Get Your Gun*. The highbrow/lowbrow theme (Lottie, the vaudevillian, loves and looks up to, but also finances, a Shakespearean actor) appears in many movies of the 1930s and 1940s, though none especially associated with the Fieldses. It is hard to say to what extent Herbert and Dorothy drew upon their father's reminiscences of just-getting-by entertainers in the last decades of the nineteenth century. Weber and Fields did their own share of Coney Island performances when they were youngsters.

There are ten numbers in act 1 of *By the Beautiful Sea*.[1] Act 2 has four new ones and reprises five from the first act. As might be expected, Shirley Booth has the most to do—three numbers in the first act and one in the second act. Mae Barnes and Wilbur Evans each have two solos—one per act. Eddie Roll, playing the juvenile romantic character Mickey Powers, has a solo in act 1. The remaining numbers are ensembles. The whole score tends to be up-tempo, almost relentlessly cheerful and surprisingly impersonal. It generally steers away from defining character. The residents of Lottie Gibson's boardinghouse are performers, and it is as if the roles they play are the whole story of their lives. They are described in the cast list as "the quartet," "acrobats," and "ballerina;" a group of singing sisters are given the names Cora Belmont, Molly Belmont, and Lillian Belmont, but they might as well have been called "trio" for all we know of their personalities. Furthermore, two of Lottie's numbers are more scene-setting than personal ("The Sea Song" and "Coney Island Boat") and one, "Please Don't Send Me Down a Baby Brother," is sung as a part of a vaudeville show; Lottie is doing an act similar to Fanny Brice in the persona of Baby Snooks. In only one song does she even come close to introspection. "I'd Rather Wake Up by Myself" is a comic review of her previous failed romances, but it tells us less about her than "He Had Refinement" told us about Cissy. Structurally, both lyrics work in a similar way—line, line, joke.

None of the women in *By the Beautiful Sea* has a romantic ballad. It is a pity that Shirley Booth was not given a chance to sing, without ironic distancing, about love. It might have been a revelation—but it also might have rocked the comic boat too much. Indeed, the creative team may well have felt that too much seriousness was what brought *A Tree Grows in Brooklyn* down. Brooks Atkinson noted that "Miss Booth's heart is not seriously involved with Wilbur Evans' concert-stage portrait of a Shakespearean actor."[2] The lack of a romantic ballad for her was probably at the root of this problem. The two romantic ballads are reserved for the male characters. They are more wistful than impassioned, and in both cases the problem for the character has to do with age. The male ingénue character worries that the girl he is drawn to, Baby Betsy Busch, is underage. She is actually a young woman, but her mother dresses her like a child so that she can take juvenile roles on stage. (Curiously, when Lottie Gibson does her specialty number in the second act, it is also in the persona of a child.) In "Old Enough to Love," Dorothy Fields borrows a "nestle-wrestle" rhyme from her earlier song, "A Fine Romance," where she had used it to better advantage.

Before Wilbur Evans was cast as Dennis Emery in *By the Beautiful Sea*, he had been singing the role of the planter, de Becque, in the London production of *South Pacific*, the role Ezio Pinza had created. His first ballad in *Sea*, "I've Been Alone Too Long," is appropriate to a character of mature years who had not expected romance to enter his life again.

Mae Barnes's first solo also brings to mind *South Pacific*—or at least the title does. "Happy Habit" is a cousin to "Happy Talk." Both songs are upbeat and are sung by the older ethnic character in the show. Barnes's second song, "Hang Up," is in a rousing gospel style. It may have been inspired by "Sit Down, You're Rocking the Boat" from *Guys and Dolls*. Each song occupies a similar near-the-end placement in its respective show.

Predictably, the reviewers adored Shirley Booth. Hawkins, in the *New York Telegram* said, "If you want to know what really being a star is, see Shirley Booth in *By the Beautiful Sea*. She is a million dollar value in show business." Chapman wrote in the *New York News*, "Miss Booth is, as always, an enchanting actress. When she is singing Dorothy Fields' wry lyrics of 'I'd Rather Wake Up by Myself,' or doing a Baby Snooks routine as a little girl who wants to remain an only child, she is a perfect entertainer." Walter Kerr of the *New York Tribune* declared, "I think there can no longer be any reasonable doubt: Miss Booth is the champ." Brooks Atkinson wrote in the *New York Times*, "Everyone has long since lost his heart to Miss Booth, who is a doll on either the dramatic or musical stage. She is in great form [in] *By the Beautiful Sea*. Friendly, unassuming and good-humored, honest with the other performers as well as with the audience, she makes a Coney Island holiday out of her part."

Reviewers also praised Mae Barnes. Hawkins remarked, "Second in line for kudos is Mae Barnes. . . . Her two songs, 'Happy Habit' and 'Hang Up' are show-stoppers." More than one reviewer indicated that this was an old-fashioned show. John McClain in the *Journal-American* called *By the Beautiful Sea* "an opulent old time musical comedy." George Freedley said it "could be called an old-fashioned musical in the best sense of the word, that is, that its performers are allowed to take full advantage of their best songs without worry about the closely integrated show which frowns on encores." The New Haven reviewer thought, "In format and execution, *Beautiful Sea* reverts to the style of musicals prevalent before the advent of allegorical, fantasy-type and ballet-integrated tune shows such as have emphasized the song-and-picture of recent seasons. In brief, its story is told simply, and vocal or terpsichorean action follows the standard routine of cues, rather than being blended into the book thread to a pronounced degree. Result is an occasion for relaxed enjoyment."[3] Perhaps a producer such as Mike Todd could have promoted the show into a major success. As it was, the show that was supposed to be an improvement on *A Tree Grows in Brooklyn* ran for exactly the same number of performances, 270.

By the Beautiful Sea was the last work in an intensely active period in Dorothy Fields's career—three Broadway musicals and four Hollywood musicals between 1950 and 1954. In the second half of the decade, she slowed down. She added lyrics to three textless songs in the Jerome Kern *Nachlass*, wrote lyrics for a made-for-television musical, and worked on the books and lyrics for one Broadway show. It is worth pointing out that this slowing down does not indicate either a falling off in quality or a retreat from new developments in the entertainment world, although it is true that *By the Beautiful Sea* seemed to be a rear-guard rather than an avant-garde work.

Whether writing rear-guard or avant-garde works, it was typical of Dorothy Fields to embrace new technologies. She was in the first wave of New York songwriters to move to Hollywood. In the 1930s, when many of her colleagues would cross the continent by train, she flew. In Hollywood in the 1930s, she enjoyed being behind the wheel of one or another of her new cars, chauffeuring such nondriving friends as Jerome Kern and Sigmund Romberg. It is not surprising, then, that while television was still in its infancy Dorothy was looking into the implications of the new medium for dramatic writers. In April 1948, Max Wilk reports, "a cadre of authors and playwrights had come together . . . under the auspices of the Authors League . . . to design and implement a new guild, one that would eventually deal with the networks and the advertising agencies and the sponsors in that brand-new, uncharted area of entertainment."[4] Dorothy was at that meeting, along with Moss Hart, Oscar Hammerstein II, Lillian Hellman, Elmer Rice, Rex Stout, John Hersey, and dozens of other writers. Her presence there points to two facets of her personality: her interest in new technologies and the enjoyment she got from meetings with her professional colleagues at the Authors League or at ASCAP.

Although Dorothy's interest in television was aroused in 1948, it was not until almost a decade later, in 1957, that she worked on a musical written especially for TV. Several other composers and lyricists had tested the waters before her. *Cinderella* by Rodgers and Hammerstein, first shown in 1957 with Julie Andrews in the title role, was perhaps the most successful and well remembered. Dorothy's friend and sometime collaborator Arthur Schwartz wrote the scores for two television musicals in 1956, *High Tor* and *A Bell for Adano*. Sammy Cahn and James Van Heusen thought their score for the television musical version of Thornton Wilder's *Our Town* contained some of their best songs. Given that "Love and Marriage" was one of these, they had a good case.

In the 1950s, television programming was receptive to experiments in musical theater that ran the cultural gamut. Among the operas written for or revised for the new medium were *Amahl and the Night Visitors* (1951) by Gian Carlo Menotti; *Trouble in Tahiti* (1952) by Leonard Bernstein; *The Marriage* (1952), by Bohuslav Martinů, based on a play by Gogol; *The Mighty Casey* (1955) by William Schuman; *Griffelkin* (1955) by Lukas Foss; *The Trial at Rouen* (1956) by Norman Dello Joio; *Sarah* (1958) by Ezra Laderman; and *Maria Golovin* (1959) by Menotti. In most years, at least one musical version of a children's story was shown, whether of *Cinderella, Heidi, Jack and the Beanstalk, Pinocchio, Peter Pan,* the *Pied Piper of Hamelin,* or *Mother Goose*. The Christmas season was deemed a particularly good time for musicals geared to family viewing.

Dorothy Fields's contribution to made-for-television musicals was *Junior Miss*, shown by CBS Friday, December 20, 1957, on the DuPont Show of the Month. The original source for *Junior Miss* was an eponymous collection of twelve short stories by Sally Benson, published in 1939. Many of the stories had previously appeared in the *New Yorker*. The stories are episodes in the life of the Graves family—"Mr. Graves, genial and successful business man in his early forties; Mrs. Graves, his charming and understanding wife; Lois, the very superior young daughter of sixteen; and in particular, Judy, just under fourteen, a little too eager, a little too fat, stepped on at every turn by her older sister, but for all that, as appealing a little job as can be found."[5]

Jerome Chodorov and Dorothy's brother Joe made these stories the basis of a play, *Junior Miss*, which reached Broadway on November 18, 1941, and had a very successful run of 710 performances. Joe Fields and Chodorov had previously made a hit play, *My Sister Eileen*, out of the *New Yorker* short stories of Ruth McKenney. In his review of *Junior Miss*, Brooks Atkinson commented, "Jerome Chodorov and Joseph Fields, who last season were writing *My Sister Eileen* out of the fecund pages of the *New Yorker*, have apparently renewed their subscription."[6] Most of Joe's plays were straight comedies, but he occasionally wrote books for musicals. In 1949, he collaborated with Anita Loos to turn *Gentlemen Prefer Blondes* into a musical. *My Sister Eileen* became *Wonderful Town* in 1953, with songs by Leonard Bernstein, Betty Comden, and Adolph Green. *The Girl in Pink Tights* opened on Broadway in 1954, three years after the death of its composer, Sigmund Romberg. Joe's last musical, done in collaboration with Rodgers and Hammerstein, was *Flower Drum Song* (1958).

Joe did not write the television script for *Junior Miss*, however; that job went to Joseph Stein and Will Glickman. The adaptation necessarily meant cutting the dialogue down to fit a ninety-minute time slot, making room for songs in the play itself and, of course, commercial breaks. This was achieved, in part, by slashing the role of the maid, Hilda. (On Broadway Hilda had been played by Paula Laurence, who later appeared with Ethel Merman in *Something For the Boys*.)

The composer for *Junior Miss* was Dorothy's longtime friend Burton Lane. Lane was born in New York in 1912 and, like his idol, George Gershwin, showed his talent for music early, both as a pianist and a composer. At the age of fifteen, he was hired by the Remick Music Corporation. He placed some of his songs in revues—*Three's a Crowd*, *The Third Little Show*, and the ninth edition of *Earl Carroll's Vanities* among them. In 1933, Lane went to Hollywood with lyricist Harold Adamson, and they soon had a big hit with their song "Everything I Have Is Yours," which was sung by Joan Crawford in the film

Dancing Lady. Dorothy had written the lyric of the title song for *Dancing Lady*, and she probably met Lane at this time, but they did not work together in Hollywood. Lane's principal lyricists in Hollywood were Frank Loesser, Ralph Freed, Ira Gershwin, and Alan Jay Lerner. One of his signal achievements in Hollywood was discovering Judy Garland (then Frances Gumm) and bringing her talent to the attention of the music department at MGM.

Over the next two decades Lane, like Fields, had a bicoastal career. He composed songs for more than thirty films and five Broadway musicals, one of which was an outstanding success. His first complete score for Broadway was *Hold On to Your Hats* (1940), which was written as a vehicle for Al Jolson. The lyricist was Yip Harburg, to whom Lane had been introduced by Ira Gershwin when Lane was still a teenager. Probably Lane's best-known and best-appreciated work was his 1947 collaboration with Harburg, *Finian's Rainbow*.

After the success of *Finian's Rainbow*, Lane's services as a composer were much in demand. Arnold Saint Subber hoped he would write the score for what became *Kiss Me, Kate*, but Lane was turning down projects left and right. The British musician and author Benny Green commented wryly, "Lane announced that he was committed to other projects, which is mystifying in view of the fact that another eighteen years were to pass before he found himself free enough to compose another Broadway score."[7] Alec Wilder wrote, "Between 1951 and 1965 the record shows that Lane had only one song of even minor interest published."[8] In 1965, Lane was persuaded by Alan Jay Lerner to write the score for what became his other Broadway hit, *On a Clear Day You Can See Forever*, which ran for 280 performances.

Lane certainly had given some thought to the reasons for his long fallow period. He said, "I have always felt I could do a show a year standing on my ear, *if* I could find things that I liked. Even though I'm willing to work on something where we'll eventually compromise, you still have to find something first where it's worth compromising."[9] When it came to writing a score for a musical, the deal breaker was generally the book. Lane said he thought it was easier for the Gershwins to write musicals in the '20s because the book was not such an issue. But he made clear that the "issue" was one specific to him. Writing music for a movie with an inadequate script was easier for "guys like Harry Warren," Lane said. "No matter what piece of junk he was working on, whatever picture, with those meaningless plots and ridiculous subjects— backstage, Argentina, whatever—Harry would always come up with some wonderful tunes."[10] Indeed, Lane himself wrote many excellent songs for undistinguished films, but he held himself to a different standard when it came to Broadway. Perhaps it was the ephemeral nature of a television musical—a work that would be seen only once, although possibly by a very large audience—and also the fact that the story they were working with had already proved itself on Broadway that allowed Lane to write a few songs with Dorothy.

Junior Miss had a fine cast. Don Ameche played Mr. Graves, Joan Bennett played Mrs. Graves, Jill St. John played older sister Lois, and Carol Lynley played Judy. Also on hand were Diana Lynn and David Wayne as a young couple whom Judy brings together. Seven songs were introduced into the play. Two of the numbers are grouped around the theme of Christmas and gift giving—"Let's Make It Christmas All Year Long," and "It's Just What I Wanted." Other songs, such as "A Male Is an Animal," "Have Feet, Will Dance" and "Junior Miss" are connected to Judy Graves' growth into young womanhood. Dorothy may have had particular fun writing the lyrics for this musical because her son, David, and daughter, Eliza, were just the same ages as the siblings in the play. The *New York Times* television reviewer, Jack Gould, thought that "I'll Buy It" (for Lynn and Wayne) was "the one bright number." On the whole, he was not impressed with the score, which he thought "for the most part consisted only of nondescript songs casually appended to the dramatic script."[11] To add insult to injury, the reviewer identified the composer as Burton Crane.

Fields's next project was *Redhead*, the last musical she and Herbert would work on together. They first had the idea for the musical that became *Redhead* in the early 1950s, but it took almost a decade to get it to the Broadway stage. In their career together as librettists, Dorothy and Herbert were sometimes the progenitors of the idea for a musical; in other instances they were approached by producers or composers who had an idea but needed a book. It is of interest, in trying to understand their creative process, to consider the starting point for a given work. *Redhead*, originally called *The Works*, began with a genre (the mystery) and an idea of time and place: a wax museum in London at the end of the nineteenth century. In this, it resembled *Up in Central Park*, which also began with the authors' sense of ambience—an idea of place and time. Other musicals they wrote books for began with the idea of a central player in a particular locale (such as Shirley Booth in *By the Beautiful Sea*), or a central player in a particular role (such as Ethel Merman as Annie Oakley). For better or for worse, what seldom seemed to have been the starting point for a libretto for the Fields siblings was an outline of a plot. The plot was constructed almost on a need-to-know basis.

Somewhere between ambience and plot is the matter of characters and characterization. The roster of very different actresses considered for the leading role in *Redhead*—Beatrice Lillie, Ethel Merman, Mary Martin, Celeste

Holm, Gisele Mackenzie—suggests that the character, at the initial stage, could be designed as needed. (This is not the same as, for example, *Hello, Dolly!* in which actresses as different as Carol Channing and Pearl Bailey could reshape the role, leaving their own imprints on it.)

There were many detours on the road to *Redhead*. Between 1951 and 1954, Dorothy was busy with *A Tree Grows in Brooklyn* and several Hollywood movies. In 1954, both Dorothy and Herbert worked on *By the Beautiful Sea*. But they did not give up on the idea of a musical-mystery, and for years they sought to line up a collaborative team. They needed a composer, and their first thought was Irving Berlin, with whom they had worked so successfully and happily on *Annie Get Your Gun*. Working with Berlin would mean, once again, that Dorothy would be a librettist only, not the lyricist. Berlin had turned down the opportunity to work on *A Tree Grows in Brooklyn*. *The Works* was even less in his normal bailiwick because it was set in England. Berlin's shows had their roots firmly in American soil, even if the Americans were transplanted to an American embassy in a mythical European state, as in *Call Me Madam* (1950), his next project after *Annie Get Your Gun*.

The Fieldses finally chose for *Redhead* a composer with whom they had not worked before, Albert Hague. A refugee from Germany, Hague came to the United States in 1939. According to his obituary, "He was born Albert Marcuse in Berlin on October 13, 1920. His father was a psychiatrist and a musical prodigy and his mother a chess champion. His family considered their Jewish heritage a liability and raised him as a Lutheran."[12] The disguise worked too well; Albert, studying music in Rome, was about to be inducted into the German army. Instead, he went to the United States, adopted by a friend of his aunt's, an eye surgeon named Elliott Hague who lived in Cincinnati. Albert enrolled in the University of Cincinnati as a music student. His skills as a pianist kept him afloat until he could establish himself as a composer. Albert Hague recalled, "When I came out of the army—the American army— I made a beeline for New York City to make my fame and fortune in the Big Apple. . . . If you want a losing proposition . . . you are going door to door trying to sell songs to music publishers in New York, who are mostly Jewish, after World War II, with a German accent." Hague acknowledged, "In retrospect maybe I shouldn't blame my accent on all this lack of success. It could be I picked lyrics that weren't as felicitous as they should be."[13] As examples of less-than-felicitous lyrics, Hague cited two of his unsuccessful songs: "When the Rats Begin to Leave My Love Boat" and "I've Got a Rock for a Pillow 'Cause You've Got a Stone for a Heart."

Hague's first hit show was *Plain and Fancy* (1955), which ran for 461 performances. The lyrics were by Arnold Horwitt, and the book by Joseph Stein and Will Glickman, who later did the television adaptation of *Junior Miss*. Set in Pennsylvania Dutch country, *Plain and Fancy* presents a when-worlds-collide situation: a modern New York City couple visiting a traditional Amish community. Described by Ethan Mordden as "more than musical comedy, yet . . . not quite a musical play, *Plain and Fancy* belongs to a form that was seeded in the 1940s and flowered in the 1950s: the 'serious' musical comedy, the 'light' musical play. In this genre, musical comedy has been strongly influenced by Rodgers and Hammerstein but not actually *Carousel*-ized."[14] The hit song of *Plain and Fancy* was "Young and Foolish."

Hague was introduced to the Fieldses by his agent, David Hocker. Hague's wife, singer Renee Orin, told a cabaret audience about her first meeting with Dorothy. "Albert has a habit of talking about me . . . especially to his lyricists. And I remember, it was their first day of work and I was very excited because I was invited to have dinner with them afterwards. So I walked up to the door of Dorothy's apartment. I rang the bell. She opened the door and she said, 'Won't you come in. I'm Dorothy Fields. What would you like to drink? I sing all my own songs.'" This anecdote seems to me a perfect encapsulation of Dorothy's combination of graciousness, hardheaded professionalism, and, perhaps, a certain opacity to the way her remarks might affect the people she spoke to. Her collaborators uniformly admired her talent, but some—Harry Warren and Cy Coleman among them—found her difficult to get along with. Hague added to this account, "Truth is, she was a brilliant lyric writer but her singing wasn't so hot. We actually never sold *Redhead* until Renee demonstrated the score."[15] Hague's uxorious version of events may be accurate. More important for moving the production of *Redhead* into high gear, though, was getting Gwen Verdon to agree to star in it.

When she was first approached to do *Redhead*, Verdon was considered a guarantee of success. Each of the previous three roles she had played on Broadway won her a Tony. Her first Tony was for best supporting actress in *Can-Can* (1953), and it was her first speaking role on Broadway. Cy Feuer, the producer of the show, recalled, "Michael Kidd staged a comic Apache dance in the second act, where Gwen, in slow motion, takes a knife out of a cheese a waiter is carrying, kills her lover, puts the knife back in the cheese as the waiter goes by again, and slow-motions off the stage."[16] The number literally stopped the show. After the set had changed and the actors were ready to go on with the next scene, the audience did not stop applauding until Verdon was brought back on stage, in a bathrobe, to take another bow. Verdon's next role was Lola in *Damn Yankees* (1955). The choreographer for this show was Bob Fosse. Verdon and Fosse had been acquainted in Hollywood, before each had moved to New York, but *Damn Yankees* was the start of their remarkable onstage and offstage partnership. Their next show together was *New Girl in Town* (1957), based on Eugene O'Neill's *Anna Christie* and directed by George Abbott. Fosse's role, as his biographer Martin Gottfried noted, "was being expanded to include musical staging as well as choreography; thus he was mastering the direction of songs—the movements of the actors singing them, and more important than that, he was learning how to stitch the musical moments smoothly into a show's dramatic fabric."[17]

When the songs for *Redhead* were auditioned for Verdon, she was enthusiastic. She had only one condition before she accepted. Bob Fosse should not only choreograph—he should direct the entire production. Fosse's artistic growth, his desire to control all the elements of a production, as well as his frustration after disagreements with George Abbott and Hal Prince about a whorehouse ballet in *New Girl in Town* made directing a natural, almost inevitable next step for him. (Michael Kidd had led the way as choreographer-director with his success with *Lil' Abner* in 1956, and Jerome Robbins followed suit with *West Side Story* in 1957.) Verdon's faith in Fosse and her increasing clout as a star opened the way for Fosse to direct. Fosse knew that when directing actors, he could not expect the same level of unquestioning obedience that he got from dancers. One of his dancers, Margery Beddow, recalled, "Although Fosse knew exactly what he wanted from the actors, I think he was a bit nervous about verbalizing it. The last day of our dance rehearsals Fosse said to us, 'Now tomorrow all those actors are going to come in here, and they're going to want to know what their motivation is. The first actor who asks that, I want you to all stand up together and say, 'Because Bobby says so!' "[8]

Bob Fosse was a shaping force, as one would expect, for the look of the show and its overall rhythm and pacing. He also asserted himself very strongly regarding the suitability of the various musical numbers, an area one might have thought was the preserve of the composer and lyricist. He was, in fact, somewhat disadvantaged musically. Hague noted, "It was very difficult to talk music with him because he didn't know music. He literally couldn't count beats."[19] Martin Gottfried recounted, "when the company moved to Washington, D.C., Hague arranged to have the sheet music of his score duplicated so that he could give it to everyone as Christmas presents. It was a lovely idea, and as he handed an autographed set to Bob, he said 'Merry Christmas,' only to receive a scowl in response. The director seemed to take the gift as a reference to his musical ignorance. 'What are you giving it to me for?' he snapped. 'You know I can't read music.' "[20] Fosse may have been touchy and defensive about his musical knowledge, but he seldom backed away from his own judgments. Of the original thirteen songs Fields and Hague auditioned, only three had survived when the show opened in New York. Essentially, Fosse had them write a whole new musical. Not surprisingly, composer and lyricist sometimes chafed under Fosse's yoke. Hague thought working with Fosse was "a little bit like going to the best dentist in town. When he works on you it hurts but when he gets through with you, you can walk out smiling proudly."[21] He also related, "We would play him a song, and he would say, 'No,' . . . and Dorothy would say, 'Well you can't just say "no." Why don't you like it?' and he would lean over to her and look her in the face and say, 'It just doesn't entertain me enough.' But he was almost always right. And Dorothy was a consummate professional."[22]

Some of the musical changes were made to meet Gwen Verdon's needs. The score was rearranged so that she would discharge all of her solo singing duties in the first half of the first act, before she did her more demanding dance routines. In the second half of the first act and in the entire second act she sang in ensembles—duos or trios—but she was not required to sustain a solo number by herself. To the extent that we hope to see a character develop in the course of the musical through the songs he or she sings (something Oscar Hammerstein II figured out brilliantly, especially for his male characters such as Billy Bigelow in *Carousel* or Joe Cable in *South Pacific*, who have soul-baring numbers before they go to their deaths), this hope is disappointed. Gwen Verdon's life and career were built on overcoming seemingly impossible obstacles—her legs were misshapen from rickets in childhood, yet she became a great dancer. Fosse judged that she could not overcome the impossible eight times a week. That is, she could not do taxing, demanding dance routines and then expect her lungs and vocal chords to get her through singing a solo. It will be remembered that the role of Essie was originally offered to performers who were primarily or exclusively singers—Bea Lillie, Ethel Merman, Mary Martin, among others. The rewriting to accommodate Gwen Verdon was extensive, even before out-of-town tryouts. Verdon sings in almost half of the numbers in the play; she was too much the star of the show to keep her offstage for long. But six of the numbers in which she sings are ensembles.

Fosse's imprint on the music is seen in other ways as well. In its setting and costumes, *Redhead* may seem to look back to *New Girl in Town*, but the structure of *Redhead* in some ways adumbrates that of *Chicago* or *Cabaret*. That is, *Redhead* is as much a revue as it is a musical play. Several of the sung musical numbers—"The Uncle Sam Rag," "Erbie Fitch's Twitch," "Two Faces in the Dark," and "We Loves Ya, Jimey"—are presented in the context of a show within a show. The lyrics are expected to be entertaining, but not advance the plot. Fosse prefers to advance the plot through the dance numbers—Essie's Vision in act 1 and the Pick-Pocket Tango in act 2. This was not a change of direction for Herbert and Dorothy Fields. *By the Beautiful Sea*, like *Redhead*, gives the heroine an opportunity to sing in a show within a show. And both of these musicals, as well as *Annie Get Your Gun*, depict the kind of popular, even lowbrow entertainment in which Lew Fields had had his roots.

Redhead is set in Edwardian London. The show begins with a coup de théâtre. We see a redheaded, red-bearded man use a purple scarf to strangle a showgirl, all in mime. The scene changes to the Simpson Sisters Waxworks where the shocking murder is now on show as a sensational wax display. The establishment is run by two elderly sisters and their spinsterish niece, Essie Whimple, who occasionally has visions. Essie falls in love at first sight with Tom Baxter, an American music-hall strongman and at one time the boy-friend of the slain showgirl. Essie believes she can win his love by helping solve the murder. There follows an assortment of disguises, music-hall acts, and chases until the murderer is finally caught. Playing opposite Gwen Verdon, in the role of Tom Baxter, was Richard Kiley, who had been the romantic lead in *Kismet* (1953). After *Redhead* he starred in Richard Rodgers's *No Strings* (1962) and had his most celebrated role as Don Quixote in *Man of La Mancha* (1965). He also worked in movies and television, winning several Golden Globe and Emmy awards.

Bob Fosse wanted entertaining lyrics from Dorothy, and that was what she delivered. In the midst of working on *Redhead*, Dorothy lost the two men closest to her—her brother and her husband.[23] It is a testimony to her profes-sionalism that while still in mourning for Herbert and Eli, she was able to write comic, witty lyrics.[24] The opening number, "The Simpson Sisters' Door," encourages us to laugh at both commercialism and the public's delight in the depiction of violence. The potential customers for the wax museum are prom-ised that they will see "much more gore than they saw at Elsinore" as well as "cadavers by the score." The word "door" has many more rhyming partners than, say, "love," and the lyricist chooses a basketful of comic rhymes for this number, including "ignore," "explore," "adore," "galore," and "before."

"Uncle Sam Rag" is a big chorus-and-dance number in the middle of the first act. In some ways it looks back to songs of the '20s and '30s that put in the lyrics a description of the dance itself, such as "The Varsity Rag." Although purportedly describing a ragtime dance, the text is perfectly apposite for Fosse's jazz-influenced choreography, particularly directions to "knock your knees" and execute a "low dip and a wiggle."

If one were to look for a sign of Dorothy's emotional distress in the lyrics of *Redhead*, one might find it in a reluctance to go below the surface emotion-ally in the solo songs. (It is also possible that these songs keep real feelings at arm's length because that is just what Fosse wanted.) Essie's regret at being a spinster is symbolically located not in her heart or her head, but rather is displaced to her hand, specifically to one finger, in "The Right Finger of My Left Hand." With great psychological insight, the lyricist allows that finger to experience some wistful envy of other fingers "smoothin' out a snowy veil or pattin' a satin gown."

When Tom Baxter first meets Essie he is underwhelmed and sings, in duet with his friend, "She's Not Woman Enough for Me." Two numbers later, he decides "My Girl Is Just Enough Woman for Me." In the second act, after he and Essie have had a disagreement he crows, "I'm Back in Circulation." The overall impression he gives in his lyrics is of emotional superficiality. Essie and Tom's duet, "Look Who's in Love" is exuberant and boisterous, but perhaps not meant to be deeply felt. In the first pair of lines, the singers express some doubt about being in love, saying, "We are—well, aren't we?" although by the end of the duet they acknowledge they are "blessed."

The critics were very enthusiastic about *Redhead*, several of them anointing it the best musical of the year. Not surprisingly, most of the praise was lavished on Gwen Verdon and Bob Fosse. Richard Watts Jr. of the *New York Post* declared, "You would have to go back to memories of Gertrude Lawrence to find a kinship in charm, skill, and authentic glamour, and even Miss Lawrence couldn't dance with Miss Verdon's humorous brilliance."[25]

The book was as good as it could be, given the circumstances. It was begun by Herbert and Dorothy. Then Herbert died, Dorothy was grieving, and the two people called in to continue work on the book, Sidney Sheldon and David Shaw, had little Broadway experience. Nevertheless, *Redhead* won eight Tony awards, including one for best book for a musical. The other awards went to Bob Fosse, Gwen Verdon, Richard Kiley, Albert Hague, Rouben Ter-Artunian (costume designer), Robert Fryer and Lawrence Carr (producers), and to *Redhead* as best musical of the year.

SWEET CHARITY

• • •

In the year 1958, death dealt Dorothy three dreadful blows. The first and most distant of the shocks was the death of Michael Todd in a plane crash on March 22, 1958. Todd was traveling in his private plane from Los Angeles to New York where he was to receive an award as "showman of the year" from the Friars Club. His plane went down in the Zuni Mountains in New Mexico. Dorothy and Herbert had worked with Todd on *Mexican Hayride* (1944) and *Up in Central Park* (1945). They had seen less of him in the 1950s, when Todd had been spending more time in Hollywood. His three-hour, star-studded film *Around the World in Eighty Days*, shown in a special widescreen process called Todd-AO, which he had helped develop, won an Academy Award in 1956. To everyone who knew him, Todd had seemed the embodiment of energy and vitality; his death at forty-nine stunned his family, friends, and associates.[1] Todd's funeral was a small, private affair, and he was buried near his father's grave in Chicago.

Much worse was to follow for Dorothy. On March 24, just two days after Michael Todd's death, her brother Herbert died of a heart attack at age sixty. Herbert was not only the sibling Dorothy was always closest to, but also a close friend, confidant, and professional collaborator. He had never married or found a lasting male partner, so to a large extent Dorothy's immediate family was his family; he was a loving and affectionate uncle to Dorothy's son and daughter. He would stay at the Lahm house in Brewster working on librettos and gardening with Dorothy. He paid for Eliza's riding lessons starting from the time she was six, and uncle and niece enjoyed talking about horses.

It had been Herb's pattern all his professional life to work collaboratively. For the first decade and a half of his theatrical career, he worked with men who had a similar sexual orientation—first Lorenz Hart and then Cole Porter. These were simply professional partnerships, but they may have given Herbert a level of comfort and security that would allow him to put himself on the line theatrically. The collaborative nature of his assignments may have intensified when his sister joined him in writing books; previously, he had not had a permanent co-librettist. Working with Dorothy may have offered comfort and security in a similar way. They began writing librettos together in 1941, and with only one exception—*A Tree Grows in Brooklyn*—every work she did for Broadway, until his death, she did with Herbert.

Herbert Fields left behind a body of librettos for more than twenty Broadway shows as well as contributions in the form of story ideas for several Hollywood musicals. In his earliest works, he and his partners Richard Rodgers and Lorenz Hart saw themselves as innovators, even pioneers. They wrote smart, modern musical comedies, in touch with the youth of the Roaring Twenties, that were willing to laugh at social absurdities and unafraid to touch on delicate or titillating sexual subjects. The greatest hits of the Rodgers-Hart-Fields partnership were *Dearest Enemy* (1925), *Peggy-Ann* (1926), and *A Connecticut Yankee* (1927). Their disintegration as a team began in the late 1920s, and by the time they were all in Hollywood, in the 1930s, Herbert Fields's divorce from the team of Rodgers and Hart was complete. Herbert's career in Hollywood was active but less distinguished. He was regularly employed, earning enough to live very comfortably and contribute to the support of his parents. But there was no memorable film accomplishment comparable to his Broadway hits.

With Cole Porter, he created a number of stage successes—*Fifty Million Frenchmen* (1929), *Du Barry Was a Lady* (1939), and *Panama Hattie* (1940). He also teamed with George and Ira Gershwin, writing the libretto for a notable flop, *Pardon My English* (1933). One theater historian writes that Herbert Fields was "consistent and reliable, but only within the narrow demands of a musical comedy book. . . . With the exception of *Annie Get Your Gun* Fields never changed: his last book was for *Redhead* in 1959, with Gwen Verdon and Bob Fosse, but it could easily have been his first."[2]

Dorothy must have received a flood of messages of condolence. She saved two, both from women friends. Ellin McKay Berlin wrote on March 25:

Dearest Dorothy—
Irving and I can't believe, can't realize that Herbie is gone. And we want to send you all our love, all our sorrowful sympathy.
Nobody knows anyone else's heart, but I know a little how you must feel as I have always been very close to my brother—I also know that you have had a special closeness to Herbie, through your work and in many ways—And that this separation is harder for you than it would be for any sister. Dear Dorothy, I am so terribly sorry for you and I love you very much.

Irving and I have talked so much about Herbie, of his talent, of his kindness, of his gaytie [*sic*]. We will miss him very much—All our love, dear

Devotedly,
Ellin

In a letter dated March 26, Dorothy Hammerstein wrote: "There is nothing I can say to you Darling that you don't already know. You know I love you deeply and sincerely. You know I loved Herbie and respected him too. And although we see each other far too little we both must know that there is nothing we wouldn't do for each other. This isn't just talk. I have only about four *real* friends and you are the most real."[3]

The next calamity to strike Dorothy in 1958 was the death of her husband just a few months later. In the words of their daughter, "I think they think it was a cerebral hemorrhage. It was extremely sudden. He was with my mother. They were in New York. They were staying at my Uncle Herbie's apartment for some reason.[4] And he got up in the middle of the night. And he knocked a lamp over. That's what woke up my mother. And then in the bathroom he vomited in the tub and then he collapsed and he died. She was right there. It was horrible. He'd just been to the doctor about a week before and gotten a clean bill of health."[5] His obituary in the *New York Times* was brief. "David Eli Lahm, a manufacturer of women's wear associated with Dove Blouse, Inc. 1375 Broadway, died yesterday of a heart attack in his home, 12 East Sixty-Ninth Street. His age was 66. Surviving are his widow, Dorothy Fields, lyricist and playwright, a son, David F.; a daughter, Eliza, and a brother, Mortimer."[6]

Soon after, Dorothy made plans to sell their home in Brewster. It was a large house with a seventy-five-by-twenty-five-foot swimming pool, and it was set on more than a hundred acres of land. Herbert was dead, Eli was dead, David was about to start college at Amherst. Dorothy saw no reason to maintain such a large property. For several years, the interlocking lives of the Fields and Lahm families—nuclear and extended—had been expressed in a number of complicated living arrangements. The family had maintained an apartment in Manhattan as well as the house in the country. For one year, Eliza went to school in Brewster, New York, and David stayed in the city with his father and his Uncle Mortimer. In the latter half of the 1950s, the family moved back and forth between the east side and the west side of Manhattan; the Lahms resided, successively, at 300 Central Park West, 565 Park Avenue, 470 Park Avenue, and the Beresford on Central Park West. Herb's apartment was at 12 East Sixty-ninth Street.[7]

It appeared for a while that Dorothy Fields's career had come to an end after the deaths of her brother and husband. *Redhead* had swept the Tonys in all the musical categories except conductor of a musical. Nevertheless, for more than five years, there was no Broadway show, no television musical, no movie featuring songs with new lyrics by Dorothy Fields.

Dorothy's return to activity on the Broadway musical was serendipitous. Cy Coleman told the story. "'How would you like to write a song?' With this brash question I approached veteran lyricist Dorothy Fields at a songwriters' meeting in her home and waited nervously while the writer of such songs as 'The Way You Look Tonight,' 'Remind Me,' 'I Can't Give You Anything but Love,' 'Sunny Side of the Street,' and countless others looked at me and said, 'Why not?' This was the beginning of a collaboration that was destined to go far beyond the tune I had in mind at that moment."[8]

Coleman had some reason to be diffident. Fields was twenty-five years older than he and a generation further up the ladder of success. But he had used the same approach—"How would you like to write a song with me?"— with good results on Bronx compatriot Carolyn Leigh. Leigh had written, with composer Mark Charlap, some of the songs for the 1954 version of *Peter Pan*, which starred Mary Martin. She had also written, with composer Johnny Richards, "Young at Heart," recorded by Frank Sinatra in 1954, and Leigh Coleman wrote the scores for *Wildcat* (1960) and *Little Me* (1962).

Cy Coleman was born Seymour Kaufman in New York on June 14, 1929. His parents had emigrated from Bessarabia, a region in Eastern Europe incorporated, at various times, into Moldavia, Romania, the Soviet Union, and Ukraine. His father found work as a carpenter while his mother managed to amass enough capital to purchase a few tenement buildings. Neither his parents nor his elder siblings had shown any musical talent. "'Did you have any musical relatives?' [an interviewer] asked. 'No,' he responds with a charming non sequitur, 'my family couldn't even speak English.'"[9]

It was his mother's entrepreneurial skills in the midst of the Depression, rather than her linguistic or musical abilities, that brought a piano into the household. Coleman related, "We owned two houses in the Bronx. One day somebody skipped on the rent and left behind an upright piano, which was moved into our home. Our milkman sent over his son's piano teacher, Constance Talerico. She offered my mother two free lessons if she'd pay for one."[10]

Seymour was a precocious student, and he had performed at Steinway Hall, Town Hall, and Carnegie Hall by age nine. By his teen years he was studying with Adele Marcus at the New York College of Music, and he owned a Steinway grand, which he kept all his life. After graduation from the High School of Music and Art, his restless and exploratory nature led him to popular music and jazz. He played in nightclubs in Chicago, Detroit, Las Vegas, Miami Beach, and, of course, New York. For a while he owned his own jazz club in Greenwich Village, called the Playroom. He was being groomed, he claimed, as a society pianist—the next Eddy Duchin.

Without abandoning his performing career, Cy Coleman began to put his energies into composition. In his typically expansive fashion, he tested the waters in popular song, film, and theater. Working with Carolyn Leigh, he had a significant hit with "Witchcraft," which was recorded in 1957 by Frank Sinatra. Tony Bennett recorded their songs "I Walk a Little Faster" (1957), "Firefly" (1958), and "The Best Is Yet to Come" (1959). Coleman's first creations for Broadway were not songs, but background music for the show *Compulsion*. He placed some songs in retrospective reviews—*John Murray Anderson's Almanac* and a version of *Ziegfeld Follies* starring Tallulah Bankhead. His first full score for Broadway was for *Wildcat* (1960), Lucille Ball's Broadway debut. His next show, again built around a nonsinging television comic was *Little Me* (1962), starring Sid Caesar. Coleman's lyricist for both shows was Carolyn Leigh, but with *Little Me*, he made other associations, which would carry over into the Fields years. The book for *Little Me* was written by Neil Simon. Bob Fosse choreographed and shared the director's job with Cy Feuer. After these shows, Coleman went to Hollywood, where he scored the films *Father Goose* (1964) and *The Art of Love* (1965).

It was neither Cy Coleman nor Dorothy Fields who first conceived the idea for the show that was to become *Sweet Charity*, but rather Bob Fosse. Gwen Verdon recalled, "One night we had nothing to do, so we went to see that Fellini film *Le notti di Cabiria*. Well, I just hated it—so depressing—but Bob, he's the movie buff in the family, just loved it. He couldn't sleep. So he woke me up at 6 A.M. with a nine-page Americanization of it."[11]

Between *Redhead* in 1959 and *Sweet Charity* in 1966, Bob Fosse had been involved with one enormous success, one mild success, and one total flop. The enormous success was *How to Succeed in Business without Really Trying* (1961), for which he did the musical staging. The show was directed by its librettist, Abe Burrows. It ran for 1,417 performances, won numerous awards and was made into a movie in 1967. The mild success was *Little Me* (1962), which ran for 257 performances. Fosse choreographed and codirected the show, which was written as a vehicle for the versatile comedian Sid Caesar. Among Fosse's coworkers on the show were Neil Simon, who wrote the book, and Cy Coleman, who wrote the music. Simon and Coleman were later recruited by Fosse for *Sweet Charity*. After *Little Me*, Fosse collaborated with Frank Loesser, the composer of *How to Succeed in Business*, on *Pleasures and Palaces*. Fosse was asked to both choreograph and direct the show, as he had done for *Redhead* but had not done since then. He was looking forward to having greater artistic control, but the show suffered from an overabundance of artistic viewpoints. Fosse commented, "We were all doing different things. [Librettist Sam] Spewack was doing a Shavian comedy, Loesser was doing an opera, and I was doing a Russian version of *A Funny Thing Happened on the Way to the Forum.*"[12] (*Pleasures and Palaces* is set in Russia during the reign of Catherine the Great.) The show closed after tryouts in Detroit in 1965, without even reaching Broadway.

Fosse was also active as a performer at this time. In 1961 and again in 1963 he played the title role in revivals of Rodgers and Hart's *Pal Joey* at City Center. The critics were extremely enthusiastic. One declared, "He is the best lead in *Pal Joey* I've seen. His dancing . . . was one of those incredible mixtures of art and gymnastics. He was marvelous."[13]

The years from 1960 to 1966 were less active professionally for Gwen Verdon. There had been talk of turning *Redhead* into a film, but nothing came of that. She made a few television appearances, and she had to undergo surgery on her knee. Though her professional life was in low gear, changes in Verdon's private life went into high gear. In 1960, while *Redhead* was on tour, Fosse and Verdon got married in Chicago—Fosse's hometown. It was the second marriage for Verdon, who was thirty-five, and the third for Fosse, who was thirty-two. Fosse's biographer Kevin Grubb reported that "in 1962 Verdon— already a grandmother from her son James Jr.—and Fosse began adoption proceedings that were interrupted when Verdon discovered she was pregnant. . . . The baby girl, born in March 1963, was named Nicole Providence, the first name taken from a character in F. Scott Fitzgerald's *Tender Is the Night*, the second name proffered by lyricist Dorothy Fields because, she reasoned, it was providence that had intervened when doctors had told Verdon and Fosse they might not be able to have children."[14] We can see from this that Dorothy remained a close friend of Fosse's and Verdon's after *Redhead* closed; their attachments were not just professional but also personal.

One can posit many reasons why *Nights of Cabiria* (*Le notti di Cabiria*) stimulated such sympathetic resonance in Bob Fosse. The heroine of the film, Cabiria, is a prostitute in Rome who is frequently mistreated by men but who manages to keep her inner dignity and to hope for a better future. Memories of Fosse's early work in vaudeville and in bump-and-grind houses may have been awakened by the neorealist scenes of Roman street life. The collaboration of Federico Fellini and Giulietta Masina—husband and wife, director and star—mirrored Fosse's collaboration with Verdon. I believe that one of the things that attracted Fosse to the movie is that dance is Cabiria's most natural, honest, and truthful form of expression. Cabiria dances three times in the movie. First, while she is on the streets in the evening hoping for customers, someone turns on a car radio, and Cabiria begins to mambo. She loses herself in the dance, and although earlier that day she was robbed and almost drowned, the dance recovers her spirits. The second dance episode is in a nightclub with a famous actor. Here again the dance is used to show Cabiria's vitality and capacity for enjoyment, particularly in contrast with the disinterested, dispirited actor. Finally, Cabiria dances while in a trance. She has been disappointed at a religious pilgrimage after which, tellingly, other people dance at a picnic but she does not. She goes to a seedy theater, is hypnotized, and dances a gentle, chaste waltz with an imaginary suitor. Here we see an innocent, vulnerable Cabiria: Cabiria without her protective shell.

Fosse's "nine-page Americanization" of *Le notti di Cabiria* was his first venture into authorship. Fosse enjoyed the company of authors. Several writers, including Paddy Chayevsky and E. L. Doctorow, were among his close friends. Doctorow wrote that Fosse "loved good writing. As the child of a vaudevillian he had spent most of his school years on the stages of burlesque and variety houses, and he had the pious regard for language and literature, and the humility in its presence, that is typical of stars who've grown up in show business—and that makes the best of the passionate autodidacts."[15] He had meant to start small with the story of Cabiria—he envisioned a pair of one-act musicals, the second being Elaine May's *Robbers and Cops*. But *Robbers and Cops* was dropped, and Cabiria, renamed Charity, grew. Fosse's skills were not up to writing a book for a two-act musical, and he turned to Neil Simon for help. At the time, Simon was in Italy working on two projects—an original screenplay, *After the Fox,* and a film adaptation of his play *Barefoot in the Park.* Simon told Fosse he would read the script and make a few adjustments, but he was too busy to do more than that. Simon recalled, "I sat down and spent one long night removing the lines that didn't work and inserting new and what I hoped were funnier ones. . . . Three days later, another phone call from New York. Fosse again.

'I love the new lines. You can't stop now.'

'Bob, I just don't have the time. I can barely get *Barefoot* done.'

'I'm not letting you off the hook. You owe me one.'

'For what?'

'I'll think of something.'

'Bob, you know if I could . . .'

'I'll find a way to convince you.' "[16]

The way Fosse found to convince Simon was to show up in Rome with a tape recorder and a tape of some of the songs that already had been written for the show. "He put on the tape. We heard the first beats of the rhythm section, and the girls began to sing and talk to the unseen customers: 'So you want to have fun, fun, fun. . . . So you want to have laughs, laughs, laughs. . . .' Joan [Simon's wife] and I were pulled into the number immediately. You knew this was something special, something we hadn't heard in musical comedy before. Bob positioned himself as each new girl sang with all her seediness, lust, and hopeless sadness, yet there was remarkable humor to it. The minute they blared out, '*Hey, big spender, spend . . . a little time with me,*' I was sold. It was Cy Coleman's music at its best, and with it were Dorothy Fields' great lyrics—tough, funny, and Brechtian. Before I could say a word to Bob, he motioned for me to be quiet. The tape started again. The next number was Latin, angry, filled with emotion, and strong earthy determination as three forlorn dance-hall girls began to sing 'There's Gotta Be Something Better Than This.'"[17] Fosse also played "I'm a Brass Band" for Simon, and he was hooked. That Dorothy did not pitch in to help write the book may suggest that writing libretti was something she did mainly to keep her brother Herbert company. She was able to produce serviceable—or even excellent—books with Herbert. But I suspect that the pleasure in doing those books came from the collaboration with her brother. When it came to writing lyrics, on the other hand, the joy was in the work itself.

When she took on *Sweet Charity*, Dorothy Fields leapt into the present both in subject matter and in musical style. Her previous five Broadway musicals were all set well in the past—times that Dorothy could research but that did not connect with her own living memory. Moreover, the composers Dorothy had worked with up until she joined forces with Cy Coleman (Jimmy McHugh, Jerome Kern, Sigmund Romberg, Arthur Schwartz) established themselves in what is sometimes called the Golden Age of popular song, which both Alec Wilder and Allen Forte see as ending around 1950. Coleman's music absorbs more contemporary elements, which show up in his use of jazz riffs, complex rhythms, and electronic instruments.

Fields's and Coleman's personal styles of working did not mesh perfectly. For one thing, Cy was a night owl, and Dorothy a lark. As he described it, "I'm a late riser. I don't have any compunctions about sleeping late. . . . Dorothy was one of those people who was up at 6 o'clock, sharpened her pencils at 6:30, and then she used to champ at the bit to get on the telephone with me. And we had *terrible* arguments about things. She'd get this kind of funny tone in her voice, you know, imperious. It was the only time she was like that, and she'd say: 'You're still in bed?' And I would be *furious*."[18] But the music and the lyrics of the songs for *Sweet Charity* are perfectly mated. Ethan Mordden noted, "As for Dorothy Fields, this wonderful talent may be the only lyricist in musical-theatre history who sounded more youthful as time ran on. Her first show had come along in 1928, when Cy Coleman was running around in a propeller beanie. Yet, in *Sweet Charity*, Fields has the ear of a teenage prodigy."[19]

There is a tension in *Sweet Charity*, both in the libretto and in the musical numbers, between progress—or at least change—and cyclical repetition. The most obvious example of cyclical repetition, of ending up just where one began, is Charity getting pushed into the lake in Central Park at the beginning of act 1 and at the end of act 2. Cy Coleman defended this ending by saying. "We got criticized for the ending. So many people said, 'You had no right to have him dump her.' But we *had* to, because this poor idiot was going to continue to go through life just that way. She was going to do it again and again and again, and she was never, ever going to stop that pattern."[20] The situations are not exactly the same. In act 1, Charity is pushed into the lake by a leech-like boyfriend who steals her purse. In act 2, Oscar is not trying to take Charity's money, and she ends up in the lake accidentally. But this hardly counts as progress.

The distribution of the musical numbers in the two acts of *Sweet Charity* show a remarkable balance and symmetry, unlike that seen in any other musical Dorothy Fields worked on. Each number in the first act has a parallel number in the second act which reflects how things have changed. *Sweet Charity* is one of the rare shows in which the second act is as strong or stronger, musically, than the first act.

Charity has three numbers in each act. Once in each act she is bolstering the ego of a man—giving what she has not received. In addition, there are two songs Charity sings when she is at the bottom of her luck and two when she is on top of the world. Each time, the second song trumps the first. When Charity sings her soliloquy in the first act, we get to know her as the girls in the Fan-dango Ballroom know her, and we are encouraged to laugh at her naiveté. As she describes her latest failed romance, in the number called "Charity's Soliloquy," an assortment of Latin dance rhythms, echoes of the dance hall, no doubt, accompany her narration.[21] The text flows seamlessly between quasi-prose lines, such as, "He moves in with his Jockey shorts in a paper bag," and rapid-rhyme lines pairing "brothering" with "mothering" and "hugging me" with "bugging me." When Charity gets to the end of her tale and declares things will change, we have no reason to believe her.

Charity does not make the same mistake again. In the second act, the man she fears she will lose is not someone who has gotten tired of bilking her of her hard-earned money. She has told Oscar, the sweet, kindly, and very strait-laced man she has met that she works in a bank, and she fears that if he should discover that she is a dance hostess he would leave her. The song she sings in the second act, "Where Am I Going," analyzes not just her affair but her life and her own responsibility for her happiness or unhappiness. Charity in fact has made remarkable personal progress, progress that any analyst— had she ever seen an analyst—would praise her for. She no longer sees herself as the hapless victim of the "fickle finger of fate," which was her only explanation for her life's plan in the first act. Charity no longer resorts to pat explanations or excuses. Instead, this text is made up almost entirely of acute and probing questions about herself and her life. Her acknowledgment that "No matter where I run I meet myself there" anticipates the title of a best-selling 1994 book on mindfulness meditation, *Wherever You Go There You Are.*[22]

Similarly, the way Charity experiences happiness is different in the two acts. When she has "landed in a pot of jam," as she describes it in "If My Friends Could See Me Now," she knows that her happiness is temporary, transitory, and not of her own making. In some sense, it is for this reason that she wishes she had witnesses.[23]

In the second act, Charity's happiness does not come from a momentary circumstance but from what she believes will be a complete change in her life. The style is musical comedy, but the content is what heroes and heroines in Wagnerian opera undergo—transformation through love. Charity's vocabulary and diction have altered. There are no more "Wows" and "Holy cows." Her friends are no longer "stumble bums" or "riff and raff" or a "dusty little group" or "thrift shop cats." In the first-act song she refers to herself as "the lowest brow." In the second-act song "I'm a Brass Band," she speaks of harpsichords and the Philadelphia Orchestra and the Modern Jazz Quartet.[24] Charity is ennobled through these lyrics. Transformed into music, she sings, "All kinds of music is pouring out of me."

The starting point of Charity's alteration is heard in the first act trio "There's Gotta Be Something Better Than This," sung by Charity and her coworkers, Nickie and Helene. The tension between stasis and change found in the entire musical is encapsulated in this single number. The trio is notable for its honesty and psychological acuity, qualities one does not ordinarily look for in a fast-paced song-and-dance number. Learning that Charity has spent the night with a famous movie star and has come way with nothing but a top hat, a cane, and an autographed photo, Nickie remarks, "It was your big chance, baby, and you blew it." and Helene adds, "It ain't no use flapping your wings 'cause we are caught in the flypaper of life." Their shared frustration at Charity's missed opportunity provokes the trio, "There's Gotta Be Something Better Than This." Their speech is unpretentious, colloquial, straightforward, and direct. The music to which the words are set is exuberant, with a Hispanic flavor coming in part from the orchestration and in part from the conflict of 3/4 and 6/8 rhythms. (Coleman may have taken as his model "America" from *West Side Story*. There is nothing in the book that demands Spanish music here, but it does not seem out of character.) The second set of lines is set to the same music, but there is a psychological shift. The anger, which was directed outward to the world in general in the first verse, is suddenly directed inward as the words move from "something easy to learn" to the harsher "something a half-wit can learn." In the next set of lines, set to a new melody, anger is directed outward again, but this time the target is specific rather than generalized, and the emotional language is stronger. Nickie, Helene, and Charity admit that they hate the men they have to dance with. The lyricist comes up with eight gerunds to describe the physical indignities the dance-hall girls endure, some alliterative ("groping, grabbing") and some rhyming ("clinching" and "pinching"). The music of the first verse returns after this, making a traditional A A B A pattern, but the emotional trajectory that has begun cannot be turned around. Charity, Nickie, and Helene have moved from generalized discontent, through anger directed inward and outward, to an urgent attempt to fend off despair—"There's gotta be some good reason to live."

This emotional outburst liberates a pair of fantasies for Nickie and Helene. Nickie imagines what it would be like to be a receptionist, sitting at a desk in a "copy of a copy of a copy of Dior." Helene envisions being a hatcheck girl, and here Dorothy Fields indulges in some playful variations on the verb "check," from "check your hat," to "check your eyes," to "check and see if you are free," to "I'll check you, and you check me." Charity, tellingly, does not supply a dream of her own.

The context of the trio—the strophic setting of the text and the exuberant dancing—encourages us to ignore the truths that Charity, Nickie, and Helene are stating. It is appropriate that the psychological clarification that occurs in this number goes by almost unnoticed. The inability to be introspective is one of Charity's most conspicuous character traits. But Charity is capable of approaching psychological insight when led by her friends. The music and dancing, energetic and propulsive, belies or at least disguises their ability to understand their feelings more fully. Although we expect music to reveal the psychological motivations of characters and reveal feelings they cannot express or articulate, in "There's Gotta Be Something Better Than This" the situation is reversed. It is Dorothy Fields's lyrics that encourage us to believe that these singing, dancing, wisecracking women have more depth than they care to show.

The second act commentary on "There's Gotta Be Something Better Than This" is the duet "Baby Dream Your Dream," sung by Nickie and Helene.[25]

Having imagined their own dreams of a better future, her two friends imagine what Charity's life as a housewife might be like. This seems to be "I Can't Give You Anything but Love" territory. However, the duet is not sung by a pair of penniless lovers but, despite the first-person and second-person pronouns, by friends of Charity's indulging in daydreaming, prompted by the fact that Charity has finally met a man who treats her well.

Charity interacts with three men in the musical. The first, who robs her and pushes her into the lake, does not speak or sing. The second, the screen star Vittorio Vidal, is entirely self-absorbed. His solo, "Too Many Tomorrows," has points of contact with "Alone Too Long" from *By the Beautiful Sea*. The text, which taken on its own has the possibility of being strongly felt and deeply emotional, is undercut by the situation. The song is sung to Vittorio's returning girlfriend while Charity watches from the clothes closet into which she has been pushed (a drier version of being pushed into a lake) to conceal her from the girlfriend. The third man, Oscar, addresses a song to Charity that declares him to be transformed by love. His song both contrasts with "Too Many Tomorrows" and forecasts "I'm a Brass Band."

Each act of *Sweet Charity* has a large production number danced by a relatively anonymous group of characters who are strangers to Charity. The first-act number, "Rich Man's Frug," is a study of detachment and alienation. Fosse's biographer Martin Gottfried notes, "This dance is an exploration of visual dissonance. Everyone seems to be going in a different direction, leaning and tilting, angular and arch."[26] The dance is in four sections, each one bearing a title. The second section is called "The Aloof," but a lack of passion is part of all the sections—even the one in which the dancers simulate a boxing match. A dancer in the 1986 revival of *Sweet Charity* described Fosse coming up to her after a performance, furious with her because she had been smiling during the dance. "He said, 'It's not about smiling and selling it! I should never see your teeth. There's always a smile in your eyes, but you've got to be cool—aloof and sophisticated. You would *never* smile or show your teeth!'"[27]

In the second act, the comparable number is "The Rhythm of Life." Unlike "Rich Man's Frug," this number is full of enthusiasm. It mocks the fervor of 1960s populist new religions with the line, "There's a million pigeons ready to be hooked on new religions." The choreography of this number is less characteristic of Fosse's style. But in the overall symmetry of the numbers in the two acts, "Rhythm of Life" is far more positive than "Rich Man's Frug."

The other pair of ensemble numbers are sung and danced by Charity's coworkers, and they too have a trajectory from pessimism to optimism. "Big Spender" is meant to shock.[28] The women of the Fan-dango Ballroom, standing behind a bar on which they drape themselves in poses that are at once awkward and sexy, stare out at the audience with vacant expressions. The tone is established by Coleman's first riff—both figuratively and literally brassy—and by Fields's first words, "The moment you walked in the joint." "Big Spender" does on an expanded, professional level what Charity had been doing in the song preceding it, "You Should See Yourself," that is, servicing the egos of men who probably do not have much to give in return.

In the second-act number "I Love to Cry at Weddings," the tone has shifted. The staff of the Fan-dango Ballroom sincerely wish Charity all the best. As with "Rhythm of Life," the happiness seems a bit mindless. On the other hand, the very title hints at complexity of feeling, or at least ambivalence. "I love to go to weddings" would be a simpler statement, as would be "I can't help crying at weddings," although that would have the wrong number of syllables for the tune. But "I Love to Cry at Weddings" suggests that the employees and manager of the Fan-dango Ballroom, who spend most of their time enmeshed in false feelings or no feelings at all (as evident from "Big Spender") are delighted to experience a genuine emotion, even a chaotic one. The number is fast-paced and played for laughs, but once again the lyrics hint at a greater depth of feeling.

Given the unusual symmetry in which each song in the first act is countered by a more hopeful and optimistic number in the second act, the ending of the show, in which Charity, just as at the beginning, finds herself flailing in the lake in Central Park is all the more shocking. Walter Kerr, enlisting "attentiveness above and beyond the call of duty," examined this problem in an essay printed in the *Herald Tribune* two weeks after the show's opening night. "It is just this triumphant animation, in the staging and the star, that forbids us to have second thoughts, subtle thoughts, sympathetically, sober thoughts, while the band wagon is rolling by. . . . The drive of the staging, exhilarating in itself, destroys any other kind of attentiveness. It waves aside, and makes us wave aside, anything that doesn't seem to fit its own tempo, until we are forced to face up to the by now mysterious ending. Suddenly we are baffled. Where, for heaven's sake, did bittersweet come from?"[29]

Fields and Coleman wrote twenty-seven songs for *Sweet Charity*—about twice as many as were used. Some songs were dropped or replaced in rehearsals; others were removed during the Philadelphia and Detroit tryouts.[30] "Poor Everybody Else" and "I'm Way Ahead" found a home in Fields and Coleman's next musical, *Seesaw*. "Did You Ever Look at You" was considered for *Seesaw* but was dropped from that show as well. "Pink Taffeta Sample Size Ten" has become a favorite with cabaret singers, including Sylvia Syms. One critic called this song "one of Fields' most dramatic and touching lyrics," and another considered the lyric "a dream of lightness and sentiment."[31] Very likely, good as it is, the sweet and reflective story song slowed the pace of action that Fosse intended to maintain.

Sweet Charity opened in the refurbished Palace Theatre on January 29, 1966. In addition to Gwen Verdon, the cast included Helen Gallagher and Thelma Oliver as Charity's friends Nickie and Helene; John Wheeler as their boss, Herman; James Luisi as Vittorio; John McMartin as Oscar; and Arnold Soboloff as Big Daddy Johann Sebastian Brubeck. The costumes were designed by Irene Sharaff, and the scenery and lighting were designed by Robert Randolph. The critics were, for the most part, enthusiastic, and Sweet Charity ran for 608 performances, amply repaying its investors. It was nominated for eight Tony awards, but received only one, for Bob Fosse in his capacity as choreographer. Gwen Verdon, John McMartin, and Helen Gallagher lost to Angela Lansbury, Frankie Michaels, and Beatrice Arthur, all in the cast of Mame. This was the only time Gwen Verdon failed to win a Tony for which she was nominated. Man of La Mancha won the awards for musical, director, scenic designer, and composer and lyricist, categories in which Sweet Charity was nominated.

One week after the opening, the cast of Sweet Charity gathered at Columbia Studios to record the complete score. In October 1966, Universal Pictures paid $500,000 for rights to turn Sweet Charity into a movie. The movie, begun the end of January 1968 and completed mid-June of that year, was Bob Fosse's first opportunity to direct a film. At the insistence of the producers the role of Charity was played not by Gwen Verdon but by Shirley MacLaine. John McMartin reprised his stage role as Oscar, but he was the only holdover from the show. James Luisi was replaced by Ricardo Montalban; the role of Big Daddy Johann Sebastian Brubeck went to Sammy Davis Jr.; Charity's friends were played by Chita Rivera and Paula Kelly; and Herman by Stubby Kaye. The score was changed somewhat for the movie. The first number, "You Should See Yourself" was replaced by "My Personal Property." The duet sung when Charity and Oscar are trapped in an elevator, "I'm the Bravest Individual," was replaced by "It's a Nice Face," sung by Charity alone after Oscar has fainted. The title song, "Sweet Charity," was revised. "Charity's Soliloquy," "Baby Dream Your Dream," and "Too Many Tomorrows," all more reflective numbers, were dropped.

Two different endings were shot for the film. In one, Charity, rejected by Oscar, has spent the night on a bench in Central Park. In the morning, she is awakened by flower children serenading her. As the camera draws back for a very long overhead shot, across the screen are emblazoned the words "and she lived hopefully ever after." The alternate ending, shot but not used, shows

Oscar "having a claustrophobia attack in his apartment, rushing out to the Park to ask her forgiveness and falling off the bridge—from which Charity also jumps to join him."[32] Either ending is gentler to Charity than that of the stage musical, but perhaps they both are a little too pat or condescending. The film was not a financial success, but it has attained a kind of cult status. Film critic Derek Elley lists it as one of the eleven most important movie musicals made in the 1960s.[33]

"IT'S WHERE YOU FINISH . . ."

• • •

Barely a month after the reviews of *Sweet Charity* indicated it was going to be a resounding success, Dorothy Fields got distressing news from California. On March 3, 1966, Joseph Fields, at age 71, died of heart disease in Beverly Hills, where he and his wife, Marion, were spending the winter. Herbert had died in March eight years earlier; Dorothy would also die in March, eight years later. During the 1920s, when he was a successful businessman dealing in perfumes, Joe wrote theater sketches as an avocation. The stock market crash and subsequent bank failures took most of his money, and so he made his hobby his real work, following Herbert and Dorothy to Hollywood.

Unlike his siblings, Joseph did not work on musicals in Hollywood. For the most part, Joe wrote screenplays for light comedies such a *$1,000 a Minute* (1935), *When Love Is Young* (1937), *Fools for Scandal* (1938), and *Rich Man, Poor Girl* (1938). Occasionally he tried his hand at courtroom dramas, such as *Grand Jury* (1936) and *The Spellbinder* (1939), and once did a horror film, *The Walking Dead* (1936). His most important screen credit during this period was the story for *Annie Oakley* (1935), which starred Barbara Stanwyck. Perhaps the most significant benefit of the time Joseph spent in Hollywood was that he met Jerome Chodorov, with whom he would collaborate on several successful Broadway shows. Like Joseph, Jerome had a sibling in show business. His older brother Edward was active in Hollywood and on Broadway.

In 1944, Joseph married Marion Feinberg. It was the second marriage for both of them. Marion's children from her first marriage, Ralph and Marjorie, took their stepfather's surname. Marion and Joseph did not have more children.

Joseph's greatest successes came in the 1940s and 1950s, after he left Hollywood for Broadway. *My Sister Eileen* (1940) and *Junior Miss* (1941), both of which he wrote with Jerome Chodorov, ran for 865 and 710 performances, respectively. *My Sister Eileen* was also the source for *Wonderful Town* (1953) with music by Leonard Bernstein, lyrics by Comden and Green and book by Fields and Chodorov. In 1954, they worked on another musical, *The Girl in Pink Tights*, which opened three years after the death of its composer, Sigmund Romberg, and had a relatively short run. Fields and Chodorov also worked together on *Anniversary Waltz* (1954) and *The Ponder Heart* (1956). Like his siblings, Joseph preferred working collaboratively. He teamed up with Peter DeVries to turn DeVries' novel *Tunnel of Love* into a 1957 play by the same name. He also worked on the screenplays for many of his Broadway hits. His last Broadway project was the book, written in collaboration with Oscar Hammerstein II, for the Rodgers and Hammerstein musical *Flower Drum Song* (1958).

Dorothy Fields's last three musicals were separated by long intermissions. There were seven years between *Redhead* and *Sweet Charity* and another seven years between *Sweet Charity* and *Seesaw*, her final musical, written in collaboration with Cy Coleman. The source for the musical was William Gibson's play *Two for the Seesaw*, "a comedy-drama in three acts." That play had opened at the Booth Theatre on January 16, 1958, starring Henry Fonda and Ann Bancroft, and ran for 750 performances.

Building a musical from a well-built play that was a proven hit would seem a good idea. After all, Dorothy and Herbert had, three decades earlier, totally transformed a 1925 farce, *The Cradle Snatchers*, to create the musical hit *Let's Face It*. In the case of *Seesaw*, it is not clear whose idea it was. (And in the end, it was not clear whose book it was, but more about that later.)

Musicals had been getting more and more expensive to produce. Higher ticket prices and longer runs (generally, more than 400 performances) were needed to earn back investment costs and the cost of keeping the show running. Perhaps that was part of the appeal of *Two for the Seesaw*: it had only two characters and one set. And the idea of a simple two-person play had an encouraging precedent: the musical *I Do, I Do* (1966) had only two characters—originally played by Mary Martin and Robert Preston—and ran for 560 performances.

Jerry Ryan and Gittel Mosca, the characters in *Two for the Seesaw*, have many points of contact with Charity and Oscar in *Sweet Charity*. Both men have conventional jobs—Oscar is an actuary for an insurance company, and Jerry is a lawyer. And both, to differing degrees, are emotionally ill at ease. In contrast, Charity and Gittel are both struggling financially and are far too generous emotionally. Early in their relationship, Jerry tells Gittel, "You don't look out for yourself." In the second act, he puts the point more strongly. "You don't get by, you only tell yourself lies. From day to day, sure, job to job, man to man, you get by. And nothing sticks—You pay the freight, and every bum climbs on for a free ride. And you never know why the ride is over, do you? I'll tell you why. When a man offers you a hand up you put a donation into it."[1] In *Sweet Charity* it is coworkers, rather than a new boyfriend, who are dismayed by Charity's inability to profit materially from her relationships with men. The similarity between Gittel and Charity is underscored by the fact that both roles were played in their film versions by the same actress. Shirley MacLaine played Gittel in the movie version of *Two for the Seesaw* in 1962 and Charity in the movie version of *Sweet Charity* in 1969.

In the early stages of *Seesaw*, Michael Stewart converted the Gibson play into a book for a musical. Stewart's career path had started at the top. The first Broadway show he wrote a book for was *Bye Bye Birdie* (1960), which ran for 607 performances. He followed that with the books for *Carnival* (1961; 719 performances) and *Hello, Dolly!* (1964; 2,844 performances). In all of these shows, he worked with choreographer-director Gower Champion. Cy Coleman was at first hoping that the role of Gittel would go to a major star such as Barbra Streisand or Liza Minnelli. The role was given to Lainie Kazan, who had had considerable success as a cabaret singer and had been Barbra Streisand's understudy for *Funny Girl*. Ken Howard had played in *Promises, Promises* (1968) and *1776* (1969) before he was chosen to play Jerry Ryan.

During the Detroit tryouts, there were changes and adjustments that turned into an avalanche of alterations. Lainie Kazan was fired—it's unclear whether this was because she did not learn her role, because she was uncooperative or confrontational, or because she was overweight. If the weight problem caused her to be fired it would be ironic because in *Two for the Seesaw*, Gittel has stopped dancing, she says, because the diet she needs to be on to treat her ulcer has made her gain too much weight. Cy Coleman, who had helped Kazan get the part, complained, "I felt at one point I couldn't control her any more. I felt we were going in different directions."[2] Kazan was replaced by Michele Lee.[3] Both women had worked together in *Bravo, Giovanni* in 1962, Lee in a starring role and Kazan in the chorus.

These changes were just the tip of the iceberg. The original director, Edwin Sherin, was replaced. The original choreographer, Grover Dale, was demoted to make room for Michael Bennett, who had choreographed Stephen Sondheim's *Follies* in 1971 and codirected it with Harold Prince. According to Ethan Mordden, "The Detroit tryout was not going well, and that's when Michael Bennett took over. While *Seesaw* played through its tryout unchanged, Bennett and his Gang of Four—Bob Avian, Baayork Lee, Thommie Walsh, and Tommy Tune—rehearsed a new *Seesaw* for Broadway. This show drove hard and looked wild and fancy, albeit with a gritty realism stressing race and crime, the New York not of musicals but of life."[4]

Michael Stewart withdrew from the enterprise and asked that his name be taken off the list of credits. Cy Coleman related, "When we got to New York and started previews, we persuaded Neil Simon to do what turned out to be an incredible job of rewriting the book. Only he didn't want credit [Simon insisted that his only contribution to the book was to make about thirty minutes' worth of cuts]. Since we didn't want to open without any authorship, we persuaded Dorothy Fields, my collaborator, to take credit. But then, two days later, she said she couldn't do it after thinking it over. So, finally we persuaded Michael Bennett to lend his name to the book."[5]

Naturally, the music needed to be rewritten as well. Dorothy said, "We had a helluva hard time getting *Seesaw* on the boards. We spent eight months writing it, and six and a half weeks in Detroit where we all had the flu. Cy and I took a box of Kleenex apiece, propped them on the piano, and coughed into each other's faces and wrote three new songs in one week. I defy anybody to match that record!"[6] Cy Coleman recollected, "That show had more trials and tribulations than 'The Perils of Pauline.' . . . I did an entire rewrite job with the London flu, sitting there with a scarf around my neck. In two weeks we went through the most radical change I ever went through."[7] Considering that for *Sweet Charity* Dorothy and Cy discarded as many songs as they kept, this seems a very strong statement. But it probably reflects the fact that the whole nature of the show changed under Bennett's direction. Not surprisingly, the revised show featured dance much more prominently. One sign of this is that no fewer than four choreographers are credited: Michael Bennett as choreographer, Grover Dale as co-choreographer, and Bob Avian and Tommy Tune as associate choreographers. This gives a special twist to the line the character David speaks to Gittel in the second act: "You're gonna be right there with me as soon as I can work it out. . . . I mean, look, why can't the assistant have an assistant?"[8] In the spoken play, Gittel has given up dancing, but the first place we see her in the musical is in a dance studio. Gittel's dancing and choreographing friend, who is just a presence on the other end of the phone in *Two for the Seesaw*, is incarnated and named David in *Seesaw* and given two major numbers in the second act: "Chapter 54, Number 1909," in which he taps to a legal text, and "It's Not Where You Start," a major production number. David's success means that by the end of the show, Gittel is left behind both by her buddy and by her lover. The role of David introduced Tommy Tune to the world; he went on to choreograph and direct a number of shows, including *The Best Little Whorehouse in Texas*, *Nine*, *My One and Only*, *Grand Hotel*, and *The Will Rogers Follies*.

Douglas Watt, writing for the *New York Daily News* commented, "*Seesaw* is an intimate, bittersweet comedy and a big, brassy musical. You get two shows for the price of one."[9] This was meant as high praise, although being two shows in one—a comic first half and a serious second half—was something critics complained about when *A Tree Grows in Brooklyn* opened on Broadway. While all of the activities in *Two for the Seesaw* take place in Gittel's or Jerry's apartments, the musical places them in ten different locations, including Lincoln Center, Spanish Harlem, St. Vincent's Hospital, Central Park, and a nightspot called the Banana Club. As if playing for an audience suffering from attention deficit disorder, the stage picture changes every few minutes. Act 1 calls for ten changes of scene, and act 2 calls for seven. Sometimes sets and props are rolled on in full sight of the audience, and sometimes scene changes are projected on a screen. One can speculate that Michael Bennett needed to get past a phase of playing with stage toys before he could go on to placing his next show, *A Chorus Line*, on an almost bare stage.

Seesaw is peopled by contemporary characters—a sexually experienced single woman, a man in the middle of a divorce, a homosexual dancer—but in some ways it presents itself more as an old-fashioned revue than as a musical drama. Some of the large musical numbers, such as "Spanglish" or "Ride Out the Storm," feature characters who will be seen only once in the show and have little or no effect on the dramatic action. In other ways, *Seesaw* is like an old-fashioned "Let's-put-on-a-show" musical. In addition to the early scene in a dance studio, there's a scene in the middle of the show that has David rehearsing while Jerry is studying for the New York bar exam, and a scene near the end has David performing the big dance number that lands him a job on Broadway. In all of these scenes, Gittel and Jerry are secondary characters or simply spectators.

By the end of *Seesaw*, the male characters have been more fortunate than Gittel. Jerry is reconciled with his wife in Nebraska on his terms; David has an opportunity to be a choreographer's assistant on Broadway; Gittel is left alone. Only two of these resolutions are marked musically; David and Gittel get final numbers, but Jerry does not. He is returned to the prosaic world both figuratively and literally. David's final number, "It's Not Where You Start," is a big showpiece. In some ways it parallels "I'm a Brass Band" in *Sweet Charity*. Charity's number is prompted by Oscar telling her he loves her. David's number is his reaction to a Broadway choreographer asking him to be his assistant. David exclaims, "He liked! He liked it! He really liked it!" The stage directions state: "He runs madly around the stage, whooping loudly and somehow magically triggering bright, multi-colored lights, all this accompanied by building music."[10] The lyric for this number is very serviceable and, at the same time, a little impersonal. David expresses himself in clichés such as "a hundred-to-one shot" and "cream of the crop." David dances up a staircase, and Dorothy obliges with a lyric that advises "conserve your fine endurance" and "take it rung after rung after rung after rung." The stage directions instruct that there will be a "big ending, resplendent with balloon, streamers, confetti, lights, high-kicks, etc."[11] Clearly, a finely wrought, subtle lyric would be wasted here.[12]

While David's number is extroverted and exuberant, Gittel's final number, "I'm Way Ahead," is personal, internal, sung alone. In the course of her career, Dorothy had written several songs designed to lift the spirits, such as "On the Sunny Side of the Street" or "Pick Yourself Up." In contrast, "I'm Way Ahead" is more like a smiling-through-tears torch song. There is some question if Gittel believes what she is singing, or if we are meant to believe her. Perhaps it is the extra syllable after the rhyme that catches the listener up: "forget" rhymes with "regret it," "lost" rhymes with "cost me," "night" rhymes with "fighting." Or perhaps the fact that the melody falls the interval of a sixth when Gittel sings "my chin is up" warns the listener not to take her words at face value.[13]

In the Detroit tryouts, "I'm Way Ahead" was the last number in the show. In the libretto that represents the Broadway performance, the end of the song segues into the opening "Seesaw" number followed by a reprise of "It's Not Where You Start." Clearly, Bennett did not want to risk having the audience feel too much sympathy for Gittel. In some sense, the ending of *Seesaw* adumbrates the ending of Bennett's biggest hit, *A Chorus Line*, which forces the audience to lose track of who the winners and the losers of the audition are. It is an aesthetic in which spectacle trumps feeling.

The first few lines of the opening number give an apt description of the opening weeks of the show on Broadway. "Ev'rybody's travelin' on a crazy see-saw, Going up . . . down . . . up . . . down." The critics gave *Seesaw* mostly favorable reviews. But the production had become so expensive, in part because of changes in cast, sets, and costumes, that it appeared there would not be enough money to carry the show through the first week. The cast agreed to take pay cuts, and Dorothy Fields put up $30,000 of her own money to keep *Seesaw* afloat. A *New York Times* article reported, "By Wednesday the *Seesaw* company got involved and just before the matinee, led by dancer Tommy Tune, they performed numbers from the musical in front of the Uris Building on Broadway, while stagehands and musicians passed out *Seesaw* flyers to pedestrians."[14] Even the mayor of New York City, John Lindsay, helped out. On Friday night, he appeared onstage during the opening number, "My City." The *New York Times* reported the next day, under the headline "Lindsay Wows 'Em in Broadway

Debut That's Simply Boffo": An unscheduled walk-on stole the show at last night's performance of the musical *Seesaw*—much to the delight of the audience, which greeted the novice with surprise and applause. The actor was Mayor Lindsay, and he made his Broadway debut shortly after the curtain rose at the Uris Theater . . . explaining later that he did so at the invitation of producers to help the city's theaters and tourism."[15] The demand for tickets picked up considerably after that. But *Seesaw* was too expensive a show to make a profit. According to a notice in *Variety* on December 12, 1973, *Seesaw* closed "after a run of 25 previews and 296 regular performances at a loss of its entire $750,000 investment and, according to an audit of last June 30, an additional $521,000."

The following March, Dorothy Fields died. *The New York Times* listed heart attack as the cause of death. As was the case with her husband, there was no long, lingering illness. About a year earlier Rex Reed had asked her if she had plans for retirement. She replied, "Are you crazy? Listen, honey, I've got songs coming out of me I haven't even thought about yet. I plan to write till I can no longer hold a pencil."[16] And that was the way it was. On Thursday, March 28, 1974, she had attended rehearsals for the road company of *Seesaw*. That evening she was scheduled to be at a benefit for the Young Adult Institute. It was a splendidly typical day in her life, in which professional work and charitable work were comfortably intertwined.

Dorothy Fields's death was sudden and unexpected. Her daughter, Eliza, had spoken with her by phone that morning. Eliza said, "My mother called me every morning around eight and that morning was no different. We talked for about ten minutes and of course she wanted to know how her grandson, David, was. [David was eleven months old at that time.] About seven that evening I got a call from Bobby Weinstein, a very good friend of my mom's who also lived in the Beresford. He told me that when the maid brought in my mother's supper, she found her dead on the floor in her bedroom, and called Bobbie."[17] The funeral service took place in the Frank Campbell Funeral Chapel in New York City. Joe Fields's widow, Marion, took charge of the reception following the funeral.

The same issue of *Variety* that carried Dorothy Fields's obituary (April 3, 1974) also listed the Tony Award nominations for that year. *Seesaw* received seven nominations. In addition to nominations in the categories for best musical and best musical score, Michele Lee was nominated as best actress in a musical, and Tommy Tune was nominated and won as best supporting actor. Michael Bennett was nominated as choreographer, director, and librettist, and he won in the choreographer category.

Dorothy Fields left behind her a rich body of work—more than four hundred songs, mostly distributed in nineteen Broadway shows and more than thirty films, as well as librettos for nine musicals. With a typical blend of modesty and professionalism, she told an interviewer in 1959, "This is my sixteenth show, some good and some bad. I've been very lucky—just three of them, I'd say, were duds."[18] There were also a number of projects that did not come to fruition. Most important among these was a musical on the life of Eleanor Roosevelt. She and Cy Coleman wrote a full score—fifteen numbers—and a star, Jane Alexander, had been chosen.[19] But backing could not be found. In addition, the producer Robert Fryer wrote to her to express his disappointment that she would not be working on a projected *Dodsworth* musical, another show that never saw the light of day.

Her son, David Lahm, gave her papers to the Museum of the City of New York. Among these are a number of letters thanking her for assorted acts of generosity and kindness. She sent gifts of plants to people who were convalescing. Her Aunt Rosalind thanked her for an anthurium and Dimitri Mitropoulos was grateful "to have spring itself come and visit me in the form of such beauty as you have sent me." She also had thank-you notes from politicians. After she introduced New York Secretary of State Caroline Simon at a Fashion Institute dinner in 1959, Simon wrote to Dorothy, asking, "May I have a copy of that introduction to re-read at low moments?" A more formal letter came from Mamie Eisenhower thanking Dorothy for writing the song "The Happy Heart" to benefit the Heart Fund. Dorothy was an enthusiastic giver of gifts. Max Dreyfus wrote to thank her for a lounging suit and for shirts. Dorothy Hammerstein expressed her appreciation for a handbag and a blue glass box. One suspects that the notes she saved—for whatever reason—were just a small sample of those she received. She knew she had given a great deal to a great number of people, and she knew she was appreciated. One friend summarized, "Dorothy Fields . . . was not only a brilliant lyricist; there was also a lyrical quality to her character. She was constantly giving of her talent, of her heart, of her thoughtfulness, of her time. She worked unsparingly for worthy causes in and out of the theater and came to the aid of scores of her friends who were ill or in trouble. . . . One of her many memorable and popular songs was 'I Can't Give You Anything but Love, Baby.' Dorothy could give much more—comfort, fun, talent, companionship. But her greatest gift was love and she gave it unstintingly to all who knew and loved her well but rarely as wholeheartedly and selflessly as Dorothy loved them."[20]

Those of us who never knew her personally are also beneficiaries of the life and work of Dorothy Fields. Without the benefit of a banner or a movement, she made the field of songwriting more woman-friendly, teaching by example. Some commentators continue the debate over whether her lyrics are distinctly female, but to me her body of work makes the question pleasantly irrelevant. For millions who know her lyrics but do not know who wrote them, she made an anonymous gift. She had a knack for starting with mundane and commonplace phrases—"Grab your coat and get your hat," "Don't blame me," "If my friends could see me now"—and placing them in the perfect verbal and musical setting to allow them to feel new, fresh, telling. She had a gift for staying just the right distance from the expression of emotion so that the listener could understand a feeling—joy or sorrow or anger or love—without being overwhelmed by it. And she seemed to have a boundless supply of optimism to share: "Pick yourself up, brush yourself off, and start all over again."

APPENDIX 1 LIST OF SONGS

The following is a list of 411 songs with lyrics by Dorothy Fields, arranged in alphabetical order. The minimal information given is the title, the composer, and the year of copyright. For most songs, I also list the title of the play, film, or television show in which the song first appeared, or for which it was intended. For some songs, I give the name of the singer or singers who first performed it. I note when a lyric is reprinted in one of the following three books: *Their Words Are Music* (referred to as Engel), *Reading Lyrics* (referred to as Gottlieb and Kimball), and *On the Sunny Side of the Street* (referred to as Winer). Complete bibliographical information for these books is given in the notes. Songs are included in this list if they appear in at least one of the following sources: the list of songs by Dorothy Fields in the Copyright Division of the Library of Congress; the list of songs in the ASCAP Ace Title Search; and Ken Bloom's list of songs by Dorothy Fields, which is included in *On the Sunny Side of the Street*.

After Forty It's Patch, Patch, Patch; Cy Coleman; 1970; *Eleanor*

Ain't It the Truth; Jimmy McHugh; 1932

All the Time; Arthur Schwartz; 1939; *Stars in Your Eyes*; first performed by Richard Carlson and Tamara Toumanova

Alone Too Long; Arthur Schwartz; 1954; *By the Beautiful Sea*; first performed by Wilbur Evans

Andiamo; Harold Arlen; 1951; *Mr. Imperium*; first performed by Ezio Pinza

Any One Else; Jimmy McHugh; 1930; *Kelly's Vacation*

April Fooled Me; Jerome Kern; 1956; lyric printed in Winer

April Snow; Sigmund Romberg; 1945; *Up in Central Park*; first performed by Maureen Cannon and Wilbur Evans

Arabian Lover; Jimmy McHugh; 1929; *Cotton Club Parade*

As Long as We're in Love; Jimmy McHugh; 1928; *Hello Daddy*

As of Today; Arthur Schwartz; 1939; *Stars in Your Eyes*

At Sea; Jimmy McHugh; 1933; *Clowns in Clover*

Baby; Jimmy McHugh; 1928; *Blackbirds of 1928*; first performed by Adelaide Hall

Baby, Dream Your Dream; Cy Coleman; 1966; *Sweet Charity*; first performed by Helen Gallagher and Thelma Oliver; lyric printed in Engel

Back in My Shell; Jerome Kern; 1940; *One Night in the Tropics*

Bandana Babies; Jimmy McHugh; 1928; *Blackbirds of 1928*; first performed by Adelaide Hall

Because I Love Nice Things; Jimmy McHugh; 1929; *Ziegfeld Midnight Frolic*

Behave Yourself; Albert Hague; 1959; *Redhead*; first performed by Gwen Verdon, Cynthia Latham, Doris Rich, and Richard Kiley

The Big Back Yard; Sigmund Romberg; 1945; *Up in Central Park*

Big Fat Heart; Cy Coleman; 1973; cut from *Seesaw*

The Big Papoose Is on the Loose; Jimmy McHugh; 1930; *The International Revue*

Big Spender; Cy Coleman; 1966; *Sweet Charity*; first performed by Helen Gallagher, Thelma Oliver, and ensemble; lyric printed in Engel, Winer

The Birds and the Bees; Sigmund Romberg; 1945; *Up in Central Park*; first performed by Maureen Cannon, Betty Bruce, Charles Irwin, Walter Burke

Blue Again; Jimmy McHugh; 1930; *The Vanderbilt Revue*; lyric printed in Gottlieb and Kimball

Bojangles of Harlem; Jerome Kern; 1936; *Swing Time*; first performed by Fred Astaire; lyric printed in Gottlieb and Kimball

Bon Soir Cherie; Jimmy McHugh; 1928

Boss Tweed; Sigmund Romberg; 1945; *Up in Central Park*

Boys Are Better Than Girls; Arthur Schwartz; 1952; *The Big Song and Dance*

The Bride Wore Something Old; Arthur Schwartz; 1951; cut from *A Tree Grows in Brooklyn*

Button Up Your Heart; Jimmy McHugh; 1930; *The Vanderbilt Revue*

The Call of the South; Jimmy McHugh; 1928; *Blackbirds of 1928*

Call On Your Neighbor; Arthur Schwartz; 1951; cut from *A Tree Grows in Brooklyn*

Can You Spell Schenectady; Harold Arlen; 1953; *The Farmer Takes a Wife*

The Carnie's Pitch; Harry Warren; 1951; *Texas Carnival*; first performed by Red Skelton

Carousel in the Park; Sigmund Romberg; 1945; *Up in Central Park*

Chapter 54, Number 1909; Cy Coleman; 1973; *Seesaw*; first performed by Ken Howard, Michele Lee, and Tommy Tune

Charge; Cy Coleman; 1970; *Eleanor*

Charity's Soliloquy; Cy Coleman; 1966; *Sweet Charity*; first performed by Gwen Verdon

Cheerio; Jimmy McHugh and Herbert Stothart; 1931

El Choclo; Jimmy McHugh and A. P. Villoldo; 1934

Cinderella Brown; Jimmy McHugh; 1930; *The International Revue*

Clean as a Whistle; Jimmy McHugh; 1933; *Meet the Baron*

Close as Pages in a Book; Sigmund Romberg; 1945; *Up in Central Park*; first performed by Maureen Cannon and Wilbur Evans; lyric printed in Engel, Winer

Clowns in Clover; Jimmy McHugh; 1933; *Clowns in Clover*

Collegiana; Jimmy McHugh; 1929; *The Time, the Place, and the Girl*; lyric printed in Winer

Coney Island Boat; Arthur Schwartz; 1954; *By the Beautiful Sea*; first performed by Shirley Booth, Robert Jennings, and ensemble

A Cow and a Plough and a Frau; Morton Gould; 1950; *Arms and the Girl*; first performed by Georges Guetary

Cuban Love Song; Jimmy McHugh and Herbert Stothart; 1931; *Cuban Love Song*; first performed by Lawrence Tibbett; lyric printed in Winer

Currier and Ives; Sigmund Romberg; 1945; *Up in Central Park*

Cut In; Jimmy McHugh; 1930; *The Vanderbilt Revue*

Dance Fool, Dance; Jimmy McHugh; 1930

Dance Me Around; Arthur Schwartz; 1952; *The Big Song and Dance*

Dance Till Dawn; Jimmy McHugh; 1931; *Flying High*

Debutante; Jimmy McHugh; 1934

Did You Ever Look at You; Cy Coleman; 1966; cut from *Sweet Charity*; *Seesaw*

Diga Diga Doo; Jimmy McHugh; 1928; *Blackbirds of 1928*; first performed by Adelaide Hall

Dinah's Daughter; Jimmy McHugh; 1934

Dinner at Eight; Jimmy McHugh; 1933; *Meet the Baron*

Dixie; Jimmy McHugh; 1928; *Blackbirds of 1928*; first performed by Aida Ward

Do I Know Why; Jimmy McHugh; 1930; *Kelly's Vacation*

Doin' the New Low-down; Jimmy McHugh; 1938; *Blackbirds of 1928*; first performed by Bill Robinson

Don't Be Afraid; Arthur Schwartz; 1951; *A Tree Grows in Brooklyn*; first performed by Johnny Johnston

Don't Blame Me; Jimmy McHugh; 1933; *Meet the Baron*; lyric printed in Gottlieb and Kimball, Winer

Don't Mention Love to Me; Oscar Levant; 1935; *In Person*; first performed by Ginger Rogers

Don't Talk; Morton Gould; 1950; *Arms and the Girl*; first performed by Georges Guetary

Dreaming; Jimmy McHugh; 1930; *Kelly's Vacation*

Drumming Out; Jimmy McHugh; 1933; *Meet the Baron*

The End Begins; Fritz Kreisler; 1936; *The King Steps Out*; first performed by Grace Moore

Erbie Fitch's Twitch; Albert Hague; 1959; *Redhead*; first performed by Gwen Verdon; recorded by Renee Orin with the composer at the piano; lyric printed in Winer

Every Little Moment; Jimmy McHugh; 1935

Every Night at Eight; Jimmy McHugh; 1935; *Every Night at Eight*

The Evils of Drink; Harold Arlen; 1953; cut from *The Farmer Takes a Wife*

Exactly Like You; Jimmy McHugh; 1930; *The International Revue*; first performed by Gertrude Lawrence and Harry Richman; lyric printed in Winer

Examination Number; Jimmy McHugh; 1931; *Flying High*

Face in the Fish Tank; Cy Coleman; 1966; cut from *Sweet Charity*

Farandola; Jerome Kern; 1940; *One Night in the Tropics*

A Fine Romance; Jerome Kern; 1936; *Swing Time*; first performed by Ginger Rogers and Fred Astaire; lyric printed in Gottlieb and Kimball, Winer

The Fireman's Bride; Sigmund Romberg; 1945; *Up in Central Park*; first performed by Maureen Cannon and Betty Bruce

Five O'clock Sky; David Lahm; 1968

For One Another; Jimmy McHugh; 1929

Free Thought in Action Class Song; Cy Coleman; 1966; cut from *Sweet Charity*

Freeze an' Melt; Jimmy McHugh; 1929; *Cotton Club Parade*

Futuristic Rhythm; Jimmy McHugh; 1928; *Hello Daddy*

Get a Horse; Arthur Schwartz; 1951; *Excuse My Dust*

Gimme a Raincheck; Cy Coleman; 1966; cut from *Sweet Charity*

A Girl with a Flame; Morton Gould; 1950; *Arms and the Girl*; first performed by Nanette Fabray

Go Home and Tell Your Mother; Jimmy McHugh; 1930; *Love in the Rough*; lyric printed in Winer

Goin' Steady; Arthur Schwartz; 1951; *Excuse My Dust*

Goin' with the Birds; Arthur Schwartz; 1952; *The Big Song and Dance*

A Good Impression; Cy Coleman; 1966; cut from *Sweet Charity*; *Eleanor*

Good Time Charlie; Arthur Schwartz; 1954; *By the Beautiful Sea*

Goodbye Blues; Jimmy McHugh; 1934; *Strictly Dynamite*; lyric by Dorothy Fields and Arnold Johnson

Got a New Lease on Life; Oscar Levant; 1935; *In Person*; first performed by Ginger Rogers

Growing Pains; Arthur Schwartz; 1951; *A Tree Grows in Brooklyn*; first performed by Johnny Johnston and Nomi Mitty; lyric printed in Engel

Gypsy Love; Jimmy McHugh; 1930; *The International Revue*

Hail to the Baron Munchausen; Jimmy McHugh; 1933; *Meet the Baron*

Hang Up; Arthur Schwartz; 1954; *By the Beautiful Sea*; first performed by Mae Barnes

Happy Habit; Arthur Schwartz; 1954; *By the Beautiful Sea*; first performed by Mae Barnes

The Happy Heart; Burton Lane; 1957; *Junior Miss*

Happy the Bride the Sun Shines Upon; Harold Arlen; 1953; *The Farmer Takes a Wife*

Happy Times; Jimmy McHugh; 1932; *Radio City Music Hall Opening*

Harlem at It Best; Jimmy McHugh; 1935

Harlem River Quiver; Jimmy McHugh; 1928

Harlemania; Jimmy McHugh; 1931

Have Feet Will Dance; Burton Lane; 1957; *Junior Miss*; lyric printed in Gottlieb and Kimball

He Had Refinement; Arthur Schwartz; 1951; *A Tree Grows in Brooklyn*; first performed by Shirley Booth; lyric printed in Winer

He Will Tonight; Morton Gould; 1950; *Arms and the Girl*; first performed by Nanette Fabray

He's Goin' Home; Arthur Schwartz; 1939; *Stars in Your Eyes*; first performed by Jimmy Durante

He's Good for Me; Cy Coleman; 1973; *Seesaw*; first performed by Michele Lee

Heavenly Party; Jerome Kern; 1938; *The Joy of Living*

Here Comes My Blackbird; Jimmy McHugh; 1928; *Blackbirds of 1928*; first performed by Adelaide Hall

Hey, Young Fella!; Jimmy McHugh; 1932; *Clowns in Clover*

Hooray for George the Third; Arthur Schwartz; 1954; *By the Beautiful Sea*

Hooray for Love; Jimmy McHugh; 1935; *Hooray for Love*

Hospitality; Cy Coleman; 1973; cut from *Seesaw*

Hot Chocolate; Jimmy McHugh; 1929

Hot Feet; Jimmy McHugh; 1929; *Cotton Club Parade*

Hottentot Tot; Jimmy McHugh; 1929

How's Your Uncle?; Jimmy McHugh; 1931; *Shoot the Works*

I Can't Give You Anything but Love; Jimmy McHugh; 1928; *Blackbirds of 1928*; first performed by Aida Ward; Lyric printed in Engel, Gottlieb and Kimball, Winer

I Can't Let You Down; Cy Coleman; 1966; cut from *Sweet Charity*

I Can't Let You Go; Cy Coleman; 1970; *Eleanor*

I Can't Wait; Jimmy McHugh; 1929; *Ziegfeld Midnight Frolic*

I Can't Waltz Alone; Max Steiner; 1935; *Alice Adams*

I Could Cook; Harold Arlen; 1953; cut from *The Farmer Takes a Wife*

I Could Go for You; Jimmy McHugh; 1930; *The International Revue*

I Did It and I'm Glad; Arthur Schwartz; 1952; *The Big Song and Dance*

I Dream Too Much; Jerome Kern; 1935; *I Dream Too Much*; first performed by Lily Pons; lyric printed in Engel, Winer

I Feel a Song Comin' On; Jimmy McHugh; 1935; *Every Night at Eight*; lyric by Dorothy Fields and George Oppenheimer; first performed by Frances Langford; lyric printed in Engel, Winer

I Feel Merely Marvelous; Albert Hague; 1959; *Redhead*; first performed by Gwen Verdon

I Got Love; Jerome Kern; 1935; *I Dream Too Much*; first performed by Lily Pons

I Like It Here; Morton Gould; 1950; *Arms and the Girl*; first performed by Georges Guetary

I Love Gardenias; Jimmy McHugh; 1934

I Love to Cry at Weddings; Cy Coleman; 1966; *Sweet Charity*; first performed by John Wheeler and Michael Davis; lyric printed in Engel, Winer

I Must Have That Man; Jimmy McHugh; 1928; *Blackbirds of 1928*; first performed by Adelaide Hall; lyric printed in Winer

I Struck Out; Cy Coleman; 1970; *Eleanor*

I Want Plenty of You; Jimmy McHugh; 1928; *Hello Daddy*

I Was Wearin' Horseshoes; Harold Arlen; 1953; cut from *The Farmer Takes a Wife*

I Won't Dance; Jerome Kern; 1935; *Roberta*; lyric by Oscar Hammerstein II, revised by Dorothy Fields; first performed by Fred Astaire; lyric printed in Gottlieb and Kimball, Winer

I'd Like to Take You Out Dreaming; Arthur Schwartz; 1951; *Excuse My Dust*

I'd Rather Wake Up by Myself; Arthur Schwartz; 1954; *By the Beautiful Sea*; first performed by Shirley Booth

I'll Be Hard to Handle; Jerome Kern; 1952; *Lovely to Look At*; lyric by Bernard Dougall and Dorothy Fields

I'll Buy It; Burton Lane; 1957; *Junior Miss*; first performed by David Wayne and Diana Lynn; lyric printed in Winer

I'll Buy You a Star; Arthur Schwartz; 1951; *A Tree Grows in Brooklyn*; first performed by Johnny Johnston; lyric printed in Engel

I'll Make a Happy Landing the Lucky Day I Land You; Jimmy McHugh; 1931; *Flying High*

I'll Never Learn; Morton Gould; 1950; *Arms and the Girl*; first performed by Nanette Fabray

I'll Never See You Again; Morton Gould; 1950; cut from *Arms and the Girl*

I'll Pay the Check; Arthur Schwartz; 1939; *Stars in Your Eyes*; first performed by Ethel Merman; lyric printed in Engel

I'll Take Any Man; Cy Coleman; 1966; cut from *Sweet Charity*

I'll Try; Albert Hague; 1959; *Redhead*; first performed by Gwen Verdon and Richard Kiley

I'm a Brass Band; Cy Coleman; 1966; *Sweet Charity*; first performed by Gwen Verdon; lyric printed in Winer

I'm a Broken Hearted Blackbird; Jimmy McHugh; 1926

I'm Back in Circulation; Albert Hague; 1959; *Redhead*; first performed by Richard Kiley

I'm Dancing on a Rainbow; Nacio Herb Brown; 1933; *Stage Mother*

I'm Doin' That Thing; Jimmy McHugh; 1930; *Love in the Rough*

I'm Feelin' Blue; Jimmy McHugh; 1930; *Rhapsody in Black* (cut from *The International Revue*)

I'm Full of the Devil; Jimmy McHugh; 1933; *Fugitive Lovers*

I'm in a Highly Emotional State; Cy Coleman; 1973; cut from *Seesaw*

I'm in Love All Over Again; Jimmy McHugh; 1935; *Hooray for Love*

I'm in the Mood for Love; Jimmy McHugh; 1935; *Every Night at Eight*; first performed by Frances Langford; lyric printed in Engel, Gottlieb and Kimball, Winer

I'm Learning a Lot from You; Jimmy McHugh; 1930; *Love in the Rough*

I'm Like a New Broom; Arthur Schwartz; 1951; *A Tree Grows in Brooklyn*; first performed by Johnny Johnston; lyric printed in Engel

I'm Livin' in a Great Big Way; Jimmy McHugh; 1928; *Hello Daddy*; lyric printed in Gottlieb and Kimball

I'm Proud of You; Arthur Schwartz; 1952; *The Big Song and Dance*

I'm Scared; Morton Gould; 1950; *Arms and the Girl*

I'm So Backward and She's So Forward; Jimmy McHugh; 1931

I'm the Bravest Individual; Cy Coleman; 1966; *Sweet Charity*; first performed by Gwen Verdon and John McMartin

I'm the Echo, You're the Song That I Sing; Jerome Kern; 1935; *I Dream Too Much*; first performed by Lily Pons

I'm Way Ahead; Cy Coleman; 1966; *Seesaw* (cut from *Sweet Charity*); first performed by Michele Lee

I've Got a Bug in My Head; Jimmy McHugh; 1930; *The International Revue*

I've Got a Date with Kate; Jimmy McHugh; 1932

I've Got a New Lease on Life; Oscar Levant; 1935; *In Person*

I've Got a Roof over My Head; Jimmy McHugh; 1933

I've Got the Blues; Jimmy McHugh; 1930; *The International Revue*

I've Tried Everything; Cy Coleman; 1966; cut from *Sweet Charity*

If My Friends Could See Me Now; Cy Coleman; 1966; *Sweet Charity*; first performed by Gwen Verdon; lyric printed in Engel, Winer

If You Haven't Got a Sweetheart; Arthur Schwartz; 1951; *A Tree Grows in Brooklyn*; first performed by Delbert Anderson

In the Little White Church on the Hill; Jimmy McHugh; 1933

In Tune; Cy Coleman; 1973; *Seesaw*; first performed by Michele Lee and Ken Howard

International Rhythm; Jimmy McHugh; 1930; *The International Revue*

Introduce Me; Jerome Kern; 1956

Is That My Prince; Arthur Schwartz; 1951; *A Tree Grows in Brooklyn*; first performed by Shirley Booth and Albert Linville

Isn't Nature Wonderful; Jimmy McHugh; 1930; *A Social Success*

It Costs Nothing to Dream; Jimmy McHugh; 1931

It Couldn't Happen to Two Nicer People; Arthur Schwartz; 1951; *Excuse My Dust*

It Doesn't Cost You Anything to Dream; Sigmund Romberg; 1945; *Up in Central Park*; first performed by Maureen Cannon and Wilbur Evans

It Doesn't Take a Minute; Albert Hague; 1959; cut from *Redhead*

It's a Nice Face; Cy Coleman; 1968; *Sweet Charity*; first performed by Shirley MacLaine

It's All Mine; Arthur Schwartz; 1954; cut from *By the Beautiful Sea*

It's All Yours; Arthur Schwartz; 1939; *Stars in Your Eyes*; first performed by Ethel Merman and Jimmy Durante; lyric printed in Engel, Gottlieb and Kimball

It's Dynamite; Harry Warren; 1951; *Texas Carnival*; first performed by Ann Miller

It's Great to Be in Love Again; Jimmy McHugh; 1935; *Every Night at Eight*

It's Just What I Wanted; Burton Lane; 1957; *Junior Miss*

It's Not in the Cards; Jerome Kern; 1936; *Swing Time*

It's Not Where You Start; Cy Coleman; 1973; *Seesaw*; first performed by Tommy Tune; lyric printed in Winer

It's Not Where You Start; Arthur Schwartz; 1954; cut from *By the Beautiful Sea*

It's the Darndest Thing; Jimmy McHugh; 1931; *Singin' the Blues*

It's Up to You; Arthur Schwartz; 1954; cut from *By the Beautiful Sea*

A Japanese Dream; Jimmy McHugh; 1929

A Japanese Moon; Jimmy McHugh; 1929

The Jockey on the Carousel; Jerome Kern; 1935; *I Dream Too Much*; first performed by Lily Pons

Johnny Cake; Morton Gould; 1950; *Arms and the Girl*

Journey's End; Jimmy McHugh; 1932; *Radio City Music Hall Opening*

Junior Miss; Burton Lane; 1957; *Junior Miss*; first performed by Don Ameche

Just a Little Bit More; Arthur Schwartz; 1939; *Stars in Your Eyes*; first performed by Ethel Merman

Just for Once; Albert Hague; 1959; *Redhead*; first performed by Gwen Verdon, Richard Kiley, and Leonard Stone

Just Let Me Look at You; Jerome Kern; 1938; *The Joy of Living*

Keep It in the Family; Cy Coleman; 1966; cut from *Sweet Charity*; *Eleanor*

Keys to Your Heart; Jimmy McHugh; 1930; *The International Revue*

A Lady Needs a Change; Arthur Schwartz; 1939; *Stars in Your Eyes*; first performed by Ethel Merman; lyric printed in Engel, Winer

Lafayette; Jerome Kern; 1952; *Lovely to Look At*

Learn How to Lose; Fritz Kreisler; 1936; *The King Steps Out*; first performed by Grace Moore

Let Me Look at You; Harold Arlen; 1951; *Mr. Imperium*; first performed by Ezio Pinza

Let Me Sing before Breakfast; Jimmy McHugh; 1929

Let's Have an Old Fashioned Christmas; Harold Adamson; 1945

Let's Make It Christmas All Year Long; Burton Lane; 1957; *Junior Miss*; first performed by Don Ameche, Joan Bennett, Carol Lynley, and Jill St. John

Let's Sit and Talk about You; Jimmy McHugh; 1928; *Hello Daddy*

Let's Sit This One Out; Jimmy McHugh; 1933

Let's Whistle a Waltz; Jimmy McHugh; 1933

Like Kelly Can; Jimmy McHugh; 1930; *Love in the Rough*

Little Old Cabin Door; Morton Gould; 1950; *Arms and the Girl*

Lolita; Jimmy McHugh; 1931

Look Who's Been Dreaming; Harold Arlen; 1953; *The Farmer Takes a Wife*

Look Who's Dancing; Arthur Schwartz; 1951; *A Tree Grows in Brooklyn*; first performed by Marcia Van Dyke and Shirley Booth

Look Who's in Love; Albert Hague; 1959; *Redhead*; first performed by Gwen Verdon and Richard Kiley

Looking For Love; Jimmy McHugh; 1929; *Ziegfeld Midnight Frolic*

Lorelei Brown; Arthur Schwartz; 1951; *Excuse My Dust*

Lost in a Fog; Jimmy McHugh; 1934; *Have a Heart*

Love and Logic; Cy Coleman; 1970; *Eleanor*

Love Is a Lovely Word; Harry Warren; 1951; cut from *Texas Carnival*

Love Is the Reason; Arthur Schwartz; 1951; *A Tree Grows in Brooklyn*; first performed by Shirley Booth and Nat Frey; lyric printed in Engel

Love Magician; Jimmy McHugh; 1931

Lovely to Look At; Jerome Kern; 1935; *Roberta*; lyric printed in Gottlieb and Kimball, Winer

Lucky Duck; Jimmy McHugh; 1934

Lucky Fella; Jimmy McHugh; 1933; *The Prizefighter and the Lady*

Madly in Love; Fritz Kreisler; 1936; *The King Steps Out*

Magnolia's Wedding Day; Jimmy McHugh; 1928; *Blackbirds of 1928*

Make the Man Love Me; Arthur Schwartz; 1951; *A Tree Grows in Brooklyn*; first performed by Marcia Van Dyke and Johnny Johnston; lyric printed in Engel, Gottlieb and Kimball, Winer

Make Up Your Mind; Jimmy McHugh; 1930; *The International Revue*

A Male Is an Animal; Burton Lane; 1957; *Junior Miss*; first performed by Carol Lynley and Susanne Sidney

A Man on Earth Is Worth Half a Dozen on the Moon; Jimmy McHugh; 1930; *Kelly's Vacation*

Marcha del Toros; Jerome Kern; 1957

The Margineers; Jimmy McHugh; 1930; *The International Revue*

Maybe Means Yes; Jimmy McHugh; 1928; *Hello Daddy*

Me and Pollyanna; Arthur Schwartz; 1954; cut from *By the Beautiful Sea*

Meat and Potatoes; Cy Coleman; 1970; *Eleanor*

Mine 'til Monday; Arthur Schwartz; 1951; *A Tree Grows in Brooklyn*; first performed by Johnny Johnston

Mister Washington! Uncle George!; Morton Gould; 1950; *Arms and the Girl*

Moments from Shakespeare; Arthur Schwartz; 1954; cut from *By the Beautiful Sea*

Mona from Arizona; Arthur Schwartz; 1954; *By the Beautiful Sea*

Moonlight on the Riviera; Jimmy McHugh; 1934

More Love Than Your Love; Arthur Schwartz; 1954; *By the Beautiful Sea*; first performed by Wilbur Evans

More People Like You; Cy Coleman; 1973; cut from *Seesaw*

The Most Exciting Night; Jerome Kern; 1952; *Lovely to Look At*

Music in My Heart; Jimmy McHugh; 1935; *The Nitwits*

My City; Cy Coleman; 1973; *Seesaw*; first performed by Ken Howard

My Dancing Lady; Jimmy McHugh; 1933; *Dancing Lady*

My Favorite Person; Jimmy McHugh; 1933; *Clowns in Clover*

My Gal's a Mule; Albert Hague; 1959; cut from *Redhead*

My Girl Is Just Enough Woman for Me; Albert Hague; 1959; *Redhead*; first performed by
    Richard Kiley; Cf. She's Not Enough Woman for Me

My Lady's Fan; Jimmy McHugh; 1928; *Hello Daddy*

My Love an' My Mule; Harold Arlen; 1951; *Mr Imperium*; first performed by Lana
    Turner (dubbed by Trudi Irwin)

My Personal Property; Cy Coleman; 1968; *Sweet Charity*; first performed by Shirley
    MacLaine

Never a Dull Moment; Arthur Schwartz; 1939; *Stars in Your Eyes*

Never Gonna Dance; Jerome Kern; 1936; *Swing Time*; first performed by Fred Astaire;
    lyric printed in Gottlieb and Kimball, Winer

Nice to Be Near; Jerome Kern; 1956

Nobody Does It Like Me; Cy Coleman; 1973; *Seesaw*; first performed by Michele Lee;
    lyric printed in Winer

Nobody's Fool; Jimmy McHugh; 1931

Nothin' for Nothin'; Morton Gould; 1950; *Arms and the Girl*; first performed by Pearl
    Bailey

Now Is Wonderful; Arthur Schwartz; 1952; *The Big Song and Dance*

Oh! Say Can You See; Sigmund Romberg; 1948; *Up in Central Park*; first performed by
    Deanna Durbin

Okay for Sound; Arthur Schwartz; 1939; *Stars in Your Eyes*

Old Enough to Love; Arthur Schwartz; 1954; *By the Beautiful Sea*; first performed by
    Larry Howard

The Old Kitchen Sink; Cy Coleman; 1970; *Eleanor*

On the Erie Canal; Harold Arlen; 1953; *The Farmer Takes a Wife*

On the Sunny Side of the Street; Jimmy McHugh; 1930; *The International Revue*; first
    performed by Gertrude Lawrence and Harry Richman; lyric printed in Engel,
    Gottlieb and Kimball, Winer

One Brief Moment; Arthur Schwartz; 1939; *Stars in Your Eyes*

One More Waltz; Jimmy McHugh; 1930; *Love in the Rough*

One More You; Arthur Schwartz; 1951; *Excuse My Dust*

Opening Night; Jerome Kern; 1952; *Lovely to Look At*

Our Song; Jerome Kern; 1937; *When You're in Love*

Out of Sight, Out of Mind; Oscar Levant; 1935; *In Person*; first performed by Ginger
    Rogers

Out Where the Blues Begin; Jimmy McHugh; 1928; *Hello Daddy*

Over on the Jersey Side; Jimmy McHugh; 1934

Oysters in July; Arthur Schwartz; 1951; cut from *A Tree Grows in Brooklyn*

Palsie Walsie; Jimmy McHugh; 1935; *Hooray for Love*

Party Line; Jimmy McHugh; 1928; *Hello Daddy*

The Party's on Me; Cy Coleman; 1973; *Seesaw* (added for tour)

Payday; Arthur Schwartz; 1951; *A Tree Grows in Brooklyn*

Pick Up the Pieces; Cy Coleman; 1973; cut from *Seesaw*

Pick Yourself Up; Jerome Kern; 1936; *Swing Time*; first performed by Fred Astaire and
    Ginger Rogers; lyric printed in Gottlieb and Kimball, Winer

Pink Taffeta Sample, Size 10; Cy Coleman; 1966; cut from *Sweet Charity*; lyric printed in Winer

Places, Everybody; Arthur Schwartz; 1939; *Stars in Your Eyes*

Plantation in Philadelphia; Morton Gould; 1950; *Arms and the Girl*

Play Half a Chorus; Jimmy McHugh; 1933; *Clowns in Clover*

Please Don't Send Me Down a Baby Brother; Arthur Schwarz; 1954; *By the Beautiful Sea*; first performed by Shirley Booth

Poor Everybody Else; Cy Coleman; 1966; *Seesaw* (cut from *Sweet Charity*); first performed by Michele Lee; lyric printed in Engel, Winer

Porgy; Jimmy McHugh; 1929; *Blackbirds of 1928*; first performed by Aida Ward

Positively Love You; Jimmy McHugh; 1933; *Clowns in Clover*

Pride of the Mountainside; Jimmy McHugh; 1933

The Profezzor; Arthur Schwartz; 1952; *The Big Song and Dance*

Raisin' the Roof; Jimmy McHugh; 1929; *Ziegfeld Midnight Frolic*

Red Hot Tomatoes; Cy Coleman; 1970; *Eleanor*

Remind Me; Jerome Kern; 1940; *One Night in the Tropics*; lyric printed in Gottlieb and Kimball, Winer

The Rhythm of Life; Cy Coleman; 1966; *Sweet Charity*; first performed by Harold Pierson, Eddie Gasper, and Arnold Soboloff

Ride Out the Storm; Cy Coleman; 1973; *Seesaw*; first performed by Cecilia Norfleet and LaMonte Peterson

The Right Finger of My Left Hand; Albert Hague; 1959; *Redhead*; first performed by Gwen Verdon

Rip Van Winkle; Sigmund Romberg; 1945; *Up in Central Park*

Rosalie; Jimmy McHugh; 1930

Salt; Cy Coleman; 1973; cut from *Seesaw*

Say How D'ya Do-a to Kalua; Jimmy McHugh; 1934

Schnapps; Harry Warren; 1951; cut from *Texas Carnival*

The Sea Song; Arthur Schwartz; 1954; *By the Beautiful Sea*; first performed by Shirley Booth

Seesaw; Cy Coleman; 1973; *Seesaw*

Self-Made Man; Arthur Schwartz; 1939; *Stars in Your Eyes*; first performed by Jimmy Durante

Serenade for a Wealthy Widow; Jimmy McHugh and Reginald Forsythe; 1934

Sergeant Housewife; Joseph Meyer; 1945

She's Exciting; Morton Gould; 1950; *Arms and the Girl*; first performed by Georges Guetary

She's Not Enough Woman for Me; Albert Hague; 1959; *Redhead*; first performed by Richard Kiley and Leonard Stone; Cf. My Girl Is Just Enough Woman for Me

Shuffle Your Feet and Just Roll Along; Jimmy McHugh; 1928; *Blackbirds of 1928*; first performed by Ruth Johnson and Margie Hubbard

Simple Philosophy; Jerome Kern; 1940; *One Night in the Tropics*

The Simpson Sisters' Door; Albert Hague; 1959; *Redhead*

Sing You a Couple of Choruses; Jimmy McHugh; 1934

Singin' the Blues; Jimmy McHugh; 1931; *Singin' the Blues*

Sixty Per Cent of the Accidents; Cy Coleman; 1970; *Eleanor*

So What Now; Cy Coleman; 1970; *Eleanor*

Somethin' Real Special; Harold Arlen; 1953; *The Farmer Takes a Wife*; first performed by Betty Grable and Dale Robertson

Spain; Jimmy McHugh; 1930; *The International Review*

Spanglish; Cy Coleman; 1973; *Seesaw*; first performed by Michele Lee, Ken Howard, Giancarlo Esposito, and Cecilia Norfleet

Speaking Confidentially; Jimmy McHugh; 1935; *Every Night at Eight*; first performed by Frances Langford

Spring Fever; Jimmy McHugh; 1930

Spring Has Sprung; Arthur Schwartz; 1951; *Excuse My Dust*

Squeaky Shoes; Jimmy McHugh; 1929; *Ziegfeld Midnight Frolic*

Stars in My Eyes; Fritz Kreisler; 1936; *The King Steps Out*; first performed by Grace Moore

Step In; Jimmy McHugh; 1934

Sweet Charity; Cy Coleman; 1966; *Sweet Charity*; first performed by John McMartin

Swing Left, Sweet Chariot; Ray Henderson; 1939; *Sticks and Stones*

Swing Low, Swing High; Jerome Kern; 1936; *Swing Time*

Take It Easy; Jimmy McHugh; 1935; *Every Night at Eight*

Tell Me; Jimmy McHugh; 1934

Terribly Attractive; Arthur Schwartz; 1939; *Stars in Your Eyes*; first performed by Jimmy Durante and Mildred Natwick

Thank You for a Lovely Evening; Jimmy McHugh; 1934; *Have a Heart*

That's for Children; Arthur Schwartz; 1951; *Excuse My Dust*

That's How It Goes; Arthur Schwartz; 1951; *A Tree Grows in Brooklyn*

That's My Fella; Morton Gould; 1950; *Arms and the Girl*; first performed by Nanette Fabray

That's the Hollywood Low-Down; Jimmy McHugh; 1935; *Every Night at Eight*

That's What I Told Him Last Night; Morton Gould; 1950; *Arms and the Girl*

That's Why We're Dancing; Jimmy McHugh; 1930; *The International Review*

Then You Went and Changed Your Mind; Jimmy McHugh; 1932

Then You've Never Been Blue; Jimmy McHugh; 1935; *Every Night at Eight*; first performed by Frances Langford

There Must Be Somethin' Better Than Love; Morton Gould; 1950; *Arms and the Girl*; first performed by Pearl Bailey; lyric printed in Gottlieb and Kimball

There's a Kick in the Old Girl Yet; Jimmy McHugh; 1930; *March of Time*

There's Gotta Be Something Better Than This; Cy Colman; 1966; *Sweet Charity*; first performed by Gwen Verdon, Helen Gallagher, and Thelma Oliver

There's Love in the Air; Jimmy McHugh; 1931

Thinking of You Thinking of Me in the Moonlight; Jimmy McHugh; 1929

Thirty Weeks of Heaven; Arthur Schwartz; 1954; cut from *By the Beautiful Sea*

This Is It; Arthur Schwartz; 1939; *Stars in Your Eyes*; first performed by Ethel Merman

Three Little Maids from School; Jimmy McHugh; 1928; *Hello Daddy*

Throw the Anchor Away; Arthur Schwartz; 1954; *By the Beautiful Sea*

Today I Love Everybody; Harold Arlen; 1953; *The Farmer Takes a Wife*; first performed by
 Betty Grable; lyric printed in Winer

Too Many Tomorrows; Cy Coleman; 1966; *Sweet Charity*; first performed by James Luisi

Topsy and Eva; Jimmy McHugh; 1930

Tramps at Sea; Jimmy McHugh; 1931; *Cuban Love Song*; first performed by Lawrence
 Tibbett

Tuscaloosa; Arthur Schwartz; 1951; cut from *A Tree Grows in Brooklyn* and *By the
 Beautiful Sea*

Tutu and Tights; Cy Coleman; 1973; cut from *Seesaw*

Two Faces in the Dark; Albert Hague; 1959; *Redhead*; first performed by Bob Dixon

The Uncle Sam Rag; Albert Hague; 1959; *Redhead*; first performed by Leonard Stone

Up from the Gutter; Sigmund Romberg; 1945; *Up in Central Park*; first performed by
 Betty Bruce

Visitors; Cy Coleman; 1973; cut from *Seesaw*

Waltz in Swingtime; Jerome Kern; 1936; *Swing Time*

The Way You Look Tonight; Jerome Kern; 1936; *Swing Time*; first performed by Fred
 Astaire; lyric printed in Gottlieb and Kimball, Winer

We Loves Ya, Jimey; Albert Hague; 1959; *Redhead*; first performed by Gwen Verdon, Jay
 Nichols, and Pat Ferrier

We'll Dance until the Dawn; Jimmy McHugh; 1931; *Red-Headed Woman*; Cf. Dance Till
 Dawn

We're Doin' It for the Natives in Jamaica; Harold Arlen; 1953; *The Farmer Takes a Wife*

We're in Business; Harold Arlen; 1953; *The Farmer Takes a Wife*

We've Got It; Cy Coleman; 1973; *Seesaw*; first performed by Ken Howard

Wearin' of the Green; Jimmy McHugh; 1930; *Kelly's Vacation*

Welcome to Holiday Inn; Cy Coleman; 1973; *Seesaw*; first performed by Michele Lee

What a Whale of a Difference Just a Few Lights Make; Jimmy McHugh; 1929; *Ziegfeld
 Midnight Frolic*

What Do I Do; Cy Coleman; 1970; *Eleanor*

What Is There about You; Jimmy McHugh; 1933

What Shall Remain; Fritz Kreisler; 1936; *The King Steps Out*; first performed by Grace
 Moore

What's Good about Good-Night; Jerome Kern; 1938; *The Joy of Living*

When Did You Know; Cy Coleman; 1966; cut from *Sweet Charity*; *Eleanor*

When I Close My Door; Harold Arlen; 1953; *The Farmer Takes a Wife*

When She Walks in the Room; Sigmund Romberg; 1945; *Up in Central Park*

When We Were Very Young; Jerome Kern; 1952; *Lovely to Look At*

Where Am I Going; Cy Coleman; 1966; *Sweet Charity*; first performed by Gwen Verdon;
 lyric printed in Winer

Where Can I Run from You; Arthur Schwartz; 1951; *Excuse My Dust*

Where Do I Go from You; Arthur Schwartz; 1952; *The Big Song and Dance*

Where There Is Love; Quincy Jones; 1968; *The Hell with Heroes*

Whisper in the Moonlight; Jimmy McHugh; 1932

Whisper on the Winds; Cy Coleman; 1970; *Eleanor*

The Whistling Boy; Jerome Kern; 1937; *When You're in Love*

Who Said That Dreams Don't Come True; Jimmy McHugh; 1934

Whoa, Emma; Harry Warren; 1951; *Texas Carnival*; first performed by Howard Keel

Why Am I Happy?; Harold Arlen; 1953; *The Farmer Takes a Wife*

With a Feather in Your Cap; Jimmy McHugh; 1932; *Radio City Music Hall Opening*

With the Sun Warm upon Me; Harold Arlen; 1953; *The Farmer Takes a Wife*; first performed by Dale Robertson

Yes!; Harold Arlen; 1953; *The Farmer Takes a Wife*

You and Your Kiss; Jerome Kern; 1940; *One Night in the Tropics*

You Can't Get over the Wall; Sigmund Romberg; 1945; *Up in Central Park*

You Can't Lose 'em All; Cy Coleman; 1966; cut from *Sweet Charity*

You Couldn't Be Cuter; Jerome Kern; 1938; *The Joy of Living*; first performed by Irene Dunne; lyric printed in Gottlieb and Kimball, Winer

You Kissed Me; Morton Gould; 1950; *Arms and the Girl*; first performed by Georges Guetary

You Should See Yourself; Cy Coleman; 1966; *Sweet Charity*; first performed by Gwen Verdon; lyric printed in Winer

You Wanna Bet; Cy Coleman; 1966; cut from *Sweet Charity*

You're a Lovable Lunatic; Cy Coleman; 1973; *Seesaw*; first performed by Ken Howard

You're an Angel; Jimmy McHugh; 1935; *Hooray for Love*

You're Devastating; Jerome Kern; 1952; *Lovely to Look At*; lyric by Otto Harbach and Dorothy Fields

You're the Better Half of Me; Jimmy McHugh; 1930; *The Vanderbilt Revue*

You've Got a Face Full of Wonderful Things; Harry Warren; 1951; *Texas Carnival*

Young Folks Should Get Married; Harry Warren; 1951; *Texas Carnival*; first performed by Howard Keel

Your Disposition Is Mine; Jimmy McHugh; 1928; *Hello Daddy*

APPENDIX 2
LIST OF THEATER WORKS AND MOVIES

The following is a list, in alphabetical order, of the musicals and movies in which songs by Dorothy Fields first appeared or for which she wrote the script or libretto. For the musicals, I give production information and information on the original cast as well as the dates of the first and last performances of the original run. I also tell if there is an original cast recording or some other recording of note, but I have not attempted a complete discography. For movies, I give production information and information on the cast.

Alice Adams (RKO, 1935)
Producer: Pandro S. Berman
Director: George Stevens
Screenplay: Dorothy Yost and Mortimer Offner
Score: Max Steiner and Roy Webb
Cast: Katharine Hepburn, Fred MacMurray, Fred Stone, Evelyn Venable
One song, "I Can't Waltz Alone," by Max Steiner and Dorothy Fields, possibly cut from the film. According to Kenneth Bloom, "The song might have been written for exploitation only."

Annie Get Your Gun
Music and lyrics: Irving Berlin
Book: Herbert and Dorothy Fields
Producers: Richard Rodgers and Oscar Hammerstein II
Director: Joshua Logan
Choreographer: Helen Tamiris
Cast: Ethel Merman, Ray Middleton, Marty May, William O'Neal, Betty Ann Nyman, Lou Penman
Opened in New York at the Imperial Theatre, May 16, 1946, and ran for 1,147 performances, closing February 12, 1949
Original production recording with cast substitutions: Decca 8001

Annie Get Your Gun (MGM, 1950)
Producer: Arthur Freed
Director: George Sidney
Screenplay: Sidney Sheldon
Musical direction: Adolph Deutsch and Roger Edens
Cast: Betty Hutton, Howard Keel, Edward Arnold, J. Carrol Naish, Louis Calhern

Arms and the Girl
Music: Morton Gould
Lyrics: Dorothy Fields

Book: Herbert and Dorothy Fields and Rouben Mamoulian, based on *The Pursuit of Happiness*, by Lawrence Langner and Armina Marshall

Producer: Theatre Guild

Director: Rouben Mamoulian

Choreographer: Michael Kidd

Cast: Nanette Fabray, Georges Guetary, Pearl Bailey, John Conte

Opened in New York at the Forty-sixth Street Theatre on February 2, 1950, and ran for 134 performances, closing May 27, 1950

Original cast recording: CBS X-14879

The Big Song and Dance (Paramount, 1952)

This film had eight songs written for it by Arthur Schwartz and Dorothy Fields; it was never produced.

Blackbirds of 1928

Music: Jimmy McHugh

Lyrics: Dorothy Fields

Producer and director: Lew Leslie

Sketches: Uncredited

Cast: Adelaide Hall, Bill Robinson, Aida Ward, Tim Moore, Elizabeth Welch

Opened in New York at the Liberty Theatre, May 9, 1928, and ran for 518 performances, closing August 1929

Recording made in 1932–33 with Bill Robinson, Adelaide Hall, Ethel Waters, Cab Calloway, the Mills Brothers, the Cecil Mack Choir, re-released on Columbia DL-6770

By the Beautiful Sea

Music: Arthur Schwartz

Lyrics: Dorothy Fields

Book: Herbert and Dorothy Fields

Producers: Robert Fryer and Lawrence Carr

Director: Marshall Jamison

Choreographer: Helen Tamiris

Sets and Lighting: Jo Mielziner

Costumes: Irene Sharaff

Cast: Shirley Booth, Wilbur Evans, Mae Barnes, Thomas Gleason, Richard France

Opened in New York at the Majestic Theatre, April 8, 1954, and ran for 270 performances, closing November 27, 1954

Original cast recording: Capitol, S-531

Clowns in Clover

Music: Jimmy McHugh

Lyrics: Dorothy Fields

Based on the revue *Clowns in Clover*, music by Noel Gay, which opened in London in 1927 at the Adelphi Theatre

Opened in Chicago, at the Apollo Theatre, 1932.

Cotton Club Parade
Music: Jimmy McHugh
Lyrics: Dorothy Fields
1929
Several shows with the title *Cotton Club Parade*, with contributions by various composers and lyricists, were written between 1923 and 1939. By 1931, there were two editions of *Cotton Club Parade* each year.

Cuban Love Song (MGM, 1931)
Producer: Albert Lewin
Director: W. S. Van Dyke
Screenplay: Gardiner Sullivan, Meredyth Bass et al.
Musical Score: Herbert Stothart
Songs by Jimmy McHugh and Dorothy Fields, and others
Cast: Lawrence Tibbett, Lupe Velez, Jimmy Durante, Ernest Torrence

Dancers in the Dark (Paramount, 1932)
Director: David Burton
Screenplay: Herman Mankiewicz
Songs by Jimmy McHugh and Dorothy Fields, Richard Whiting and Ralph Rainger, and others
Cast: Jack Oakie, Miriam Hopkins, William Collier, George Raft, Lyda Roberti

Dancing Lady (MGM, 1933)
Producer: David O. Selznick
Director: Robert Z. Leonard
Screenplay: Allen Rivkin and P. I. Wolfson
Songs by Jimmy McHugh and Dorothy Fields; Burton Lane and Harold Adamson; and others
Musical direction: Louis Silvers
Cast: Joan Crawford, Clark Gable, Franchot Tone, May Robson, Fred Astaire

Dinner at Eight (MGM, 1933)
Producer: David O. Selznick
Director: George Cukor
Screenplay: Frances Marion, Herman J. Mankiewicz et al.
Title song, by Jimmy McHugh and Dorothy Fields, not used in film.
Cast: Jean Harlow, John Barrymore, Lionel Barrymore, Billie Burke, Wallace Beery

Eleanor
Complete score written by Cy Coleman and Dorothy Fields in 1970. Never produced.

Every Night at Eight (Paramount, 1935)
Producer: Walter Wanger
Director: Raoul Walsh
Screenplay: Gene Towne, Graham Baker, and Bert Hamlon

Songs by Jimmy McHugh and Dorothy Fields
Cast: George Raft, Alice Faye, Frances Langford, Patsy Kelly

Excuse My Dust (MGM, 1951)
Producer: Jack Cummings
Director: Roy Rowland
Screenplay: George Wells
Choreographer: Hermes Pan
Songs by Arthur Schwartz and Dorothy Fields
Cast: Red Skelton, Macdonald Carey, Sally Forrest (dubbed by Gloria Grey), Monica Lewis

The Farmer Takes a Wife (TCF, 1953)
Producer: Frank P. Rosenberg
Director: Henry Levin
Screenplay: Joseph Fields, Sally Benson, Walter Bullock
Choreographer: Jack Cole
Songs by Harold Arlen and Dorothy Fields
Cast: Betty Grable, Dale Robertson, Thelma Ritter, Eddie Foy Jr., John Carroll

Father Takes a Wife (RKO, 1941)
Producer: Lee Marcus
Director: Jack Hively
Screenplay: Herbert and Dorothy Fields
Musical score: Roy Webb and Aaron Gonzales
Cast: Adolph Menjou, Gloria Swanson, Desi Arnaz, Helen Broderick

Flying High (MGM, 1931)
Director: Charles Riesner
Screenplay: A. P. Younger and Robert E. Hopkins
Choreographer: Busby Berkeley
Songs by Jimmy McHugh and Dorothy Fields, and others
Cast: Bert Lahr, Charlotte Greenwood, Pat O'Brien, Hedda Hopper, Guy Kibbe

Fugitive Lovers (MGM, 1934)
Producer: Lucien Hubbard
Director: Richard Boleslawski
Screenplay: Albert Hackett and Frances Goodrich
Songs by Jimmy McHugh and Dorothy Fields, and others
Cast: Robert Montgomery, Madge Evans, Ted Heely

Have a Heart (MGM, 1934)
Producer: John W. Considine Jr.
Director: David Butler
Screenplay: B. G. DeSylva, Florence Ryerson et al.
Songs by Jimmy McHugh and Dorothy Fields
Cast: Jean Parker, James Dunn, Una Merkel

The Hell with Heroes (Universal, 1968)
Producer: Stanley Chase
Director: Joseph Sargent
Screenplay: Hallsted Wells and Harold Livingston
Song by Quincy Jones and Dorothy Fields
Cast: Rod Taylor, Kevin McCarthy, Claudia Cardinale

Hello Daddy
Music: Jimmy McHugh
Lyrics: Dorothy Fields
Book: Herbert Fields, based on *The High Cost of Loving*, by Frank Mandel
Producer: Lew Fields
Director: Alexander Leftwich
Choreographer: Busby Berkeley
Cast: Lew Fields, Wilfred Clark, George Hassell, Alice Fischer
Opened in New York at the Mansfield Theatre, December 26, 1928, and ran for
26 weeks, closing June 15, 1929

Hooray for Love (RKO, 1935)
Producer: Felix Young
Director: Walter Lang
Screenplay: Lawrence Hazard and Ray Harris
Choreographer: Sammy Lee
Songs by Jimmy McHugh and Dorothy Fields
Cast: Ann Sothern, Gene Raymond, Bill Robinson, Fats Waller

I Dream Too Much (RKO, 1935)
Producer: Pandro S. Berman
Director: John Cromwell
Screenplay: Edmund North and James Gow
Choreographer: Hermes Pan
Songs by Jerome Kern and Dorothy Fields
Cast: Lily Pons, Henry Fonda, Eric Blore, Osgood Perkins

In Person (RKO, 1935)
Producer: Pandro S. Berman
Director: William A. Seiter
Screenplay: Allan Scott
Choreographer: Hermes Pan
Songs by Oscar Levant and Dorothy Fields
Cast: Ginger Rogers, George Brent, Alan Mowbray

The International Revue
Music: Jimmy McHugh

Lyrics: Dorothy Fields
Sketches: Nat Dorfman and Lew Leslie
Choreographers: Busby Berkeley and Harry Crosley
Producer: Lew Leslie
Director: Edward Clarke Lilley
Principals: Gertrude Lawrence, Harry Richman, Jack Pearl, Florence Moore, Anton Dolin
Opened at the Majestic Theatre February 25, 1930, and closed May 17, 1930

The Joy of Living (RKO, 1938)
Producer: Felix Young
Director: Tay Garnett
Screenplay: Gene Towne, Graham Baker, Allan Scott
Songs by Jerome Kern and Dorothy Fields
Cast: Irene Dunne, Douglas Fairbanks Jr., Eric Blore, Lucille Ball

Junior Miss
Music: Burton Lane
Lyrics: Dorothy Fields
Book: Joseph Stein and Will Glickman
Cast: Don Ameche, Joan Bennett, Carol Lynley, David Wayne, Diana Lynn, Jill St. John
DuPont Show of the Month, shown on television December 20, 1957

Kelly's Vacation
According to Ken Bloom (Winer, 248) this work opened in 1930 and contained five songs by Fields and McHugh. I can find no further information on this work.

The King Steps Out (Columbia, 1936)
Producer: William Perlberg
Director: Josef von Sternberg
Screenplay: Sidney Buchman
Songs by Fritz Kreisler and Dorothy Fields
Cast: Grace Moore, Franchot Tone, Victor Jory

Let's Face It
Music and lyrics: Cole Porter
Book: Herbert and Dorothy Fields
Producer: Vinton Freedley
Director: Edgar MacGregor
Choreographer: Charles Walters
Cast: Danny Kaye, Eve Arden, Benny Baker, Mary Jane Walsh, Edith Meiser, Vivian Vance, Nanette Fabray
Opened in New York at the Imperial Theatre, October 29, 1941, and ran for 547 performances

Lew Leslies' Blackbirds of 1928
See *Blackbirds of 1928*

Love in the Rough (MGM, 1930)
Director: Charles Reisner
Screenplay: Joe Farnham and Robert E. Hopkins
Songs by Jimmy McHugh and Dorothy Fields
Cast: Robert Montgomery, Benny Rubin, Dorothy Jordan, Dorothy McNulty

Lovely to Look At (MGM, 1952)
Producer: Jack Cummings
Director: Mervyn LeRoy
Screenplay: Harry Ruby and George Wells
Choreographer: Hermes Pan
Songs by Jerome Kern; the lyrics of seven of them were written or revised by Dorothy Fields
Cast: Kathryn Grayson, Howard Keel, Red Skelton, Ann Miller, Marge and Gower
Champion

March of Time (MGM, 1930)
Producer: Charles Reisner
Director: Harry Rapf
Song by Jimmy McHugh and Dorothy Fields
This film, begun at MGM in 1930, was intended to be a gala review in three parts of
famous stage screen performers. It was never completed.

Meet the Baron (MGM, 1933)
Producer: David O. Selznick
Director: Walter Lang
Screenplay: Allen Rivkin, P. J. Wolfson et al.
Songs by Jimmy McHugh and Dorothy Fields
Cast: Jack Pearl, Jimmy Durante, ZaSu Pitts

Mexican Hayride
Music and lyrics: Cole Porter
Book: Herbert and Dorothy Fields
Producer: Michael Todd
Director: Hassard Short and John Kennedy
Choreographer: Paul Haukon
Cast: Bobby Clark, Jane Havoc, George Givot, Wilbur Evans, Edith Meiser
Opened in New York at the Winter Garden, January 28, 1944, and ran for 481
performances, closing March 17, 1945
Original cast recording: Decca 10" 5232; CBS x-14878

Mr. Imperium (MGM, 1951)
Producer: Edwin H. Knopf

Director: Don Hartman
Screenplay: Edwin H. Knopf and Don Hartman
Musical score: Bronislaw Kaper
Songs by Harold Arlen and Dorothy Fields, and others
Cast: Ezio Pinza, Lana Turner (dubbed by Trudy Erwin), Debby Reynolds, Marjorie Main

The Nitwits (RKO, 1935)
Producer: Lee Marcus
Director: George Stevens
Screenplay: Fred Guiol and Al Boasberg
Songs by Jimmy McHugh and Dorothy Fields
Cast: Bert Wheeler, Robert Woolsey, Betty Grable, Evelyn Brent

One Night in the Tropics (Universal, 1940)
Producer: Leonard Spiegelgass
Director: Edward Sutherland
Screenplay: Gertrude Purcell and Charles Grayson
Songs by Jerome Kern, Dorothy Fields, Oscar Hammerstein II, Otto Harbach
Cast: Bud Abbott, Lou Costello, Allen Jones, Gertrude Purcell, Nancy Kelly

The Prize Fighter and the Lady (MGM, 1933)
Producer: Hunt Stromberg
Director: W. S. Van Dyke
Screenplay: John Lee Mahin and John Meehan
Songs by Jimmy McHugh and Dorothy Fields and others
Cast: Myrna Loy, Max Baer, Jack Dempsey, Primo Carnera, Walter Huston

Radio City Music Hall Inaugural Program
December 27, 1932

Redhead
Music: Albert Hague
Lyrics: Dorothy Fields
Book: Herbert Fields, Dorothy Fields, Sidney Sheldon, David Shaw
Producers: Robert Fryer and Lawrence Carr
Director and choreographer: Bob Fosse
Cast: Gwen Verdon, Richard Kiley, Leonard Stone, Doris Rich, Cynthia Latham
Opened in New York at the Forty-sixth Street Theatre, February 5, 1959, and ran for
452 performances, closing March 19, 1960
Original cast recording: RCA Victor, 09026-61995-2

Rhapsody in Black
Music: Jimmy McHugh, George Gershwin, and others
Lyrics: Dorothy Fields and others
Producer: Lew Leslie

Principals: Ethel Waters, Valaida, Blue McAllister, Al Moore, Cecil Mack's Choir
Opened at the Sam H. Harris Theatre on May 4, 1931, and closed in
July 1931

Roberta (RKO, 1935)
Producer: Pandro S. Berman
Director: William A. Seiter
Screenplay: Jane Murfin, Sam Mintz, and Allan Scott
Choreographer: Hermes Pan
Songs by Jerome Kern, Otto Harbach, Dorothy Fields
Cast: Irene Dunne, Randolph Scott, Ginger Rogers, Fred Astaire

Seesaw
Music: Cy Coleman
Lyrics: Dorothy Fields
Book: Michael Bennett, based on the play *Two for the Seesaw* by William Gibson
Producers: Joseph Kipness, Lawrence Kasha, James Nederlander, George
Steinbrenner III
Director and choreographer: Michael Bennett
Cast: Michele Lee, Ken Howard, Tommy Tune
Opened in New York at the Uris Theatre, March 18, 1973, and ran for 25 previews
plus 296 regular performances, closing December 8, 1973
Original cast recording: DRG Records, CDRG6108

Shoot the Works
Songs by Jimmy McHugh and Dorothy Fields, Irving Berlin, and others
Sketches by Dorothy Parker, E. B. White, and others
Producer: Heywood Broun
Director: Ted Hammerstein
Choreographer: Johnny Boyle
Principals: Heywood Broun, Jack Hazzard, Johnny Boyle, Imogene Coca, George
Murphy
Opened in New York at the George M. Cohan Theatre on July 21, 1931, and closed
on October 3, 1931

Singin' the Blues
Music: Jimmy McHugh
Lyrics: Dorothy Fields
Book: John McGowan
Producers: Alex A. Aarons and Vinton Freedley
Director: Bertram Harrison
Choreography: Sammy Lee
Cast: Frank Wilson, Mantan Moreland, Fredi Washington, Maud Russell
Opened in New York at the Liberty Theatre on September 16, 1931, and closed on
October 24, 1931

A Social Success (1930)
According to Ken Bloom (Winer, 248), this film contains one song by Jimmy McHugh and Dorothy Fields.

Something for the Boys
Music and lyrics: Cole Porter
Book: Herbert and Dorothy Fields
Producer: Michael Todd
Director: Hassard Short
Cast: Ethel Merman, Paula Laurence, Bill Johnson, Betty Garrett, Betty Bruce, Allen Jenkins
Opened in New York at the Alvin Theatre on January 7, 1943, and ran for 422 performances, closing on January 8, 1944

Stars in Your Eyes
Music: Arthur Schwartz
Lyrics: Dorothy Fields
Book: J. P. McEvoy
Producer: Dwight Deere Wiman
Director: Joshua Logan
Choreographer: Carl Randall
Cast: Ethel Merman, Jimmy Durante, Tamara Toumanova, Richard Carlson, Mildred Natwick
Opened in New York at the Majestic Theatre, February 9, 1939, and ran for 127 performances, closing May 27, 1939
Original production recording (six songs): AEI-CD001

Sticks and Stones
According to Ken Bloom (Winer, 250), this show opened in 1939 with one song by Ray Henderson and Dorothy Fields. I can find no further information.

Strictly Dynamite (RKO, 1934)
Producer: H. N. Swanson
Director: Elliott Nugent
Screenplay: Maurine Watkins, Ralph Spence et al.
Choreographer: Hermes Pan
Songs by Jimmy McHugh and Dorothy Fields, and others
Cast: Jimmy Durante, Lupe Velez, Norman Foster

Sweet Charity
Music: Cy Coleman
Lyrics: Dorothy Fields
Book: Neil Simon, based on the movie *Le Notti di Cabiria* (*Nights of Cabiria*)
Producer: Robert Fryer, Lawrence Carr, Sylvia and Joseph Harris
Director and choreographer: Bob Fosse

Cast: Gwen Verdon, John McMartin, Helen Gallagher, Thelma Oliver, James Luisi

Opened in New York at the Palace Theatre, January 29, 1966, and ran for 608 performances, closing July 15, 1967

Original cast recording: Columbia Records, CK 2900

Sweet Charity (Universal, 1968)
Producer: Robert Arthur
Director and choreographer: Bob Fosse
Screenplay: Peter Stone
Eleven songs by Cy Coleman and Dorothy Fields, of which three were newly written for the movie
Cast: Shirley MacLaine, John McMartin, Chita Rivera, Paula Kelly, Sammy Davis Jr., Ricardo Montalban, Stubby Kaye

Swing Time (RKO, 1936)
Producer: Pandro S. Berman
Director: George Stevens
Screenplay: Howard Lindsay and Allen Scott
Choreographer: Hermes Pan
Songs by Jerome Kern and Dorothy Fields
Cast: Fred Astaire, Ginger Rogers, Victor Moore, Helen Broderick, Eric Blore

Texas Carnival (MGM, 1951)
Producer: Jack Cummings
Director: Charles Walters
Screenplay: Dorothy Kingsley
Choreographer: Hermes Pan
Musical score: David Rose
Songs by Harry Warren and Dorothy Fields
Cast: Red Skelton, Esther Williams, Howard Keel, Ann Miller, Keenan Wynn

The Time, the Place, and the Girl (Warner Bros., 1929)
Director: Howard Bretherton
Screenplay: Frank R. Adams
Songs by Jimmy McHugh and Dorothy Fields, and others
Cast: Grant Withers, Betty Compson, James Kirkwood
According to the Internet Movies Database, the film is believed to be lost.

A Tree Grows in Brooklyn
Music: Arthur Schwartz
Lyrics: Dorothy Fields
Book: Betty Smith and George Abbott
Producers: George Abbott and Robert Fryer
Director: George Abbott
Choreographer: Herbert Ross

Cast: Marcia Van Dyke, Johnny Johnston, Shirley Booth, Nomi Mitty, Lou Wills Jr., Nathaniel Fry

Opened in New York at the Alvin Theatre, April 19, 1951, and ran for 270 performances, closing December 8, 1951

Original cast recording: Sony Broadway, SK 48014

Up in Central Park
Music: Sigmund Romberg
Lyrics: Dorothy Fields
Book: Herbert and Dorothy Fields
Producer: Michael Todd
Director: John Kennedy
Choreographer: Helen Tamiris
Cast: Wilbur Evans, Maureen Cannon, Betty Bruce, Noah Beery, Maurice Burke, Charles Irwin, Robert Rounseville

Opened in New York at the New Century Theatre on January 27, 1945, and ran for 504 performances, closing April 13, 1946

Original production recording, with cast substitutions: JJA Records 19782; Decca 8016

Up in Central Park (Universal, 1948)
Producer: Karl Tunberg
Director: William A. Seiter
Screenplay: Karl Tunberg
Choreographer: Helen Tamaris
Musical score: Johnny Green (uncredited)
Songs by Sigmund Romberg and Dorothy Fields, one newly written for the film
Cast: Deanna Durbin, Dick Haymes, Vincent Price, Albert Sharpe

The Vanderbilt Revue
Music: Jimmy McHugh, Jacques Fray, Mario Braggiotti
Lyrics: Dorothy Fields, Yip Harburg, and others
Sketches: Kenyon Nicholson, Sig Herzig, Ellis Jones, and Joseph Fields
Producers: Lew Fields and Lyle Andrews
Choreographer: Jack Haskell
Cast: Lulu McConnell, Joe Penner, Evelyn Hoey

Opened in New York at the Vanderbilt Theatre on November 5, 1930, and ran for two weeks

When You're in Love (Columbia, 1937)
Producer: Everett Riskin
Director: Harry Lachman and Robert Riskin
Screenplay: Robert Riskin
Choreographer: Leon Leonidoff

Songs by Jerome Kern and Dorothy Fields
Cast: Grace Moore, Cary Grant, Thomas Mitchell

Ziegfeld Midnight Frolic
Music: Jimmy McHugh
Lyrics: Dorothy Fields
Producer: Florenz Ziegfeld Jr.
Musical director: Paul Whiteman
Cast: Helen Morgan, Lillian Roth, Tamara Geva
Opened in New York at the cabaret of the New Amsterdam Theatre,
February 6, 1929

NOTES

ABBREVIATIONS

Bordman	Bordman, Gerald. *Jerome Kern: His Life and Music*. New York: Oxford University Press, 1982.
CUOHROC	Columbia University Oral History Research Office Collection.
Engel	Engel, Lehman. *Their Words Are Music*. New York: Crown Publishers, 1975.
Evening	*An Evening with Dorothy Fields*, DRG Records (DRG 5167), recorded live April 9, 1972, from the stage of the Kaufmann Concert Hall of the Ninety-second Street YM-YWHA in New York City as part of the Lyrics and Lyricists series.
Fields and Fields	Fields, Armond, and L. Marc Fields. *From the Bowery to Broadway: Lew Fields and the Roots of American Popular Theater*. New York: Oxford University Press, 1993.
Fordin	Fordin, Hugh. *Getting to Know Him*. New York: Random House, 1977; repr., New York: Ungar, 1986.
Gottlieb and Kimball	Gottlieb, Robert, and Robert Kimball, eds. *Reading Lyrics*. New York: Pantheon Books, 2000.
Hemming	Hemming, Roy. *The Melody Lingers On: The Great Songwriters and Their Movie Musicals*. New York: Newmarket Press, 1986.
Lahr	Lahr, John. *Notes on a Cowardly Lion*. New York: Alfred A. Knopf, 1970; repr., Berkeley: University of California Press, 2000.
Musical Stages	Rodgers, Richard. *Musical Stages: An Autobiography*. New York: Random House, 1975; repr., New York: Da Capo, 1995.
Nolan	Nolan, Frederick. *Lorenz Hart: A Poet on Broadway*. New York: Oxford University Press, 1994.
NYT Film	*The New York Times Film Reviews, 1913–1968*. New York: New York Times and Arno Press, 1970.
Shipton	Shipton, Alyn. *I Feel a Song Coming On: The Life of Jimmy McHugh*. Urbana: University of Illinois Press, 2009.
Suskin	Suskin, Steven. *Opening Night on Broadway*. New York: Schirmer Books, 1990.
Wilder	Wilder, Alec. *American Popular Song: The Great Innovators, 1900–1950*. New York: Oxford University Press, 1972.
Wilk	Wilk, Max. *They're Playing Our Song*. New York: Atheneum, 1973; repr., Mount Kisco, N.Y.: Moyer Bell, 1991.
Winer	Winer, Deborah Grace. *On the Sunny Side of the Street: The Life and Lyrics of Dorothy Fields*. New York: Schirmer Books, 1997.

PREFACE

1. Dorothy's father was born in Poland, but her mother was born in Troy, New York. There is no simple locution for someone who is a first-generation American on her father's side and a second-generation American on her mother's side.

2. Engel, p. 81.

CHAPTER 1: THE WORLD OF HER FATHER

1. Wilk, p. 53.

2. Irving Howe, *The World of Our Fathers* (New York: Simon and Schuster, 1976), p. 6.

3. Howard M. Sachar, *A History of the Jews in America* (New York: Random House, 1993), p. 160.

4. B. J. Woolf, "Golden Jubilee of a Famous Team," *New York Times Magazine*, September 4, 1932, p. 9.

5. Fields and Fields, p. 69.

6. Quoted in Felix Isman, *Weber and Fields* (New York: Boni and Liveright, 1924), pp. 84–85.

7. Ibid., pp. 131–32.

8. This is the figure given in Fields and Fields. Isman claimed their salary was $500 a week.

9. Fields and Fields, p. 146.

CHAPTER 2: THE WORLD OF HER FAMILY

1. Unidentified newspaper clipping, July 16, 1904, in Robinson Locke scrapbook, v. 198, p. 11, New York Public Library, Billy Rose Theatre Collection.

2. Frank Lea Short, "A Talk with Lew Fields," *Christian Science Monitor*, June 24, 1924, p. 11.

3. Lahr, pp. xviii–xix.

4. Reminiscences of Dorothy Fields (November 1958), part 1, p. 6, in CUOHROC.

5. Ibid.

6. Ibid., p. 11.

7. Fields and Fields, p. 209.

8. Ibid., pp. 151–52.

9. Felix Isman, *Weber and Fields* (New York: Boni and Liveright, 1924), pp. 309–10.

10. As quoted in Fields and Fields, p. 290.

11. Reminiscences of Dorothy Fields (November 1958), part 1, p. 10, in CUOHROC.

12. Ibid., p. 9.

13. *Evening*, track 2

14. *New York Times*, August 25, 1914, p. 9.

CHAPTER 3: THE TEEN YEARS

1. Unidentified newspaper clipping, in Robinson Locke scrapbook, v. 198, p. 112, New York Public Library, Billy Rose Theatre Collection.

2. *Theatre Magazine*, July 1918, p. 24.

3. Ibid., p. 23.

4. Ibid., August 1918, p. 96.

5. Philip Furia, *Irving Berlin: A Life in Song* (New York: Schirmer Books, 1998), pp. 82–83.

6. Unidentified newspaper clippings in Robinson Locke scrapbook, v. 198, pp. 50, 65, New York Public Library, Billy Rose Theatre Collection.

7. *New York Times*, September 28, 1927, p. 28.

8. Fields and Fields, p. 349.

9. Reminiscences of Dorothy Fields (November 1958), part 1, p. 1, in CUOHROC.

10. *Musical Stages*, pp. 29–30.

11. Nolan, p. 15.

12. As quoted in Fields and Fields, p. 289.

13. Reminiscences of Dorothy Fields (November 1958), part 1, pp. 6–7, in CUOHROC.

14. *Musical Stages*, p. 25.

15. Dorothy Hart and Robert Kimball, eds., *The Complete Lyrics of Lorenz Hart* (New York: Da Capo Press, 1995), p. 21.

16. *Musical Stages*, pp. 40–41.

17. Ibid., p. 50.

18. Reminiscences of Dorothy Fields (November 1958), part 1, p. 3, in CUOHROC.

19. Fields and Fields, p. 362.

20. *New York Times*, June 5, 1919, p. 15.

21. Ibid., November 21, 1920, p. 21.

CHAPTER 4: MARRIAGE AND THE START OF A CAREER

1. Wilk, p. 54.

2. Fields and Fields, p. 441.

3. Winer, p. 41.

4. As quoted in Fields and Fields, p. 361.

5. Fordin, p. 51.

6. Ethan Mordden, *Broadway Babies* (New York: Oxford University Press, 1983), p. 72.

7. As quoted in Nolan, p. 59.

8. *Musical Stages*, p. 80.

9. Fields and Fields, p. 449.

10. Mordden, *Babies*, p. 95.

11. As quoted in William G. Hyland, *Richard Rodgers* (New Haven, Conn.: Yale University Press, 1998), p. 47.

12. Fields and Fields, p. 435.

13. Ibid., p. 456.

14. *Musical Stages*, p. 114.

15. Gerald Bordman, *Days to Be Happy, Years to Be Sad* (New York: Oxford University Press, 1982), pp. 101–2.

16. Fields and Fields, p. 459.

17. Reminiscences of Dorothy Fields (November 1958), part 1, p. 3, in CUOHROC.

18. *Evening*, track 2.

19. Reminiscences of Dorothy Fields (November 1958), part 1, pp. 3–4, in CUOHROC.

20. Jack Burton, *The Blue Book of Tin Pan Alley* (Watkins Glen, N.Y.: Century House, 1950), p. 277.

21. *Evening*, track 2.

22. Ibid.

23. Wilk, pp. 54–55.

24. *Evening*, track 2.

25. Reminiscences of Jimmy McHugh (June 1959), pp. 7, 9, in CUOHROC.

26. Ibid., p. 13.

27. Ibid., p. 19.

28. Wilk, p. 54.

29. Shipton, p. 81.

30. Ibid., p. 79.

CHAPTER 5: WHAT'S BLACK AND WHITE AND HEARD ALL OVER?

1. Jack Burton, *The Blue Book of Broadway Musicals* (Glens Falls, N.Y.: Century House, 1958), p. 161.

2. "Jelly Fish Ballet in 'Delmar's Revels,'" *New York Times*, November 29, 1927, p. 30.

3. Unpublished manuscript in McHugh papers, as quoted in Shipton, p. 82.

4. Wilk, p. 55.

5. Lahr, p. 91.

6. As quoted in Shipton, p. 84.

7. Maurice Waller and Anthony Calabrese, *Fats Waller* (New York: Schirmer Books, 1977), p. 164.

8. Shipton, pp. 83–84.

9. Barry Singer, *Black and Blue: The Life and Lyrics of Andy Razaf* (New York: Schirmer, 1992), p. 210.

10. Philip Furia, *The Poets of Tin Pan Alley* (New York: Oxford University Press, 1990), pp. 216–17.

11. The complete text of "Where's That Rainbow" is printed in *The Complete Lyrics of Lorenz Hart*, edited by Dorothy Hart and Robert Kimball (New York: Da Capo Press, 1995), pp. 88–89.

12. The full text of "I Can't Give You Anything but Love" is printed in Engel, pp. 81–82; Winer, p. 31; and Gottlieb and Kimball, p. 379.

13. Furia, *Poets*, p. 31.

14. Fields and Fields, p. 463.

15. Lewis A. Ehrenberg, *Steppin' Out: New York Nightlife and the Transformation of American Culture, 1890–1930* (Chicago: University of Chicago Press, 1981), p. 239.

16. Ibid., p. 254.

17. Jim Haskins, *The Cotton Club* (New York: New American Library, 1977), p. 41.

18. Edward Jablonski, *Harold Arlen* (Boston: Northeastern University Press, 1996), p. 40.

19. Dempsey J. Travis, *The Duke Ellington Primer* (Chicago: Urban Research Press, 1996), p. 26.

20. Stuart Nicholson, *Reminiscing in Tempo: A Portrait of Duke Ellington* (Boston: Northeastern University Press, 1999), p. 118.

21. Ibid., pp. 81–82.

22. Lee "Harlemania" Posner, "Let's Go Places: Night Life of New York," November 22, 1929, in "Nightclubs" folder in New York Public Library, Schomburg Center for Research in Black Culture.

23. Italics mine. Abel Green, review, *Variety*, December 7, 1927, pp. 54, 56, as quoted in Mark Tucker, ed., *The Duke Ellington Reader* (New York: Oxford University Press, 1993), p. 31.

24. Reminiscences of Jimmy McHugh (June 1959), p. 13, in CUOHROC.

25. Wilk, p. 55.

26. Fields and Fields, p. 470.

27. As quoted in Winer, p. 28.

28. Reminiscences of Jimmy McHugh (June 1959), p. 15, in CUOHROC.

29. Ibid., p. 17.

30. Wilk, p. 55.

31. Hy Kraft, "Lyrics by Dorothy Fields," *ASCAP Today*, January 1974, p. 8.

32. *Evening*, track 2.

33. Fields and Fields, p. 473; Winer, p. 28.

34. Green, as quoted in Tucker, p. 31.

35. Nicholson, p. 70.

36. Reminiscences of Jimmy McHugh (June 1959), pp. 21–22 in CUOHROC.

37. Klaus Stratemann reproduced programs, front pages of programs, and advertisements for several Cotton Club shows between 1928 and 1938 in his book *Duke Ellington: Day by Day and Film by Film* (Copenhagen: JazzMedia, 1992), pp. 685–97. Unfortunately, there seems to be no program for the show that premiered in December 1927.

38. Haskins, p. 79.

39. Tucker, p. 54.

40. Reminiscences of Jimmy McHugh (June 1959), pp. 23–24, in CUOHROC.

CHAPTER 6: GIVE MY REFRAINS TO BROADWAY

1. Reminiscences of Jimmy McHugh (June 1959), p. 24, in CUOHROC.

2. As quoted in Allen Woll, *Black Musical Theatre from Coontown to Dreamgirls* (Baton Rouge: Louisiana State University Press, 1989), p. 106.

3. As quoted in Woll, pp. 96–97.

4. Woll, p. 123.

5. Reminiscences of Jimmy McHugh (June 1959), p. 28, in CUOHROC.

6. Wilk, p. 55.

7. Reminiscences of Jimmy McHugh (June 1959), pp. 31–32, in CUOHROC.

8. The text of "I Must Have That Man" is printed in Winer, p. 33.

9. The lyric of "Baby" can be heard sung by Adelaide Hall on the *Smithsonian Collection of Recordings: American Songbook Series—Dorothy Fields*, track 3.

10. Wilk, p. 55.

11. Miles Kreuger, liner notes dated March 8, 1968, for recording of *Lew Leslie's Blackbirds of 1928*, Columbia Records, Mono OL 6770.

12. Wilk, p. 55.

13. *Evening*, track 3.

14. *Musical Stages*, p. 120.

15. Various reviews from the *Hello Daddy!* clippings file, New York Public Library, Billy Rose Theatre Collection.

16. *Evening*, track 3.

17. Winer, p. 58.

18. The text of "On the Sunny Side of the Street" is printed in Engel, p. 82; Winer, p. 58; and Gottlieb and Kimball, p. 382.

19. The text of "Exactly Like You" is printed in Winer, p. 54.

20. Wilder, p. 407.

21. Gerald Bordman, *American Musical Theatre: A Chronicle* (New York: Oxford University Press, 1978), p. 459.

22. *New York Sun*, December 3, 1933, as quoted in Woll, p. 155.

23. Undated clipping in Dorothy Fields's scrapbook in the theater collection of the Museum of the City of New York.

24. Fields and Fields, p. 500.

25. *Evening*, track 5.

CHAPTER 7: HELLO TO HOLLYWOOD

1. Ian Hamilton, *Writers in Hollywood, 1915–1951* (New York: Harper and Row, 1990), p. 30.

2. Preston Sturges, *Preston Sturges on Preston Sturges*, reprinted in *The Grove Book of Hollywood*, ed. Christopher Silvester (New York: Grove Press, 1998), p. 158.

3. Richard Rodgers, *Letters to Dorothy (1926–1937)*, ed. William W. Appleton (New York: New York Public Library, 1988), p. 60. Herbert was an enthusiastic horseman and for a time owned several thoroughbreds named after characters in operas by Richard Wagner.

4. The lyrics are reproduced in Winer, p. 67.

5. Mordaunt Hall, "The Screen: Golf and Song," *NYT Film*, Vol. 1, p. 657.

6. Reminiscences of Dorothy Fields (November 1958), part 2, p. 1, in CUOHROC.

7. *NYT Film*, Vol. 1, p. 657.

8. As quoted in Winer, p. 49. The complete lyric appears in Winer, p. 51.

9. The lyric is printed in Dorothy Hart and Robert Kimball, eds., *The Complete Lyrics of Lorenz Hart* (New York: Knopf, 1986), p. 25.

10. Mordaunt Hall, "Dancing Lady," *NYT Film*, Vol. 2, pp. 1005–6.

11. Rodgers, *Letters to Dorothy*, p. 151.

12. Arthur Knight, *Disintegrating the Musical: Black Performance and American Musical Film* (Durham, N.C.: Duke University Press, 2002), p. 20.

13. C.R.P., "Hooray for Love," *NYT Film*, Vol. 2, p. 1191.

14. *Musical Stages*, p. 138.

15. Rodgers, *Letters to Dorothy*, p. 107.

16. *Musical Stages*, p. 114.

17. Stephen Citron, *Noel and Cole: The Sophisticates* (New York: Oxford University Press, 1992), pp. 102–3.

18. Fields and Fields, p. 502.

19. *Musical Stages*, p. 143.

20. As quoted in Meryle Secrest, *Somewhere for Me: A Biography of Richard Rodgers* (New York: Alfred A. Knopf, 2001), p. 146.

21. *Musical Stages*, p. 145.

CHAPTER 8: CHANGE PARTNERS AND WRITE

1. Ken Bloom, "Song List," in Winer, p. 249; Jack Burton, *The Blue Book of Hollywood Musicals* (Watkins Glen, N.Y.: Century House, 1953), p. 53; Hemming, p. 144.

2. Philip Furia, *The Poets of Tin Pan Alley* (New York: Oxford University Press, 1990), p. 218; Burton, *Blue Book*, p. 53.

3. Wilder, p. 408.

4. Furia, *Poets*, p. 218.

5. Dick Jacobs and Harriet Jacobs, *Who Wrote That Song?* (Cincinnati: Writer's Digest Books, 1994), pp. 168–69.

6. The lyric is reprinted in Winer, p. 71, and Gottlieb and Kimball, pp. 377–78.

7. R.C.P., "Every Night at Eight," *NYT Film*, Vol. 2, p. 1196.

8. Allen Forte, *The American Popular Ballad of the Golden Era* (Princeton, N.J.: Princeton University Press, 1995), p. 251.

9. The lyric is reprinted in Engel, p. 82; Winer, p. 78; and Gottlieb and Kimball, p. 380.

10. The lyric is reprinted in Engel, p. 82, and Winer, p. 77.

11. Reminiscences of Jimmy McHugh (June 1959), p. 79, in CUOHROC.

12. Wilk, p. 56.

13. Shipton, p. 104.

14. Ibid., p. 103. Italics mine.

15. Ibid., p. 123.

16. Clipping from *Evening Sun*, July 25, 1928, in the Dorothy Fields clippings file, New York Public Library, Billy Rose Theatre Collection.

17. Gary Marmorstein, *Hollywood Rhapsody* (New York: Schirmer Books, 1997), p. 197.

18. Shipton, p. 137.

19. Marmorstein, pp. 82, 106.

20. Oscar Levant, *A Smattering of Ignorance* (New York: Doubleday, 1940), pp. 106–7.

21. Ibid., p. 101.

22. Louis Lochner, *Fritz Kreisler* (New York: Macmillan, 1950), p. 89.

23. Ibid., pp. 87–88.

24. Richard Barrios, *A Song in the Dark: The Birth of the Musical Film* (New York: Oxford University Press, 1995), p. 428.

25. Pauline Kael, *5001 Nights at the Movies* (New York: Henry Holt, 1991), p. 397.

26. The lyric can be heard on the CD *An Evening with Dorothy Fields*, track 14.

27. Levant, *Smattering*, p. 103.

28. As quoted in *Halliwell's Film Guide,* 7th ed. (New York: Harper and Row, 1989), p. 509.

29. *The Complete Lyrics of Ira Gershwin*, edited by Robert Kimball (New York: Alfred A. Knopf, 1993), p. 193.

30. Fields and Fields, p. 510.

31. Ibid., quoted on p. 516.

CHAPTER 9: THE BEST OF HOLLYWOOD

1. *Musical Stages*, p. 28.

2. *Evening*, track 2.

3. The principal sources include: Max Wilk, *They're Playing Our Song* (Mount Kisco, N.Y.: Moyer Bell, 1991), p. 56; reminiscences of Dorothy Fields (November 1958), part 2, p. 3, in CUOHROC; and "Jerome Kern: The Man and His Music," *NBC News Biography in Sound*, November 1945, tape in the Museum of Television and Radio, New York, my own transcription.

4. *NBC News Biography in Sound*.

5. Lee Davis, *Bolton and Wodehouse and Kern: The Men Who Made Musical Comedy* (New York: J. H. Heinman, 1993), p. 321.

6. The lyric is reprinted in Winer, p. 87, and Gottlieb and Kimball, p. 379. In addition, the film *Roberta* is readily available on DVD.

7. *NBC News Biography in Sound*.

8. Ibid.

9. The lyric is reprinted in Winer, p. 85, and Gottlieb and Kimball, p. 381.

10. *NBC News Biography in Sound*.

11. Hemming, p. 93.

12. Quoted in Leslie Halliwell, *Halliwell's Film Guide*, 7th ed. (New York: Harper and Row, 1989), p. 861.

13. Andre Sennewald, "Roberta," *NYT Film*, Vol. 2, p. 1153.

14. Wilder, pp. 31–32.

15. Wilk, p. 36.

16. Ibid., p. 34.

17. *The Complete Lyrics of Ira Gershwin*, ed. Robert Kimball (New York: Alfred A. Knopf, 1993), p. xiv.

18. *The Complete Lyrics of Ira Gershwin*, p. xvi.

19. Wilk, p. 39.

20. *NBC Biography in Sound*.

21. These were *She's a Good Fellow*, 1919; *The Night Boat*, 1920; *Hitchy-Koo of 1920*; *Good Morning, Dearie*, 1921; *The Bunch and Judy*, 1922; *Stepping Stones*, 1923; *The City Chap*, 1925; and *Criss Cross*, 1926.

22. *NBC News Biography in Sound*.

23. Ibid.

24. Undated clippings from Dorothy Fields's scrapbook in the Museum of the City of New York.

25. Andre Sennewald, "I Dream Too Much," *New York Times*, November 29, 1935, p. 24.

26. The lyric is reprinted in Winer, p. 97, and Gottlieb and Kimball, p. 383. In addition, *Swing Time* is readily available on DVD.

27. John Mueller, *Astaire Dancing: The Musical Films* (New York: Alfred A. Knopf, 1985), p. 109.

28. Ibid. The lyric for "Bojangles of Harlem" is printed in Gottlieb and Kimball, p. 377.

29. Bordman, p. 358.

30. The lyric is reprinted in Winer, p. 101, and Gottlieb and Kimball, p. 378.

31. Winer, p. 136.

32. The lyric is reprinted in Winer, p. 107, and Gottlieb and Kimball, p. 385.

33. The lyric is reprinted in Winer, p. 105, and Gottlieb and Kimball, p. 382.

34. As quoted in Arlene Croce, *The Fred Astaire and Ginger Rogers Book* (New York: Vintage Books, 1972), p. 109.

CHAPTER 10: END OF AN ERA

1. George S. Kaufman, as quoted in Deena Rosenberg, *Fascinating Rhythm: The Collaboration of George and Ira Gershwin* (New York: Dutton, 1991), p. 368.

2. Sam Kashner and Nancy Schoenberger, *A Talent For Genius: The Life and Times of Oscar Levant* (Los Angeles: Silman-James Press, 1994), p. 183.

3. Bordman, p. 368.

4. Ibid.

5. Fields and Fields, p. 517.

6. As quoted in Leslie Halliwell, *Halliwell's Film Guide*, 7th ed. (New York: Harper and Row, 1989), p. 544.

7. Frank S. Nugent, "The Joy of Living" *NYT Film*, Vol. 2, p. 1497.

8. In *Swing Time*, Ginger Rogers is shampooing her hair when Fred Astaire enters her hotel suite and begins to sing "The Way You Look Tonight." Entranced by the song, she walks up to him as he gets to the final line, "just the way you look tonight." He looks up at her, sees her in her bathrobe with a towel around her neck and soapsuds in her hair, and they are both startled out of their romantic reverie.

9. Hemming, p. 103.

10. Michael Freedland, *Jerome Kern* (New York: Stein and Day, 1978), p. 129.

11. Bordman, pp. 385–86.

12. *Back in the Tropics* is available on DVD. To my knowledge, the lyric for "Back in My Shell" has not been reprinted.

13. Winer, p. 114.

14. The lyric is reprinted in Winer, p. 115, and Gottlieb and Kimball, p. 383.

15. Meryle Secrest, *Stephen Sondheim: A Life* (New York: Alfred A. Knopf, 1998), p. 19.

16. Ibid., p. 18.

17. Fordin, p. 144.

18. *New York Times*, August 1, 1958, p. 21.

19. Ibid., March 29, 1967, p. 29.

CHAPTER 11: HOLLYWOOD THROUGH A BROADWAY LENS

1. The figures for productions per season are: 207 in 1931–32; 174 in 1932–33; 151 in 1933–34; 149 in 1934–35; 135 in 1935–36; 118 in 1936–37; 111 in 1937–38; 98 in

1938–39. Musicals make up only a small portion of the total number of productions in any given year. (The figures are taken from Gene Brown, *Show Time* [New York: Macmillan, 1997]).

2. *Musical Stages*, p. 148.

3. Ibid., p. 169.

4. As quoted in Benny Green, *Let's Face the Music* (London: Pavilion Books, 1989), p. 111.

5. Ibid., p. 95.

6. Stanley Green, *Broadway Musicals Show by Show*, 4th ed. (Milwaukee: Hal Leonard, 1994), p. 74.

7. *Musical Stages*, p. 174.

8. Joshua Logan, *Josh: My Up-and-Down In-and-Out Life* (New York: Delacorte Press, 1976), p. 141.

9. Ethan Mordden, *Better Foot Forward: The History of American Musical Theatre* (New York: Grossman Publishers, 1976), p. 195.

10. James Robert Parish and Michael R. Pitts, *Hollywood Songsters* (New York: Garland Publishing, 1991), p. 470.

11. *Musical Stages*, p. 175.

12. All of the following critical comments are taken from clippings in the *Stars in Your Eyes* file, New York Public Library, Billy Rose Theatre Collection.

13. "Eadie Was a Lady," by DeSylva, Brown, and Whiting, was sung by Merman in *Take a Chance* (1932); "Sam and Delilah," by George and Ira Gershwin, was sung by Merman in *Girl Crazy* (1930); "You're the Top" and "I Get a Kick out of You," by Cole Porter, were sung by Merman in *Anything Goes* (1934).

14. As quoted in Parish and Pitts, *Songsters*, p. 470.

15. The complete lyric is printed in Robert Kimball, ed., *The Complete Lyrics of Cole Porter* (New York: Knopf, 1983), p. 207.

16. The lyric is reprinted in Engel, p. 83, and Winer, p. 123.

17. The lyric can be heard on the CD *Ethel Merman: Red, Hot, and Blue*, and *Stars in Your Eyes*, AEI CD 001.

CHAPTER 12: LIBRETTOS INSTEAD OF LYRICS

1. Lahr, p. 205.

2. Irving Drutman, "Lew Fields Left behind Him a Talented Family," *New York Herald Tribune Magazine*, 1941. Article in Dorothy Fields's scrapbook in the Museum of the City of New York.

3. *Wonderful Town* was successfully revived on Broadway, opening on November 23, 2003, and closing on January 30, 2005, a run of 497 performances.

4. Drutman, "Lew Fields Left Behind."

5. "The Fabulous Fields Family," *Life* magazine, February 8, 1943.

6. Drutman, "Lew Fields Left Behind."

7. As quoted in William McBrien, *Cole Porter: A Biography* (New York: Alfred A. Knopf, 1998), p. 223.

8. Ethan Mordden, *Oh, What a Beautiful Mornin'* (New York: Oxford University Press, 1999), pp. 14–15.

9. Wolcott Gibbs, "Our Miss Merman," *New Yorker*, January 16, 1943, p. 30.

10. Cole Porter scrapbook, Yale University Archives and Department of Special Collections.

11. Michael Todd Jr., *A Valuable Property* (New York: Arbor House, 1983), p. 13.

12. Mordden, *Beautiful Mornin'*, p. 37.

13. Ibid., p. 41.

14. Ibid., p. 200.

15. As quoted in Suskin, p. 435.

16. Wilk, p. 58.

17. *Variety* clipping in the Cole Porter scrapbook, Yale University Archives and Department of Special Collections.

18. T. S., "Film Version of 'Let's Face It,' in Which Bob Hope Is Enlisted to Help Provide Hot-Weather Fare, Appears at Paramount," *New York Times*, August 5, 1943, p. 18.

19. Bosley Crowther, "Something for the Boys," *New York Times*, November 30, 1944, p. 19.

20. McBrien, *Cole Porter*, p. 280.

21. Bosley Crowther, "Mexican Hayride," *New York Times*, January 12, 1949, p. 33.

22. Personal communication from Eliza Brewster, September 8, 1995.

CHAPTER 13: UP IN CENTRAL PARK

1. *Musical Stages*, p. 38.

2. Ibid., p. 39.

3. Fordin, p. 90.

4. Gerald Mast, *Can't Help Singin'* (New York: Overlook Press, 1987), p. 32.

5. Bordman, p. 361.

6. This and all of the following excerpts of reviews are taken from reviews found in the clippings file for *Up in Central Park*, New York Public Library, Billy Rose Theatre Collection.

7. William McBrien, *Cole Porter* (New York: Knopf, 1998), p. 279.

8. Herbert and Dorothy Fields, "Digging Up the 'Big Back Yard,'" essay in souvenir program booklet, unpaginated, without date.

9. Ibid.

10. Michael Todd Jr., *A Valuable Property* (New York: Arbor House, 1983), p. 129.

11. Ward Morehouse, "Mr. Romberg Talks Theatre," essay in souvenir program booklet of *Up in Central Park*, unpaginated, without date.

12. "The Story of Sigmund Romberg," unsigned article in Sigmund Romberg clippings file, New York Public Library, Billy Rose Theatre Collection.

13. Bordman, p. 364.

14. Todd, *Valuable Property*, p. 132.

15. Mordden, *Beautiful Mornin'*, p. 156.

16. The lyric is reprinted in Engel, p. 85, and Winer, p. 143.

17. The lyric can be heard on the CD Decca Broadway Original Cast Album of *Up in Central Park*, B0000554–02.

CHAPTER 14: ANNIE GET YOUR GUN

1. *Evening*, track 15.

2. Wilk, p. 285.

3. Credit for the story is given to Joseph Fields and Ewart Adamson; the screenplay for the film was by Joel Sayre and John Twist.

4. Andrea Most, *Making Americans: Jews and the Broadway Musical* (Cambridge, Mass.: Harvard University Press, 2003), p. 119.

5. Recall that in *I Dream Too Much* (see chap. 10), the heroine likewise seems to have relatively little ego connection to her extraordinary talent.

6. Mordden, *Beautiful Mornin'*, p. 115.

7. Wilk, p. 285.

8. Fordin, p. 242.

9. Philip Furia, *Irving Berlin: A Life in Song* (New York: Schirmer Books, 1998), p. 217.

10. Wilk, pp. 285–86.

11. Fordin, p. 242.

12. *Musical Stages*, p. 246.

13. Wilk, p. 286.

14. Ethel Merman with Pete Martin, *Who Could Ask for Anything More?* (Garden City, N.Y.: Doubleday, 1955), p. 185.

15. Ethel Merman with George Eells, *Merman* (New York: Simon and Schuster, 1978), p. 138.

16. Wilk, p. 286.

17. Merman and Eells, *Merman*, p. 139.

18. *Musical Stages*, p. 246.

19. Fordin, p. 236.

20. Bordman, p. 404.

21. Fordin, p. 237.

22. In 1973 Welfare Island's name was changed to Roosevelt Island. City Hospital on Roosevelt Island was demolished in 1994.

23. Bordman, p. 406.

24. *Musical Stages*, p. 246.

25. Wilk, p. 286.

26. *Musical Stages*, p. 246.

27. Ibid.

28. Ibid, p. 235.

29. Ibid., p. 247.

30. As quoted in Alexander Woollcott, *The Story of Irving Berlin* (New York: G.P. Putnam's Sons, 1925), p. 215.

31. Wilk, p. 286.

32. Ibid.

33. *Musical Stages*, p. 248.

34. Ibid.

35. Fordin, p. 244.

36. *Musical Stages*, p. 248.

37. Wilk, p. 288.

38. I am grateful to Jeffrey Magee for information about the early draft of the libretto in the Library of Congress.

39. The titles of these songs in the final version are "You Can't Get a Man with a Gun" and "Doin' What Comes Natur'lly."

40. Mary Ellin Barrett, *Irving Berlin: A Daughter's Memoir* (New York: Simon and Schuster, 1994), p. 234.

41. Herbert and Dorothy Fields, "Authors of 'Annie Get Your Gun' Come Clean," *New York Herald Tribune*, April 21, 1946, in Dorothy and Herbert Fields clippings file, New York Public Library, Billy Rose Theatre Collection.

42. Jeffrey Magee, *Irving Berlin* (forthcoming).

43. Herbert and Dorothy Fields, "Authors of 'Annie Get Your Gun' Come Clean."

44. Barrett, *Daughter's Memoir*, pp. 238–39.

45. *Musical Stages*, p. 249.

46. As quoted in Suskin, pp. 55–56.

CHAPTER 15: MORE MOVIES

1. Laurence Bergreen, *As Thousands Cheer: The Life of Irving Berlin* (New York: Viking, 1990), p. 460. Stanley Green, in *Hollywood Musicals Year by Year* (Milwaukee: Hal Leonard, 1990), p. 159, says the rights brought $700,000.

2. These duets were not included in the original cast recording or the 1966 revival. "I'll Share It All With You" was first recorded in 1991 in the McGlinn reconstruction.

3. Gerald Clarke, *Get Happy: The Life of Judy Garland* (New York: Random House, 2000), p. 253.

4. Reminiscences of Dorothy Fields (November 1958), part 2, p. 5, in CUOHROC.

5. Wilk, p. 121.

6. Tony Thomas, *The Hollywood Musical: The Saga of Songwriter Harry Warren* (Secaucus, N.J.: Citadel, 1975), p. 266.

7. Ibid., p. 267.

8. Wilk, p. 124.

9. Ibid., p. 147.

10. Reminiscences of Dorothy Fields (November 1958), part 2, p. 7, in CUOHROC.

11. Wilk, p. 150.

12. Ibid., pp. 144–45.

13. Susan Loesser, *A Most Remarkable Fella: Frank Loesser and the Guys and Dolls in His Life* (New York: Donald Fine, 1993), p. 34.

14. Wilk, p. 151.

15. Edward Jablonski, *Harold Arlen* (Boston: Northeastern University Press, 1996), p. 226.

16. Desmond Shawe-Taylor, "Ezio Pinza," *The New Grove Dictionary of Music and Musicians*, ed. Stanley Sadie (London: Macmillan, 1980).

17. *Musical Stages*, p. 263.

18. Wilder, p. 284.

19. Winer, p. 252. Jablonski, in his biography *Harold Arlen*, pp. 376–77, lists twelve titles.

20. Bosley Crowther, "The Farmer Takes a Wife," *NYT Film*, p. 2703.

21. Reminiscences of Dorothy Fields (November 1958), part 2, p. 11, in CUOHROC.

22. The lyric is reprinted in Winer, p. 191.

CHAPTER 16: COLONIAL AMERICA AND BROOKLYN

1. Winer, p. 162.

2. Maurice Zolotow, "Mamoulian Directs a Musical," *New York Times*, January 29, 1950, section 2, p. 1.

3. Ibid., p. 4.

4. Ibid., p. 1.

5. The lyrics discussed on the following pages can be heard on the CD issued on the Decca Broadway label of the original Broadway cast performance.

6. "There Must Be Somethin' Better Than Love" is reprinted in Gottlieb and Kimball, p. 384.

7. Suskin, p. 62.

8. Betty Smith, *A Tree Grows in Brooklyn* (New York: Harper Perennial Modern Classics, 2005), p. 236.

9. The lyrics of *A Tree Grows in Brooklyn* can be heard on the CD issued on the Sony Broadway label of the original Broadway cast performance.

10. Smith, *Tree*, p. 4.

11. Ibid., p. 22.

12. "Make the Man Love Me" is reprinted in Engel, p. 88; Winer, p. 177; and Gottlieb and Kimball, p. 382.

13. *Evening*, track 16.

14. The lyric is reprinted in Engel, p. 88.

15. Ethan Mordden, *Coming Up Roses* (New York: Oxford University Press, 1998), p. 40.

16. The lyric is reprinted in Engel, p. 85.

17. The lyric is reprinted in Winer, p. 175.

18. Reaching further back in literature, Ovid in book IV of *Metamorphoses* speaks of unending youth and eternal boyhood. Several Jungian analysts have discussed a *puer* complex, which manifests itself as a man's reluctance to go beyond adolescent patterns of behavior.

19. Mark Steyn, *Broadway Babies Say Goodnight: Musicals Then and Now* (New York: Routledge, 1999), p. 232.

20. The lyric is reprinted in Engel, p. 86.

21. This and the following quotes from the critics are all gathered from Suskin, pp. 674–78.

22. Brooks Atkinson, "A Tree Grows in Brooklyn, Made Into an Affable Musical Drama," *New York Times*, April 20, 1951, p. 24.

23. Mordden, *Coming Up Roses*, p. 42.

24. Ken Mandelbaum, "A Tree Grows in Brooklyn," liner notes for the reissue on CD by Sony of the original Broadway cast album, p. 10.

CHAPTER 17: SOMETHING OLD, SOMETHING NEW

1. There is an original cast recording of *By the Beautiful Sea* that was remastered on the DRG label.

2. The *New York Times Theater Reviews, 1920–1970* (New York: New York Times and Arno Press, 1971), Vol. 6, without pagination, April 9, 1954.

3. Reviews of *By the Beautiful Sea* are taken from Suskin, pp. 111–12.

4. Max Wilk, *The Golden Age of Television* (New York: Delacorte Press, 1976), p. 1.

5. This description is taken from the dust jacket of the 1941 Random House publication of *Junior Miss*.

6. *The New York Times Theater Reviews, 1920–1970*, Vol. 4, without pagination, November 18, 1941.

7. Benny Green, *Let's Face the Music* (London: Pavilion Books, 1989), p. 69.

8. Wilder, p. 342.

9. Wilk, *Song*, p. 211.

10. Ibid., p. 210.

11. Jack Gould, "Musical of *Junior Miss* on Channel 2," *New York Times*, December 21, 1957, p. 39.

12. Douglas Martin, "Albert Hague, Tony-Winning Composer, Dies at 81," *New York Times*, November 15, 2001, p. D10.

13. Albert Hague and Renee Orin, *Still "Young and Foolish": Live from the Cinegrill* (LML CD-105, 1998), track 14.

14. Ethan Mordden, *Coming Up Roses* (New York: Oxford University Press, 1998), p. 127.

15. Hague and Orin, "Young and Foolish," track 5.

16. Myrna Katz Frommer and Harvey Frommer, *It Happened on Broadway* (New York: Harcourt Brace, 1998), p. 152.

17. Martin Gottfried, *All His Jazz: The Life and Death of Bob Fosse* (New York: Da Capo Press, 1998), p. 104.

18. Margery Beddow, *Bob Fosse's Broadway* (Portsmouth, N.H.: Heinemann, 1996), p. 17.

19. Gottfried, *All His Jazz*, p. 113.

20. Ibid., p. 114.

21. Hague and Orin, "Young and Foolish," track 2.

22. Winer, p. 200.

23. This will be discussed further in the next chapter.

24. The lyrics of *Redhead* can be heard on the original cast recording issued on the RCA Victor label and reissued on CD by BMG Classics, 09026-61995-2.

25. Reviews of *Redhead* reprinted in Suskin, pp. 570–72.

CHAPTER 18: SWEET CHARITY

1. The actress Elizabeth Taylor had married Todd just over a year before his death. His daughter with Taylor was an infant. His son by his first marriage, Michael Todd Jr., was twenty-eight when his father died.

2. Mark Steyn, *Broadway Babies Say Goodnight: Musicals Then and Now* (New York: Routledge, 1999), p. 70.

3. Both of these letters are in the collection of Dorothy Fields materials in the Museum of the City of New York. I am grateful to the staff there, particularly the licensing manager, Faye Haun, for permission to reproduce the contents of these letters.

4. Since this was soon after Herbert's death, they may have been engaged in the dreary task of figuring out what to do with the things in his apartment.

5. Personal communication from Eliza Lahm Brewster, September 8, 1995.

6. *New York Times*, August 1, 1958, p. 21.

7. I am grateful to David Lahm for supplying this information.

8. Cy Coleman, "The Art of Scoring with Music," *New York Journal American*, August 29, 1965. This, and the following two references, are from articles in the Cy Coleman clippings file, New York Public Library, Billy Rose Theatre Collection.

9. Wilfrid Sheed, "With a Song in His Heart," *Time*, February 24, 1992, p. 66.

10. Harry Haun, "Broadway Music Maker," *Playbill*, December 1989, p. 18.

11. As quoted in Kevin Boyd Grubb, *Razzle Dazzle: The Life and Work of Bob Fosse* (New York: St. Martin's Press, 1989), p. 120.

12. Ibid., p. 112.

13. Frank Aston, *New York World Telegram and Sun*, June 1, 1969. In the Bob Fosse clippings file, New York Public Library, Billy Rose Theatre Collection.

14. Grubb, *Razzle Dazzle*, p. 114.

15. *New York Times*, October 4, 1987, section 2, p. 6.

16. Neil Simon, *Rewrites: A Memoir* (New York: Simon and Schuster, 1996), p. 215.

17. Ibid., p. 216.

18. Sharon Rosenthal, "A Life in the Day of Cy Coleman," *Daily News*, December 9, 1960. In Cy Coleman clippings file, New York Public Library, Billy Rose Theatre Collection.

19. Ethan Mordden, *Open a New Window: The Broadway Musical In the 1960s* (New York: Palgrave, 2001), pp. 221–22.

20. Norma McLain Stoop, "The Composite Cy Coleman," *After Dark*, March 1979, p. 38.

21. The lyrics of this musical can be heard on the original cast recording of *Sweet Charity* issued by Columbia Records.

22. The lyric is printed in Winer, p. 225.

23. The lyric is printed in Engel, p. 89, and Winer, p. 214.

24. The lyric is printed in Winer, p. 229.

25. The lyric is printed in Engel, pp. 90–91.

26. Martin Gottfried, *All His Jazz: The Life and Death of Bob Fosse* (New York: Da Capo Press, 1998), p. 181.

27. Grubb, *Razzle Dazzle*, p. 127.

28. The lyric is printed in Engel, pp. 88–89, and Winer, p. 209.

29. Walter Kerr, "A Sudden Dose of Bittersweet," *New York Herald Tribune*, February 13, 1966, p. 25.

30. Ken Bloom lists the following songs as having been cut from *Sweet Charity*: "Did You Ever Look at You," "Free Thought in Action Class Song," "Gimme a Raincheck," "A Good Impression," "I Can't Let You Down," "I'll Take Any Man," "I'm Way Ahead," "I've Tried Everything," "Keep It in the Family," "Pink Taffeta Sample Size 10," "Poor Everybody Else," "When Did You Know," "You Can't Lose 'em All," and "You Wanna Bet." In Winer, p. 253.

31. Dwight Blocker, program booklet accompanying "Dorothy Fields," in the *American Songbook Series* (Smithsonian Collection of Recordings), p. 11; David Jenness and Don Velsey, *Classic American Popular Song: The Second Half-Century, 1950–2000* (New York: Routledge, 2006), p. 153.

32. Derek Elley, "Cult Movies: *Sweet Charity*," in *Sweet Charity* clippings file, New York Public Library, Billy Rose Theatre Collection.

33. Ibid.

CHAPTER 19: "IT'S WHERE YOU FINISH . . ."

1. William Gibson, *Two for the Seesaw: A Comedy-Drama in Three Acts* (New York: Samuel French, 1956), pp. 44–45.

2. Rex Reed, "Finally, Fickle Fame Calls on Cy," *Daily News*, May 8, 1977; in the Cy Coleman clippings file, New York Public Library, Billy Rose Theatre Collection.

3. Lainie Kazan presented her side of the story in a letter the editor printed in the "Drama Mailbox" in the *New York Times*, April 29, 1973, section 2, p. 7.

4. Ethan Mordden, *One More Kiss: The Broadway Musical in the 1970s* (New York: Palgrave Macmillan, 2004), p. 11.

5. Reed, "Fickle Fame."

6. Rex Reed, "She Gives Broadway Something to Sing About," *Sunday News*, April 29, 1973; in the Dorothy Fields clippings file, New York Public Library, Billy Rose Theatre Collection.

7. Reed, "Fickle Fame."

8. Michael Bennett, *Seesaw: A Musical* (New York: Samuel French, 1975), p. 56.

9. In the *Seesaw* clippings file, New York Public Library, Billy Rose Theatre Collection.

10. Bennett, *Seesaw*, p. 53.

11. Ibid., p. 55.

12. The chorus of the lyric is printed in Winer, p. 244.

13. The lyric can be heard on the original cast recording of *Seesaw*, released by DG Records, CDRG6108, by special arrangement with Notable Music. A volume of vocal selections from *Seesaw* was published by Notable Music in co-publication with Aldi Music Co., New York, 1973.

14. Patricia Bosworth, "The Fight to Save 'Seesaw,'" *New York Times*, April 8, 1973, p. 1.

15. *New York Times*, March 24, 1973; in *Seesaw* clippings file, New York Public Library, Billy Rose Theatre Collection.

16. Reed, "She Gives Broadway."

17. Personal communication from Eliza Brewster, January 17, 2010.

18. Reminiscences of Dorothy Fields (November 1958), p. 14, in CUOHROC.

19. Jane Alexander got to play Eleanor Roosevelt in two made-for-television movies—*Eleanor and Franklin* (ABC, 1976) and *Eleanor and Franklin: The White House Years* (ABC, 1977). She also played Franklin Delano Roosevelt's mother, Sarah, in the HBO movie *Warm Springs*, a performance that won her an Emmy in 2005.

20. Dorothy Fields clippings file, New York Public Library, Billy Rose Theatre Collection.

INDEX OF SONGS, SHOWS, AND MOVIES

"Free Thought in Action Class Song," 229
"Freeze an' Melt," 59, 229t
From Dover to Dixie, 57, 60, 61, 62
"From the Halls of Montezuma," 77
Fugitive Lovers, 244
Funny Girl, 219
Funny Thing Happened on the Way to the Forum, A, 207
"Futuristic Rhythm," 67, 68, 229

Garrick Gaieties, 36, 37, 38, 40, 120
Gay Divorce, 121, 135
Gay Divorcée, The, 97, 104
Gay Ranchero, The, 172
Gentlemen Prefer Blondes, xii, 182, 193
Gentlemen Unafraid, 113
George White's Scandals, 54, 61
"Get a Horse," 168, 229
Gilligan's Island, 94
"Gimme a Raincheck," 229
Girl Crazy, 122, 160
Girl Friend, The 38, 39, 40
Girl from Utah, The, 22, 25
Girl in Pink Tights, The, 144, 193, 217–18
"Girl That I Marry, The," 159
"Girl with a Flame, A," 179, 229
"Go Home and Tell Your Mother," 76, 229
"Goin' Steady," 168, 229
"Goin' with the Birds," 229
Gone with the Wind, 77, 120
"Good Impression, A," 230
Good News, 82
"Good Time Charlie," 230
"Goodbye Blues," 230
"Goodbye Mama, I'm Off to Yokohama," 42
"Got a New Lease on Lif," 93, 230
Grand Hotel, 220
Grand Jury, 95, 217
Grand Street Follies, 120
Greenwich Village Follies, The, 61
Griffelkin, 192
"Growing Pains," 184, 186, 230
Guys and Dolls, 185, 190
Gypsy, 134
"Gypsy Love," 230

"Hail to the Baron Munchausen," 230
Hallelujah, I'm a Bum, 82

Hands Across the Table, 94
Hands Up, 25, 26, 138
"Hang Up," 190, 191, 230
Happy Birthday, 152
"Happy Habit," 190, 191, 230
"Happy Heart, The," 224, 230
"Happy Talk," 190
"Happy the Bride the Sun Shines Upon," 230
"Happy Times," 230
"Harlem at It Best," 59, 230
"Harlem River Quiver," 59, 230
"Harlemania," 59, 230
Harry Delmar's Revels (see *Delmar's Revels*), 47 (see *Delmar's Revels*)
Harvey Girls, The, 170, 176
"Has Anybody Seen My Gal," 50
Have a Heart, 244
"Have Feet Will Dance," 195, 230
Hazel Flagg, 182
"He Had Refinement," 125, 184, 185, 190, 230
"He Will Tonight," 230
"He's Goin' Home," 230
"He's Good for Me," 230
"Heat Wave," 119
"Heavenly Party, A," 112, 113, 230
Heidi, 192
Hell with Heroes, The, 245
Hello Daddy, 66–69, 111, 219, 245
Hello, Dolly! 196
"Hello My Baby," 51
"Here Comes My Blackbird," 230
"Hey, Young Fella!" 75, 230
High Button Shoes, 178, 182
High Cost of Loving, The, 67
"High Flyin' Man," 58
High Tor, 192
High, Wide and Handsome, 111
Hit the Deck! 41
Hold On to Your Hats, 194
"Hooray for George the Third," 230
"Hooray for Love," 230
Hooray for Love, 78, 79, 88, 96, 105, 235
Hooray for What! 119, 170
"Hospitality," 230
"Hot Chocolate," 59, 230
Hot Chocolates, 59

GENERAL INDEX

Gray, Dolores, 162, 164
Great Depression. *See* Depression, the
Greeley, Horace, 143
Green, Abel, 40, 55, 57–59
Green, Adolph, 177, 185, 193, 217
Green, Benny, 194
Green, Richard, 101
Green, Johnny, 101
Green, Stanley, 121
Greer, James, 47
Greer, Sonny, 54
Griffith, D. W., 7
Grofé, Ferde, 54
Grubb, Kevin, 207
Guernsey Jr., Otis, 147
Guetary, Georges, 178–80
Guggenheim, Emily, 28

Haakon, Paul, 143
Hague, Albert, xvii, 87, 196–99, 201
Hague, Elliott, 196
Hale, Alan, 111
Hall, Adelaide, xvi, 62, 63, 170
Hall, Mordaunt, 76, 78
Hamlin, Fred, 9
Hamm, Charles, 139
Hammerstein, Arthur, 37
Hammerstein, Dorothy, 12, 115, 116, 156, 204, 224
Hammerstein, James, 116, 154
Hammerstein, Oscar, 8, 10
Hammerstein Oscar II, xv, 20, 27, 28, 31, 37, 64, 97, 103, 111, 114–16, 133, 139, 140, 141, 143, 144, 152–58, 160, 168, 170, 179, 180, 192, 199, 218
Hammerstein, Theodore J., 70
Harbach, Eloise, 156
Harbach, Otto, 37, 96, 97, 102, 156, 174
Harburg, Yip, xv, 70, 88, 93, 119, 122, 167, 170, 171, 176, 194
Hardwick, Otto, 57
Harlem, 52, 53, 55, 62, 105, 221
Harms, T. J., 38, 99
Harnick, Sheldon, xi
Harrigan and Hart, 51, 142
Harrington, Hamtree, 66
Harris, Herbert, 17, 18, 22–24, 33, 36, 52, 81

Harris, Rose. *See* Fields, Rose Harris
Hart, Dorothy, 133
Hart, Larry. *See* Hart, Lorenz
Hart, Lorenz, xv, xvi, 20, 21, 26–28, 36–41, 49, 51, 52, 58, 60, 63, 66, 67, 72, 77, 82, 83, 85, 96, 115, 120, 125, 133, 155, 156, 166, 177, 179, 180, 184, 202, 203
Hart, Moss, 120, 192
Hart, Teddy, 20
Hartman, Don, 171
Haskell, Jack, 70
Haskins, Jim, 53, 57, 58
Havoc, June, 133, 134
Hawkins, William, 180
Hayes, Helen, 149
Haymes, Dick, 163, 164
Healy, Dan, 53
Hearst, William Randolph, 9
Heath, Thomas, 4
Hebrew Sheltering and Immigrant Aid Society, 22
Hecht, Ben, 72
Hellman, Lillian, 192
Hemming, Roy, 84, 98, 113
Henderson, Ray, 70, 88
Hepburn, Katharine, 90, 110, 149
Herbert, Victor, 51, 139, 140
Herrmann, Bernard, 89
Hersey, John, 192
Herzig, Sig, 70
Heuberger, Victor, 138
Heyman, Edward, 92, 167
Heyward, Dorothy, 64
Heyward, DuBose, 64
Heyward, Leland, 187
Higgins, Billy, 64
Hill, Lethia, 58
Hines, Earl, 54
Hit Parade, 170
Hocker, David, 197
Hoey, Evelyn, 70
Hollywood Bowl, 109
Holm, Celeste, 195–96
Hope, Anthony, 29
Hope, Bob, 97, 135, 136
Hopper, De Wolf, 10
Horan, Edward, 70

Universal Funeral Chapel, 133
Universal Pictures, 73, 111, 113, 114, 135, 163, 215
University of Cincinnati, 196
University of Michigan, 180
Uris Building, 222
USO canteen, 137

Valentino, Rudolph, 43, 139
Vallee, Rudy, 85
Van Druten, John, 152
Van Dyke, Marcia, 187
Van Heusen, James, 192
Vance, Vivian, 130
Vanderbilt Theatre, 38, 51, 52, 70
Vanity Fair, 142
Variety, 40, 41, 71, 79, 98, 111, 134, 143, 146, 147, 149
Vassar College, 33
Velez, Lupe, 76
Verdon, Gwen, 173, 197–201, 203, 206, 207, 215
Vienna Imperial Academy of Music, 89
Villon, François, 28
Vivaldi, Antonio, 91
von Sternberg, Josef, 91
von Tilzer, Al, 70
Vreeland, Frank, 40

Wagner, Richard, 33, 107, 211
Waldorff, Wilella, 124
Walker, Jimmy, 54, 61
Wallenda Brothers, 75
Waller, Fats, 48, 49, 79
Waller, Maurice, 48
Walsh, Raoul, 85
Walsh, Thommie, 219
Walters, Charles, 166
Walters, Teddy, 70
Ward, Aida, xvi, 57, 63
Warfield, David, 10, 11, 60
Warner Brothers, 72, 73, 74, 79, 82, 91, 111, 119, 168
Warren, Harry, 73, 74, 99, 108, 118, 154, 155, 168–70, 175, 176, 194, 197
Warschauer, Morris, 13
Washington, George, 177
Waters, Ethel, xvi, 64, 69, 70, 119, 149

Waterson, Berlin, and Snyder, 7, 44
Watt, Douglas, 221
Watts, Richard Jr., 124, 186, 201
Waxman, A. P., 152
Waxman, Franz, 89
Wayburn, Ned, 36
Wayne, David, 195
Wayne, Mabel, 43
Weber, Joe, 2, 3, 5, 11–13, 19, 23, 117, 128
Weber, Lillian, 19
Weber and Fields, xii, xvi, 3–11, 18–20, 25, 27, 35, 75, 96, 117, 130, 142, 150, 189
Weber and Fields music hall, 9, 60
Weber and Fields' Own Company, 7, 8
Weill, Kurt, 119
Weill, Lloyd, 115
Weiner, Ed, 70
Weingart Institute, 20
Weinstein, Bobby, 223
Welfare Island, 155
Weller, Chas, 48
Welles, Orson, 121, 141, 145
Wellesley College, 33
Wells, George, 174
West, Mae, 110
Westchester Kennel Club, 55
Wheeler, John, 215
Wherever You Go, There You Are, 211
White, George, 46, 54
White, Jack, 54
White, Sammy, 38–39
White, Stanford, 9
Whiteman, Paul, 54, 61, 70
Whiting, Richard, 64, 118, 168
Who Wrote That Song, 85
Wiener, Jack, 34, 35, 56, 101, 116
Wieniawski, Henryk, 91
Wilder, Alec, 69, 84, 99, 139, 172, 194, 209
Wilder, Thornton, 192
Wilk, Max, 86, 149, 168, 192
Williams, Bert, 61
Williams, Clarence, 43
Williams, Esther, 169
Williams, Tennessee, 72
Williamson Music, 152
Wilson, Earl, 145, 178
Wilson, Edith, 57, 69
Wiman, Dwight Deere, 121, 123